Academics in Court

Academics in Court

The Consequences of
Faculty Discrimination Litigation

George R. LaNoue and Barbara A. Lee

Ann Arbor   The University of Michigan Press

1990   1989   1988   1987   4   3   2   1

Library of Congress Cataloging-in-Publication Data

LaNoue, George R.
  Academics in court.

  Bibliography: p.
  Includes index.
  1. College teachers—Legal status, laws, etc.—
United States—Cases.   2. Discrimination in
employment—Law and legislation—United States—
Cases.   I. Lee, Barbara A.   II. Title.
KF4240.A7L36 1987   344.73'01133'0269   87-5047
                       347.30411330269
ISBN 0-472-10086-6 (alk. paper)
ISBN 0-472-08070-9 (pbk. : alk. paper)

Preface

One role of the social scientist is to reexamine the lenses through which we view the social phenomena that surround and affect us. As our organizations and communities become more complex, this social science task becomes more significant. In order to function well, we need theories and models about what is important so that we can sort out the essential from the nonessential and make sense of our world. All of us use lenses based on experience and intuition, but social scientists seek to use evidence and logic to build more precise and more clearly articulated theories and models. It is not so much that a particular conceptual approach will be the correct or most useful one for all times or places, but that by being aware that different lenses are possible, we enrich our perspective and increase the probability that we will use the right approach for the understanding we seek.

This book uses a different lens to view the growing phenomenon of civil litigation in the United States. We are not essentially concerned with the legal rules that have emerged from these cases. In fact, most lawsuits contribute very little to the development of such rules. Nor is this book about the capacity of the courts to act when such cases are presented or the legitimacy of such actions. Nor are we primarily concerned with the national debate about the cumulative effects of litigation on American culture, although that question provides a context for our work. Instead, we are concerned with what happens to the particular people and institutions that get caught up in the litigation process. In 1983 there were about 13 million civil lawsuits in the United States. For the participants, these cases involved an enormous amount of time, energy, expense, and often anxiety. Litigation in our society has assumed an unusal role in conflict resolution, and it is important to describe and, eventually, to measure the consequence of this process. This requires a new social science lens, which this book develops and applies.

Of course, it is impossible to study litigation generally. Our focus is on a type of litigation that has emerged since the amendments to the Equal Pay Act and the Civil Rights Act in 1972. These amendments opened the door for college and university faculty who thought their institutions discriminated against them: they could now seek redress in federal courts. Hundreds of such cases have been filed; many are pending; some have been settled. More than three hundred have been decided. Our sample was drawn from this latter category. These cases are substantively important because they touch the vital personnel processes of academic institutions. Because of their academic setting, they have been remarkably accessible for intensive research. Although they are not necessarily typical of other types of litigation, we can use them to create a research framework. By pointing to the consequences of the process in this one area, other researchers may use this lens to examine other legal problems.

Analyzing the impact of litigation that may have involved scores of people on both sides over a period of several years is not a simple matter. One of our concerns has been the financial, emotional, and vocational consequences of the process for plaintiffs. We have also sought to explore lawyer-client relationships, the significance of support networks, the role of the plaintiff in pretrial research and decision making, and the plaintiff's perception of the process before and after litigation. Equally important, though more difficult to research, is the impact on the defendants. What are the consequences of being personally accused of discrimination or of being used for comparison purposes during a trial? How are the institutions' decisions about seeking legal representation or settlement made? What is the effect of litigation on the defendants' personnel policies and bureaucratic structures? Finally, the litigation process affects lawyers, litigating agencies, and judges, and some of these impacts are explored. All these matters are discussed in the conclusion (chap. 8).

Most of our data are drawn from six case studies (five are reproduced in this book) and two national surveys of plaintiffs and university attorneys. A description of the methodology employed in this research and the reasons for selecting these cases can be found at the end of chapter 2. This chapter also provides an overview of the academic discrimination case law that will be helpful in establishing the legal context of the specific cases we have researched. Chapter 1 discusses the development of litigation in the United States and places the perspective of this book in the framework of other literature about judicial process.

In understanding the litigation process, the authors have benefited from their previous experience. Lee is an attorney and teaches both higher education and employment law. LaNoue teaches constitutional law and has served as a trial expert for federal agencies and private parties in a number of academic discrimination cases.

Modern social science is frequently a collaborative enterprise, and this book has been the result of a team effort much larger than the work of the coauthors. We have been the grateful beneficiaries of a grant from the Carnegie Corporation of New York. Karin Egan and Sara Engelhardt were our foundation contacts, and they have been gracious, supportive, and patient throughout the research. Particularly important to the project have been the members of our advisory committee, who were chosen because of their status in and knowledge of this field and because we wanted to draw upon diverse interests in the process of designing the research and eliciting comments on the manuscript. The members are: Phillip M. Grier, Esq., Executive Director of the National Association of College and University Attorneys; Jeffrey H. Orleans, Esq., formerly Special Assistant to the President and University Counsel of the University of North Carolina system and now Executive Director of the Council of Ivy League Presidents; Dr. Jack W. Peltason, formerly President of the American Council on Education and now Chancellor of the University of California, Irvine; Dr. Bernice Sandler, Director of the Project on the Status and Education of Women, Association of American Colleges; and Dr. Irving J. Spitzberg, Jr., formerly General Secretary of the American Association of University Professors and now Executive Director of the Council for Liberal Learning. Each of them would have written a somewhat different book from the one that has finally emerged, but all made valuable suggestions. Several other colleagues have made valuable suggestions in reading the manuscript, including Hugh Davis Graham, Jack Pemberton, and Steve Sfekas. Several students provided valuable assistance at various stages of the research; they are: Deborah Fajer, Isaac Sperka, Janet Moran, Beverly Brossoie, and Elizabeth Kight. To all of the above and to the hundreds of people who consented to be interviewed for this project, sometimes about subjects that were delicate, even painful, to recall, we owe our thanks. Finally, we express our gratitude to our families, colleagues, students, and friends, who had to defer some of their own needs so that we might complete this three-year research. We are thankful that despite all the inconveniences and schedule readjustments, all disputes were settled without resort to litigation . . . so far.

George R. LaNoue
University of Maryland Baltimore County

Barbara A. Lee
Rutgers University

Contents

Chapter 1
Litigation: The Participants' Perspective

In the last decade Americans have become increasingly aware of the growing significance of litigation and courts in their collective and individual lives. Both the scholarly and the popular press have commented on the new forms and amounts of litigation. For example, a 1977 *Newsweek* cover story, "Too Much Law," asserted that the impatience of reformers with the slowness of legislative change, the discovery by Americans of "rights" newly created by courts or legislatures, and the ever-increasing willingness of elected officials and private citizens to let the courts settle matters that were once settled by legislatures, executives, parents, teachers (or chance) had led to a litigation explosion.[1] Two years later, a *Time* cover story, "Judging the Judges," described the relationship between increasing litigation and increasing frustration in judicial ranks.[2] According to United States Circuit Court of Appeals Judge Edward Allan Tamm, "Federal judges are working harder than they ever did in private practice, but they never can get their heads above water."[3] In 1979, over sixteen thousand cases had been pending for more than three years in federal courts, double the backlog of a decade before. Harvard Law School Professor Lawrence Tribe predicted, "If court backlogs grow at their present rate, our children may not be able to bring a lawsuit to conclusion in their lifetime. Legal claims might then be willed on, generation to generation, like hillbilly feuds, and the burdens of pressing them would be contracted like a hereditary disease."[4]

Network television also picked up the story. A 1980 CBS documentary titled "See You in Court" chronicled the sad cases of a divorcing couple financially devastated by attorney fees, of small towns that disincorporated because they could no longer afford legal liability insurance, and of sports equipment manufacturers whose product liability insurance costs had driven them out of markets. As a counterpoint, the documentary examined the role of litigation in obtaining remedies for workers who suffered from asbestosis. This often fatal lung disease was contracted by thousands of workers, even though some industry executives knew handling of asbestos was dangerous. Lawyers using the powerful discovery mechanisms of modern litigation unearthed the story, proved culpability, and have begun the process of gaining compensation for the workers affected. Still, justice has been elusive. Johns-Manville, the largest asbestos producer, has declared bankruptcy. The asbestos litigation threatens to overwhelm the judicial system. Some twenty thousand cases have been filed, and if it takes only twelve days to hear each one, the federal courts could do nothing else for two years.[5]

By 1985, the general problem of the loss or cost of legal liability insurance, which threatened to close or make prohibitively expensive many services and goods, had moved to center stage in the legislative arena. Almost every state considered enacting laws to limit tort awards or regulate insurance or both. President Reagan, noting that between 1975 and 1985 the average award in medical malpractice cases had increased 350 percent, to over $1 million, and in product liability cases 400 percent, to over $1.8 million, declared, "Twisted and abused, tort law has become a pretext for outrageous legal outcomes . . . that impede our economic life, not promote it. . . . These problems have begun to eat away at the fabric of American life."[6]

Some scholars doubt whether there has been a litigation explosion. Marc Galanter, writing in the *U.C.L.A. Law Review,* suggests that the fear of "hyperlexis" is exaggerated.[7] For one thing, many people who have potential claims decide not to pursue them or settle them in nonjudicial forums. Furthermore, when litigation is formally begun, "the vast majority of suits are disposed of by abandonment, withdrawal, or settlement, without full-blown adjudication and often without any authoritative disposition by the court."[8] The role of litigation in these instances is not to determine the outcome but to focus attention on the problems and to create an environment in which the parties can work out a solution. Comparing the amount of litigation in the United States to that in other countries is difficult, because the data are not uniform. In general, Galanter found that the American rate is probably in the same range as those in England, Australia, Denmark, and New Zealand, somewhat higher than those in Germany and Sweden, and far higher than those in Japan, Spain, and Italy.

Galanter's caveats are a useful antidote to exaggerated claims. The facts show that overall there has been a rapid increase in the amount of litigation in the United States but that in the most recent years there may have been some decline in some state courts. The data are imperfect because the American court system is so decentralized and until recently has not been very inclined to gather or publish statistics. Even the definition of what is a case is not uniform. The best data on state cases are published by the National Center for State Courts.[9] Its most up-to-date, comprehensive publication shows that in 1981 there were 11,626,849 civil cases filed in the District of Columbia and the forty states for which there were comparable data. That total represents an increase of 23 percent from the 1977 figures. In the same period, the median population growth in these states was 4.8 percent. Since the remaining ten states are somewhat smaller in population than the average and since there is a .94 correlation between population size and the amount of litigation,[10] it seems reasonable to believe that the total civil litigation in the states was about 13,000,000 cases at the beginning of the decade. Preliminary data from the period 1981–84, however, suggest a slight decline in the number of cases filed from the previous three-year period.[11] The number of civil cases filed in federal district courts, however, has grown steadily and rapidly.[12] There were 138,567 civil suits filed in 1977; 180,576 in 1981 (a 30 percent increase); and 261,485 in 1984 (a 92 percent increase). Civil appellate court cases rose in number from 16,768 in 1975 to 31,490 in 1984, an increase of 93 percent.

Worry over the quantity of litigation is not a modern phenomenon. In his book *The Daily Life of Rome,* Jerome Carcopino notes, "From the reign of one emperor to another, litigation was a rising tide which nothing could stem, throwing on the public courts more work than men could master."[13] Consequently, Augustus had to convert a forum he built into a court to relieve judicial congestion in the year 2 B.C. Nor is the observation that Americans are a particularly litigious people a novel one. In 1835, the French chronicler of American politics and mores, Alexis de Tocqueville, wrote his famous dictum that "there is hardly a political question in the United States that sooner or later does not turn into a judicial one."[14] Still, although the concern over excessive litigation is hardly new, there is a consensus that modern Americans are suing each other more often about more things than ever before. As Jethro Lieberman puts it in his thoughtful analysis, *The Litigious Society,* "Judicial decrees have changed the face of the social order and Americans seemingly take to the courtroom at the merest whisper of an insult."[15]

The principal scholarly debate about the growth of litigation has focused on its implication for courts. What kind of a policy role is legitimate for the judiciary in a democracy? Do the courts have the organizational capacity to play this role?

More lawsuits mean more decisions by the courts, sometimes crowding out the role of other more accountable governmental bodies. The judicial activism/judicial restraint debate has long existed inside and outside the courts.[16] Although the classical judicial restraint position has been forcefully asserted by modern scholars such as Raoul Berger[17] and Nathan Glazer,[18] much of the recent literature has been about the capacity of courts. The problem of judicial workloads has been of concern to many, but the most effective spokesperson for this cause has been Warren Burger. In addition to being chief justice, he was the closest thing we have had to a chief administrator of the federal court system. Shortly after Burger took his seat on the Court, he made a dramatic speech to the American Bar Association, complaining, "In a supermarket age we are trying to operate the courts with cracker-barrel grocer methods and equipment—vintage 1900."[19] This antiquated judicial machinery confronts a flood of new civil suits and criminal trials that are made increasingly complex by new procedural safeguards. Indeed, Burger predicted that if the percentage of criminal defendants who pleaded guilty dropped much below 90 percent, the whole system would break down. At first Burger's proposals for reform were modest, but in later years he advocated eliminating juries in some civil cases, requiring judicial impact statements for new legislation, and creating a new national court of appeals to help the Supreme Court screen cases. Others seek to solve the problems by decriminalizing some activities (prostitution, gambling, marijuana use) or by shifting some disputes into nonjudicial forums (neighborhood justice centers, arbitration, mediation).

Recently some scholars have explored the relationships between the legitimacy and capacity questions. Clearly, courts should not decide issues judges cannot understand or make rulings that cannot be implemented. In *The Courts and Social Policy,* Donald Horowitz advanced the argument that litigation is not a good vehicle for making complex policy judgments.[20] Lawsuits, he argued, are too focused on specific facts, are too erratic to provide continuity of policy development, and do not provide for review of their intended and unintended impacts. Furthermore, according to Horowitz, judges are generalists who cannot focus on a policy area, have very small professional staffs, and are bound by rigid rules of evidence in the adversary process.

A challenging response has been created by Michael A. Rebell and Arthur R. Block in their book *Educational Policy-Making and the Courts.*[21] Based on their analysis of a sample of federal court educational decisions and two case studies, they came to the conclusion that judicial policy making was both more flexible and more responsible than critics had maintained. Most education-related cases, they noted, were based firmly on controversies about some legal principle usually involving minority rights and, therefore, were appropriate for judicial decision. Moreover, the courts had adapted to this new role by creating new rules for class actions, by making it easier for multiple parties to participate, and by developing remedies with unobtrusive monitoring devices. The authors did not find that, compared to state legislatures, federal courts were less able to understand complex factual situations.

Whether or not courts have the capacity to play their expanded role in society, the search for alternatives to litigation for resolving legal disputes will continue. But these are unlikely to be panaceas. In *Justice Without Law,* historian Jerold S. Auerbach points out that alternatives have been advocated most often when relatively disadvantaged persons have suddenly begun to litigate effectively (in consumer complaints, prisoners' grievances, medical malpractice claims, and juvenile problems, for example).[22] He emphasizes the danger that shoving these issues into alternative dispute mechanisms may deprive disadvantaged persons of the potent tools of discovery and the equity powers of the bench that litigation provides, thereby gradually freezing the status quo.

So the dilemma remains. We do not like so much litigation, but we may need it. As Auerbach wrote in an earlier article, "Litigation is the modern equivalent of the Darwinian struggle for survival. As in any jungle, the fittest are the most aggressive, conniving, and selfish—or they possess our civilized equivalent, money. The unfit will be devoured."[23]

But Lieberman counters, "Until the day when our institutions can be trusted to serve us as fiduciaries and when we can be educated to understand the limitations of the world we have constructed, litigation will remain the hallmark of a free and just society."[24]

The Traditional Study of Law

Since litigation plays so many roles in modern America, what are appropriate scholarly approaches? Only a fraction of the 290,000 federal cases and an even smaller number of the 13,000,000 state cases in a particular year have any consequential impact on public policy. Yet every case has some effect (financial, emotional, occupational) on the individuals and organizations who become parties, and it is estimated that 20 percent of all adult Americans have been parties to a civil suit.[25] Given the scope of contemporary litigation, understanding the impact of the process on these participants is an important task. But the existing approaches to the study of litigation, and consequently the resulting literature, are not very helpful.

When lawyers research the results of litigation, they traditionally examine case law. Each year hundreds of law journal articles analyze, criticize, and synthesize judicial decisions. This writing attempts to state what the law is or should be. Generally, the actual plaintiffs and defendants are only shadowy figures—essentially, stage props used to rehearse the facts—who vanish before the important outcome, which is the rule of law the judge announces in his or her decision.

Considering the consistency and inconsistency of judicial opinions and predicting their impact is a useful activity in a country that seeks to live under the rule of law. But it provides a very limited perspective for describing the full consequences of litigation on individuals and society. Surely scholars would not seek to understand the social phenomena of marital discord or labor-management relations by focusing only on divorce decrees or collective bargaining contracts. Similarly, to examine printed case opinions exclusively is to look at the litigation process through a very narrow lens. Many judicial decisions in state and even federal courts are never published and are therefore generally not available for the lawyer's textual analysis. Even when opinions are published, the rules of evidence specifically or the adversary process generally sometimes excludes events or data important to a social science understanding of the conflict. Further, judges report the facts in the record selectively when they write a decision. Some facts they think not legally important, although they may be of considerable social consequence, while other facts may not be consistent with the argument the judge wishes to advance. Moreover, consequences of litigation that occur before and after the decision are unseen. Because social scientists have documented that, at least in the controversial cases, implementation of judicial decisions is slow and partial, focusing on the judge's opinion will not even reveal the operational law. Ten years after *Brown v. Board of Education,* not a single black child attended classes in any of the four districts that were original parties in the suit.

Awareness of the limitations of traditional legal scholarship has led social scientists to expand their decision perspective to include other components in the judicial process. The so-called judicial systems model is an adaptation of the general systems model developed by David Easton, a professor at the University of Chicago.[26] Easton suggested that any social system can be analyzed by identifying the following components: inputs (demands and supports), gatekeepers, convertor, outputs, and feedback loop. As conceptualized by Sheldon Goldman and Thomas P. Jahinge[27] and others, the judicial systems model is composed of litigants who make demands and supports on the system, lawyers who are the gatekeepers, courts who act as convertors, judicial decisions, which are the output, and, finally, the implementation process, which is the feedback loop. From this viewpoint, it is important not only to study what judges have said, but to examine the role of bar associations, prosecutors and other law enforcement officers, litigating agencies and public lawyers, judges as individuals shaped by their social backgrounds and ideologies (and while on the appellate bench, influenced by that small group setting). Literature based on this perspective is now large and sophisticated and greatly advances our knowledge about the legal process.

Still, the judicial systems model also has its limitations. Although the lawyer is concerned primarily with specific judicial pronouncements and their relationships, and the social scientist focuses the judicial process model on the macrosystem and the relationship of its components, something very important is left out.[28] What is the impact of litigation on the individuals and organizations who get caught up in the process as parties?

Searching for Clues about the Consequences of the Litigation Process

Litigation produces more than legal rules or even employment and social roles for lawyers, prosecutors, and judges. The litigation process itself alters the lives of the participants and their environment apart from the effects of any particular decision. Litigation makes some parties wealthy and bankrupts others. For some plaintiffs it is an exhilarating experience of personal triumph, vindication, or revenge. For others it is frustrating, frightening, and bitter. Merely being sued causes some organizations to jettison long-standing policies, alter organizational procedures, and change leadership. Other organizations respond by becoming fortresses, by restricting internal and external communication, and by giving expensive lawyers a mandate to win at all costs. What causes these alternative responses? What strategies and behaviors are developed and emerge from the litigation experience? On these questions, the existing literature is not well developed.

We have only fragments found in studies focused on other subjects to guide us.[29] For example, what leads people to respond to problems by litigating? Once they become plaintiffs, how does the process affect them, and how do they feel about it? Is it true that litigation, in Lieberman's phrase, often stems from the "merest whisper of an insult," or that plaintiffs perceive the process, in Auerbach's metaphor, as survival of the fittest in a legal jungle?

Two different scholarly studies have investigated the question why people initiate court actions. In 1969, Herb Jacob wrote a book called *Debtors in Court: The Consumption of Government Services.*[30] Jacob was interested in what impelled debtors to make the decision to seek a bankruptcy proceeding and what caused lenders to use court-enforced garnishments. He concluded that legal rules regarding standing and justiciability, available economic resources, perception of the relevance of court proceedings, and the socioeconomic status of the parties all affected their willingness to consume court services. These factors may generally affect the initiation of litigation, but bankruptcy and garnishments are special forms of court activity—more like administrative proceedings than other forms of civil litigation.[31]

A more recent and extensive study has been conducted by Wisconsin scholars connected with the Civil Litigation Research Project. They conceptualized the transformation of injury to lawsuit as a process of naming, blaming, and claiming.[32] They noted that a very large number of injuries go unperceived and that even when an awareness of damage develops, frequently nothing happens. The victim "lumps it" because of the hassle or because the danger of pursuing the claim is too high. Even when a grievance is pursued, it is more likely taken up with the offending party than in a court.

The most colorful study of why people initiate litigation is Marlene Adler Marks's *The Suing of America*.[33] The book begins with the nineteenth-century humanist Ambrose Bierce's definition: "law suit n. a machine in which you go into as a pig and come out as a sausage."[34] Marks, however, finds that plaintiffs' purposes are more differentiated and sometimes more noble than Bierce's cynicism suggests. The chapters in her book (which is rich in anecdote but not undergirded by systematic research) are organized around seven motivations that she claims instigate litigation: protest, grief, political and social change, money, vindication, harassment, and last resort.

Aside from the particular verdict in a case, what are the consequences of participation in litigation for plaintiffs?[35] Marks reports that "involvement in 'cause' lawsuits makes people feel good, useful, even patriotic." Twenty-five years after *Brown v. Board of Education,* the landmark Supreme Court case desegregating public schools, the participants recalled the event "as being the high point of their lives, like being on Mount Sinai when the Commandments were delivered."[36]

How typical are the *Brown* plaintiffs? Does this good feeling stem from the virtue of their cause, the historical significance of their case, or simply from the fact that they won so dramatically? An earlier civil rights plaintiff, Dred Scott, was not so fortunate. After the proslavery decision in his case, Scott was freed according to a previous agreement by Sanford, his owner. But without a means of support, he died a year later of consumption, in poverty, and ignored by those who once championed his cause.

Sometimes litigation is the device for finding meaning and support in the face of tragedy. Gerald Stern, plaintiff's lawyer and author of *The Buffalo Creek Disaster,*[37] tells the story of what happened after 125 people died when a defective coal company dam broke and flooded a West Virginia town in 1972. In this instance, the process of litigation served as a focus for community organization, therapeutic recognition of loss for the bereaved, and release of anger. The $13.5 million settlement was the basis for rebuilding both collective and personal lives. "Still," Stern reported, "some people just didn't want to let go. For them the end of the lawsuit was a sad occasion. It signaled the loss of camaraderie, the end of battle."[38] Perhaps even sadder were those who immediately accepted the coal company's original offer. They had missed the two-and-a-half-year catharsis of litigation.

But what about plaintiffs in cases of less notoriety? In an article titled "Litigation as a Means of Improving Treatment: Is It the Best Approach?" Roger Peale (a doctor) argues that lawsuits have some negative effects:

> The adversary process also may be introduced among patients (plaintiffs), their relatives, and their clinicians. Communication is kept to a

minimum to avoid providing any material that might be used in court. That obviously is not a good basis for a clinician-patient relationship.[39]

Another doctor, Donald M. Naftulin, has taken up a similar theme regarding a different group of patients. In his article, "Psychological Effects of Litigation on the Industrially Impaired Patient," he writes:

> Perhaps as much as the injury, labels such as "litigant," "claimant," and "insured" can undermine the workman's self-esteem. . . . The result is often a sense of less control over his own life. One then asks whether the industrially injured patient pays too high a psychological price for the system evolved that attempts to reduce the consequences of his injury.[40]

We still know very little about this process. Naftulin's article, subtitled "A Research Plea," calls for further empirical investigation.

Though there is little research on the subject, it is plausible to suppose that the impact of litigation on plaintiffs depends in part on whether they are actually in control of the lawsuit. Sometimes lawyers or litigating agencies will seek out nominal plaintiffs for a case they intend to bring anyway. The plaintiffs will lend their names, but it is not expected that they will make any litigation strategy decisions or bear the financial costs. Sometimes these plaintiffs will be virtually invisible; other times they are chosen because they have media-appealing personalities or stories, and they become celebrities of a sort. Still other cases are brought by plaintiffs who are engaged in one-man or one-woman crusades. In that instance, the plaintiff sets the legal goals, represents the case before the media, and finds a lawyer who will go along. Litigation surely will have a different impact on the plaintiff who is really responsible for the suit and has much at stake in it than on the plaintiff whose name is used merely because he or she fits the legal definition of someone who has standing.

Another factor is whether the plaintiff is able to construct an adequate support network or falls into an existing one. As Clement Vose discovered and wrote about in his book *Caucasians Only,* a litigating agency such as the NAACP may be building the intellectual and financial support for a case for a decade before the lawsuit is actually begun.[41] On the other hand, it wasn't until Karen Silkwood's death that a support network formed around her case.[42] Two local Catholic priests and a host of friends investigated every lead, keeping the case alive after the Justice Department and congressional inquiries finished. Eventually, a coalition of labor unions, feminist groups, and antinuclear organizations formed to bring the litigation that resulted in a

$10.5 million jury verdict for Silkwood's heirs. Equally important to the coalition was a new precedent holding a nuclear power plant responsible for low-level contamination of employees. But many plaintiffs attract little or no formal or informal support. Or if they have it in the beginning, it withers away as the lawsuit develops. In those instances the plaintiff must not only bear all the litigation costs personally but also cope with the feelings of alienation and isolation that involvement with the lawsuit brings. We have no systematic research, but many experienced lawyers are aware that plaintiffs experience dramatic personality shifts during the course of the litigation.

What about defendants? Marks asserts:

> Being sued—whether you are the average citizen or President of the United States—is like being sent a dead fish by the Mafia. It marks you as a misfit, a transgressor on other's rights.[43]

She continues:

> From the standpoint of the defendant . . . all lawsuits are harassing, whether or not the plaintiff intends it that way. The entire labyrinthine process is excruciating, and even if the defendant wins his case, the headaches incurred along the way rob him of most of the joy in his victory. Lawsuits spell trouble, and that is why some plaintiffs love them.[44]

Consequently:

> Defendants and would-be defendants sometimes start their barricade building long before the plaintiff even has a lawsuit in mind. There's a come-and-get-me dare to their actions as they warm up for battle.[45]

But some lawsuits are avoidable, and some organizations, large corporations in particular, invest considerable time and energy in litigation prevention. Sometimes this is done by seeking careful compliance with antitrust, environmental protection, or equal employment opportunity laws. Other times an effective public relations campaign is thought to be cheaper or more in line with the companies' competitive goals than actual compliance. Still, in the large, multifaceted organizations, compliance with complex modern regulations is often elusive, even with the best intentions. In a speech to the American Bar Association, Robert S. Hatfield, chairman and chief executive officer of the Continental Group (insurance), described the intensive education process his company engages in to avoid antitrust exposure. But as Hatfield pointed out, it was not only a concern that the company comply with the law that led to such efforts:

An effective compliance program can help prevent the enormous human suffering experienced by corporate managers charged with violations of criminal antitrust laws. They and their families live sometimes for years in fear of the ruin of their life's work. If a company compliance program succeeds in saving some of its managers from this fear or this fate, it will accomplish an important social and human service.[46]

There is some literature on how defendants react once the litigation has begun. For some who are sued frequently, litigation is just a cost of doing business, and there are special bureaucracies and budgets set aside to handle it. After being a defendant often enough, you may be immunized against any emotional impact. But in other instances, high financial stakes, potential criminal sanctions, or stubborn institutional pride can cause a fierce defendant response.

However, despite some valuable case studies, we really have little systematic data and no theories to explain defendant behavior. Indeed, it is difficult to generalize about the impact of litigation on either plaintiff or defendant from the existing literature. Still needed are concepts and data to measure the cost and benefits of litigation for the participants.

Even the most dramatic part of the process, the trial itself, has not been investigated for its impact on the parties. There is some concern about the stress trials place on lawyers. Wayne D. Brazil has written an article called "The Attorney as Victim: Toward More Candor about the Psychological Price Tag of Litigation Practice."[47] Brazil describes the manipulation of people, the distortion of data, and the search for the opponents' psychological, as well as legal, vulnerability that often characterize litigation tactics. Gradually, Brazil argues, such tactics alter the lawyer's perception of himself, other people, and even purely social situations. Wanting to avoid being "distorted and scarred by many of the kind of things I had to do to give our clients competitive representation," Brazil resigned his practice as "professional combatant" and became a law professor.

Generally the lawyers' professional ethos overlooks this dimension. James B. Stewart's book *The Partners* contains a series of case studies about the tactics used by blue chip firms in some of the great law wars of our time (the government antitrust actions against IBM, the takeover of Kennecott Copper Company, and others). These are marvelous stories full of high stakes, near misses, and herculean hours (fully billable, of course), but the impact of litigation on the participants is not of much interest to the authors. After Cravath, Swaine and Moore's victory in the twelve-year-long IBM case, which Stewart called "the model for complex litigation at nearly every other major firm," the presiding partner suggested that those involved in the case had earned some time off. But the macho style of the firm prevailed, and Stewart reports that one by one each of the young partners decided not to take any vacation. Stewart's only comment was, ''In the wake of such an unqualified victory, it was easy to forget that the IBM litigation had taken a toll on the firm and its lawyers that no victory could entirely erase, a toll most evident in the high divorce rate among the IBM lawyers.''[48]

If preparing and conducting trials creates stress for the attorneys who are doing all the manipulating and attacking, what does litigation do to the plaintiffs and defendants? We know intuitively that the oath ''the truth, the whole truth, and nothing but the truth'' is not a term of normal discourse. Anxiety must follow from having every word, hesitation, and evasion recorded by the implacable court reporter. Cross-examination is probably one of the most intellectually intimidating experiences the average citizen can undergo. Yet we know very little about reactions to that process. Among other things, it is important to investigate the consequences of the loss of control over matters critical to them that both parties experience during litigation. As Marks says, ''No one who has ever participated in or witnessed a court in session can avoid the conclusion that the process does punish both sides.''[49]

There is one stage in the litigation process about which substantial research does exist: the implementation of judicial decisions. Two decades ago, political scientists discovered that judicial rulings were often diverted, ignored, or evaded. Given that reality, the conditions under which implementation does occur is a question of considerable importance. Subsequent research has suggested that judicial decisions are most likely to be implemented if the judges are unanimous, the prestige of the court is high, the executive supports the decisions, and powerful interest groups monitor the implementation process.

The focus of the implementation studies, however, is on the achievement of the public policy option the court has selected. The researchers have been less concerned with how implementation affects the participants in the litigation. Consequently, the level of our understanding is still that expressed by Jethro Lieberman in his foreword to *The Litigious Society:* ''[T]here is not a great deal known about litigiousness as a social phenomenon.''[50] But there is a price to be paid for our ignorance. Wayne Brazil was writing from the attorney's perspective, but his comments apply equally well to the other participants in litigation. He said, ''The failure to acknowledge and to explore the implications of the [litigation] costs leaves legal education woefully deficient in a crucial area and renders analysis of the pros and cons of civil dispute resolution systems superficial and incomplete.''[51]

Alternative Approaches for Researching the Impact of the Litigation Process

There are, of course, some substantial case studies of particular lawsuits. Historian Richard Kluger has given us *Simple Justice*[52] (*Brown v. Board of*

Education), and journalist Anthony Lewis wrote *Gideon's Trumpet*,[53] (*Gideon v. Cochran*) to name two splendid examples. Alan Westin has described *Youngstown v. Sawyer*,[54] while his fellow political scientist, Allan Sindler, has done a full case study of *Bakke v. California*.[55] These are rich narratives of cases of enduring significance. Here the plaintiffs and defendants are clearly drawn, the strategies developed, and the impact of the issues fully considered. But these cases are really sui generis. There are no comparative data in these studies, no hypotheses, and no models. The authors intended to do no more than to tell the stories that led to the Supreme Court decisions. As worthy as that aim is, it does not lead to a better understanding of the impact of the litigation process on the participants. If we seek to understand litigation from that·perspective, we need an analytical framework specifically designed to organize that inquiry. That does not presently exist.

There are, of course, some models of the litigation process in the literature. Some are purely descriptive. The President's Commission on Law Enforcement and the Administration of Justice adapted Easton's system model to the specifics of the criminal justice system.[56] Jean G. Taylor and others, of the Institute for Defense Analysis, then went a step further to use the critical path method to permit analysis of the flow of cases in a particular criminal justice system.[57]

In a textbook called *Legal Systems,* Blair J. Kolasa and Bernadine Meyer use a technique they call decision analysis.[58] Each decision point in the civil or criminal litigation process is identified, and the choices are discussed in hypothetical case vignettes. The authors used this approach for pedagogical purposes, to "walk students through the legal system." It could also be used for research, though, as we have emphasized here, understanding the impact of litigation involves far more than analyzing decision points.

Other models focus on strategy considerations for litigation. Stephen Shavell, a professor at Harvard Law School, has developed a litigation model to be used in evaluating settlement versus trial options given varying methods for allocating legal costs.[59] Using decision theory, Shavell shows that the American policy of having each side pay its own legal costs deters settlement. Robert Mnookin, professor of law at the University of California, Berkeley, and Lewis Kornhauser, professor of law at New York University School of Law, have created a framework for considering how court rules and procedures affect the bargaining process that occurs between divorcing couples outside the courtroom.[60] The authors concluded that judicial practice powerfully affects bargaining, but that we currently have no theory or systematic data to describe the phenomenon. Since bargaining "in the shadow of law" is common in many contexts, the authors suggest the need for research about this process and the effect that alternative dispute resolution mechanisms would have on settlements.

Also in the literature are manuals for litigators that contain implicit models, or at least indicate the stages of the process and some of the tactical considerations at each stage. In *The Rule of Reason: A New Approach to Corporate Litigation,* attorney and author Milton R. Wessel outlines an idealized approach, describing the behavior of some of the litigation participants.[61] However, Wessel's purpose is to advise corporations on the management of litigation, not to examine the consequences of that process.

Scholars of the policy-making process have found it useful to distinguish among the various phases or stages of a process even if in reality the segments are not completely discrete. One of the most well-known conceptualizations using this approach is by Charles O. Jones, who has labeled the stages identification, formulation, legitimation, application, and evaluation.[62] Articulating the stages of a process for descriptive or analytical purposes is now commonplace in the public policy literature,[63] but it has not been done for the litigation process. Focusing on stages (rather than on specific decision points, as in the Kolasa and Meyer approach) encourages researchers to examine the interrelationship of the multiple decisions and participants in each stage. The real world of litigation, particularly its effect on the parties involved, is much messier and less rational than portraying a series of linearly related decision points would imply. In the litigation process, participants may face clusters of interrelated decisions rather than discrete decision points. For example, whether a litigant can afford a particular attorney may be related to the availability of a support network. But the reverse may be true as well. The attorney one retains may determine whether the plaintiff has access to an existing support network or can construct a new one.

Ideally, an analytical tool would be both descriptive and predictive, but in the initial development of a research area, description is the priority. A good descriptive tool should not only aid the researcher in sorting out the relevant facts and events from the welter of actions that characterize any complex social phenomenon, but should also generate new insights and hypotheses in the area it seeks to illuminate. To develop an analytical framework for describing the consequences of litigation, we have borrowed the "stages" approach from public policy research. Figure 1 represents a ten-stage litigation analytical framework, which is described in more detail in chapter 2.

By segmenting the litigation process into stages, it is possible to study plaintiff and defendant behavior as they parallel one another. We can examine how each party perceives the initial conflict, establishes the "facts," creates a support network, acquires legal representation, participates in strategy, fundraising, and research, bears up under testimony, cross-examination, and the other rigors of trial, and emerges after the judge's decision is made. We can show who participates at which stages and who controls strategy at each stage. We can measure the time, financial, psychological, and organizational costs of litigation, and also its benefits. We can inquire in the aftermath about

	1. Triggering Incident	2. Perception of Alleged Discrimination	3. Problem Evaluation and Informal Consultation	4. Use of Internal Remedies	5. Settlement or Litigation Decision	6. Litigation Preparation	7. Pretrial Impacts	8. Trial Impacts	9. Decision Impacts	10. Posttrial Impacts
Plaintiff										
Defendant										

Fig. 1. Stages of litigation. This framework of the litigation process provides not only a chronological sequence but also, by delineating the stages involved, an analytical focus for examining changes in issues, actors, tactics, and impacts as the litigation progresses.

how it might have been done differently. Were opportunities for settlement missed? In any event, would settlement have benefited the parties? Could the cost/benefit ratio have been more favorable for one or both parties?

Although this framework does not have predictive capacity, it may improve social scientists' ability to describe the litigation process comprehensively. By focusing on the impacts of that process on the participants, we may gain insights that could make the process more rational and more humane.

NOTES

1. "Too Much Law," *Newsweek,* January 10, 1977, p. 42.
2. "Judging the Judges: An Outsized Job Getting Bigger," *Time,* August 20, 1979, p. 49.
3. Ibid., p. 55.
4. Ibid., p. 51.
5. Stephen Sfekas, defense attorney in asbestos cases, interview with author, July 13, 1983. Of course, courts cannot give all of their time for a single issue, no matter how pressing the claim. In Mississippi, where six hundred asbestos claims are pending, the courts are disposing of one such case a year. The saga of these cases is told by Paul Brodeur in "The Asbestos Industry on Trial," *New Yorker,* June 10, 17, 24, July 1, 1985, pp. 49, 45, 37, 36.
6. Ronald Reagan, Address to the American Tort Reform Association, *Washington Post,* May 31, 1986, p. A9.
7. Marc Galanter, "Reading the Landscape of Disputes: What We Know and Don't Know about Our Allegedly Contentious and Litigious Society," *U.C.L.A. Law Review* 31 (October, 1983): 4–71; the Civil Litigation Research Project at the University of Wisconsin, which sponsored some of Galanter's research, has a number of projects measuring the characteristics of litigation in our society. See David Trubeck et al., "Civil Litigation Research Project: Final Report" (University of Wisconsin, 1983).
8. Galanter, "Reading the Landscape," p. 26.
9. Victor E. Flango et al., *The Business of State Trial Courts* (Williamsburg, Va.: National Center for State Courts, 1983), p. 68.
10. Ibid., p. 64.
11. Robert T. Roper, "A Preliminary Examination of Available Civil and Criminal Trend Data in State Trial Courts for 1978, 1981 and 1984" (National Center for State Courts, Williamsburg, Va., April, 1986).
12. The federal statistics are taken from the annual reports of the director of the Administrative Office of the United States Courts, Government Printing Office. As the number of federal cases has increased, so has the backlog. In 1975 district courts had 119,767 cases pending. By 1984, the backlog had grown to 250,292. The comparable numbers for circuit courts are 12,128 and 22,785, respectively.
13. Jerome Carpocino, *The Daily Life of Rome* (New Haven: Yale University Press, 1940), p. 186.

14. Alexis de Tocqueville, *Democracy in America,* ed. J. P. Mayer and M. Lerner (New York: Harper and Row, 1966), p. 248.

15. Jethro K. Lieberman, *The Litigious Society* (New York: Basic Books, 1981), p. 3.

16. See, for example, Stephen C. Halpern and Charles M. Lamb, *Supreme Court: Activism and Restraint* (Lexington, Mass.: Lexington Books, 1982), and Aryeh Neier, *Only Judgement* (Middletown, Conn.: Wesleyan University Press, 1982).

17. Raoul Berger, *Government by Judiciary* (Cambridge, Mass.: Harvard University Press, 1977).

18. Nathan Glazer, "Toward an Imperial Judiciary," *Public Interest* 41 (1975): 104–23.

19. Warren Burger, Address to the American Bar Association, August 10, 1970, reprinted in Howard James, *Crisis in the Courts* (New York: David McKay Co., 1971), p. iv.

20. Donald Horowitz, *The Courts and Social Policy* (Washington, D.C.: Brookings Institution, 1977).

21. Michael A. Rebell and Arthur R. Block, *Educational Policy-Making and the Courts* (Chicago: University of Chicago Press, 1982).

22. Jerold S. Auerbach, *Justice Without Law? Resolving Disputes Without Lawyers* (New York: Oxford University Press, 1983).

23. Jerold S. Auerbach, "Welcome to Litigation," *New Republic,* January 17, 1983, p. 21.

24. Lieberman, *Litigious Society,* p. 190.

25. F. Bennack, Jr., *The American Public, the Media, and the Judicial System,* Hearst Corporation Report (New York: Hearst Corporation, 1983), p. 23.

26. David Easton, *A Systems Analysis of Political Life* (New York: John Wiley and Sons, 1965).

27. Sheldon Goldman and Thomas P. Jahinge, *The Federal Judicial System* (New York: Holt, Rinehart and Winston, 1968), p. 4.

28. The literature on a judicial systems model is not very helpful. Neither Goldman and Jahinge (*Federal Judicial System* and *The Federal Courts as a Political System* [New York: Harper and Row, 1971]) nor Jay A. Sigler (*An Introduction to the Legal System* [Homewood, Ill.: Dorsey Press, 1968]) discusses the impact of litigation on the parties at all. The richest literature to date is anthropological. In the preface to *The Disputing Process—Law in Ten Societies* (New York: Columbia University Press, 1978), the editors, Laura Nader and Harry F. Todd, Jr., write:

> As part of our focus on interactional aspects, the Berkeley Law Project group has stressed that the perspective of the litigant must be treated as of at least equal importance to that of a third party—the judge, for example. . . . People who write about the judicial process and the judicial decisions as if the outcome were solely the product of a third party, a judge, miss the sociological relevance of the courtroom as an interactive arena. (P. 22)

Unfortunately, for our purposes, most of this anthropological research focuses on cultures that are not comparable to our own and on processes not nearly as formal and complex as federal litigation.

29. A survey of this literature was conducted for us by Deborah Fajer, a student at the University of Maryland Law School.

30. Herb Jacob, *Debtors in Court: The Consumption of Government Services* (Chicago: Rand McNally, 1969).

31. As Jacob points out (*Debtors in Court*, p. 118), garnishments are generally handled in the clerk's office with little formality. This proceeding usually takes less than thirty minutes. Although a bankruptcy proceeding takes place in a courtroom, the whole thing is over in a few minutes, unless it is opposed by creditors (which is rare).

32. William L. F. Felsteiner, Richard L. Abel, and Austin Sarat, "The Emergence and Transformation of Disputes: Naming, Blaming, Claiming . . . ," *Law and Society Review* 15 (1980–81): 632–54. See also Richard E. Miller and Austin Sarat, "Grievances, Charges and Disputes: Assessing the Adversary Culture," *Law and Society Review* 15 (1980–81): 526–65; Lynn Mather and Barbara Yngvesson, "Language, Audience, and the Transformation of Disputes," *Law and Society Review* 15 (1980–81): 775–824; and Keith O. Boyum, "Theoretical Perspectives on Court Caseloads: Understanding the Earliest Stages, Claim-Definition," in Keith O. Boyum and Lynn Mather, eds., *Empirical Theories about Courts* (New York: Longman, 1983).

33. Marlene Adler Marks, *The Suing of America* (New York: Seaview Books, 1981).

34. Ibid., p. 1.

35. Jacob reports (*Debtors in Court*, pp. 116–29), that debtors who become involved in either bankruptcy or garnishment actions had lower feelings of self-confidence in the judicial realm and were more critical of the courts than a control group. On the other hand, these debtors felt more self-confidence about the larger political system than did the control group.

36. Marks, *Suing of America*, p. 81.

37. Gerald Stern, *The Buffalo Creek Disaster* (New York: Random House, 1977).

38. Ibid., pp. 65–66.

39. Roger Peale, "Litigation as a Means of Improving Treatment: Is It the Best Approach?" *Hospital and Community Psychiatry* 26, no. 3 (March, 1975): 171.

40. Donald M. Naftulin, "Psychological Effects of Litigation on the Industrially Impaired Patient," *Industrial Medicine and Surgery* 39, no. 4 (April, 1970): 26.

41. Clement Vose, *Caucasians Only: The Supreme Court, the NAACP and the Restrictive Covenant Case* (Berkeley: University of California Press, 1959).

42. Ciji Ware, "The Silkwood Connection," *New West*, June 18, 1979, p. 25.

43. Marks, *Suing of America*, p. 8.

44. Ibid., p. 174.

45. Ibid., p. 201.

46. Robert S. Hatfield, "The Impact of Antitrust on the Large Corporation," *Vital Speeches* 45, no. 22 (September, 1979): 700.

47. Wayne D. Brazil, "The Attorney as Victim: Toward More Candor about the Psychological Price Tag of Litigation Practice," *Journal of the Legal Profession* 3 (1978): 107.

48. James B. Stewart, *The Partners* (New York: Simon and Schuster, 1983), p. 112.

49. Marks, *Suing of America*, p. 175.

50. Lieberman, *Litigious Society,* p. xi.

51. Brazil, "Attorney as Victim," p. 107.

52. Richard Kluger, *Simple Justice* (New York: Alfred A. Knopf, 1975).

53. Anthony Lewis, *Gideon's Trumpet* (New York: Vintage Books, 1964).

54. Alan Westin, *Youngstown v. Sawyer* (New York: Macmillan Co., 1958).

55. Allan Sindler, *Bakke, De Funis, and Minority Admissions* (New York: Longman, 1978).

56. President's Commission on Law Enforcement and Administration of Justice, *Challenge of Crime in a Free Society* (Washington, D.C., 1967).

57. Jean G. Taylor et al., *Data Analysis and Simulation of the District of Columbia Trial Court Systems for the Processing of Felony Defendants* (Arlington, Va.: Institute for Defense Analysis, 1968).

58. Blair J. Kolasa and Bernadine Meyer, *Legal Systems* (Englewood Cliffs, N.J.: Prentice-Hall, 1978).

59. Steven Shavell, "Suit, Settlement, and Trial: A Theoretical Analysis under Alternative Methods for the Allocation of Legal Costs," *Journal of Legal Studies* 11 (January, 1982): 435–58.

60. Robert H. Mnookin and Lewis Kornhauser, "Bargaining in the Shadow of the Law: The Case of Divorce," *Yale Law Journal* 88 (1979): 950–97.

61. Milton R. Wessel, *The Rule of Reason: A New Approach to Corporate Litigation* (Boston: Addison-Wesley Publishing Co., 1976).

62. Charles O. Jones, *An Introduction to the Policy Process* (North Scituate, Mass.: Duxbury Press, 1977), p. 13.

63. Garry D. Brewer and Peter de Leon (*The Foundations of Policy Analysis* [Homewood, Ill.: Dorsey Press, 1983]) use a six-stage model—initiation, estimation, selection, implementation, evaluation, and termination—while Judith V. May and Aaron B. Wildavsky (*The Policy Cycle* [Beverly Hills: Sage, 1978]) describe a similar concept in a somewhat different language.

Chapter 2
Academic Discrimination Litigation as a Research Vehicle

Measuring the effects of the litigation process is difficult because the issues, facts, and parties vary in each lawsuit. Some of the effects might be measured quantitatively, but not much data have been gathered. Other important factors are not easily quantifiable. Furthermore, at the early stage of research development the first task is to identify important questions and to describe the impacts of the process in order to lay the foundation for the theory building that will follow. The best vehicle for question formulation and process description is a set of case studies in which effects can be described in detail and compared in general. The litigation stages framework described in chapter 1 is a device for organizing this kind of research.

We decided to use cases that were recent (so the parties and documents were still available), were of intrinsic importance, and were in an area of law with which we were familiar.[1] Finally, it was essential to gain access to the people and data involved. For all these reasons, we chose the body of cases in which faculty plaintiffs have charged higher education institutions with discriminating against them in some aspect of employment.

Since Title VII and the Equal Pay Act were amended in 1972, there have been more than three hundred federal decisions on such cases involving college faculty. Most plaintiffs are white women, but a significant number involve blacks or other ethnics, or whites of both sexes suing black institutions; there are also scattered cases involving age discrimination or other issues. Several hundred more cases are pending in courts and administrative agencies.

These cases raise issues of considerable substantive importance and increasing financial significance. Employment discrimination is, of course, a major domestic problem. Yet despite the powerful tools available in civil rights litigation, the racial and gender configurations of the American professoriat have changed little in the past decade. In case after case, courts have conceded the difficulty of determining, in the academic setting, whether inadequate performance or institutional discrimination have caused plaintiffs to suffer a negative personnel decision. Several commentators have pointed out that the courts seem to have bent civil rights law itself in order to avoid becoming enmeshed in the complexity of these cases.[2] On the other hand, the United States possesses higher education institutions that are more numerous, more diverse and, some would argue, of higher quality than those anywhere else in the world. It would be no small matter, then, should the courts decide that hiring, promotion, and compensation systems in American universities must be radically restructured.

Academic institutions also seemed an appropriate setting for this research for several other reasons. Universities historically have not been sued frequently, so examining recent employment discrimination cases can highlight different institutional responses to litigation. Academic personnel procedures, management structures, and communication systems are not well designed to defend against lawsuits. The degree of decentralization of faculty personnel decisions and the lack of accountability of peers for their recommendations makes Weick's concept of these organizations as "loosely-coupled" particularly appropriate.[3] Judges often find it difficult to distinguish administrative peculiarities from discrimination. One of the purposes of this research is to determine whether litigation has caused academic institutions to "tighten the coupling" by making their administrative patterns and power alignments more accountable and hierarchical.

Being sued or just threatened with a lawsuit can have harmful effects on the informal cultural context of the institution as well as on its more formal structures. Today's university can be sued in its capacity as employer, contractor, research manager, housing authority, and educator/evaluator of students. In addition to the financial burden of defending lawsuits, it is also costly to prevent them by continuously adding procedural or documentary requirements for decision making. These expenses compete for resources traditionally devoted to teaching and other core academic concerns. University of Delaware Dean Helen Gouldner has written:

> The burden of legal negotiations and litigation on school officials' time and energy makes it increasingly difficult for them to attend to the regular affairs of the university and to do the necessary planning for the future. Being in court, preparing for cases, and trying to stay out of court have all become an integral part of the university's regular affairs. . . .
>
> Professors and students have also found that litigation has made increasing demands on their time. As a consequence, it is more and more difficult to get them to serve on personnel and grievance committees— the rumors of the amount of time it takes are well-founded. Strong faculty

and student governance is difficult to come by at best, but as litigation places extra demands on participants in campus self-government, fewer faculty members and students are willing to engage in it.[4]

Although Gouldner's view is echoed by numerous administrators and faculty, others argue that litigation has resulted in beneficial and long-overdue change in academic personnel practices and that extra time and effort are a small price to pay for such gains.[5]

Compared to other plaintiffs, faculty members are often unusually active and articulate in pursuing their cases. Yet a lawsuit in an academic setting frequently means challenging one's colleagues as well as administrators. This can be painful, since the plaintiff's performance will be publicly exposed to criticism throughout the litigation. No one is perfect in the trinity of academic obligation: teaching, scholarship, and service. Self-doubt is a constant companion. Furthermore, very few professors have the financial or political resources to lighten the cost of litigation.

This study examines the consequences of the academic discrimination litigation process and does not attempt to determine which party "deserved" to prevail. Judges have made their decisions in these cases, and it would be pointless for us to second-guess them. What we suspected, however, was that while a judge's decisions lead to critical tangible outcomes (e.g., reinstatement or non-reinstatement to a job, or who pays attorney fees), the litigation process itself has other less apparent but also important impacts on both winning and losing parties. We set out to study those impacts.

From our perspective, the different problems academic institutions and faculty face add interest to the case studies, but the relative openness of these institutions to researchers was also an important consideration. Respect for research is traditional in this environment. Academic institutions are decentralized and lack control over faculty employees, so information is relatively more accessible than in corporate, governmental, or health care organizations. But, of course, all of the distinctive advantages of choosing academic discrimination cases mean these cases are not necessarily typical of litigation in other settings. We will be commenting on the relationship of this research to other areas of litigation in the last chapter, but first it will be useful to outline the distinctive characteristics of this particular body of litigation.

One of the characteristics of modern academic life is increased contentiousness over the terms and conditions of faculty employment. The tight job market has closed the traditional option for the dissatisfied—moving to another campus. Furthermore, changes in the ethos and organization of universities have made it possible to stand and fight. Sometimes disputes are resolved by human relations officers, ombudsmen, grievance procedures, or collective-bargaining mechanisms, but not infrequently the parties litigate.

When a lawsuit occurs, one of its most common forms is a claim that the institution has discriminated against an individual or a class of faculty because of sex, race, national origin, religion, age, or handicap. The conflicts may be over hiring, promotion, tenure, salary, fringe benefits, pensions, or working conditions.

Faculty litigation over discrimination is a relatively new phenomenon. Despite all of the turmoil of the sixties, federal courts decided only one such case. (Cary Lewis, a black business educator, sued Chicago State University in 1969 for failure to promote him to full professor and lost.) Then, in 1972, Congress amended Title VII of the Civil Rights Act of 1964 and the Equal Pay Act to cover faculty, and that changed the legal environment dramatically. In the seventies there were 145 decisions by federal courts in academic discrimination cases. During the eighties, there has been an average of 34 such decisions per year. What are the characteristics of these decisions?

Survey of Decisions

Let us turn first to the conventional analysis of who sued and who was sued, who won and who lost. When Congress amended the Civil Rights Act and the Equal Pay Act, it was because it was widely believed that women in particular were discriminated against in higher education. In the legislative history of the Title VII amendments, Congress said,

> Discrimination against minorities and women in the field of education is as pervasive as discrimination in any other area of employment. . . . When women have been hired into educational institutions, particularly institutions of higher education, they have been relegated to positions of lesser standing than their male counterparts.[6]

Social scientists researching employment policies and practices in higher education reached similar conclusions.[7]

Consequently, it is not surprising that most discrimination lawsuits have been brought by women. Table 1 describes the characteristics of plaintiffs and the issues on which they sued. Table 2 groups the defendant institutions by type and control and by the types of personnel decisions on which each was sued. The data demonstrate that most institutional types have been sued about most types of issues. Generally, institutions have been sued about in proportion to the number of faculty they hire. The exception is community colleges, which have attracted little litigation. It may be that the more centralized decision-making systems at community colleges either are perceived as fairer

TABLE 1. Plaintiffs and Issues in Academic Discrimination Cases Decided on the Merits, 1970–84

Plaintiff and Claim Category	Hiring	Promotion	Tenure	Nonrenewal/ Discharge	Salary	Pension	Working Conditions	Retirement
Sex								
Female								
Individuals	3	11	21	18	7	2	4	0
Class	5	7	3	0	13	1	2	0
Male								
Individuals	1	1	0	1	2	0	0	0
Class	0	0	0	0	2	0	0	0
Race/National Origin								
Individuals	7	11	13	18	7	0	5	0
Class	2	1	1	0	0	0	0	0
Age								
Individuals	1	1	0	3	1	1	0	2
Class	0	0	0	0	0	0	0	1
Handicap								
Individuals	0	0	1	1	0	0	0	0
Class	0	0	0	0	0	0	0	0
Religion								
Individuals	1	3	3	1	3	0	0	0
Class	0	0	0	0	0	0	0	0
Total Charges[a]	20	35	42	42	35	4	11	3

Note: Limited to cases filed by faculty under Title VII of the Civil Rights Act, the Age Discrimination in Employment Act, the Rehabilitation Act, and the Equal Pay Act. Does not include First Amendment cases or discrimination lawsuits filed by nonfaculty plaintiffs.

[a]It is not uncommon for cases to have multiple plaintiffs and for individual plaintiffs to raise multiple issues.

TABLE 2. Defendants and Issues in Academic Discrimination Cases Decided on the Merits, 1970–84

Defendant[a]	Hiring	Promotion	Tenure	Nonrenewal/ Discharge	Salary	Pension	Working Conditions	Retirement	Total Defendants[b]
Research/Doctoral University									
Public	5	11	10	8	10	1	5	2	52
Private	2	3	12	6	5	0	1	0	29
Comprehensive University									
Public	7	11	6	12	9	0	2	0	47
Private	0	0	1	1	0	1	2	1	6
Liberal Arts College									
Public	0	0	0	0	0	0	0	0	0
Private	0	2	4	6	3	1	1	0	17
Two Year Institution									
Public	5	2	0	0	1	1	2	0	11
Private	0	0	0	0	0	0	0	0	0
Professional School									
Public	0	0	0	0	1	0	0	0	1
Private	0	1	1	1	1	0	2	0	6
Total Issues	19	30	34	34	30	4	15	3	

[a]This classification system follows the Carnegie categories as found in The Carnegie Council on Policy Studies in Higher Education, *A Classification of Institutions of Higher Education: Revised Edition* (Berkeley, Calif.: Carnegie Council, 1976).

[b]Some defendants were charged with more than one violation.

TABLE 3.   Federal Judicial Decisions on Higher Education Faculty Discrimination Based on Procedural and Jurisdictional Issues, 1971–77

1971	1972	1973	1974
	Braden v. *Univ. of Pittsburgh* (D) League of Academic Women v. *Regents, Univ. of California* (D)	*Johnson* v. Univ. of Pittsburgh (D) *Braden* v. Univ. of Pittsburgh (A)	Gresham v. *Chambers (Nassau Comm. College)* (A) *EEOC* v. Univ. of New Mexico (A) Peters v. *Middlebury College* (D) O'Connell v. *Teachers College of Columbia* (D) *Pendrell* v. *Chatham College* (D) Kaplowitz v. *Univ. of Chicago* (D) Rackin v. *Univ. of Pennsylvania* (D) Scott v. *Univ. of Delaware* (D) Jaroch v. *Univ. of Wisconsin* (D) Cohen v. *Illinois Inst. of Tech.* (D) *Presseisen* v. Swarthmore College (D) *Taliaferro* v. *Dykstra (Va. State Council of Higher Education)* (D) Clark v. *Atlanta Univ.* (D)

Notes: Names of winning parties appear in italics; in split decisions, names of both parties appear in italics; A = appellate court; D = district court.

or actually create less opportunity for discrimination. Or it may be that two-year institutions have better internal procedures for conflict resolution through collective bargaining or other mechanisms.

Although there are few surprises regarding who comes to court, the results of judicial decision making have not been so predictable. Considering

1975	1976	1977
Braden v. Univ. of Pittsburgh (D)	Wagner v. *Long Island Univ.* (D)	*Braden* v. Univ. of Pittsburgh (A)
Hanshaw v. Delaware Tech (D)	Rubenstein v. *Univ. of Wisconsin* (D)	*Perham* v. *Ladd (Chicago State Univ.)* (D)
Byron v. *Univ. of Florida* (D)	*Solin* v. SUNY (D)	*Al-Hamdami* v. SUNY (D)
Cohen v. *Illinois Inst. of Tech.* (A)	Sanday v. *Carnegie-Mellon* (D)	Kutska v. *California State College* (D)
Sanday v. *Carnegie-Mellon* (D)	Savage v. *Kibbee (Hunter College)* (D)	*Gilinsky* v. Columbia Univ. (D)
Cole v. *Univ. of Hartford* (D)	*Usery* v. Memphis State Univ. (D)	*Lamphere* v. Brown Univ. (A)
McKillop v. *Regents, Univ. of California* (D)	*Lamphere* v. Brown Univ. (D)	Lamb v. *Rantoul (R.I. School of Design)* (A)
Weise v. Syracuse Univ. (A)	*Sobel* v. Yeshiva Univ. (D)	Bireline v. *Seagondollar* (A)
Strunk v. *West Kentucky Univ.* (D)	Bennun v. *Rutgers* (D)	*Guerra* v. Board of Trustees (Calif. State Univ. and Colleges) (A)
Winsey v. *Pace College* (D)	Theodore v. *Elmhurst College* (D)	*Cap* v. *Lehigh Univ.* (D)
Jackson v. *Univ. of Pittsburgh* (D)	Egelston v. *SUNY Geneseo* (A)	Clark v. *Atlanta Univ.* (A)
Scott v. Univ. of Delaware (D)	Melanson/Lamb v. *Rantoul (R.I. School of Design)* (D)	
Savage v. *Kibbee (CUNY)* (D)	*Marshall* v. Kent State (D)	
	Leake v. *Univ. of Cincinnati* (D)	
	Board of Governors (Wayne State Univ.) v. *Perry* (D)	
	Gellman v. State of Maryland (A)	
	Scott v. Univ. of Delaware (D)	

only those cases litigated under Title VII of the Civil Rights Act, the Equal Pay Act, the Age Discrimination in Employment Act, and the Rehabilitation Act that ended in a published opinion by a federal court between 1971 and 1984, there have been 156 decisions on procedural and jurisdictional issues and 160 decisions that have reached the merits. Tables 3, 4, 5, and 6 present the results in simple chronological form. All these cases and their citations are listed in the Appendix.

TABLE 4. Federal Judicial Decisions on Higher Education Faculty Discrimination Based on Procedural and Jurisdictional Issues, 1978–84

1978	1979	1980	1981	1982	1983	1984
Duncan v. Maryland (D)	Jacobs v. Board of Regents (Florida) (D)	Guertin v. Hackerman (Rice Univ.) (D)	MSU Faculty Assoc. v. Michigan State Univ. (D)	Baruah v. Young (Univ. of Maryland) (D)	Zahorik v. Cornell Univ. (D)	Pime v. Loyola Univ. of Chicago (D)
Hermmann v. Moore (Brooklyn Law School) (A)	Francis-Sobel v. Univ. of Maine (A)	Manning v. Tufts Univ. (A)	Lucky v. Board of Regents (Florida) (D)	Sanders v. Duke Univ. (D)	Berry v. Board of Supervisors, LSU (A)	Cohen v. Temple Univ. (D)
EEOC v. Mississippi College (D)	Shawer v. Indiana Univ. (A)	EEOC v. Southwest Baptist Seminary (D)	Vaughn v. Regents, Univ. of California (D)	Penk v. Oregon State Board of Education (D)	Ghosh v. NYU Medical Center (D)	Duke v. Univ. of Texas, El Paso (A)
Marshall v. Kent State (A)	Abramson v. Univ. of Hawaii (A)	Chai v. Michigan Tech. Univ. (D)	Franklin v. Herbert Lehman College (D)	Adler v. John Carroll Univ. (D)	Soble v. Univ. of Maryland (D)[a]	Beverly v. Douglas (Cornell Univ. Medical College) (D)
Sweeney v. Board of Trustees (Keene State College) (A)	Ricks v. Delaware State College (A)	Sobel and EEOC v. Yeshiva Univ. (D)	Denny v. Westfield State College (D)	Carpenter v. Board of Regents (Univ. of Wisconsin) (D)	Chang v. Univ. of Rhode Island (D)	McAdoo v. Toll (D)
Whitaker v. Board of Higher Education (City of New York) (D)	Ottaviani v. SUNY (New Paltz) (D)	EEOC v. Univ. of Pittsburgh (D)	Lazic v. Univ. of Pennsylvania (D)	EEOC v. Univ. of Notre Dame (D)	Billings v. Wichita State Univ. (D)	St. Louis v. Alverno College (A)
Rajender v. Univ. of Minnesota (D)	Rajender v. Univ. of Minnesota (D)	Haugh v. Iona College (D)	Meehan v. New England School of Law (D)	EEOC v. Troy State Univ. (A)	Abrams v. Baylor College of Medicine (D)	Pande v. Johns Hopkins Univ. (D)
Hudak v. Curators of Univ. of Missouri (A)	Karlen v. New York Univ. (D)	EEOC v. Mississippi College (A)	Ottaviani v. SUNY (New Paltz) (D)	Lyon v. Temple Univ. (D)	Felton v. Trustees of California State Univ. (A)	
Marshall v. Univ. of Texas, El Paso (D)	Henry v. Texas Tech Univ. (D)	Ritter v. Mt. St. Mary's College	McAloon v. Bryant College (D)	Russell v. Belmont College (D)	EEOC v. Univ. of Notre Dame (A)	
Townsel v. Univ. of Alabama (D)	Eichmann v. Indiana State Univ. (A)	Jepsen v. Florida Board of Regents (A)	Al-Khazraji v. St. Francis College (D)	Spaulding v. Univ. of Washington (D)	Behlar v. Smith (Univ. of Arkansas) (A)	
	Leake v. Univ. of Cincinnati (A)	Ricks v. Delaware State College (S)	Penk v. Oregon State Board of Education (D)	Sessum v. Houston Comm. College (D)	Zaustinsky v. Univ. of California (D)[a]	
	Muhich v. Allen (A)	Hoth v. Grinnell College (D)		Behlar v. Smith (Univ. of Arkansas) (D)	Garcia v. Univ. of Kansas (A)	
	Hunter v. Ward (Univ. of Arkansas) (D)					

Hyatt v. Agricultural and Technical College (SUNY) (D)

Lamphere v. Brown Univ. (A)

Sobel v. Yeshiva Univ. (D)

Veeder v. Trustees of Boston College (D)

Jacobs v. College of William and Mary (D)

Larsen v. Kirkham (L.D.S. Business College) (D)

Lynn v. Board of Regents (Univ. of Calif.) (A)

Bickley v. Univ. of Maryland (D)

Zahorik v. Cornell Univ. (D)

Middleton-Keirn v. Stone (Jacksonville State) (A)

Black Faculty Assoc. v. San Diego Comm. College District (A)

Duke v. Univ. of Texas, El Paso (A)

Rivas v. State Board for Comm. Colleges (Pikes Peak Comm. Coll.) (D)

Rubin v. Univ. of Minnesota (A)

EEOC v. Univ. of Pittsburgh (A)

EEOC v. Southwest Baptist Seminary (A)

Lyon v. Temple Univ. (D)

Gray v. Board of Higher Education (CUNY) (D)

Sanders v. Duke Univ. (D)

Weise v. Syracuse Univ. (D)

Bernhard v. Dutchess Comm. College (D)

Gray v. Board of Higher Education (CUNY) (A)

Notes: Names of winning parties appear in italics; in split decisions, names of both parties appear in italics; A = appellate court; D = district court; S = Supreme Court.

[a]Affirmed 1985

TABLE 5. Federal Judicial Decisions on Higher Education Faculty Discrimination Based on the Merits, 1971–77

1971	1972	1973	1974
Green v. *Board of Regents (Texas Tech.)* (D)		Green v. *Board of Regents (Texas Tech.)* (A) Shipley v. *Fisk Univ.* (D) Faro v. *New York Univ.* (D)	Van de Vate v. *Boling (Univ. of Tennessee)* (A) Faro v. *New York Univ.* (A)

Notes: Cases containing issues involving both merits and procedure are included; names of winning parties appear in italics; in split decisions, names of both parties appear in italics; A = appellate court; D = district court.

aAffirmed 1985

It is clear that federal courts have responded to the plaintiffs' procedural and jurisdictional claims in a very different way from claims on the merits.[8] Of the 156 procedural/jurisdictional decisions, 58 have been in favor of the plaintiff and 77 for the defendant, and 21 have been split decisions in which both parties have won and lost on different issues. On the other hand, plaintiffs have won only 34 of the 160 decisions that reached the merits (6 were split). One can speculate that where academic plaintiffs have raised procedural/jurisdictional issues that were part of the mainstream of civil rights law, they have been relatively successful. But where they have raised claims that touched the distinctive nature of the academic personnel process, judges

1975	1976	1977
Spieldoch v. *Maryville College* (D)	Dyson v. *Lavery (Va. Poly. Inst.)* (D)	Cussler v. *Univ. of Maryland* (D)
EEOC v. Tufts Univ. (D)	Peters v. *Middlebury College* (D)	Johnson v. *Univ. of Pittsburgh* (D)
Labat v. *Board of Higher Education (New York City)* (D)	Kutska v. *California State College* (D)	Presseissen v. *Swarthmore College* (D)
Chung v. *Morehouse College* (D)	Davis v. *Weidner (Univ. of Wisconsin-Green Bay)* (D)	Molthan v. *Temple Univ.* (D)[a]
Sime v. *Trustees, California State Univ. and Colleges* (A)	Mosby v. *Webster College* (D)	EEOC v. *Colby College* (D)
Board of Regents *(Univ. of Nebraska)* v. Dawes (D)	Keyes v. *Lenoir Rhyne College* (D)	Huang v. *College of Holy Cross* (D)
	Mecklenberg v. Montana State Univ. (D)	Keyes v. *Lenoir Rhyne College* (A)
	Cramer v. Virginia Commonwealth Univ. (D)	Mosby v. *Webster College* (A)
	Board of Regents (Univ. of Nebraska) v. *Dawes* (A)	United States v. *Univ. of Maryland* (D)
	Silverman v. *Lehigh Univ.* (D)	Citron v. *Jackson State Univ.* (D)
	Chambliss v. *Foote* (D)	Klain v. *Pennsylvania State Univ.* (D)
	Jawa v. *Fayetteville State Univ.* (D)	Chambliss v. *Foote* (A)
		Kutska v. *California State College* (A)
		Jepsen v. *Florida Board of Regents* (D)

have been reluctant to intervene. The classic statement of that position occurred when the Second Circuit Court of Appeals said, "[E]ducation and faculty appointments are probably the least suited for federal court supervision."[9] Judges have frequently repeated that sentiment when they have chosen not to intervene.

The matter is more complex when one examines the characteristics of the plaintiff winners. The most common kind of case is the single white female plaintiff suing a predominantly white institution—the kind the congressional supporters of the 1972 amendment envisioned when the legislation was changed. Out of the 116 cases decided on the merits, 47 are of this type.[10] In only 9 of these cases has the individual plaintiff prevailed. In two special instances, however, women have won. Class actions have been more successful. Female class plaintiffs have won 5 out of 12 times. The other suc-

TABLE 6. Federal Judicial Decisions on Higher Education Faculty Discrimination Based on the Merits, 1978–84

1978	1979	1980	1981	1982	1983	1984
Cap v. Lehigh Univ. (D)	Sweeney v. Board of Trustees (Keene State College) (A)	Barding v. Board of Curators (Lincoln Univ.) (D)	Cooper v. Univ. of Texas, Dallas (A)	Greer v. Univ. of Arkansas (D)	Melani v. Board of Higher Education (City of New York) (A)	Craik v. Minnesota State Univ. Board (A)
Powell v. Syracuse Univ. (A)	Scott v. Univ. of Delaware (A)	Jacobs v. College of William and Mary (D)	Carton v. Trustees of Tufts College (D)	Dewey v. Univ. of New Hampshire (A)	Hooker v. Tufts Univ. (D)	Tolliver v. Yeargan (Univ. of Arkansas) (A)
Sweeney v. Board of Trustees (Keene State College) (A)	Fisher v. Flynn (Bridgewater State) (A)	Timper v. Board of Regents (Univ. of Wisconsin) (D)	Timper v. Board of Regents (Univ. of Wisconsin) (D)	EEOC v. Cleveland State Univ. (D)	Turgeon v. Howard Univ. (D)	Abrams v. Baylor College of Medicine (D)
EEOC v. Colby College (A)	Laborde v. Regents, Univ. of California (A)	Laborde v. Regents, Univ. of California (D)	Riley v. Univ. of Lowell (A)	Elias v. El Paso County Comm. College Dist. (D)	EEOC v. McCarthy (Framingham State College) (D)	Walton v. St. Louis Comm. College (D)
Kunda v. Muhlenberg College (D)	Davis v. Weidner (Univ. of Wisconsin-Green Bay) (A)	Fisher v. Dillard Univ. (D)	Davis v. State Board for Comm. Colleges (D)	Johnson v. Michigan State Univ. (D)	Ende v. Board of Regents (Northern Illinois Univ. (D)[b]	Zahorik v. Cornell Univ. (A)
Craig v. Alabama State Univ. (D)	Ishigami v. Univ. of Hawaii (D)	Kunda v. Muhlenberg College (A)	Meehan v. New England School of Law (D)	Leftwich v. Harris-Stowe State College (D)	Kumar v. Univ. of Massachusetts (D)[c]	Winkes v. Brown Univ. (A)
Scott v. Univ. of Delaware (D)	Lynn v. Board of Regents (Univ. of Calif.) (D)	Whiting v. Jackson State Univ. (A)	Lamb v. Rantoul (R.I. School of Design) (D)	Scagnelli v. Whiting (N.C. Central Univ.) (D)	Kureshy v. CUNY (D)	Langland v. Vanderbilt Univ. (D)[b]
Hill v. Nettleton (Colorado State Univ.) (D)	Spirt v. T.I.A.A. (D)	Manning v. Tufts Univ. (A)	Valentine v. Smith (Arkansas State Univ.) (A)	Melanson v. Rantoul (R.I. School of Design) (D)	Lincoln v. Board of Regents (Savannah State) (A)	Spaulding v. Univ. of Washington (A)
Citron v. Jackson State Univ. (A)	Smith v. Univ. of North Carolina (D)	Marshall v. Georgia Southwestern College (D)	Acosta v. Univ. of the District of Columbia (D)	Lamphere v. Brown Univ. (A)	McMillan v. Rust College (A)	Spirt v. T.I.A.A. (A)
Presseisen v. Swarthmore College (A)	Lieberman v. Gant (Univ. of Connecticut) (D)	Campbell v. Ramsey (Univ. of Arkansas) (A, D)	Gupta v. East Texas State Univ. (A)	Laborde v. Regents, Univ. of California (A)	Planells v. Howard Univ. (D)	Ford v. Nicks (A)
	Cooper v. Univ. of Texas, Dallas (D)	Gilinsky v. Columbia Univ. (D)	Hernandez-Cruz v. Fordham Univ. (D)	Spirt v. T.I.A.A. (D)	Sobel v. Yeshiva Univ. (D)	Coser v. Moore (A)
	Peters v. Wayne State Univ. (D)	Banerjee v. Smith College (D)	Guertin v. Hackerman (Rice Univ.) (D)	Hein v. Oregon College of Education (A)	Taylor v. Southern Univ. of New Orleans (D)	Lewis v. St. Louis Univ. (A)
	Wilkens v. Univ. of Houston (D)	Smith v. Univ. of North Carolina (A)		Taylor v. Southern Univ. of New Orleans (D)	Hou v. Slippery Rock State College (D)	Palmer v. Dist. Board of Trustees (St. Petersburg Jr. College) (A)
		Lamb v. Scripps College (A)				Carpenter v. Board of Regents (Univ. of Wisconsin) (A)
		Mittelstaedt v. Univ. of Arkansas (D)				

Lieberman v. Gant Univ. of Connecticut) (A)

Schwartz v. Florida (D)

Croushorn v. Board of Trustees of Univ. of Tennessee (D)

Lamphere v. Brown Univ. (D)

Craig v. Alabama State Univ. (A)

Cohen v. Comm. College of Philadelphia (D)

Cramer v. Virginia Commonwealth Univ. (D)

Jepsen v. Florida Board of Regents (A)

Joshi v. Florida State Univ. (D)

Mitchell v. Visser (Emporia State Univ.) (D)

Kim v. Coppin State College (A)

White v. Univ. of Massachusetts (D)

Jamerson v. Board of Trustees (Univ. of Alabama) (A)

Wilkens v. Univ. of Houston (A)

Banerjee v. Smith College (A)

Levine v. Fairleigh Dickinson Univ. (A)

Jacobs v. College of William and Mary (A)

Gilinsky v. Columbia Univ. (D)

Joshi v. Florida State Univ. (A)

Lewis v. Central Piedmont Comm. College (A)

Peters v. Wayne State Univ.[a] (A)

Tolliver v. Yeargan (Univ. of Arkansas) (D)

Johnson v. Michigan State Univ. (A)

Meehan v. New England School of Law (A)

Greer v. Univ. of Arkansas Board of Trustees (A)

Berry v. Board of Supervisors, LSU (A)

Coser v. Moore (D)

Wilkens v. Univ. of Houston (A)

Leftwich v. Harris-Stowe State College (A)

Lewis v. St. Louis Univ. (D)

Felton v. Trustees of California State Univ. (A)

Araujo v. Trustees of Boston College (D)

Harmond v. Board of Regents (Armstrong State College, Ga.) (D)

Notes: Names of winning parties appear in italics; in split decisions, names of both parties appear in italics; A = appellate court; D = district court.

[a] Vacated and remanded, 1983 (Supreme Court)

[b] Affirmed on appeal, 1985

[c] Reversed on appeal, 1985

cessful category is white females who have sued black institutions. They have won 4 out of 4 times. Indeed, the only environment in which plaintiffs have generally been successful is when whites sued black institutions. In these cases plaintiffs, both male and female, have won 8 out of 12 times. On the other hand, when blacks (11) or other ethnic minorities (12) have sued white institutions, they have almost always lost. This is certainly not an outcome anyone would have predicted when the congressional amendments were passed in 1972.

Legal Procedures in Academic Discrimination Cases

Why have the decisions in this area of litigation been so negative for the plaintiffs? Partly it is because of a long-standing judicial deference to the decisions of academic administrators and trustees. Although litigation against colleges and universities for any reason was comparatively rare until the mid-twentieth century, prevailing judicial views regarded higher education as a privilege rather than a right, and plaintiffs almost always lost when they challenged academic decisions.[11] In 1929 a court even upheld the expulsion, without notice of charges or hearing, of a state teachers college coed who rode in a car on the lap of a male student and smoked a cigarette.[12] Students' rights have advanced considerably since then.

One might have thought the civil rights movement and the enforcement powers in the legislation it stimulated would have had an impact on faculty personnel practices comparable to those in other employment areas that have been dominated by white males. Depending on their complaints, plaintiffs potentially have four major legal devices with which to attack an allegedly discriminatory employment practice. They can argue that their rights under the Fourteenth Amendment, the Civil Rights Acts of 1866 and 1871 (sections 1981, 1983, and 1985), Title VII of the Civil Rights Act of 1964, or the Equal Pay Act were violated. In some cases, the federal provisions against discrimination on the grounds of age or handicap will also be involved. In still other cases, state statutes will be used.

To prevail in any case, a plaintiff must meet the burden of proof as set by the particular statutes under which the suit is brought and the judicial precedents interpreting it. This burden varies substantially from statute to statute, and these variations dictate the strategies of both sides in the case. Public institutions can be sued for employment discrimination on the grounds that they have violated due process and equal protection clauses of the Fourteenth Amendment. Such suits do not occur very often, however, because the Supreme Court in *Washington v. Davis*[13] ruled that intentional discrimination must be proved in order for the plaintiff to prevail on equal protection grounds. In the modern era, employment discrimination is generally well hidden, so proving intent is exceedingly difficult. Under section 1981 of the Civil Rights Act, intentional discrimination must be proven as well, while under section 1983, although public officials may be held personally liable for violating a plaintiff's civil rights, they are covered by a qualified good-faith immunity and are held liable only if their conduct was blatantly and intentionally illegal.[14] Unless a defendant has been indiscreet enough to state publicly that the action was based solely on discrimination, or unless such an admission has been captured by a tape recorder, proving intentional, knowing discrimination is extremely difficult for plaintiffs.

Consequently, most suits alleging employment discrimination are brought under Title VII of the Civil Rights Act. This act permits plaintiffs to recover if they can show discriminatory impact as well as discriminatory intent. Impact is the easier test, particularly if the suit is a class (group) action, which Title VII encourages, since statistics can be used to make or buttress a case.

Whether or not it occurs in the context of an academic organization, employment discrimination litigation under Title VII is specialized and complicated and requires substantial evidence for a plaintiff to prevail. An elaborate order of proof has been developed following the Supreme Court's decision in *McDonnell-Douglas Co. v. Green.*[15] Furthermore, litigation over employment decisions involving professionals or high-level executives requires judicial review of subjective evaluations of those employees' competence, a review with which judges are uncomfortable because it places them in a position of second-guessing the decisions of individuals who have specialized expertise and knowledge the judge does not.[16] For that reason, judges hearing claims of employment discrimination by professionals or high-level, white-collar employees will generally review the fairness of the procedures used to evaluate the employee and make the decision; they will not inquire into the accuracy of the decision or the appropriateness of the criteria used to judge the individual.[17] That is also the case in higher education litigation, where the courts generally review the fairness and sufficiency of the decision-making procedures but refuse to "sit as a super-tenure review committee" and review the substance of the decision.[18]

Characteristics of Faculty Employment Decisions

The courts' discomfort with scrutinizing the accuracy of employment decisions made in academe is not surprising, given the complexity (and some would say the medieval nature) of the decision-making process used. Academic norms require that the initial evaluation and recommendation be made by the faculty member's peers, a process normally carried out in secrecy, sometimes without giving the candidate for reappointment, promotion, or tenure an opportunity to provide the decision-making group with appropriate materials regarding his or her performance.[19] Furthermore, the deliberations of peer review groups are frequently informal and use broad criteria that can be interpreted in various ways. Many institutions also solicit the views of specialists outside the employing college or university who are familiar with the candidate's scholarship and professional status. In an effort to encourage candor on the part of the external evaluators, their letters are usually not revealed to the candidate, even if the peer group or higher administrative levels rely on them to support a negative employment decision.[20]

The problems of academic personnel decision making do not rest solely with the faculty peer review groups. In higher education, administrators responsible for academic issues are trained generally as scholars in a particular discipline rather than as managers.[21] Therefore, many department chairs, deans, and academic vice-presidents hold the same norms and values as the faculty peer groups whose decisions they review, but may have little understanding or appreciation for the *institutional* ramifications of improperly made peer review decisions. The delegation of faculty employment decisions to the department level combined with the lack of accountability of peer review groups, when added to the lack of training or knowledge of academic administrators concerning the legal and practical requirements of personnel decision making, have often resulted in institutional practices that are difficult to defend in court.

Given the limited demand for faculty in most disciplines, a particular denial of tenure[22] or refusal to hire decision may terminate or severely alter careers so that litigation may seem a necessary option. On the other hand, since plaintiffs frequently challenge basic assumptions in the faculty employment process (secrecy of peer review, requirement of a Ph.D. or publication) as well as the merits of a particular decision, defendants often see themselves as protecting general academic principles as well as the unique characteristics of their previous decision. For both sides the stakes in these cases are often high enough to make them pursue the lawsuits vigorously.

It is not surprising, then, that academic discrimination cases are complicated and lengthy, require extensive collection of documentary and testimonial evidence, and result in frustration and heavy expenses for both parties, no matter who prevails. For this reason, it is important for both faculty plaintiffs and defendant colleges to understand the requirements of litigating an academic employment discrimination case. Furthermore, the details of the case studies in the next five chapters will be more meaningful when the evidentiary and procedural requirements of an academic employment discrimination case are understood.

Legal Requirements of an Academic Discrimination Case

Despite the merit of a faculty plaintiff's position or the conviction a college or university may feel in making a negative employment decision, both must produce extensive information to support their claims. The plaintiff has the burden of proof throughout the litigation. The court[23] must be convinced that he or she was not only qualified for the position (or the promotion or tenure), but that the reason for the negative decision was discrimination and not a neutral business reason that would be permissible despite the individual's qualifications. The defendant college or university must demonstrate that the decision was made for a neutral reason and must support that allegation with sufficient proof to convince the judge that its behavior was appropriate. Therefore, the order and burden of producing evidence are important to an understanding of the litigation of these cases and the types of evidence used by each party.

The plaintiff is responsible for first establishing a prima facie case of discrimination. In order to establish such a case, the plaintiff must prove

1. that he or she belongs to a class protected by Title VII.
2. that the plaintiff sought and was qualified for reappointment, promotion, tenure, or whatever is at issue.
3. that the plaintiff was not reappointed, promoted, or awarded tenure.
4. that, in hiring or reappointment cases, the college sought applicants with qualifications similar to the plaintiff's to fill the plaintiff's position, or in the case of promotion or tenure, the employer promoted or awarded tenure to other persons possessing similar qualifications at approximately the same time.[24]

Over the fifteen years in which faculty have been litigating negative employment decisions, the courts have decided that the plaintiff has proven the prima facie case if he or she can demonstrate through objective evidence that the four requirements have been met. In other words, the plaintiff need only show that he or she had the same paper qualifications (degrees, experience, and so on) as successful candidates for hiring, promotion, or tenure; the issue of whether the plaintiff was subjectively qualified (i.e., the appropriateness of the college's assessment of the plaintiff's performance and abilities) is left for the second stage of the discrimination case and must be demonstrated by the defendant college. Although some judges have criticized applying only objective criteria to the prima facie case,[25] the prevailing practice is to leave the analysis of the plaintiff's subjective qualifications to the defendant college's rebuttal.

Once the plaintiff has successfully established a prima facie case of discrimination, the evidentiary burden shifts to the defendant to "articulate some legitimate, nondiscriminatory reason" for the negative employment decision.[26] The college need not prove that the neutral reason was the deciding factor, but only that there were sufficient neutral grounds for denying further employment (or promotion) to the faculty member. At this point, the institution must produce evidence that the faculty member was unqualified for further employment or that some neutral institutional reason (such as a new curriculum the plaintiff was not qualified to teach or a decision no longer to award tenure to individuals teaching in departments where student enrollment was declining) was responsible for the negative decision.

In many academic discrimination cases, institutions attempt to prove that the faculty plaintiff did not meet one or more of the criteria for reappointment, promotion, or tenure: scholarship, teaching, and service to the college or to the profession. Typically, the institution attempts to establish that the individual faculty member was a mediocre or poor teacher or scholar or that he or she failed to meet the performance standards in some other way. Furthermore, institutions have successfully argued that a plaintiff's incompatibility with departmental colleagues, either on a personal level or in terms of the plaintiff's research or teaching specialty, is a sufficiently neutral reason to support a negative employment decision.[27]

After the defendant college has completed its rebuttal, the plaintiff must prove one final issue: that the "legitimate nondiscriminatory reason" for the negative decision was not the reason supporting the decision but was, in fact, a pretext for discrimination. Academics have only occasionally been successful in proving the college's reasons pretextual, for they must show either that "a discriminatory reason more likely motivated the employer" or that "the employer's proffered explanation is unworthy of credence."[28] Judges generally accept the college's proffered reason for the negative employment decision, especially if it involves a determination that the plaintiff's performance was inadequate in some respect. In the few cases in which individual plaintiffs have prevailed, they have been able to show considerable conduct by the defendant college that was inconsistent with the negative employment decision, such as awarding promotions or salary increases to less qualified faculty, or treating similarly situated majority class members more favorably than the plaintiff.

Generally speaking, if a defendant college or university can demonstrate that the individuals and groups responsible for making recommendations or decisions on faculty employment issues have used the stated criteria, have followed their stated procedures, have documented the reasons for the negative decision, and have treated similar faculty members in the same way that the plaintiff was treated, the institutions have prevailed. Even in situations where statistical evidence demonstrates that women or racial minorities are severely underrepresented within the institution, or where no women or minorities have attained promotion or tenure in the past, the courts still review the fairness and reasonableness of the particular action of the defendant college, and, absent evidence of differential treatment or intentional bias, the college usually prevails.

Recent developments in class litigation involving claims of salary discrimination have been more favorable to plaintiffs. The courts have been forced to rely on statistical studies of salary fairness, usually based on regression analysis, in order to separate the effects of legitimate salary decision criteria, such as years of experience and degree held, from impermissible criteria, such as race or sex. These cases have truly become battles of the experts, with federal judges left to decide which expert was the most convincing.

Litigation alleging salary discrimination has been especially troublesome for institutions of higher education because salary decisions, like decisions concerning promotion and tenure, are often made using subjective and poorly defined criteria. Unless the institution has a uniform salary schedule for faculty (which is not unusual in two-year institutions but is rare in four-year colleges and universities), decisions about starting salaries or annual salary increases are usually made by department chairs or deans. This may result in substantial discrepancies in salaries between departments and among faculty members. The decentralization of salary decisions and the tendency for women faculty to be clustered in disciplines in which faculty receive lower average salaries (e.g., nursing, social sciences, and the humanities) may lead to lower salaries for women without intentional discrimination on the institution's part.

Nevertheless, institutions may be held accountable for salary differences that disfavor women. Although female plaintiffs have lost several sizable class action suits,[29] they have won in others, and the potential judgments assessed against their institutions are, in some cases, enormous. For example, in *Melani v. Board of Higher Education,*[30] women faculty and administrators alleged that sex discrimination infected the hiring, promotion, and salary decisions at the City University of New York, using statistical data exclusively to present their case. The trial judge agreed and ruled that the university must provide back pay and salary adjustments for members of the plaintiff class, an outcome which may cost the university in excess of $60 million.[31]

One special problem related to salary equity litigation is the ill-defined nature of academic work. For example, accurate results in a regression analysis of faculty salaries depend upon correct assumptions about the factors involved in setting salary levels and the identification of measurable variables that can be included within the regression. The productivity of individual faculty members may be a factor in arriving at salary decisions, but neither legal scholars, statisticians, nor experts on faculty issues have been able to agree on how to measure productivity in a way that can be incorporated in a regression analysis. How does one measure the value of an award-winning book as compared with five articles in respected scholarly journals? Because regression analysis and other statistical models that seek to separate the effects of discrimination from the effects of neutral decision-making criteria depend on quantitative, or measurable, indicators rather than the subjective criteria normally used to evaluate faculty performance, attempts to use statistical tools to ascertain the equity of academic salaries have been inadequate in many respects.[32]

Consequently, whether the issue is tenure, promotion, or salaries, academic discrimination litigation is particularly complex, presenting difficult challenges to the parties, their lawyers, and, ultimately, the courts.

Analyzing the Consequences of Academic Discrimination Litigation

Examining decisions to determine procedural rules, who sued and who was sued, what the issues were, and who won and who lost is a conventional way to look at a field of litigation, but it can be a highly misleading gauge of the real impact of litigation. As pointed out in chapter 1, many lawsuits are settled before a trial occurs, so there is no decision. But even when a decision is reached, it may not be published and thus cannot be counted in surveys like the one we have conducted. Furthermore, when decisions are printed, the judge is interested in articulating and applying legal rules and not in the impact of the process on those who have appeared before him or her. Yet litigation frequently spans several years, costs thousands of dollars, takes up the time of scores of people, and inflicts anxiety on winners and losers alike. None of this may be reflected in the judicial decision. Worse, the decision may distort reality. Egon Brenner, executive vice-president of Yeshiva University, remarked about the famous Supreme Court case involving his institution that curtailed the formation of faculty unions, "The Yeshiva of the Supreme Court's decision is not associated with the real Yeshiva. The Court's Yeshiva is just a piece of paper."[33]

The mere act of litigation may have political, organizational, financial, and emotional consequences. Careers may be broken; personnel policies may be improved or made more devious; academic units may become more cohesive or divided; governance may become more centralized or decentralized; institutions may become more autonomous or accountable to external bodies. Yet our systematic knowledge of these consequences of the litigation process is almost nil. To understand them, we must delve beneath the decision to understand the context and cross-currents of the lawsuit. For that case studies are necessary.

Methodology

We used several considerations in selecting particular cases for detailed investigation. About half of the 316 academic discrimination decisions are based on procedural or jurisdictional questions and do not reach a determination on whether discrimination occurred. These cases may be very important in the development of the law, but they are usually duels between teams of lawyers with little involvement of or practical impact on other participants. These cases are listed in tables 3 and 4, but they were excluded as possibilities for full-scale case studies. Of the remaining cases, which were decided on the merits, we had the resources to investigate fully six for our report to the Carnegie Corporation of New York. To make this book of manageable length, we have presented five of the case studies in full (*Acosta* has been omitted), although we have drawn insights from all six. In choosing cases for study, we decided against a random selection because that procedure might have turned up too many cases that were substantively uninteresting or that did not reflect an appropriate diversity. In the end, we created a stratified sample (modified for reasons of access and geographical considerations) aimed at representing the major types of issues, plaintiffs, defendant institutions, and judicial outcomes.

The cases selected were:

I. Individual women

A. Defendant prevailed: *Lieberman v. Gant*[34] (University of Connecticut).

This was one of the most prominent cases of that large category where female faculty have challenged the denial of tenure. In addition to the issue of Lieberman's personal qualifications as a candidate for tenure in English, the case was fiercely contested over the kind of evidence about male counterparts that could be introduced and considered. Judge Henry Friendly finally wrote for the Second Circuit that federal courts should not engage in "tired-eye review" of academic personnel decisions. This principle, if followed, may foreclose other tenure appeals.

B. Plaintiff prevailed: *Kunda v. Muhlenberg College*.[35]

Kunda is the first instance where courts ruled in favor of a woman in a tenure case. On appeal, which the college lost two to one, several national organizations filed amicus curiae briefs regarding the trial judge's award of "conditional tenure."

II. Minorities

A. Defendant prevailed: *Scott v. University of Delaware*.[36]

This case, brought by a black sociologist, had potentially major ramifications. The university had been de jure segregated and still had few blacks among the students or faculty. With the aid of the Equal Employment Opportunity Commission (EEOC), Scott sought not only a tenured position for himself but also a court order requiring the university to hire the same percentage of blacks as resided in the state. He also challenged the university's subjective tenure criteria, its decentralized procedures, and its Ph.D. requirements. Scott was unsuccessful in certifying the class and also lost on the merits.

B. Plaintiff prevailed: *Acosta v. University of the District of Columbia*.[37]

Acosta, a Puerto Rican, sued over denial of promotion. The judge found the university's personnel procedures entirely unsatisfactory and ordered the promotion.

III. Class actions

A. Plaintiff prevailed: *Mecklenberg v. Montana State University*.[38]

This case is the most comprehensive victory women plaintiffs have ever won. Not only did several individual plaintiffs win remedies, but the final order restructured university governance, personnel procedures, and the salary system. The case is unusual in the judge's reliance on a posttrial agreement hammered out by the opposing parties and by the willingness of the university to cooperate in the agreed-upon change.

B. Settled: *Rajender v. University of Minnesota*.[39]

This case, brought by a female assistant professor of chemistry, eventually emerged as a 1,300-member class action suit representing all current female academic, nonstudent employees and all female past, present, and future applicants for academic, nonstudent positions at the university. The settlement, when reached, affected many categories of promotions and hiring. The case created considerable publicity because, after settlement, the court awarded fees of about $2 million to the plaintiff's attorneys.

As in all case study research, some sacrifice of quantitative validity had to be made in order to depict the uniqueness and richness of particular cases. For some research questions, however, we constructed a more comprehensive sample. For example, we wanted to know how plaintiffs dealt with their attorneys. How did they view the other parties in the university before and after the litigation? How did they estimate costs, and how did they manage them? Finally, what recommendations would they make to improve the process? For that purpose a mail questionnaire supplemented by telephone interviews was used in an attempt to reach all named plaintiffs in cases decided on the merits. We were able to obtain a 50 percent response rate for 110 plaintiffs.[40]

In addition, we sought to answer questions about the importance of academic discrimination litigation in the role of university attorneys and for faculty personnel procedures in institutions that have been sued. Consequently, we used another telephone-supplemented questionnaire for university attorneys. Here the response rate was 60 percent.

Our case study method was to seek answers to a structured set of questions generated by our litigation stages framework and by our experience with academic discrimination lawsuits. This enables the researcher and the reader to discover the common elements in each case, while not obscuring its special dimensions.

Although discrimination litigation against universities and colleges has occurred more frequently in recent years, every institution is different, and there are particular characteristics of each one that may strongly affect the way the litigation is developed and the impact of the process. Challenging a tenure or a salary decision at a research university creates problems that are different from those involved in attacking such decisions at a community college. To understand the impact of this process, therefore, one must be aware of the special circumstances of the institution. In the introduction to each case, the issues we describe are institutional history, organizational structure, political and social context, and the nature of the personnel process.

1. Triggering Incident

The first stage in the framework calls for an examination of the event(s) that led to the lawsuit. Academic discrimination cases have been brought over failure to hire, denial of tenure or promotion, and unfair salaries, benefits, or working conditions. They have been based on race, gender, ethnic, and age discrimination. Often the cases raise more than one issue. Since all the ensuing strategies and legal decisions are based on the triggering incident, it is important to understand the facts as the parties see them.

2. Perception of Alleged Discrimination

It is perception more often than fact that causes a lawsuit. In a major university, if salary adjustments are included, there will be thousands of personnel decisions annually. Many will not meet faculty expectations, others will be very disappointing, and some will be career threatening. Yet, even in this litigious era, most will be quietly accepted. A lawsuit represents an extreme response. Therefore, we are interested in how the plaintiff sees his or her environment and personal circumstances as being affected by discrimination. What combinations of self-interest and ideology lead to a decision to confront the decision makers? On the other hand, because so many personnel decisions arise every year, not all of them are based on good data, careful consideration, or dispassionate review. It is important, then, to know how the potential plaintiff is viewed by institutional decision makers and how their environment affects objectivity.

3. Problem Evaluation and Informal Consultation

For almost all academics, contemplating litigation or even instigating some other formal challenge is a first-time occurrence. Their professional training usually has provided them with no relevant experience or information. How does one proceed? Who can advise? Should one turn to family, colleagues, institutional officials (such as affirmative action officers), lawyers, advocacy groups? If one is serious about litigation, a lawyer is necessary. When should an attorney be sought? How is one eventually found? What contractual arrangements should be made? Should a network be developed for emotional or financial support? From the defendant's perspective, when is a routine faculty personnel problem about to turn into something much more formal, in which the institution must behave in a more defensive and coordinated manner? When and how does an institution find out that it may have a lawsuit on its hands? Who is alerted and who is consulted?

4. Use of Internal Remedies

In almost all academic institutions there will be some sort of appeal process. Some are carefully formulated, with broad remedial powers. Others are quite informal and are taken seriously by nobody. But beyond the institution, appeals may be taken to city, state, or federal agencies. In a few cases, professional or other private organizations can be involved. Potential plaintiffs must consider whether to use these other avenues. How are those decisions made?

From the defendant's perspective, the problem is often whether to encourage or cooperate with a plaintiff who is interested in a nonjudicial remedy. Or if that avenue is taken, should the institution honor the results if they are not satisfactory? If one wishes to assess the costs of the litigation process, it is important to understand whether other procedures were tried and, if so, why they failed to prevent the lawsuit.

5. Settlement or Litigation Decision

Most civil litigation is settled before a judicial decision is rendered. Since trials are so costly and unpredictable, there are powerful incentives for both sides to settle. Consequently, it is important to consider how and why both sides make the settlement or litigation decision. Who is consulted? What constraints exist? What strategies are employed? As the cases show, the role of the judge is often important.

6. Litigation Preparation

Academic discrimination cases, even where they do not involve class suits, are generally complex and require considerable preparation. What role do plaintiffs and their support networks play in trial preparation? Are they consulted about costs and strategies? Does the nature of their participation make a difference in the way the process affects plaintiffs? Do an attorney's philosophy and experience affect the relationship with clients? On the defendant side, a decision must be made about who will represent the institution. What difference does the choice of staff attorney, state attorney general (for public defendants), or outside counsel make? What is the character of the working relationship between the academic defendant and its legal counsel? What issues are discussed? Who is consulted? Who makes which decisions?

Also, both sides will have to decide on the use of experts and the use of quantitative data, which are often very important in civil rights cases.

7. Pretrial Impacts

From the triggering incident to the first day of trial, it is not uncommon for the process to drag on for several years. During that period, there will be flurries of activity (depositions, interrogatories, motions, briefs, pretrial hearings) and periods of silence. From the plaintiff's viewpoint, the pretrial period almost always takes too long. From the defendant's perspective, delay may be an ally.

For the plaintiff, the pretrial process will almost always have a considerable impact. What are the pretrial financial, career, and emotional costs? For the defendants, the costs are not so certain. Is the suit seen as one of many potential impediments to the efficient, autonomous operation of the institution? Can it be easily handled by existing bureaucratic mechanisms? Or has the pretrial process created substantial problems of adverse publicity, weakened public support, damaged staff morale, or resulted in high legal costs, future financial uncertainties, and a diversion of administrative attention to nonacademic pursuits?

The pretrial process will have an impact on the lawyers. Has it drained their income, channeled their energy away from other projects, antagonized judges or other attorneys, created conflicts with their clients?

8. Trial Impacts

In an academic discrimination trial, the plaintiff will be asked, under oath during examination and cross-examination, to prove the value to the institution of his or her performance. The defendant administrators and other officers, under similar adverse conditions, will have to prove the legality or at least the reasonableness of decisions made. Other academics, often only tangentially related to the case, will be brought in to have the validity of their information and even the comparative worth of their careers questioned. Experts will be produced, not all of whom always emerge with their reputations intact. But the experts are well-paid and often experienced. What is the impact of the trial process on other academics who serve involuntarily as witnesses? What is the impact on the parties and their institutions of the trial strategies employed? What is the impact of the role the judge chooses to play?

9. Decision Impacts

Although social scientists have generally not given much attention to the impact of the litigation process, there is considerable literature on the impact of the decision. What is not always recognized, however, is that decisions may have multiple impacts on different actors (some not even parties to the event or even within the jurisdiction of the court). We will be interested in the cases' rule and remedy, of course, but also on the tangible and intangible impacts on plaintiffs, defendants, and others. What were the immediate impacts on the plaintiff's finances and employment? How did the decision affect the defendant's personnel policies and procedures, governance structure, and financial obligations?

10. Posttrial Impacts

The impacts of a major lawsuit may linger long after the trial is over and in areas only indirectly touched by the decision. What is the cumulative impact on the parties of the years of being involved in litigation and the problems of implementing the remedy? What has been the effect on families and other emotional relationships? On career choices? On political, professional, and social status? How do plaintiffs view the fairness of the academic decision-making process and the legal system? In hindsight, do they believe litigating was a mistake? What would they do differently? What is the impact of the litigation process on collegial governance and the faculty's willingness to participate in peer review? Has litigation led institutions to make their personnel processes more accountable, better documented, more centralized? What has been done to avoid future litigation or better defend should it occur? What has been litigation's effects on the roles of administrators, affirmative action officers, and legal counsel? What is the effect of this type of litigation on judges, litigating agencies, and lawyers generally?

These are the questions this research will seek to answer through comprehensive descriptions of five cases and by analyzing the results of two national surveys. Not every case will be suitable to answer every question. Nor are the data consistently available even when a question is relevant to a case. Case studies, even supplemented by our larger samples, will not always provide the data to make definitive generalizations about each question. But most of these questions have never been researched before, or have been a part of micro-studies that do not relate the questions to one another or follow a case through more than one stage. This book is intended to provide a comprehensive framework for combining microstudies about specific aspects of litigation with the traditional narrative chronological case study. The focus for this study is the impact of the process on participants. This perspective and the data generated may lead to new hypotheses that can be refined and eventually tested more systematically.

Answers to these questions come from a number of sources. The court papers, where they were complete, were a marvelous compilation of depositions, interrogatories and their responses, and complaints, motions, testimony, and rulings. In the cases we chose there were often thousands of pages of such records. Such documents have the advantages of being public, chronologically arranged, sworn, and tested in the adversary process. They are, therefore, relatively reliable. Academic institutions, by their nature, produce paper—memos, committee minutes and reports, campus newspaper stories, and the like. Often these were useful sources, particularly where the university archives were complete and well organized. Always, however, the richness and texture of a case study came from interviews. For almost all cases, we interviewed the plaintiffs, their attorneys, members of support networks, defendant administrators and faculty, other institutional officers, and defense attorneys. Where they were particularly important to a case, we interviewed experts, judges, and friends and colleagues of the main participants as well. When the case studies were completed in draft form, the manuscripts were sent to many of those interviewed for their comments and corrections.

All these sources have been invaluable in our attempt to portray the impact of the litigation process more comprehensively than ever before.

NOTES

1. Both authors have written articles exploring the legal rules that have emerged in these cases. For example, Barbara A. Lee, "Balancing Confidentiality and Disclosure in Faculty Peer Review: Impact of Title VII Litigation," *Journal of College and University Law* 9 (1982–83): 279–314; "Raising the Hurdles: Judicial Response to Heightened Standards for Promotion and Tenure," *Education Law Reporter* 20 (1984): 357–64. George R. LaNoue, "Tenure and Title VII," *Journal of College and University Law* 1 (Spring, 1974): 206–21; "The Federal Judiciary, Discrimination and Academic Personnel Policy," *Policy Studies Journal* 10 (September, 1981): 105–23.
2. See George R. Kramer, "Title VII on Campus," *Columbia Law Review* 82 (1982): 1206–35.
3. Karl E. Weick, "Educational Organizations as Loosely-Coupled Systems," *Administrative Science Quarterly* 21 (1976): 1–19. "Loosely coupled" may be an overly polite term: Michael Cohen and James March have described educational governance as a "garbage can" in which goals are unclear, strategies are inconsistent, and decision making is erratic and unpredictable (*Leadership and Ambiguity* [New York: McGraw-Hill, 1976]).
4. Helen Gouldner, "The Social Impact of Campus Litigation," *Journal of Higher Education* 51, no. 3 (1980): 329, 331.
5. Harry T. Edwards, *Higher Education and the Unholy Crusade Against Governmental Regulation* (Cambridge, Mass.: Institute for Educational Management, 1980), and Walter C. Hobbs, "The Courts," in *Higher Education and American Society,* ed. P. G. Altbach and R. O. Berdahl (Buffalo: Prometheus Books, 1981), pp. 181–98.
6. 1972 U.S. Code Congressional and Administrative News 2155.
7. See, for example, Theodore Caplow and Reese McGee, *The Academic Marketplace* (New York: Doubleday and Co., 1965); Michael A. Lasorte, "Academic

Women's Salaries: Equal Pay for Equal Work?'' *Journal of Higher Education* 42 (1971): 265–78.

8. Although the procedural/jurisdictional and merit distinction is useful for analytical purposes, it is important to note that the categories are not completely separate. Losing on procedural or jurisdictional grounds may make it difficult or even impossible for the plaintiff to prevail on the merits, and so the case may be dropped or settled. On the other hand, once the plaintiff has prevailed on the procedural/jurisdictional question, the defense may be induced to settle. Cases dropped or settled are not reported, and so do not appear in table 1 or 2. Since some cases resulted in both trial and appellate court decisions, the 116 merit cases generated 160 different decisions.

9. Faro v. New York University, 502 F.2d 1229, 1231–32 (2d Cir. 1974).

10. Each case may involve one, two, or more decisions. Cases are used as the unit of analysis for this discussion, as a measure of the relative success (or lack thereof) of plaintiffs in academic discrimination litigation.

11. William A. Kaplin, *The Law of Higher Education,* 2d ed. (San Francisco: Jossey-Bass, 1985), pp. 4–7.

12. Tanton v. McKinney, 197 N.W. 510 (Mich. 1929).

13. 426 U.S. 229 (1976).

14. Wood v. Strickland, 420 U.S. 308 (1975).

15. 411 U.S. 792 (1973).

16. Elizabeth Bartholet, ''Application of Title VII to Jobs in High Places,'' *Harvard Law Review* 95 (1982): 945–1027; Andrea R. Waintroob, ''The Developing Law of Equal Employment Opportunity at the White Collar and Professional Level,'' *William and Mary Law Review* 21 (1979–80): 45–119.

17. Waintroob, ''Developing Law of Equal Opportunity.''

18. Keddie v. Pennsylvania State University, 412 F. Supp. 1264 (M.D. Pa. 1976).

19. Johnson v. University of Pittsburgh, 435 F. Supp. 1328 (W.D. Pa. 1977).

20. Note, ''Preventing Unnecessary Intrusions on University Autonomy: A Proposed Academic Freedom Privilege,'' *California Law Review* 69 (1981): 1538–68. Note, ''Academic Freedom, Secrecy, and Subjectivity as Obstacles to Proving a Title VII Sex Discrimination Suit in Academia,'' *University of North Carolina Law Journal* 60 (1982): 438–50.

21. Peter M. Blau, *The Organization of Academic Work* (New York: John Wiley and Sons, 1973).

22. The United States Supreme Court has ruled that legally a denial of renewal, promotion, or tenure should not be viewed as a denigration of a faculty member's abilities or performance. Board of Regents v. Roth, 408 U.S. 564 (1972). Nevertheless, as a practical matter in today's academic marketplace, such denials are very damaging.

23. Title VII cases are tried without a jury. However, if other claims are appended to the Title VII claim, a jury is sometimes used.

24. Smith v. University of North Carolina, 632 F.2d 316 (4th Cir. 1980), modifying the *McDonnell-Douglas* order of proof to accommodate the circumstances of academic employment decisions.

25. Lieberman v. Gant, 630 F.2d 60 (2d Cir. 1980).

26. McDonnell-Douglas Co. v. Green, 411 U.S. 792, 802 (1973). In these cases, the reader may wish to keep in mind the difference between the ultimate burden of proof and the temporary burden of producing evidence. At the end of the trial, unless the preponderance of evidence is on the plaintiff's side, he or she will lose, but according to the *McDonnell-Douglas* rules, the plaintiff can shift the immediate evidentiary burden to the defendant by establishing a prima facie case.

27. Lee, "Balancing Confidentiality and Disclosure," p. 291.

28. Texas Department of Community Affairs v. Burdine, 450 U.S. 248, 253 (1981).

29. Wilkens v. University of Houston, 654 F.2d 388 (5th Cir. 1981); Sobel v. Yeshiva University, 566 F. Supp. 1166 (S.D.N.Y. 1983).

30. Melani v. Board of Higher Education, 561 F. Supp. 769 (S.D.N.Y. 1983).

31. Robert D. McFadden, "U.S. Court Rules Against City U. in Sex-Bias Suit," *New York Times*, March 19, 1983, p. 1.

32. Thomas R. Pezzullo and Barbara E. Brittingham, *Salary Equity: Detecting Sex Bias in Salary Among College and University Professors* (Lexington, Mass.: D.C. Heath-Lexington, 1979).

33. Beverly Watkins, "What the High Court's 'Yeshiva' Decision Has Meant to Yeshiva University Itself," *Chronicle of Higher Education*, February 29, 1985, pp. 27–28.

34. 474 F. Supp. 848 (D. Conn. 1979), *aff'd*, 630 F.2d 60 (2d Cir. 1980).

35. 463 F. Supp. 294 (E.D. Pa. 1978), *aff'd*, 621 F.2d 532 (3d Cir. 1980).

36. 385 F. Supp. 937 (D. Del. 1974), 68 F.R.D. 606 (D. Del. 1975), 16 Fair Employment Practices Cases 737 (D. Del. 1976), 455 F. Supp. 1102 (D. Del. 1978), *modified*, 601 F.2d 76 (3d Cir. 1979), *cert. denied*, 444 U.S. 931 (1979).

37. 528 F. Supp. 1215 (D.D.C. 1981).

38. 13 Employment Practices Decisions ¶ 11,438 (D. Mont. 1976).

39. 20 Employment Practices Decisions ¶ 30,214, 24 Fair Employment Practices Cases 1045 (D. Minn. 1978), 20 Employment Practices Decisions ¶ 30,225, 24 Fair Employment Practices Cases 1051 (D. Minn. 1979), 546 F. Supp. 158 (D. Minn. 1982), 563 F. Supp. 401 (D. Minn. 1983).

40. A discussion of sample bias and its impact on our results can be found in chapter 8.

Chapter 3
A Faculty Wife Who Was Not a Gentleman

Lieberman v. Gant[1]

In this case, an individual woman plaintiff fought a denial of tenure for nearly ten years. Important legal issues included the admissibility of personnel files for "comparable" male faculty as well as the significance of inconsistent evaluation procedures as an indicator of discriminatory motive.

The University of Connecticut is located in a rural area in the eastern portion of the state, approximately twenty-five miles from Hartford, the state capital, and fifty miles from Providence, Rhode Island. Storrs, the community in which the university is located, has one main street, a handful of stores, a movie theater, and two restaurants geared to the tastes of college students (pizza and health food, respectively). As the state's land grant institution, the university has a campus that sprawls over rolling hills and contains a working dairy farm, three modern engineering classroom and laboratory buildings, and a range of other academic and residential buildings. The university enrolls twenty-six thousand students, and the Storrs campus is its flagship.

Until the 1960s, promotion and tenure were routinely awarded even to faculty who had few or no publications. During that decade, however, the university turned its attention to improving the quality of its graduate programs, and the emphasis on research and publication began to increase. At about the same time, the university began to be criticized for the very obvious underrepresentation of women and minorities on its faculty. It was in this environment of change and criticism that Marcia Lieberman sought a faculty position in the English department.

Triggering Incident

Ironically for an ardent feminist and committed career professional, Marcia Lieberman was employed by the university because of the scholarly reputation of her husband. The university had been anxious to recruit Philip Lieberman, an expert in intonation, speech, and transformational-generative grammar and a student of Noam Chomsky at the Massachusetts Institute of Technology (MIT), to the newly organized Department of Linguistics at the university. In the spring of 1967, the dean of the College of Liberal Arts and Sciences, Kenneth Wilson, who also held a faculty position in the English

51

department, corresponded with the Liebermans concerning an appointment at the associate professor level for Philip Lieberman and detailed his efforts to find the funds and to secure a position for Marcia Lieberman in the Department of English. Although Marcia Lieberman remembers a conversation with Kenneth Wilson in which he discouraged her from attempting to secure a full-time position at the university (saying that he did not believe in hiring faculty wives), Wilson apparently broke his own rule against employing spouses and campaigned for a position for her, even offering to provide the funds to the English department in order that she might be hired.

The English department employed a number of part-time instructors (who were not eligible for tenure), several of whom were wives of faculty members in other departments at the university. Lieberman was told that a part-time lecturer position for one semester was all that was available, and she was appointed to that position effective September, 1967, teaching one course for the sum of one thousand dollars.

Lieberman had just completed her doctorate in English at Brandeis University and had two small sons aged three and five when she and her husband moved to Storrs. She admits that she was naive about the academic tenure track system and did not understand the significance of tenure track versus non–tenure track status, nor in which category she was employed, until sometime later. There were many untenured faculty teaching in the department; some were on the tenure track and others were not. Until she had been employed by the department for several years, she was not aware that there were two classes of untenured faculty. At the time of her hiring, the forty-three-member English department (two women) did not have explicit standards for the scholarly productivity of its faculty, whether tenured or untenured. When she later attained a tenure track position, Lieberman was the department's third female faculty member.

A full-time position became available in the department effective at the beginning of 1968, when an assistant professor resigned midyear. Because Lieberman's initial appointment had been for only one semester, she was available to fill the spring semester vacancy that had occurred, and the department head, William Moynihan, appointed her to that position, at the rank of assistant professor rather than her initial rank of lecturer. Later that spring, Moynihan reappointed Lieberman to a second one-year temporary position, effective until mid-September, 1969.

Lieberman was understandably dissatisfied with the uncertainty of year-to-year temporary appointments and, beginning in the fall of 1968, sought a tenure track appointment at the assistant professor level. Because the department was large (it had grown to fifty-two members by 1972), hiring (as well as promotion and tenure evaluation) was done through an executive committee that made recommendations to the department chair. Lieberman contacted the committee, asking to be considered for a tenure track position. During the 1968–69 academic year, various faculty committees met and considered her request three times, and three times those committees recommended against offering her a tenure track position. Furthermore, three members of the executive committee read her doctoral dissertation during that year and found it unsatisfactory.[2] Despite the apparently frequent evaluation of Lieberman during that year, none of the members of the committees that reviewed her credentials, nor Moynihan, advised Lieberman that her teaching or her scholarship were unsatisfactory. And during the second semester of the 1968–69 academic year, the acting department head offered her yet another one-year temporary appointment.

In the fall of 1969, Lieberman again asked to be considered for a tenure track appointment. This time, Moynihan asked the departmental promotion and tenure committee to review her credentials and to recommend for or against a permanent position. The promotion and tenure committee voted against recommending such a position, as did the executive committee in early 1970. Furthermore, the executive committee decided to "pursue all candidates whose records were clearly superior" to Lieberman's.[3] The committee compiled a list of potential candidates and ranked them; Lieberman was rated thirteenth out of fifteen. Incredibly, the twelve individuals ranked above Lieberman refused the tenure track position when it was offered to each in turn, persuading Moynihan to offer the tenure track position to her. According to Lieberman, however, neither Moynihan nor any of the other faculty told her that she had ranked near the bottom of the pool of candidates for the position she finally obtained, or why the other candidates had refused the position. In fact, none of this information was communicated to her until the trial several years later.

By the time Marcia Lieberman's tenure track position began, she had taught at the university full time since January, 1968, or three and one-half years. Although that teaching was not in a tenure track position, university regulations mandated that such service be counted as part of the six-year probationary period for tenure evaluation purposes. (Lieberman had asked to start the tenure clock over at the beginning of her tenure track appointment, so that she would have more time to prove her worthiness of tenure, but her request was denied.) Therefore, at the beginning of her tenure track appointment, Lieberman had only two more years before the department would evaluate her for tenure and promotion to associate professor.

Because Lieberman had been a year-to-year temporary faculty member, her scholarship and teaching had not been evaluated formally by departmental committees, as was the practice for probationary tenure track faculty. The promotion and tenure committee met with her in the spring of 1971 and recommended that she improve her teaching and focus her scholarship on one subject instead of spreading her writing among several topical areas. They did not, however, otherwise explicitly criticize her scholarship, and she was recommended for reappointment by both that committee and the department head, Moynihan.

During the spring of 1972, Lieberman met with the promotion and tenure committee members, who criticized her scholarship for the first time in her presence. Upset by this second negative meeting, she consulted Moynihan, asking him for advice on how to respond to her colleagues' criticisms. Moynihan advised her to write one essay that her colleagues would "admire." Lieberman responded that she doubted that any essay she wrote would gain the admiration of her colleagues and questioned their competence to evaluate feminist criticism or linguistic analysis, the areas of inquiry upon which she had decided to focus.

At the end of the academic year, as was the routine practice, Moynihan forwarded the department's recommendations regarding reappointments to the dean. This time, Robert Lougee, who had succeeded Kenneth Wilson (now academic vice-president) as dean of the College of Liberal Arts and Sciences, wrote to Lieberman, advising her that her scholarship could potentially be found insufficient during her tenure review. The dean's letter was written on May 5, 1972; the tenure evaluation would take place less than six months later, hardly enough time for any faculty member to markedly increase scholarly productivity, because of the long lapses between the times articles are submitted for review, accepted for publication, and actually published. Furthermore, the information submitted to the dean had not included some of Lieberman's recently published articles. When she replied, advising the dean that her record was better than the information he had been given, she was not answered. As in previous years, Moynihan recommended her reappointment for an additional one-year term.

In addition to the problem of insufficient quantity of research, the fact that one of Lieberman's fields was feminist criticism sparked controversy over whether that is a legitimate scholarly discipline. Both on campuses and in the press, debate has been joined concerning the legitimacy of women's studies as an academic discipline; the tenure denials to feminist scholars at Harvard and Stanford universities and the University of California have been reported in the national press.[4] An opinion by the Ninth Circuit Court of Appeals declared that "a disdain for women's issues, and a diminished opinion of those who concentrate on those issues, is evidence of a discriminatory attitude toward women."[5] Nevertheless, honestly held differences of opinion persist concerning both the legitimacy of the area of study and the rigor with which it is pursued, a debate that has also occurred over the issue of black studies and ethnic studies. These differences have frequently resulted in nonrenewals or tenure denials to feminist scholars;[6] in order to avoid such an outcome, some researchers who concentrate on feminist criticism have felt compelled to publish in more traditional disciplines.

During the late 1960s and the first years of the 1970s, some of the women faculty and nonteaching professionals at the University of Connecticut had become active on behalf of women's causes. Marcia Lieberman either organized or joined several women's groups, including the Connecticut chapter of the Women's Equity Action League and the University of Connecticut Organization of Faculty, Professional and Classified Women.[7] In fact, Lieberman was cochair of the latter group, which produced a report critical of the status of women at the university and especially of the low rates of hiring and promotion for women faculty. This report has special political significance because it was released just prior to a campus visit by the Office for Civil Rights of the Department of Health, Education, and Welfare (HEW), which was conducting a contract compliance review of the university in order for the university to continue receiving federal grants. The subsequent HEW report was critical of the university's treatment of both women and minorities in hiring, promotion, and salaries and found that the university's maternity leave policy and nepotism policies discriminated against women.[8]

But probably the most discussed and perhaps the most irritating (from the perspective of some of her male departmental colleagues) activity Lieberman engaged in on behalf of women was her successful effort to gain a women's locker room in the theretofore all-male field house and gymnasium, necessitating the relocation (and reduction in size) of the men's locker room. Several of Lieberman's departmental colleagues, including Moynihan, made remarks to her about this event, some of which seemed jocular and some of which seemed hostile.

However, Lieberman was not only active on behalf of women at the university. She was elected to the university senate, an unusual occurrence for a junior faculty member, and served on several senate committees. She also served on the department's black studies committee and helped develop courses and curriculum in this new area.

Thus, at the end of Lieberman's probationary period, she had acquired a reputation as a strong advocate for women and a hard-working committee member; because she had not been advised of the reluctance with which she had been afforded a tenure track position, she was not fully aware of her colleagues' doubts about her scholarship and teaching abilities. She believed that she had followed the advice of the promotion and tenure committee to focus her research (she limited her subsequent work to feminist criticism and linguistic analysis) and to improve her teaching (her student evaluations did go up in the spring of 1973). She knew that some of her views were unpopular and probably made some of her departmental colleagues uncomfortable or angry, but she was not aware of the apparent dissatisfaction with her work, because of the lack of communication of the department's expectations.

Under university regulations, Marcia Lieberman had to be evaluated for promotion and tenure during the fall semester of 1972. The department's policies required a multistep review, beginning with a five-member, elected promotion and tenure committee. That committee was to make a preliminary evaluation and then meet with the departmental executive committee, composed of four tenured faculty members elected by the department and a nontenured faculty member appointed by the chair. The joint committee, as this combined group was called, would discuss the candidate, vote to recommend or deny tenure, and then report the vote to the tenured departmental faculty, who could either accept the joint committee's vote or ask it to reconsider its recommendation. A request for reconsideration would result in a second vote that would be reported directly to the department chair, who would then make an independent recommendation and forward it to the dean of the College of Liberal Arts and Sciences.

The dean was required to appoint an advisory council made up of faculty, which would also deliberate and vote on the worthiness for tenure of all candidates each year. The dean would then make an independent recommendation and forward the dossier to the academic vice-president. The academic vice-president and associate academic vice-president then would review the candidate's materials and recommend for or against tenure to the president, who would add his own recommendation to the others and present them to the board of trustees, who would make the final decision.

Marcia Lieberman was eligible for promotion to associate professor as well as for tenure, and thus each level of recommending authority had to address both issues. The votes were close at every level, which made the difficulty of the decision evident. In its initial deliberation, the promotion and tenure committee voted five-to-zero in favor of tenure and three-to-two against promotion, an unusual splitting of the promotion and tenure issues. The joint committee voted five-to-four in favor of tenure and seven-to-two against promotion, following the pattern of the earlier vote and suggesting that none of the members of the executive committee voted for either tenure or promotion. The departmental rules specified that a two-thirds majority was necessary to constitute a positive vote for either tenure or promotion, which meant that Lieberman did not receive a positive vote for tenure from the joint committee. When the tenured faculty met to consider the vote of the joint committee, they deadlocked fifteen-to-fifteen. The department head cast the tie-breaking vote, sending the matter back to the joint committee.[9]

On reconsideration, the joint committee voted five-to-four against tenure and seven-to-two against promotion. The committee allowed Lieberman to meet with them to present her case for tenure and to submit letters from scholars outside the university supporting her candidacy, but she was not able to gain more votes. The department chair, Moynihan, also recommended against both tenure and promotion and forwarded the tenure file to the dean's office.

Perception of Alleged Discrimination

At many research universities, the customary practice during the tenure review process is for the department to request assistance from scholars outside the university in evaluating the candidate's research and publications. External evaluations are sometimes sought because faculty members within the department are insufficiently familiar with the candidate's area of research to be able to evaluate it competently. And in most cases, external evaluations are sought to provide a more objective analysis of an individual's intellectual abilities than colleagues who work alongside that individual might be able to make. In order to encourage candid evaluations, the content and source of these letters are usually not revealed to the candidate.

Although it is not unusual for a department to seek the views of outside experts in reaching a decision to recommend or deny tenure, the English department at the University of Connecticut had not done so previously. However, Moynihan had anticipated that the Lieberman tenure decision would be a difficult one, and he had decided, in consultation with the academic vice-president and the dean, to seek outside experts to evaluate her published articles. He selected the dean of the College of Arts and Sciences at the University of Massachusetts, Donald Freeman, an old friend who was a former doctoral student of Kenneth Wilson, the academic vice-president. Freeman was a respected expert in linguistics, and Moynihan sent him Lieberman's articles dealing with linguistic issues. Moynihan sent her articles on feminist criticism to another outside expert, Isabel MacCaffrey, who was a professor of literature at Harvard University. Both were critical of the quality of the articles; Freeman wrote that the essays were "disappointing," made "obvious points," and were "trivial bordering on empty."[10] Professor MacCaffrey was equally critical, calling the essays sent to her "superficial," "uncritical . . . toward her own methods [of literary analysis]," and "mediocre."[11] Although Moynihan insisted that he solicited the letters solely for his own use, the tenured faculty asked him to read the letters at the meeting at which the decision was made to accept or remand the vote of the joint committee. Moynihan read one letter (MacCaffrey's), without identifying the author or the institution; the faculty did not ask him to read the second letter.[12]

Marcia Lieberman believed the sudden decision to use experts and Moynihan's method of soliciting their assistance was strong evidence of sex discrimination. First, outside experts had never before been used by the English department in tenure decisions, although they were used routinely for promotions to full professor. Although the university regulations permitted department chairs to consult individuals outside the department, this had never been done before by her department. Lieberman also objected to the way in which Moynihan communicated with the outside experts. His letter to one stated, "We have a particularly difficult tenure decision. Our Committee has already made its appraisal, but we'd like someone outside the university to be in on this one. Anonymity will be religiously kept."

Furthermore, Lieberman questioned the qualifications of the two experts to evaluate her work. Although Donald Freeman was an acknowledged expert in linguistics, there was a potential conflict of interest in his evaluation. Freeman's wife was serving as a part-time faculty member in the English department at the university; Lieberman believed that Freeman might, even unconsciously, evaluate her work more harshly because his wife might wish to obtain a permanent position in the department, which Lieberman's tenure denial could have facilitated. As to Professor MacCaffrey's evaluation, Lieberman believed that Moynihan had chosen an individual who was hostile to feminist criticism in general and who would be predisposed to be critical of Lieberman's work. To counter the effect of these letters, Lieberman asked Joan Hall, a colleague in the English department (and already tenured) to contact several experts in feminist criticism for additional evaluations of her work. Letters were received from Dwight Bolinger of Harvard, E. L. Epstein, the editor of a journal that had accepted one of Lieberman's articles, Samuel J. Keyser, head of the linguistics department at the University of Massachusetts, and Carol Ohmann, a professor of women's studies at Wesleyan University. Several University of Connecticut faculty who had read Lieberman's work also wrote in her support, including a professor in the linguistics department and another in the German department. Lieberman gave these letters to the members of the joint committee before their reconsideration vote, but they were apparently not persuasive.

At the dean's level, the dean's advisory council voted three-to-three on the tenure issue and voted unanimously against promotion. One of the members of the advisory council was a tenured faculty member in the English department, and he was not allowed to vote on tenure cases originating in his own department. However, the faculty member, William Rosen, was present during the advisory council's discussion of the Lieberman tenure decision and, as another member of that year's advisory council later testified in court, was critical of Lieberman to the other council members. A witness at the trial recounted Rosen's response to a question by an advisory council member about Lieberman's "behavior in the department." Rosen is alleged to have replied that her behavior "had been 'aggressive'; that her manner had been 'abrasive'; and that 'She had not conducted herself as a gentleman.'"

THE COURT. How about as a lady? Did you ask about that?

THE WITNESS. No, sir. . . . [He said] that she was unusually argumentative and occasionally strident . . . he mentioned her being strident in promoting the women's use of the gym.[13]

In addition to this discussion of Lieberman's behavior, the advisory council raised the issue of obtaining letters from other outside experts. However, according to Lieberman, when the council asked Moynihan to solicit more letters, the chair said that there was not enough time to do so without violating the requirements of the university promotion and tenure calendar. Therefore, the council split evenly, and the dean voted to recommend denial of both promotion and tenure. The academic vice-president and president concurred, and the board of trustees voted to deny both tenure and promotion to Marcia Lieberman on March 24, 1973, awarding her a terminal appointment for the 1973–74 academic year.

Lieberman believes that the differences in procedures used for her tenure evaluation were strong evidence of sex discrimination, especially on the part of her department head. Her efforts to determine the reasons for the tenure denial were frustrating, and she was dissatisfied with the responses she received to her questions. From her perspective, her review had been unfair. She wrote:

> My department head told me that I was being denied tenure because of the mediocre quality of my publications; this was a department in which for years everyone else with a Ph.D. and some publications had received tenure. He admitted that I had been productive; the quality, not the quantity, of my publications was at issue. If my articles were that poor, I asked, how could I have succeeded in publishing them in reputable journals? All the other assistant professors I knew were struggling to get their work accepted for publication. My department head replied that an article isn't necessarily good simply because it gets published . . . apparently, the department thought it could judge the quality of a person's work better than the journal editors could. . . . I reminded [the department head] that I had published as much as the last man who had received tenure and promotion; the chairman replied that they now thought that their decision to award tenure to the previous candidate had been a mistake.[14]

Problem Evaluation and Informal Consultation

After being notified of her department's negative vote in December, 1972, Marcia Lieberman decided to consult an attorney for advice. She chose Louis

Winer, then a partner in the New Haven firm of Tyler, Cooper, Grant, Bowerman and Keefe. Winer had attracted the attention of the higher education community in Connecticut for his successful representation of a Vietnam War protester, Irving Stolberg, whose contract had not been renewed by Southern Connecticut State College. Stolberg, who is now the minority leader of the Connecticut House of Representatives (and formerly its speaker), believed that his antiwar activism had been the motive for the college's decision not to renew his contract. The court agreed and ordered Stolberg reinstated. By the time reinstatement was ordered, however, Stolberg held an elected public office, and concurrent state employment at the college and in the legislature was prohibited by Connecticut law. Nevertheless, Stolberg's victory was noted in academic circles, and other academic clients asked Winer to represent them because of the expertise he had developed in higher education personnel matters and because of his success in the Stolberg case.

Lieberman went to New Haven to discuss the negative promotion and tenure decision with Winer. Winer agreed that the situation was serious, said he would represent her, and advised her not to seek another position in academe, because he believed her case was a strong one and that she would be reinstated. Lieberman, too, was sure that the tenure decision had been handled poorly and hoped that the decision would be reversed without resort to litigation.

Use of Internal Remedies

The university's procedures provided for a reconsideration process at several steps of the promotion and tenure decision-making system. First, Lieberman spoke before the joint committee of the English department, noting the supportive outside letters that had been solicited in her behalf, pointing out the improvement in her teaching, and reminding the committee that male faculty in earlier years had been promoted and tenured with similar or less impressive records (six published articles, two unpublished manuscripts, and work in progress). However, the joint committee took a vote after Lieberman's appearance before them and the vote was unchanged: five-to-four against tenure and seven-to-two against promotion.[15] Lieberman also spoke before the dean's advisory council prior to their vote, and Joan Hall spoke to them on Lieberman's behalf as well. Nevertheless, the council voted three-to-three on tenure and unanimously against promotion—a negative result for both decisions. When the decision reached the level of the vice-president for academic affairs, Lieberman was also afforded an opportunity to speak before the decision makers at that level (at that time, the provost, associate provost, and vice-president for academic affairs),[16] but these officials also reached a negative decision.

Although the University of Connecticut faculty are now unionized, the first contract between the union (the American Association of University Professors [AAUP]) and the university was not finalized until 1975. However, the university bylaws provided an appeal procedure that culminated in review by an elected faculty committee which then advised the president of the action he should take. Lieberman filed an appeal with the administration in the spring of 1973 but withdrew it on the advice of her attorney. Winer had studied the terms of the grievance procedure and had told her that it afforded her very little protection, because the university president made the final decision. Since the president had been involved in the earlier decision, Winer believed that spending time and resources on an appeal through the administrative grievance process would be unwise.

Settlement or Litigation Decision

The university's refusal to overturn the negative departmental vote gave Lieberman little choice, she believed, but to sue to regain her position at the university. Although Lieberman believed she would be successful in her litigation, she realized that there would be a time of unemployment before her reinstatement would occur and thought about seeking another academic position in the interim.

Early in her discussions with Winer, the issue of payment of attorney fees was discussed. Lieberman believes that Winer agreed to a contingent fee arrangement, while Winer states that no contingent fee arrangement was made. This discrepancy became a problem after the trial had concluded.

At the time that department head Moynihan had forwarded his negative recommendation to the dean's office, he had discussed with Lieberman the possibility of her obtaining a teaching position at another Connecticut institution. In fact, Moynihan offered to help her find a teaching position at one of the branch campuses of the university, an offer she rejected because faculty positions at branch campuses carried less status than main campus positions and because she believed that she deserved reinstatement and tenure. Moynihan's offer was the sole attempt on the university's part to discuss settlement with her. The case was an important one for the university, because the central administration believed that the decision not only had been a correct one but had been handled properly by the individuals and groups involved in the decision-making process. So the trustees decided that the university "had" to defend the case to obtain judicial ratification of its decision and to create a disincentive for other faculty members considering legal challenges to negative personnel decisions.

One factor that makes this case unusual is the number of individual defendants and the corresponding number of attorneys involved. Winer decided to sue all of the trustees individually and all the administrators (including Moynihan) who were involved in the negative decision both individually and in their official capacities. Because of potential conflicts of interest between some of the defendants, most of the trustees and administrators hired their own attorneys, resulting in twenty attorneys of record.[17] Obviously, the number of attorneys involved made the case quite expensive for the university, which ended up paying attorney fees for all defendants involved, even though the state attorney general has the responsibility for defending the university. It does not appear, however, that the number of attorneys or their combined fees were a consideration in the decision to defend the litigation, although it was reported that throughout the litigation the trustees were concerned about the mounting costs of defending the *Lieberman* case.

One additional factor important to the case deserves mention here. Winer had advised Lieberman to include a class action claim with her individual claim, a tactic often used in civil rights litigation to encourage a defendant to settle an individual claim to avoid the expense and embarrassment of defending an action involving every member of one or more protected classes. A class claim was plausible, for women were underrepresented at the university, and those who were employed in faculty positions were paid less than their male counterparts (a finding of the report Lieberman helped to write and also a conclusion drawn by the report issued by the Office of Civil Rights). Winer and Lieberman had done some preparation for the class action, but as the expenses for the individual action mounted, she decided to postpone the class litigation and focus on her individual claim. Therefore, Winer no longer pursued the class claim, although he contacted the Connecticut Women's Educational and Legal Fund (CWEALF), a public interest law firm funded with private contributions, and suggested that CWEALF litigate the class claim. Later, when Lieberman abandoned the class claim, Winer discontinued his conversations with CWEALF, and the class claim languished until several years later. Its eventual outcome will be discussed later in this chapter.

Litigation Preparation

To initiate the litigation process, Lieberman filed a complaint with the EEOC and received from them a right-to-sue letter on February 25, 1974. In the meantime, Winer had filed an action in her behalf against the university on May 23, 1973, claiming that the denial of tenure was a result either of sex discrimination or of her vocal efforts to equalize opportunities for women at the university, a denial of her First Amendment right of free speech. After receiving the EEOC's right-to-sue letter, Winer amended the complaint to include a specific Title VII claim as well as a claim that the tenure denial violated Lieberman's due process and equal protection rights (under the Fourteenth Amendment) and constituted a conspiracy to violate her civil rights, retaliation for exercise of her free speech rights, salary discrimination, and defamation.[18] Thus, although the claims were grounded primarily in federal civil rights and constitutional law, Winer added a state law tort claim, that of defamation.[19]

In addition to preparing the motions, interrogatories, and other discovery documents necessary to the litigation, Winer made several trips seeking help with the *Lieberman* litigation. He sought financial support from women's groups such as the National Organization for Women (NOW) and other groups involved in expanding educational opportunity for women. However, he was unable to obtain contributions from these organizations, and neither he nor Lieberman has been able to determine whether the lack of support stemmed from an unwillingness to endorse her particular claim, a lack of resources, or some other reason. More importantly, however, Winer attempted to obtain experts who would testify about the evaluation and personnel decision-making processes in universities and who could criticize the methods and procedures used in Marcia Lieberman's case. Winer believes that the use of expert witnesses in litigation, and especially in litigation of this sort, is extremely important and may be "90 to 100 percent dispositive" of the case because of the importance judges attach to the testimony of experts. Especially in this case, where the university was claiming that Lieberman's scholarship was unworthy and she was attempting to prove otherwise, the use of experts was critical, for judges are unwilling to substitute their judgment for the opinions of experts in the subjective evaluation of the quality of specialized professional work.[20] Therefore, Winer knew that it was extremely important to locate individuals with recognized expertise who were well prepared to testify about the issues and who had the right kind of courtroom presence to convince a judge of their credibility.

Winer needed to find experts who could testify about two issues: the level of Lieberman's scholarly work and the fairness of the English department's tenure evaluation process. He traveled to Philadelphia to consult with a psychology professor at the University of Pennsylvania, Henry Gleitman. He also sought advice from law and English professors at Yale University, and met with Bernice Sandler, director of the Project on the Status and Education of Women, in Washington, D.C. Lieberman talked with Elizabeth Dunn, an experienced consultant on discrimination and the academic selection process. As a result of these discussions, Winer decided to use three experts to testify about the quality of Lieberman's scholarship: a linguistics professor to evaluate her research and writing in linguistics, a feminist scholar on her feminist writings, and someone who could comment on the overall quality of her writing. Winer decided to use Wayne O'Neil, head of the MIT humanities department, to testify about the quality of Lieberman's scholarship as well as about the integrity of the evaluation procedures, and Sheila Tobias, associate provost at Wesleyan University, who agreed to testify about tenure procedures, discrimination, and the relationship between the two. In addition, Winer located another expert, Millicent McIntosh, who had been president of Barnard College and a trustee at Bryn Mawr and Kirkland colleges. Her area of expertise was English, and, as an experienced academic administrator, she was quite familiar with the intricacies of personnel decisions in higher education. She had agreed to testify on Lieberman's behalf, but the trial judge later refused to qualify her as an expert witness without stating the basis for this decision.

While Winer was searching for funding, political support, and expert witnesses, Lieberman was acting as his paralegal, filing court papers, doing library research, proofreading documents, and answering interrogatories. Lieberman's terminal contract ended in the summer of 1974, and, except for teaching classes and performing other job-related responsibilities, she spent most of the spring assisting Winer with the trial preparation work. She was actively involved in the discovery process, although Winer made all the decisions on litigation strategy (after explaining the issues to her). She obtained documents from the university and suggested the names of potential expert witnesses. She also obtained the personnel files of faculty who were promoted or tenured in the years preceding her case, in an attempt to gather comparative evidence concerning the relative qualifications of those about whom positive decisions were made.

Pretrial Impacts

Most of the pretrial impacts fell on the plaintiff. She had been advised by her attorney not to seek another academic position, so she was unemployed after the spring semester of 1974. Although the university's refusal to reverse its tenure denial and its decision to defend vigorously the charges of sex discrimination and suppression of academic freedom outraged the women's community at the university, their actions were more symbolic than substantive. The members of the Commission on the Status of Women, which Lieberman had cochaired, went to the administration and demanded to see her personnel folder. Students staged a sit-in in the university president's office (apparently without Lieberman's knowledge or consent). The assistant provost, Gail Shea, attempted to persuade the administration that Lieberman's evaluation had been handled improperly and that the decision should be reversed. (Shea herself was fired by the university at about the same time that Lieberman's terminal year ended; she sued the university, alleging sex discrimination, but did not prevail.)[21] Several women faculty members filed salary discrimination claims with the state Commission on Human Rights and Opportunities, challenging salary and promotion practices at the university. Although Lieberman reports that she felt much psychological encouragement from the university women, no formal support group was formed like the one that assisted Phyllis Rackin in her fight against the University of Pennsylvania, or others.[22] No formal fund-raising was conducted on campus in Lieberman's behalf, although many women kept in touch with her and some attended the first phase of her trial. (They were not in attendance two years later when the trial concluded, however—Lieberman reports that on most days of the second segment of the trial, she was the only woman in the courtroom.) Lieberman felt "let down, angry, and bitter" at the lack of overt support from the women's community during the litigation process. Some may have feared retaliation, especially those who were not tenured. Many were discouraged by the termination of two feminist leaders on campus—Marcia Lieberman and Gail Shea. Others later admitted to Lieberman that because of her decision to sue the university, they were treated more fairly than they believed she had been, and they felt that she was responsible for their attaining tenure. Lieberman stated that at the point at which she made the decision to litigate, she expected more support from the women's community and did not anticipate such a lengthy litigation process.

The pretrial impacts on the university were less substantial. Although the tenure denial and ensuing political demonstrations attracted some attention, it was of brief duration. Faculty members from other departments report that although there was a widespread belief that the English department had held Lieberman to a higher standard than males had been required to meet, there was no feeling that her research was demonstrably better than that of other department members. Department morale was only marginally affected, according to both Professors Hall and Moynihan, although tenure decisions made in the next few years were approached with great care, and the next woman tenure candidate was recommended for tenure and received it. Because both the department and the university administration believed that the department had acted appropriately, there was little impetus to change personnel policies.

Trial Impacts

The *Lieberman* trial was long and complex. It "produced a transcript of nearly 10,000 pages and almost 400 exhibits and consumed 52 days of court time. The docket entries stretch over 32 pages."[23] Among academic discrimination cases its length may be second only to that of *Johnson v. University of Pittsburgh*, which required seventy-four days of trial and 12,085 pages of testimony.[24] The large number of defendants (eighteen), the sizable number of counts (five), the variety of claims (civil rights, constitutional, state law tort, conspiracy), and the large number of witnesses, combined with the "protracted illness" of attorney Winer, produced a lengthy litigation process that demanded substantial human and financial resources from both parties. The trial began on April 20, 1976, and ended over two years later, on May 26, 1978.

Winer presented Lieberman's case in April and May of 1976. He called numerous witnesses, including faculty members from the department who supported a positive promotion and tenure decision for Marcia Lieberman. Testimony focused on the decision-making process within the English department and the various evaluations of her scholarship and teaching. Lieberman testified for several days about the facts surrounding her employment at the university and the subsequent denial of tenure. Her husband, Philip, also testified about the recruitment conducted by the university. Faculty and administrators were questioned about their views of Lieberman's scholarship and teaching and their beliefs about the fairness of the promotion and tenure decision-making process in her case. Department head Moynihan was on the witness stand for six days, and Julius Elias, who replaced Robert Lougee as dean of the College of Liberal Arts and Sciences, testified for one day. Members of the dean's advisory council testified, as did the provost, associate provost, and vice-president for academic affairs.

Lieberman's departmental colleague and supporter, Joan Hall, gave two days of testimony about the procedures used by the department to evaluate candidates for promotion and tenure. She had been a member of the department's promotion and tenure committee and had obtained much of the documentary evidence introduced in the case. The defense, in cross-examining Hall, attacked her credibility by attempting to portray her as biased in Lieberman's favor and as vindictive toward men. The defense counsel had read into the record some of Hall's feminist poetry, which appeared to encourage conspiracies among women to discredit men. The experience was a painful one for Hall. Equally awkward for her was the need to respond to a difficult question, and an important one: Did she believe that any male faculty who voted against promotion and tenure for Lieberman really believed that she was qualified, despite his negative vote? Hall answered, "No."

In addition to the university representatives, Winer presented two expert witnesses. MIT English professor Wayne O'Neil testified about the propriety of Moynihan's seeking outside letters and the manner in which those solicitations were made. O'Neil testified that the letter requesting Donald Freeman's opinion of Lieberman's work (the letter that discussed a "difficult" tenure decision and promised "anonymity") was, in his opinion, "unprofessional" because it suggested that Moynihan wanted a negative reaction from Freeman and it also suggested that the letter would be used without attribution. O'Neil testified that reading aloud a negative letter such as Freeman's without identifying the author was "outrageous" and pointed out inconsistencies in the written evaluations of Lieberman's scholarly work from year to year, concluding, "I think what is remarkable about the folder, from my point of view, is the kind of diminution of her as a scholar and as a thinker . . . that is what is so appalling about that folder; it just diminishes her achievements, although they are all granted at other places in the folder."[25]

The second expert witness, Wesleyan University associate provost Sheila Tobias, also testified about the comments made by Moynihan in Lieberman's personnel file and criticized the solicitation of anonymous letters and their use only at the level of the tenured faculty vote, without attribution. This critical testimony by two experts was an attempt to demonstrate the irregularity of the evaluation and decision-making procedures used in the Lieberman tenure denial; both Winer and Lieberman believed that this portion of the case was the most important. Defense counsel were apparently also concerned about this, for the testimony of both experts was constantly interrupted by objections from several attorneys for the defendants, especially Thomas Parker, the attorney for Kenneth Wilson, vice-president for academic affairs at the university, and the attorneys for several of the trustees.

Winer rested the plaintiff's case on December 10, 1976. Because of numerous requests for continuances, as well as the delays caused by the court's criminal trial calendar, the defendants did not begin presenting their case until March, 1978. Between the time that the trial recessed and its resumption, Louis Winer left the firm of Tyler, Cooper, Grant, Bowerman and Keefe and opened a small law firm with one other partner, Michael Sulzbach. Although the Tyler, Cooper firm offered to provide Lieberman with another attorney from the firm to complete the litigation, she decided to continue to be represented by Winer, as he had done all of the trial preparation, had questioned and cross-examined all the witnesses on her behalf, and was more familiar with her case than any other attorney.

When the trial resumed, the university's defense focused on the legitimacy of the decision to deny tenure to Marcia Lieberman based upon objective, unprejudiced evaluations of her scholarship and teaching. The university sought to convince Judge T. Emmet Clarie that the effective decision was made by the joint committee within the English department and that the committee had not known about or been read the outside letters, so that they could not have been affected by them. The defense put every member of the joint committee on the witness stand to testify about his or her opinion of Lieberman's teaching and scholarship and the reason for his or her vote on both tenure and promotion. Cross-examination attempted to demonstrate inconsistencies in the way that members of the joint committee had evaluated Lieberman in comparison with the way male faculty had been evaluated in previous years. Lieberman was contending that in the previous year two males had been tenured who had published fewer articles and whose teaching was rated no better than hers. Furthermore, the English department had recommended for tenure one faculty member who had published only one book review; he had been turned down at the dean's level.

The testimony of one witness in particular illustrates the often peculiar nature of promotion and tenure decisions and the sometimes fragile basis upon which they rest. One of the members of the English department's joint committee, Joseph Cary, had voted in favor of tenure for Lieberman. In an attempt to demonstrate that Cary was soft on tenure issues and thus discredit his positive tenure vote, the defense elicited testimony about his behavior in another tenure decision made regarding a male faculty member one year earlier. It too was a difficult decision, a close case, and yet the individual was recommended for tenure by the department. Cary had initially voted against recommending tenure for the male professor, resulting in a five-to-four vote, which was insufficient to constitute a positive recommendation for tenure. Cary, however, had appeared on Moynihan's doorstep at 7:30 A.M. the next day (a Saturday), demanding that the joint committee be permitted to take a second vote so that he could change his negative vote to a positive one. It seems that Cary had dreamed the night before that Don Quixote appeared and gave him a message that "if one must err, err on the side of charity."[26] Moynihan acceded to Cary's demand, and the second vote was six-to-three, which gave the two-thirds majority needed for a positive tenure recommendation. Furthermore, Cary testified with regard to articles Lieberman had coauthored with her husband that although he believed "her work in the area of linguistics was terrible, pretty bad . . . fifth rate" he "excused Dr. Lieberman on this and blamed her husband for it."[27] Cary also testified that he had never said anything negative about any candidate for tenure.[28] Despite this attempt to discredit one of the votes in the promotion and tenure process, the defense continued to stress the rationality and fairness of the process and assured Judge Clarie that it had been carried out properly.

The defendants required twenty-three days to present their case (the plaintiff had used twenty-four), and Judge Clarie set July 31, 1978 as the deadline for proposed findings and posttrial briefs. After requests from both sides for postponements of the due date for posttrial memoranda, the university's attorneys filed their proposed findings of fact and conclusions of law on March 5, 1979. Although the plaintiff's attorney submitted two appendixes to a posttrial brief, the brief itself was never submitted. The docket notes that Lieberman's attorney promised to submit the brief by July 6, 1979; he did not, and Judge Clarie, with only the university's brief before him, filed his opinion dismissing all of Marcia Lieberman's claims against the individual defendants and the university on August 2, 1979.

Although Lieberman had paid Winer for the expenses of the litigation (a figure she prefers not to disclose), it was her understanding that the arrangement for the legal fees had been on a contingent basis; that is, Winer would receive a proportion of the recovery, should there be one, and would receive no fees if the defendants prevailed. However, Winer disagreed, stating that no contingent fee arangement had been agreed to and that he expected to be paid for the two thousand hours (by his estimate) that he had spent on the Lieberman case. Furthermore, there was the trial transcript to be purchased so that the posttrial brief could be prepared. Lieberman states that the trial transcript cost $14,000 (her appellate attorney estimated $18,000), and she worked for a computer company for thirteen months writing manuals in order to earn the money for the transcript. She also withdrew money from a retirement fund and sold some stock that she had inherited in order to raise the funds to purchase the transcript. Another financial pressure for Lieberman was the university's decision to file a claim under rule 54(d) of the Federal Rules of Civil Procedure, which permits the prevailing party to demand payment of court costs from the losing party. In this case, the court costs approximated $25,000, according to Lieberman. Because of the substantial bill for legal fees and the university's claim for court costs, she decided to file for bankruptcy.

Decision Impacts

The opinion filed by Judge Clarie found for the defendant university on all claims. After reviewing the evidence at some length, the judge concluded that

> the procedures employed in deciding Marcia Lieberman's tenure case were entirely proper. Moreover, the Court finds that even if there were any procedural irregularities, they were not the cause of her failure to get tenure. Rather, she was denied tenure because of the perceived deficiencies in her cumulative teaching record and her scholarship. Therefore, absent a showing that she would have been granted tenure but for the procedural defects alleged in her complaint, the plaintiff is not entitled to either reinstatement or compensatory damages, even if she were able to prove that the procedures were in fact defective.[29]

Lieberman also had claimed that the department faculty judged her more harshly than candidates evaluated for tenure in previous years, including the year prior to her evaluation. During the trial, the judge refused to admit the comparative evidence Lieberman had prepared from the personnel files of faculty evaluated for tenure in recent years, saying its value was limited in comparison to the delay that would be created by permitting a rebuttal. Furthermore, he discounted the differential treatment argument, saying that

Moynihan's instructions to the joint committee were the same as he had always given and . . . neither the department nor the dean's advisory council raised the standards. . . . Moreover, any raising of standards which may have occurred over the years was the result of an effort to upgrade the quality of professors at the University, and was not directed at women generally or the plaintiff specifically.[30]

On the locker room issue, the judge found no connection between it and the negative promotion and tenure decisions.

The judge focused specifically on the testimony by Lieberman's departmental colleagues on the quality of her scholarship. He described the reluctance of the faculty to give her a tenure track position in the first place and summarized testimony by members of the joint committee (the dispositive vote at the department level) evaluating her scholarship. The defense attorneys' strategy of questioning every member of the joint committee, even those who voted in favor of Lieberman's tenure, had apparently been successful, for the judge characterized the testimony of her supporters as "unenthusiastic."[31] Therefore, Judge Clarie concluded that "Mrs. Lieberman never distinguished herself as either a scholar or a teacher. It is not likely that she would ever have been hired by the University in the first place had it not been for the desire to attract her husband."[32] Furthermore, the judge found that rather than treating Lieberman unfairly, the various actors in the decision-making chain had exerted special efforts to avoid sexual bias. Clarie wrote:

The evidence in this case discloses that at every level those who were responsible for making the decision to give Mrs. Lieberman a terminal appointment were meticulous in their deliberations and sensitive to the claims of sexual bias. The departmental committees "agonized" over the decision . . . more time was spent at the dean's level on this case than on any other, and [the dean] himself read the file ten times before reaching the decision. . . . The central administration and the Board of Trustees spend [sic] an inordinate amount of time on this case and could uncover no evidence of sexual or political bias.[33]

The judge made short work of the First Amendment and defamation claims, stating that the university's successful proof that Marcia Lieberman was not qualified to obtain tenure was sufficient evidence to deny her claim that the negative decision was in fact made in retaliation for exercise of free speech rights. The defamation claim was in response to charges by the department head, several faculty members, and the dean that Lieberman had attempted to stack the joint committee by lobbying for the election of certain faculty members (conduct labeled unprofessional by some department members).

Judge Clarie ruled that the charge of attempted stacking was true, and, because truth is an absolute defense to a defamation claim, he dismissed the claim. Furthermore, the judge noted, even had the accusation been false, the faculty and administrators would have been protected by a qualified privilege against liability because the statements were "made in good faith and in the regular course of the tenure proceedings, and there was no publication beyond those to whom the defendants were required to report their recommendations."[34]

The trial court opinion was a blow to Lieberman, who had not been able to find a permanent teaching position in a comparable institution since her employment with the University of Connecticut had ended. She was a visiting scholar at Wesleyan University during academic year 1974–75, conducting a research project on the origins of courtly love. Lieberman applied for "every teaching job east of the Hudson River" and even applied for work with detective agencies, but was not successful. She found a part-time position teaching an evening course at the University of Rhode Island but had to give that job up when she went to work for the computer company to pay for the trial transcript. She then worked as a kindergarten assistant at a religious school and taught United States history to twelfth-graders for a salary of $1,500 a year. Later on, she taught a course for one semester at a community college and secured a one-year teaching position at a small college.

Discouraged by her inability to find an appropriate position in academe, Lieberman decided that she had little to lose by appealing the trial court's negative decision. She was reluctant to switch attorneys, for the case was complicated and she knew it would take a new attorney more time to absorb all of the details of the litigation at the trial level. However, Lieberman decided to turn to CWEALF for two reasons. First, this public interest law firm had a track record of successful sex discrimination advocacy (although not at that time in higher education). And second, because it was a public interest law firm, CWEALF did not expect clients to pay legal fees, only expenses. Of course, if Lieberman succeeded on appeal, then CWEALF would seek to be reimbursed for attorney fees by the university, as provided for in Title VII.

Susan Meredith, who had been a CWEALF attorney for five years before the *Lieberman* case, was assigned to represent Lieberman, along with Phyllis Gelman, the other staff attorney. Although Meredith had represented many plaintiffs in sex discrimination cases prior to *Lieberman,* she had not taken on a higher education discrimination case before. She found Marcia Lieberman very well informed about the issues in the case and worked closely with her in developing the appellate issues.

CWEALF depends upon contributions for its operating funds and has received money from local foundations, insurance companies, and individuals as well. Because CWEALF has limited resources and many requests for its services, a litigation committee, made up of several members of CWEALF's board of trustees, had to approve requests such as Lieberman's. Although CWEALF's two staff attorneys believed that the *Lieberman* case had considerable merit, they sought the advice of Nadine Taub and Annamay Shepard, both on the faculty of Rutgers University Law School, as to the advisability of an appeal. The law professors gave the CWEALF attorneys a "cautious yes," according to Meredith. The litigation committee approved the decision, and Meredith and Gelman began preparing Marcia Lieberman's appeal.

Meredith, Gelman, and a paralegal (CWEALF's entire legal staff) worked full time for six months on the *Lieberman* appeal. Meredith and Gelman had to construct a strong argument in their appellate brief urging reversal of Judge Clarie's decision; Meredith noted that their efforts were hampered by Winer's decision not to file a posttrial brief on Marcia Lieberman's behalf.

In reading the trial transcript, Meredith found that Winer had presented a long and complicated array of issues, and she thought perhaps that the judge had not understood completely some of the points the plaintiff was attempting to make. She decided that the approach most likely to prevail would be to attack Judge Clarie's decision to exclude the comparative evidence on male faculty given promotion and/or tenure in the few years just prior to 1972–73, the year in which Lieberman was denied tenure. Meredith believed that if the appellate court reviewed the comparative data that Lieberman had assembled, they would have to conclude that discrimination was present because the evaluations of both her scholarship and her teaching were superior to the evaluations of males who had been granted tenure just prior to the negative decision for Lieberman. In other words, Meredith wished to demonstrate that Lieberman had been judged more harshly than similarly situated males, an allegation which, if proven, may be found to be dispositive of sex discrimination in employment.

Judge Clarie had excluded the comparative evidence because, in his view, its probative value was so limited as to be outweighed by the delay and waste of time engendered by permitting defense counsel to offer rebuttal evidence.[35] However, Meredith argued, this comparative evidence was the only *direct* evidence of discrimination against Lieberman, for "it would be extremely surprising to find persons of the sophistication and intellectual capacity of these defendants who would give direct evidence of discriminatory motive."[36] Meredith argued that the files Lieberman had sought to introduce (personnel files of males evaluated in the same year that Lieberman was evaluated and in previous and subsequent years) would demonstrate that she had been subjected to higher standards and evaluated with closer scrutiny and that she was better qualified both as a teacher and as a scholar than males who had been tenured and/or promoted. In several cases, males with teaching ratings similar to Lieberman's had been promoted and/or tenured, and males with the same number of publications or fewer had also been tenured. And in one case, Meredith claimed, a faculty member had been promoted to full professor on the strength of publications "in journals that literally do not exist,"[37] suggesting that Lieberman's scholarship was subjected to much closer scrutiny for promotion to associate professor than the male faculty member's scholarship was for promotion to full professor. Furthermore, a male faculty member's election to the faculty senate was noted by department chair Moynihan as "an unusual distinction for a junior faculty member," but Lieberman's tenure packet included no mention of her election to that same important body.[38] Moreover, Meredith noted, Judge Clarie refused to admit the expert testimony of three witnesses who, after having read these comparative personnel files, were ready to testify that they demonstrated the differential standards and unfair treatment accorded Marcia Lieberman.

Meredith's second argument on appeal was a challenge to Judge Clarie's exclusion of statistical evidence demonstrating the underrepresentation of women on the university faculty. The statistical evidence would have demonstrated that although on a nationwide basis 31 percent of all Ph.D.'s in English were female in the early 1970s, women comprised only 12 percent of the English department faculty at the University of Connecticut. Furthermore, the judge had refused to admit statistical evidence on the proportion of women who had obtained tenure at the university or on the 7 percent salary discrepancy between male and female faculty, because defense counsel, in objecting, claimed that in order to rebut these statistics it would be necessary to examine the qualifications of every individual faculty member in the university.[39] The court did, however, admit defense statistics on the number of female faculty hired by the English department during Moynihan's tenure as department head (nine of forty-one new hires).[40] Meredith's conclusion was that the trial judge had used a "confession standard" to evaluate the conduct of the defendants. Rather than examining the treatment of comparable faculty members or statistical evidence on the treatment of other women both within the English department and in the university as a whole, the judge would accept only direct evidence of intent to discriminate (i.e., a "confession"). At several points in the trial, the judge himself had attempted to determine whether the defendants entertained a "sincere belief" that Lieberman was unqualified for tenure. Upon the assurances of the defense witnesses that they truly held this belief, the judge, according to Meredith, inquired no further and ruled for the university.[41]

Not surprisingly, the defendants presented a different view of the judge's decision to exclude the comparative personnel folders and the summary of comparative evaluations of teaching, scholarship, and service. The defense noted that Lieberman's counsel had wished to introduce the comparative personnel files not in an attempt to demonstrate that her qualifications were equal or better than those of male faculty but in an attempt to show that the comments made about her teaching and scholarly abilities were of a different order from those comments made about the abilities of male faculty.[42] The university asserted that individuals used as comparators for scholarship were not used as comparators for teaching, meaning that the individual faculty themselves were not "comparable." The defendants argued that Lieberman was attempting to compare her qualifications not with the complete tenure files of others who were granted tenure, but with a "mosaic" compiled of partial evaluations of several different individuals.

The defense also argued that the statistical evidence Lieberman's counsel attempted to introduce was both unverifiable and irrelevant to the issue of the individual discrimination alleged in this case. The university's attorney, Thomas Parker, argued that the only statistical evidence relevant to the issue of individual discrimination was the number and proportion of male and female faculty tenured within the English department, data that had been admitted. Furthermore, with regard to Lieberman's complaint that important evidence of universitywide salary discrimination had been excluded, Parker noted that Judge Clarie had, in fact, examined the salary history of faculty hired into tenure track positions at the time of Lieberman's initial tenure track appointment and that her salary was actually higher than the salary of several comparable males. The university concluded that no reversible error had been committed.

The three-judge appellate panel that heard oral arguments and reviewed the voluminous record found little merit in Lieberman's arguments. Indeed, Judge Henry J. Friendly, who wrote the unanimous opinion, appeared impatient with the length and complexity of the trial, strongly suggesting that the plaintiff could not complain about the *amount* of justice she had received.[43] Furthermore, Friendly implied in a footnote to the opinion that judicial resources are unduly burdened by the litigation of adverse academic employment decisions by members of protected classes. His implication was that the burdens far outweigh the individual and/or societal benefits.

In the context of these views about academic discrimination litigation, Judge Friendly upheld all of Judge Clarie's findings of fact and conclusions of law. Friendly decided, however, to respond at greater length to several of Lieberman's legal arguments, "in the hope that an opinion may clarify the tests applicable in cases of this kind and suggest means of avoiding such protracted proceedings as were held in this case."[44]

Judge Friendly first turned to the issue of the plaintiff's prima facie case. As discussed in chapter 2, a plaintiff in an employment discrimination case litigated under Title VII of the Civil Rights Act must demonstrate a prima facie case of discrimination by proving that he or she was a member of a protected class, was qualified for the position, and was rejected, and that after the rejection the job either remained open or was filled by an individual no better qualified than the plaintiff. In the trial court's opinion, Judge Clarie had expressed doubt as to whether Marcia Lieberman was qualified for tenure, as the express finding of her department had been that she was not qualified, and hence the recommendation to deny tenure. However, an earlier Second Circuit case, *Powell v. Syracuse University*,[45] had asserted that a plaintiff need only prove that he or she was objectively, or minimally, qualified for the position and that the determination of the subjective quality of the plaintiff's performance was to be established during the second phase of the trial, at which time the defendant would present the "legitimate, nondiscriminatory reason" for the negative decision. Judge Clarie had noted that without the *Powell* ruling, he would have found Lieberman not to have been qualified, therefore resulting in a finding that no prima facie case had been made.[46]

Judge Friendly disagreed with Judge Clarie as to the application of *Powell*, noting that the case had involved a denial of reappointment, not tenure. Friendly believed that a tenure decision, which implied lifetime employment, justified the application of a stricter standard to the "qualified for the job" portion of the prima facie case, noting that "a candidate for tenure does not make out the elements needed for a prima facie case merely by showing qualifications for continuation as an untenured faculty member." However, because Judge Clarie's use of a lower standard of proof for Lieberman's prima facie case worked to her benefit, Judge Friendly did not address the issue further.

Judge Friendly next addressed the plaintiff's claim that the "confession standard" used by Judge Clarie was an incorrect application of Title VII standards of proof. To the contrary, Friendly wrote, the order of proof in a Title VII case requires the defendant merely to introduce some neutral reason for the negative decision, and the university had amply satisfied that obligation. Friendly catalogued the numerous factors that he believed constituted justification for the tenure denial, including the difficulty with which Lieberman attained a tenure track position in the first place, the criticism of her teaching and scholarship in the years before the tenure denial, and the consistency with which individuals at each level of the decision process viewed the quality of her work. He concluded that "the participants in the tenure decision had ample basis for honest belief that her scholarship did not measure up to the properly stringent requirement for tenure."[47]

Friendly then turned to Lieberman's arguments that comparative evidence of other English department faculty had been improperly excluded by Judge Clarie. Friendly found the university's legal arguments to be convincing, for he ruled that the evidence Lieberman attempted to introduce was not, in fact, describing "comparable" faculty. Instead, Judge Friendly wrote, the studies ''were made in such a manner as to destroy any relevancy they might otherwise have had,'' fo. they ''proved only that plaintiff, who was neither an outstanding scholar nor an outstanding teacher, had been treated less well than males who were outstanding scholars or outstanding teachers.''[48] Therefore, Friendly wrote, the trial judge had not erred in refusing

> to engage in a tired-eye scrutiny of the files of successful male candidates for tenure . . . in the absence of independent evidence of discriminatory intent or a claim that plaintiff's qualifications were clearly and demonstrably superior to those of the successful males, a claim which was not made by Dr. Lieberman because it could not have been substantiated.[49]

In other words, the appellate court ruled that comparative evidence was insufficient to prove discrimination if it was used merely to show that the plaintiff was equally well qualified, and thus its exclusion was not legally erroneous.

Friendly last reviewed the plaintiff's claim that Judge Clarie had improperly refused to admit statistical evidence that women were underutilized at the university. He again agreed with the defendant's appellate arguments, noting that data from the university's women's committee was neither verified nor perhaps able to be verified and that the plaintiff was not prejudiced, because only one figure in the entire report was relevant to her case. Friendly noted that ''whatever probative value those figures might have had, the court was not bound to admit the entire haystack simply because it contained a single needle''[50] and countered the plaintiff's argument further by noting that evidence introduced by the university had refuted any claims of departmental discrimination by proving that since Moynihan's appointment as department head, the proportion of women faculty members in the department had risen substantially. Friendly concluded by implying that even had Lieberman's evidence been admitted, it would not have refuted the university's ''compelling evidence that the reason for the defendant's denial of tenure to Dr. Lieberman was completely neutral.''[51]

Friendly's discomfort with the concept of judicial review of academic tenure cases is evident in the last paragraph of his opinion, which appears to summarize his view of the importance of academic autonomy in these decisions.

> Denial of tenure, after six years of employment in a university department, is necessarily a traumatic experience. But it is a simple fact of university life that not every appointee to the rank of assistant professor, even one who may possess some degree of qualification, can be given tenure. . . . To award tenure to marginally qualified candidates would block the road to advancement for more highly qualified prospects who

may be coming down the tenure track in the future and seriously impair a university's quest for excellence. . . . [52]

Lieberman and Meredith discussed an appeal to the Supreme Court, but Meredith recommended against it. After eight years of litigation, the individual case came to an end.

Posttrial Impacts

Because of the length of the litigation, the number of individuals involved, and the visibility of the issue on campus, the Lieberman case had numerous direct and indirect consequences for both the individuals and organizations involved. Cause and effect relationships cannot always be established with confidence, but it appears that the issues addressed by the case and its impact on several of the people have had a number of important effects.

Consequences for the Plaintiff and Her Counsel

Marcia Lieberman was deeply disappointed by the outcome of the litigation and decided to abandon her efforts to find a full-time position teaching college English. She was accepted as a student in the writing program at Brown University, where she is studying creative writing and painting. She says that she feels like "a totally different person" now and that reflecting on her difficult experience and her new academic interests have helped her "to begin to overcome the bitterness and sense of loss" she has felt for the past decade. Although she knows that other women have benefited from her litigation, the knowledge that some women were aided by her efforts is only abstractly comforting. She believes that in some respects the women's movement let her down because, although many friends provided informal support and encouragement, the women at the university did not form the kind of support group that sprang up at other institutions where women believed that they had been discriminated against. Lieberman says that the costs of the case, both personal and financial, were far greater than she ever anticipated, and the consequences far more severe. She was "financially ruined" (by the necessity to declare bankruptcy to avoid legal fee claims), lost her "health and profession," and "could have lost [her] marriage," she said, had her husband not been as supportive as he was throughout the long years of litigation.

She is especially sorry that she did not look for another academic position immediately after the end of her terminal year at the university. As is common in employment discrimination litigation, her attorney had advised her not to leave the area nor to find another academic position if she truly wished to be reinstated at the university. Lieberman acted on that advice and spent the time prior to trial helping attorney Winer in the discovery process. Her advice to prospective plaintiffs is to get the most realistic estimate of cost and time that they can, and to understand that the experience is like Russian roulette, for "anything can happen in court." Plaintiffs must be prepared, she warns, to choose a new profession and should either create a support network or make the decision not to sue. She now wishes that she had "started a new life and sought out support and *then* made the decision to sue."

As a result of her litigation, Lieberman has strongly held views of the academic personnel decision-making process and the fairness of the individuals within academe. Despite her difficult experience with litigation, she discussed its value in an essay written shortly after the Second Circuit denied her appeal.

> The most important thing for you to know is this: They will try to persuade you that you are being denied tenure (or promotion, or reappointment) because of your deficiencies. The argument most certain to take you in is the one that speaks to your self-doubt, so they will tell you that your publications are mediocre, your teaching weak. Don't believe it. . . .
>
> You will cause the least trouble to the university if you can be persuaded to doubt your own worth and to believe that your opponents are being objective. The university may also rely on your fear of what will happen to you if you resist its authority. . . . Many of us are burdened with a sense of inferiority; though we know better, we are nevertheless likely to believe authorities who assure us in a seemingly rational and objective or even benevolent tone that our work is mediocre. . . .
>
> Months of struggle and appeal, during which I was repeatedly told that my work was mediocre, left me depressed and unable to continue my research. Had I not continued to fight by filing a lawsuit after I was denied tenure, I might still be convinced, at some deep level, of my inadequacy. The lawsuit uncovered many things that were never meant to be seen in the light of day. The records made it plain to me that I was as good as or better than men who received tenure before and after me and that procedures were manipulated in order to support a predetermined negative recommendation.[53]

Susan Meredith, Lieberman's appellate attorney, is also discouraged by the outcome of the case. Although she admits that she could "probably get suckered into a really strong tenure case" now, Meredith doubts that as a sole practitioner she would agree to represent a plaintiff in Lieberman's position today. She has not litigated any academic discrimination cases since *Lieber-*

man and recently refused a tenure case. When asked whether universities have reduced the amount of discrimination present in promotion and tenure decisions, she replied that she didn't believe so but that their procedures have improved and the fact that the number of cases in which faculty plaintiffs have prevailed is small tends to discourage potential plaintiffs.

Lieberman's trial attorney, Louis Winer, has reacted somewhat differently to the case. Although he agrees that such cases are "poor prospects," he would not reject out of hand a request by a plaintiff in a similar case. He has represented several academic plaintiffs since the *Lieberman* litigation and has settled most of those cases. Despite his less negative response to the *Lieberman* case, however, Winer emphasizes the "quirkiness" of litigation and notes that even if discrimination is evident, the results are often disappointing for the plaintiff, because of the difficulty of proof and the reluctance of judges to involve themselves in employment matters.

Consequences for the University

The impacts of the litigation for Lieberman and her attorneys are fairly straightforward; the impacts on the University of Connecticut are more complex and subtle. Faculty agree that the case influenced the university to change promotion and tenure decision procedures. At least one administrator says that the specter of litigation is before him constantly when he is involved in personnel decisions, but other administrators attribute the ensuing changes to factors other than the *Lieberman* case. It may not be possible to sort out all the cause and effect relationships, but it is important to understand what changes have occurred at the university and their effects on personnel decisions.

Several of the faculty respondents reported that promotion and tenure procedures became more explicit as a result of the litigation, although recruiting and hiring practices were affected more directly by federal and state equal employment and affirmative action requirements than they were by the litigation. The English department head reports that the written procedures are identical to those in force at the time of the Lieberman tenure denial and that they are written in a manner that is "intentionally vague" in order to permit each department to develop its own guidelines. The department's use of the promotion and tenure committee and the joint committee is unchanged since the litigation.

A recent occurrence suggests that litigation lessons are not easily forgotten. The English department had a tenure track position available and conducted a search in the 1984–85 academic year to fill it. The university's affirmative action office noted that the department had "underutilized" both female and minority faculty and criticized the search process for its failure to produce any female or minority candidates. When the department asked hypothetically whether it could, in fact, offer the position to a white male, the response it received was unclear. Furthermore, a visiting faculty member (a white male) had expressed interest in a permanent position but had been told by department chair Moynihan that the department was required to hire a woman or a member of a minority group. According to university counsel Paul Shapiro, the faculty member considered suing the university under a reverse discrimination theory but found a job at another institution and left the university without litigating. The affirmative action director assured members of the English department that if the department conducted a full and fair search, the successful candidate would in all probability be approved regardless of race or gender. Since some of those faculty involved in that search had also been involved in the *Lieberman* litigation, their sensitivity to another lawsuit was heightened.

With regard to the impact of the litigation on the willingness of English department faculty to participate in peer review, faculty in the English department report a "remarkable" lack of tension within the department and an undiminished willingness to evaluate tenure candidates critically. However, the faculty concede, there is an underlying concern about litigation, and the reports that go from the department to higher decision levels are written more carefully and more collaboratively than in earlier years.

One change that has come about since the *Lieberman* litigation is the imposition of an accountability system tied to the hiring, evaluation, and promotion and tenure review process. Although previous academic vice-presidents evaluated candidates' qualifications and the fairness of collegial decisions, chairs and deans were not held accountable as administrators for the defensibility of peer judgments. Many at the university attribute an increased attention to accountability to the arrival of a new academic vice-president, A. T. DiBenedetto, in the fall of 1981. DiBenedetto was not involved in the *Lieberman* litigation, although he was a faculty member at the university at the time, and is a former president of the faculty union. Although the university required annual evaluations of untenured faculty during the time of Marcia Lieberman's employment with the university, DiBenedetto has strengthened the importance of these evaluations and states that he will hold department chairs strictly accountable for the accuracy of the evaluations.

Untenured faculty are evaluated by their departments (by both a faculty committee and the department chair) annually, just as they were in the early 1970s. These evaluations are sent to the dean, who makes an independent evaluation, as does the dean's advisory council and the academic vice-president. This process is unchanged, but the review by the academic vice-president is stricter now than in the past. He, together with the associate vice-president for academic affairs, David Carter, reads every evaluation and assesses the sufficiency of the record supporting a positive or negative evaluation. If the academic vice-president finds a negative evaluation to be supported by the individual's record of performance (or lack thereof), he sends a letter to the faculty member warning him or her of the inadequate performance. He stated that it is not uncommon for the university not to renew the contract (probationary faculty are given one-year contracts) of an untenured faculty member whose performance has been found to be inadequate.

Connecticut's Personnel Data Act requires that all materials in faculty personnel files be available to the individual, so confidentiality is not an issue in either the annual evaluations or the promotion and tenure evaluation process. Candidates are advised at every step of the process as to the recommendation made and are given copies of all written reports and recommendations. Thus, the process is an open one, and it provides even more pressure for decision makers to justify and document the decisions they reach.

Vice-president DiBenedetto's accountability system focuses on the degree to which evaluations conducted by chairs and deans are supported by evidence. If the vice-president cannot find support in the record for a excessively positive (or excessively negative) evaluation of a faculty member, he calls a meeting of the chair, the faculty member, and himself in order to obtain an accurate picture of the faculty member's performance. He believes that it is extremely difficult for faculty members to tell their colleagues directly that their performance is unsatisfactory, but "not being honest with people is expensive for the University," and the litigiousness of even a small proportion of faculty members makes it imperative, he believes, to be "fully honest and open with the employee in every aspect of the relationship," in order to protect the university.

The level of concern is such that the university is planning a training program for department chairs in the procedures and practices necessary for evaluating faculty. The vice-president's office has developed sample form letters and other guidelines for chairs so they can make the evaluation system more rational and build a record of faculty performance over the probationary period. Despite their empathy with chairs who are "do-gooders" and want to protect young faculty members, the vice-president and his staff understand that lack of documentation and overly positive evaluations make it difficult later, when a negative tenure decision is reached, to determine the motivations behind that negative decision. For that reason, the academic vice-president evaluates department chairs and deans on the basis of *their* performance in supporting and documenting the faculty evaluations they conduct.

The academic vice-president and his associate vice-president stressed the significant impact of the faculty union in rationalizing the promotion and tenure decision-making process. The faculty contract provides a grievance procedure for faculty who wish to challenge alleged violations of the promotion and tenure procedures, as catalogued in the university bylaws. Grievances may not be filed on the merits of the decision, so all procedural defects are challenged, according to several administrators, whether or not the defects affected the outcome of the decision. Therefore, according to the administrators, adherence to the written procedures is important not only to ensure fairness and accountability but to protect the university against reversal of a negative employment decision because a minor procedural violation occurred.

Despite the impact of the union's grievance process, the potential for litigation also strongly influences the behavior of the dean of the College of Liberal Arts and Sciences, Julius Elias, who approaches "every decision about personnel that [he] make[s] with grievance or litigation consequences in mind." Because of the university's experience with both litigation and grievance handling, Elias believes, individuals who are "slipshod deserve what [they] get" when carelessly documented decisions are challenged in a legal forum. However, he expresses sadness that the rigidity of the system does not permit administrative flexibility in responding to unusual cases where administrators might wish to bend the rules for a faculty member who deserves special treatment. Furthermore, Elias states, even the best of procedural guarantees does not protect an individual against "wicked colleagues" who make unfair or biased evaluations but who have followed the correct procedures. Elias believes that despite the best efforts of administrators, if the department faculty "keep their noses procedurally clean, they can get away with murder." Despite his skepticism, Elias admits that the procedures now in place at the university have "inhibited much improper, arbitrary, and capricious behavior," but "those who are guileful can wiggle their way through the system" because it is not infallible.

Elias, Moynihan, and other administrators had explicit advice for other faculty and administrators involved in promotion and tenure decisions. Among their suggestions were these:

1. Keep good records and file everything, even handwritten notes.
2. Act consistently every year in the definition and application of standards.
3. Don't be too nice to borderline or mediocre faculty members—let them know where they stand.
4. Learn to live with the situation, and don't permit the potential for grievances or litigation to make you cynical.
5. Ask administrators at higher levels, including the university counsel, to read drafts of letters or reports to faculty members, and remember that such documents can have consequences for the entire institution.

Interestingly, these recommendations are nearly identical to the responses of Marcia Lieberman when she was asked the same question. Her recommendations were as follows:

1. Institutions (and departments) should try to articulate what the standards are and what they expect of junior faculty, and make it *very* clear to faculty.
2. Give faculty members whose performance is unsatisfactory plenty of warning as to what they have to do to satisfy the expectations of the department.
3. Provide faculty members who cannot meet the department's expectations with counseling about other careers.
4. Clarify the rules and make sure that the faculty member understands them.
5. Provide lots of feedback to probationary faculty and make sure they understand exactly how their performance has been inadequate well before the time that a final decision must be made.

In addition to the combined litigation and unionization effects noted here, other changes have been made in various departments that faculty believe are a result, whether direct or indirect, of the litigation. In many departments, hiring decisions are made much more carefully, and individuals are scrutinized for their promotability as well as for their basic qualifications. In a few departments, all junior faculty members are required to serve on the department's tenure and promotion review committee during their second year so that they will understand the standards and process that will be used when they themselves are candidates for tenure.

However, some faculty warn, problems remain. For example, there is no requirement that the annual evaluations of probationary faculty be discussed with them unless the dean initiates such a discussion, nor are there explicit standards about how the evaluation is to be conducted. The variation in standards and procedures (for example, the importance of applied research or the relative quality of certain journals) that exists among departments can be confusing to a faculty advisory council acting for the entire school. Faculty who have served on such committees believe that council members should be trained about evaluation criteria and procedures and in appropriate practices in peer evaluation. And the faculty echo Elias's lament that unfair or discriminatory practices occurring informally within departments may be difficult or impossible for deans to discover and say that the responsiveness of the system relies to a great extent upon the integrity of the department head and the dean.

One other consequence of the *Lieberman* litigation deserves some discussion. Although Marcia Lieberman originally filed both an individual and a class claim, she decided not to pursue the class claim. However, the university and other defendants in the class action claim served interrogatories on Lieberman, the named plaintiff, in 1975, attempting to determine the identity of class members and requesting more specific information on the alleged discrimination. Because Lieberman decided not to pursue the class claim, no response to the interrogatories was ever filed, according to a ruling on the class action claim by Judge José Cabranes in 1981.

According to Cabranes's account,[54] the case was dormant from 1975 until December, 1980, when Elsie Fetterman, a professor in the Cooperative Extension Service at the College of Agriculture, moved to intervene as a plaintiff in the class action claim, alleging salary discrimination. She was represented by Louis Winer, who had been Lieberman's trial attorney. She then moved for certification of the class, a procedure that was delayed pending the court's determination of the propriety of Fetterman's petition to intervene. Furthermore, the bankruptcy trustee of Marcia Lieberman's estate filed a petition demanding to be joined as a plaintiff in the class action. The trustee was also represented by Winer. The university filed a motion for summary judgment (which, if granted by the court, would have resulted in a ruling in favor of the university without a trial on the merits). The parties conducted discovery, and oral arguments were held on the issue of Fetterman's intervention and the trustee's joinder in July, 1981.

The judge denied the trustee's joinder motion and also denied Fetterman's motion to intervene. Fetterman, a full professor at the university, claimed that the university's salary policies had discriminated against her because male faculty with "similar skills and experience" were paid higher salaries. Although Fetterman left the university for a full-time position at the University of Massachusetts in 1979, she wanted to preserve her salary claims against the university for the period from 1972 through 1979, which she would have accomplished had the court permitted her to intervene as a class plaintiff. Otherwise, the state statute of limitations (two years) would have extinguished any claim of hers prior to 1978.

Judge Cabranes ruled against Fetterman's motion to intervene on several grounds. First, the court was concerned about potential conflicts of interest between Fetterman and other class members because of her counsel's involvement in the earlier *Lieberman* litigation. (The judge noted that Lieberman had sent a letter to the court informing it that Winer no longer represented her and that she did not wish to be involved in the class action.) Second, because Fetterman was no longer employed by the University of Connecticut, the judge did not believe that she could effectively represent the other class members, who were still employed by the university. Furthermore, the judge ruled, the time that had elapsed between the filing of the class claim in 1974 and the motion to intervene in 1980 would make it difficult for the university to defend the litigation, as records had been destroyed and former university employees, some of them named defendants, were no longer employed by the university. And finally, Fetterman had also filed a claim against the university in state court, so she could preserve the claims occurring within the state's statute of limitations through that action. Although there were several other intervenors, the exclusion of Fetterman left the class without a named plaintiff or class representative.

With regard to the university's motion for summary judgment, Judge Cabranes granted a continuance so that other potential class plaintiffs could join the case. Two potential plaintiffs filed motions to intervene: the University of Connecticut chapter of the AAUP and Ann Linda Polcari, whose salary discrimination claim was similar to Fetterman's. However, Judge Cabranes decided that this was "a case without a plaintiff" and that the "putative intervenors have occupied a shadowy procedural role on the margins of this litigation." He denied the motions to intervene and granted the university's motion to dismiss the case on June 8, 1983.

Although the university was successful in winning the dismissal of *Lieberman II*, as the class action has been called, the issue of sex discrimination is not closed at the university. Some women faculty believe strongly that sex discrimination still exists in salaries, promotion, tenure, and hiring and speak of individual examples of discriminatory treatment. They explain that women who have been treated unfairly have refused to come forward because they fear retaliation. The women have encouraged the union to be more aggressive in negotiating contractual provisions that would deter sex discrimination. (For example, the most recent contract now lists sexual harassment as grounds for dismissal, according to one faculty member.) The union has also negotiated salary adjustments for certain women faculty who were underpaid in relation to men with similar training and performance records. And, of course, the union attempted to intervene, albeit at the last moment, in the *Lieberman II* case.

Despite the continuing dissatisfaction of some women faculty with the status of women at the university, data obtained from the university's Office of Affirmative Action show slow progress in the number of women hired and tenured in the years since the *Lieberman* litigation. According to the report issued by the University of Connecticut Organization of Faculty, Professional, and Classified Women, in the early 1970s women held 13.6 percent of all faculty positions at the university.[55] In the fall of 1983, 19.4 percent of the faculty were women, and in that year 14.9 percent of the tenured faculty were women. However, during that year nearly one-third of the faculty in tenure track positions but not yet tenured were women.[56] Although these figures suggest that women are still underrepresented among university faculty, gradual increases have occurred. Furthermore, three women have become department heads since 1981, a first according to the director of affirmative action.

After ten years of litigation in *Lieberman I* and *II*, the involvement of five judges, twenty-three attorneys, two advocacy organizations (CWEALF and AAUP), and scores of trustees, administrators, and faculty members, the legal outcome for women academics was not only a great disappointment but, in some respects, a setback. Judge Friendly's strong criticism of academic discrimination litigation in general and his deference to academic autonomy in personnel decisions have been cited in subsequent academic discrimination cases by other federal courts. In particular, the refusal of judges Clarie and Friendly to credit the relevance of "comparator" male faculty will make it difficult for plaintiffs to use such evidence in future litigation.[57] Furthermore, Judge Friendly's statements that tenure decisions should be treated more cautiously by courts and that plaintiffs should prove their subjective qualification as well as their objective qualification for tenure have made these cases more difficult for subsequent plaintiffs to win.[58]

Perhaps the administrators who insist that *Lieberman* had little impact on the university were correct, for hiring and promotion procedures have not changed appreciably in the years following Marcia Lieberman's tenure denial. In fact, the trial and appellate court opinions strongly endorsed the university's promotion practices and procedures. However, the university community is sensitized to the problem of potential discrimination in faculty employment decisions, and the administration appears to be working to make the peer evaluation and supervisory process rational, so that decisions are made accurately and fairly. Whatever lessons the university learned from *Lieberman* were expensive ones, and it is fair to assume that women faculty at the University of Connecticut did benefit from Marcia Lieberman's lawsuit, even if those benefits are indirect or not uniformly evident.

NOTES

1. 474 F. Supp. 848 (D. Conn. 1979), *aff'd*, 630 F.2d 60 (2d Cir. 1980).
2. Lieberman, 474 F. Supp. at 853.
3. Lieberman, 474 F. Supp. at 854.
4. Liz McMillen, "Legal Experts Eye 2 Sex-Bias Lawsuits Brought by Women's-Studies Scholars," *Chronicle of Higher Education*, April 9, 1986, pp. 23–24.
5. Lynn v. Board of Regents, 656 F.2d 1337, 1343 (9th Cir. 1981).
6. Sarah Slavin and Jacqueline Macaulay, "Joan Roberts and the University," in *Rocking the Boat*, ed. Gloria DeSole and Leonore Hoffman (New York: Modern Language Association, 1981), pp. 37–49.
7. Joint Appendix.
8. Lieberman, 474 F. Supp. at 871.
9. Lieberman, 474 F. Supp. at 854.
10. Joint Appendix, pp. 248a–49a.
11. Ibid., pp. 252a–54a.
12. Lieberman, 474 F. Supp. at 858.
13. Joint Appendix, pp. 420a–21a.
14. Marcia Lieberman, "The Most Important Thing for You to Know," in *Rocking the Boat*, pp. 1–7.

15. Lieberman, 474 F. Supp. at 856.
16. During the early 1980s, the positions of vice-president for academic affairs and provost were consolidated into the vice-president's position.
17. Lieberman, 474 F. Supp. at 851–52. The Connecticut legislature subsequently passed a law limiting the ability of administrators and trustees of public colleges and universities to retain their own counsel at state expense.
18. Plaintiff's Appellate Brief, p. 1.
19. This claim was based on allegations by members of the English department that Lieberman had attempted to stack the membership of a committee. Details of the claim are explained later in this chapter.
20. This issue is discussed in chapter 2.
21. Shea v. Gant, 22 Fair Employment Practices Cases 371 (D. Conn. 1979).
22. Phyllis Rackin, "Not by Lawyers Alone: Ten Practical Lessons for Academic Litigants," in *Rocking the Boat,* pp. 50–56.
23. Lieberman, 630 F.2d 60, 62 (1980).
24. Lieberman, 630 F.2d at 62.
25. Trial Transcript, pp. 3,695–96.
26. Ibid., p. 7,156.
27. Ibid., pp. 3,032, 3,034.
28. Ibid., p. 7,624.
29. Lieberman, 474 F. Supp. at 863.
30. Lieberman, 474 F. Supp. at 871.
31. Lieberman, 474 F. Supp. at 867.
32. Lieberman, 474 F. Supp. at 872.
33. Lieberman, 474 F. Supp. at 869.
34. Lieberman, 474 F. Supp. at 876.
35. Lieberman, 474 F. Supp. at 873 n. 22.
36. Plaintiff's Appellate Brief, p. 30.
37. Ibid., p. 34.
38. Ibid., p. 35.
39. Ibid., p. 40.
40. Ibid., p. 41.
41. Ibid., pp. 51–52.
42. Defendant's Appellate Brief, pp. 12–13.
43. Lieberman, 630 F.2d at 62.
44. Lieberman, 630 F.2d at 62.
45. 580 F.2d 1150 (2d Cir. 1978), *cert. denied,* 439 U.S. 984 (1978).
46. Lieberman, 474 F. Supp. at 864. For an analysis of recent judicial treatment of the issue of objective vs. subjective qualification in academic discrimination cases, see Barbara A. Lee, "Threshhold Qualifications in Academic Discrimination Litigation: How Onerous Is the Burden?" *Education Law Reporter* 30 (1986): 1–9.
47. Lieberman, 630 F.2d at 66.
48. Lieberman, 630 F.2d at 68.
49. Lieberman, 630 F.2d at 68.
50. Lieberman, 630 F.2d at 69.
51. Lieberman, 630 F.2d at 69.

52. Lieberman, 630 F.2d at 70.
53. Lieberman, "The Most Important Thing," pp. 1–7.
54. The decisions in *Lieberman II* are unpublished.
55. Plaintiff's Appellate Brief, p. 37.
56. Unpublished data, Office of Affirmative Action, University of Connecticut, 1984.
57. Plaintiffs have encountered difficulty in obtaining personnel files of potential comparator faculty (see, e.g., *EEOC v. University of Notre Dame*, 551 F. Supp. 737 (N.D. Ind. 1982), *rev'd*, 715 F.2d 331 (7th Cir. 1983). If such information is ruled irrelevant to plaintiffs' prima facie case, then prevailing in a discrimination case will be even more difficult for plaintiffs than it is presently (see table 1 and chap. 2).
58. See, e.g., *Zahorik v. Cornell University*, 579 F. Supp. 349 (N.D.N.Y. 1983), *aff'd*, 729 F.2d 85 (2d Cir. 1984). See also *Kumar v. Board of Trustees*, 566 F. Supp. 1299 (D. Mass. 1983), *rev'd*, 744 F.2d 1 (1st Cir. 1985).

Chapter 4
A Triumph for Peer Review

Kunda v. Muhlenberg College[1]

This case is important not only because it is a rare instance where an individual woman plaintiff prevailed but also because of the controversial remedy of "conditional tenure" fashioned by the trial court judge. On appeal, that ruling unleashed amicus briefs from national organizations concerned with the significance of the award of tenure for academic traditions.

The Lehigh Valley of eastern Pennsylvania is famous for the large number of small liberal arts colleges it boasts. Within a twenty-mile radius of Allentown, Pennsylvania, a town of just over one hundred thousand about sixty miles north of Philadelphia and twenty miles west of the Delaware River, are six liberal arts colleges: Allentown College, Cedar Crest College, Lafayette College, Lehigh University, Moravian College, and Muhlenberg College.

Muhlenberg College is a small, coeducational college founded by the Lutheran Church in 1848 as a college for men. The college, which admitted women for the first time in 1957, occupies a seventy-five-acre campus on the outskirts of Allentown. Although the church does not operate the college, church leaders constitute the majority of the members of the board of trustees. The college enrolled fifteen hundred full-time equivalent students in 1983–84, nearly all of whom lived on campus. The college awards undergraduate degrees only and emphasizes good teaching as one of its strengths. Because of its size and relatively placid appearance, Muhlenberg College seems an unlikely setting for a major court case concerning the propriety of a judge's awarding tenure to a faculty member.

Tenure is a central component of the academic personnel system. It was originally conceived as a series of procedural safeguards to protect faculty academic freedom,[2] but its importance goes far beyond that function. Tenure has an important role as a rite of passage, especially because an individual denied tenure must usually leave the institution or move into a nonfaculty position. In order to attain tenure at most colleges and universities, a faculty member must be found worthy in terms of the quality of his or her teaching, research, and service to the profession and institution, as well as other criteria.[3] Once tenured, a faculty member's employment may not be terminated except for cause or for reasons of financial exigency.[4] Although tenure may be denied for many reasons unrelated to the individual faculty member's competence as a teacher or scholar (such as the need to reduce the proportion of tenured faculty in a department, a shift in curricular emphasis, or the elimination of a program of study), denial of tenure is typically viewed by the academic community as a reflection on the individual's competence. Being denied tenure by one institution often makes it difficult for the individual to secure a faculty position at another college or university. Furthermore, the individual may have worked closely with faculty colleagues for six years or more, and a negative vote by a committee of one's peers usually shocks and hurts the individual deeply. Thus, tenure has important symbolic meaning beyond its more pragmatic function of a lifetime guarantee of employment.

The case of Connie Rae Kunda against Muhlenberg College raised many questions about the role of the faculty vis-à-vis the administration in determining whether faculty were qualified to receive tenure. But the case is important for other reasons as well. It was the first, and is to date the only, example of a judicial award of "conditional tenure," an award that engendered substantial controversy throughout the higher education community. Furthermore, it was the second of three charges of employment discrimination within a period of less than a decade against a college with only one hundred full-time faculty members.

Muhlenberg College may appear on the surface a small, peaceful liberal arts college, but its recent history has been anything but peaceful. During the 1970s, tension characterized the relationships between faculty and administration, students and administration, and the board and both faculty and students. The three employment discrimination cases are only one element, albeit an important one, of the conflict at Muhlenberg College over the past ten years.

Much of the tension at Muhlenberg focused on one person—its president, John Morey, who retired at the end of the 1983–84 academic year. His fifteen-year leadership at the college was eventful and controversial. Morey began his presidency at Muhlenberg in the fall of 1969, coming from the presidency of Frostburg State College, a small institution in western Maryland. The faculty at Muhlenberg had a history of self-governance and viewed the college bylaws as affording them considerable responsibility to control their own affairs (although, as is the usual case, ultimate authority rested with the trustees).

A year or two after his assumption of the presidency, Morey began to take steps to, in his words, "upgrade the quality of the faculty," and they created much controversy on campus. For example, Morey began enforcing the policy stated in the faculty handbook that a faculty member had to hold a terminal degree "or its scholarly equivalent" in order to be promoted to associate professor. The terminal degree requirement had not been followed consistently prior to Morey's arrival. In an attempt to reduce the college's high ratio of tenured faculty, a situation which made hiring new faculty nearly impossible and responding to shifting student curricular preferences extremely difficult as well, a plan was implemented in 1974 that effectively halted all new tenure track appointments unless fewer than two-thirds of the faculty in a department were tenured. The faculty handbook was "withdrawn" by the administration in the mid-1970s, and no new edition had been issued by the end of 1983.

Faculty at the college cited the above actions as attempts to reduce faculty autonomy. However, Morey points to other actions he took at the same time to widen faculty participation in academic policy matters. For example, Morey reported that when he arrived at the college in 1960, many governance committees had some elected and some appointed members; Morey insisted that all committee members be elected by the faculty. He also worked to enfranchise first-year instructors, who previously had not been allowed to vote at faculty meetings. He urged the creation of a faculty committee on the evaluation of teaching and another on faculty issues. The differences in perceptions between Morey and faculty leaders concerning his actions and his motivations help to explain the source of much of the tension on campus during the years between 1971 and 1983.

By the middle of Morey's term as president, Muhlenberg's problems began to reach the local press. A reporter for the *Allentown Call Chronicle,* always interested in the happenings at Allentown's most prominent employer, wrote:

> Muhlenberg's Student Council once called for Morey's resignation. Faculty members have said he ignores them. The Board of Trustees has suggested that he improve communications with the campus community. His press officers have thrown up their hands at his distrust and disregard of the press. And only 5 percent of the college administration and about 25 percent of the faculty and students polled in 1975 said an atmosphere of trust existed at Muhlenberg.[5]

Incidents on campus, though perhaps not atypical of the trend on other college campuses during the 1970s, seemed to have more lingering effects at Muhlenberg. For example, in 1976, Clarence Kelley, the director of the FBI, was invited to speak on campus. This was Kelley's first appearance after the arrest of Patty Hearst; a resident of eastern Pennsylvania had been killed in the shootout that took place during that incident. The local police and the FBI were prepared for campus unrest accompanying Kelley's visit, and a large number of both police and FBI were present on campus that day. Five people passed out leaflets on campus protesting FBI activities and rushed up to Kelley as he was leaving the student union, where he had been speaking. The Allentown police chief ordered the "Muhlenberg Five" arrested for trespassing. The Five were found guilty of "defiant trespass" and were fined twenty-five dollars each by an Allentown District Court judge. After several appeals to intermediate courts, the state supreme court reversed their convictions, stating that the college's refusal to permit the Five to distribute leaflets peacefully violated the state constitution, for it was arbitrary in that the college had no policies or standards related to the use of the campus as a public forum.[6]

Despite Morey's practice of meeting regularly with student officers to discuss their concerns, Muhlenberg students were critical of his leadership, and in 1978, eight hundred of the fifteen hundred students signed petitions demanding his resignation.[7] Faculty dissatisfaction took another form; in 1978, a group of faculty attempted to form a faculty union in an effort to gain a greater role in decision making at the college. The Pennsylvania State Education Association, an affiliate of the National Education Association, garnered enough faculty support to hold an election. The faculty rejected unionization, although the vote was close (forty-two-to-thirty-seven). Some faculty at the college believe that the negative votes were an expression of discomfort with the idea of a union rather than a vote of confidence for the administration; others believe that a different agent, such as the AAUP, might have been able to obtain a positive vote. Despite the results, however, the closeness of the vote was interpreted by many as criticism of Morey's leadership.

A more direct challenge to the president came later. In the spring of 1983, the Muhlenberg faculty voted no confidence in Morey by a vote of seventy-three-to-twenty-six and asked for his resignation. Although the board publicly affirmed its confidence in Morey after the faculty's negative vote, it agreed to create a committee of board members, administrators, and faculty to examine the "communication problems" on campus. Later that summer, Morey announced his retirement effective July 31, 1984.

Despite the campus criticism of Morey, the board chairman described the successes of Morey's fifteen-year tenure:

> Under his leadership over the past 14 years, we have seen the face of Muhlenberg change dramatically with the addition of the Center for the Arts, the Life Sports Center, the renovation of the Trumbower Science Building, the 60-bed addition to Prosser Hall, the renovation and enlargement of the Student Union, the development of MacGregor Village, and the 50th Anniversary renovation of the Chapel, which now is graced with a new organ. . . . [D]uring John's tenure, our development effort has generated over $19,000,000 in gifts, and our endowment has grown from $4.7 million to $15.1 million, all of this achieved during the difficult economic years of the 70's and early 80's, a period in which the College experienced balanced books and capacity enrollment each year.[8]

Praising a departing president is conventional in academic life, but the board's continuing support was in direct opposition to the views of the majority of the faculty, who saw the campus environment as one of conflict and distrust throughout Morey's presidency. The dissatisfaction of the faculty with Morey's leadership underlay many of the events leading up to and following the *Kunda* litigation.

Triggering Incident

Connie Rae Kunda was hired as an instructor in the physical education department in 1966. She was a resident of Allentown and had taught physical education in the local public schools for eleven years. She held a bachelor's degree in physical education from the Pennsylvania State University. At the time of her hiring, she received a copy of the faculty handbook and the college bylaws. The faculty handbook explicitly stated that a terminal degree "or its scholarly equivalent" was required for tenure; however, male faculty in her department had been promoted and tenured without a master's degree, and Kunda was not advised that this practice would be different in her situation.

Kunda enjoyed her job as an instructor at the college. She taught dance, team sports, and individual sports courses and directed the college's dance program. Although there was only one other woman on the faculty of the physical education department at the time (a tenured professor), Kunda did not anticipate any problems related to either her performance or her gender when her department head, Raymond Whispell, recommended that she be promoted to assistant professor.

Muhlenberg emphasizes undergraduate liberal arts education, and effective teaching has been the primary criterion for promotion or tenure. "College involvement," which includes service to the college and the local community and colleagueship, was also important; research and creative work and religious commitment were also listed in the faculty handbook as criteria for promotion and tenure. Despite its significance, teaching usually was not formally evaluated by peers, nor were student evaluations of teaching used in promotion or tenure reviews.

Although an instructor would normally have been reviewed for promotion to assistant professor after three years of employment at the college, several faculty in the physical education department were in the pipeline ahead of Kunda, and Whispell decided to wait until 1971, or five years after her initial hiring, to recommend her for promotion to assistant professor.

Relationships between the administration and the physical education department were strained in the 1970s. The board had discussed dropping the physical education requirement for graduation, although that policy was not implemented. Whispell was a key figure in the department as the longtime football coach, the department head, and the athletic director. Although he was relieved of his coaching position in 1970, he remained as department head and athletic director until 1979.

The promotion decision process in effect at Muhlenberg at the time included recommendations by the department chair, by an elected faculty committee (the Faculty Personnel and Policies Committee [FPPC]), by the dean, and by the president; the final determination fell to the board of trustees. In the fall of 1971, Kunda's department head forwarded to the dean, Philip Secor, a positive recommendation for promotion to assistant professor. This was merely a promotion decision; tenure decisions were usually not made concurrently with promotion decisions at Muhlenberg. No supporting information was appended to Whispell's recommendation,[9] and the committee was unable to evaluate Kunda's qualifications for promotion. The FPPC split three-to-three on the promotion issue, and the president recommended against her promotion. Department head Whispell appealed the promotion denial, submitted additional information to support his recommendation for Kunda's promotion, and asked that the FPPC reconsider its decision. Although the dean did not usually attend meetings of the FPPC, he did attend the one at which the reconsideration of Kunda's promotion was addressed. According to FPPC members present, he told the FPPC that the future of the physical education department was uncertain and that the interests of the college would be better served if the decision about Kunda's promotion were made at a later time. The FPPC voted four-to-two to deny the promotion.

Although Connie Kunda was surprised by the negative result, she believed that she would be promoted the following year, when the committee had more information about her qualifications. The next fall, Whispell again recommended that she be promoted to assistant professor. The dean accidentally omitted Kunda's name from the list of faculty to be considered by the FPPC for promotion. Although the cases of all the other candidates had already been acted upon by the board, the FPPC was asked to convene a special meeting to consider Kunda's promotion. The committee voted to recommend her for promotion to assistant professor. However, the president recommended against the promotion, and the board did not approve it.

The 1973–74 academic year was the year in which, according to both college bylaws and AAUP standards, Kunda had to be evaluated for tenure. Again, Whispell recommended Kunda for both tenure and promotion to assistant professor, and the FPPC voted unanimously to recommend that she be promoted and awarded tenure. The committee specifically noted that although she had not earned a master's degree, she had earned the "scholarly equivalent" through frequent activities to update and improve her skills through continuing professional education, continued study in dance, activity in local and state professional associations, publications, and community activities.

The dean recommended against tenure, admitting in his written recommendation that Kunda's performance justified tenure but that the uncertain future of the physical education department and the high percentage of tenured faculty already employed by the department militated against tenure. The president declined to recommend tenure, notified Kunda of his decision, and forwarded a terminal contract.

Perception of Alleged Discrimination

The negative tenure decision shocked Connie Kunda, for she believed that she had been "doing the right things" and had never been aware that the president intended to enforce the terminal degree requirement uniformly. Had she known of Morey's intentions to require a master's degree for tenure in her field, she said, she would certainly have obtained one, for she wanted very much to remain at Muhlenberg. She had never felt discriminated against by her faculty colleagues, and, indeed, they had recommended her for promotion the previous year and had voted unanimously to award her tenure as well. She knew that men in her department had been both promoted *and* tenured with only a bachelor's degree—indeed, her department chair, a full professor, held only a bachelor's degree. The only difference that she could ascertain between her and her male colleagues who had been treated more favorably was gender. Although she did not view herself at that time as a feminist, Kunda decided that she would go to court to try to get her job back.

As she talked with faculty colleagues about the negative decision, she learned other things that led her to conclude that her gender must have been an issue in the way she was treated. She learned that both Whispell and the dean had told two male faculty in the department that they would need to earn a master's degree in order to be promoted; however, at no time had anyone at the college so informed her. In fact, in the same year that Kunda was first considered for promotion to assistant professor (1971), a male faculty member who had discontinued work toward his master's degree was promoted to assistant professor. Other male faculty had been promoted contingent on completion of their master's degrees; that option was not offered to Kunda. Thus she concluded that the differential treatment she received could only be explained as sex discrimination.

On the other hand, the administration insisted that the tenure denial was motivated solely by the fact that Kunda lacked a master's degree. Although the college could muster no evidence that Kunda had been informed of this requirement, the president maintained that she should have known that this requirement was in effect because several colleagues close to her in the physical education department were working on master's degrees and had been counseled concerning the necessity of completing them. Furthermore, the president said, the plaintiff had been denied a promotion by her peers twice in 1971, although he acknowledged that the following year's committee apparently felt differently. [10]

The administration also disagreed with the FPPC's interpretation of the scholarly equivalent criterion for tenure. The president and the dean explained that this alternate method of qualifying for tenure was not to be used for routine personnel decisions but only in exceptional cases, for individuals who might be great authors or have special talent in other fields but did not yet possess a terminal degree. Kunda did not meet that description. Furthermore, they noted, in her additional academic work she had enrolled in classes that they viewed as continuing professional education rather than graduate-level coursework. The president admitted that earlier promotions and tenurings had been granted to individuals who had not earned master's degrees. However, the president maintained, most of these decisions were made either before or only shortly after he became president, before he had had the opportunity to review and attempt to change the methods of faculty promotion and tenure evaluation. Also, the expectations for the faculty of the physical education department had once been different, for publication had not been expected and teaching had been evaluated in a different manner. Nevertheless, the president asserted, he had determined that all individuals who wished to obtain tenure must have a terminal degree (which would be the master's degree for physical education faculty), and he enforced this requirement consistently beginning in 1971, the year that Kunda was first denied promotion.

Problem Evaluation and Informal Consultation

Connie Kunda was not alone in her surprise at the tenure denial. Her faculty colleagues, both within her department and on the faculty committees that had reviewed her credentials, had supported her attempts to be promoted and tenured and expected the decision to be a positive one. Throughout her employment at Muhlenberg College, she had never been given any indication that her performance was unsatisfactory or that there was any reason she would not be promoted or tenured. She believed, and had not been told otherwise, that her activity in professional organizations and her publications were valued and that her continued professional improvement through dance studies was viewed positively as well. She also had her own television fitness program, an educational production that aired twice weekly in the Lehigh Valley area, which she had developed, written, and conducted. Many faculty at Muhlenberg were also surprised that Kunda had been denied tenure. Some of them believe that the tenure denial was less a judgment of her capabilities than a decision to no longer grant tenure to faculty in the physical education department. They cite the history of difficult relationships between the president and Whispell, the head of the department. Some believe that what was involved was not sex discrimination but academic politics.

Use of Internal Remedies

In the fall of 1974, Kunda appealed the tenure denial decision, using the grievance process then in effect. She appeared before an elected faculty board of appeals (FBA), which decided that there had been several procedural irregularities in the earlier decision process and recommended to the president that he appoint a special committee to reconsider Kunda's case and recommend for or against tenure. The board of appeals's decision was unusual, for that committee had heard six tenure appeals and only in the Kunda case had it voted in favor of the faculty member.[11] To its surprise, the president asked the FBA to serve in the special committee's role. The FBA reviewed the dossier and other pertinent materials and voted nine-to-zero to recommend that Kunda be granted promotion and tenure. After receiving the FBA's recommendation, the president afforded Kunda an opportunity to appear before the educational policies and faculty affairs committee of the board of trustees, which would make the recommendation to the full board. The president recommended to the board that it deny tenure and promotion. The board committee reviewed Kunda's dossier and recommended that the full board vote to deny both tenure and promotion. The board did so, and Kunda's employment with the college terminated at the end of the 1974–75 academic year.

Settlement or Litigation Decision

After Kunda completed her terminal year at Muhlenberg College, she was unable to obtain a similar job at any other college in the area. She was employed sporadically as a substitute teacher in the public schools in the area, was manager of a health spa, and continued her job as hostess of the television show on fitness until the program was terminated because, she believes, the station was unwilling to make unemployment insurance payments. (Kunda had filed for unemployment compensation benefits upon leaving Muhlenberg College, and employers for whom she worked part time were required to contribute to her unemployment benefits.) She had been recently separated from her husband and was supporting two children, one who had a chronic illness that required substantial medical care and another who was about to enter college. She wanted to stay in the Lehigh Valley area but could not find employment for which her credentials qualified her. Although she knew that she might lose her assets if she sued, she regarded the college's behavior as blatant and decided to sue to get her job back. She believed that she really had no choice but to do so.

A local attorney offered to assist Kunda with her case and filed suit in county court under the state employment discrimination law. She paid him a substantial amount, but no progress was made. She then filed a claim with the Pennsylvania Human Relations Commission (the state equivalent of the EEOC), which issued a finding of probable cause on March 10, 1977. The EEOC, alerted by the Pennsylvania agency, also investigated the case, making campus visits and interviewing faculty and administrators. Meanwhile, Kunda released her local attorney and was given a right-to-sue letter by the EEOC on April 25, 1977.

Because of her inability to find full-time employment and the pressure of supporting two children, Kunda wrote to the national headquarters of NOW, in Washington, D.C., seeking either financial or legal help. She received no response to her letter. She also contacted the offices of the American Association of Health and Physical Education, as well as the regional professional associations in which she had been active, for documentation of her contributions and for legal briefs supporting her scholarly equivalent argument. Neither documentation nor briefs were forthcoming. Thus, she was quite literally alone as she prepared to challenge the negative tenure decision in federal court.

In her search for an attorney for the litigation, Kunda had little luck with the local bar. They were reluctant to take her case because of its complexity and because, in a small community like Allentown, suing the college was viewed unfavorably. Furthermore, federal litigation required local attorneys to travel to Philadelphia, which was expensive and time consuming. In any event, a friend suggested that she contact two attorneys who had just opened a practice in Philadelphia, Michael Golden and Roy Yaffe. After consulting with Golden and Yaffe, Kunda retained them as counsel. This time her choice of legal help was more fortunate.

Golden and Yaffe had both had previous experience with employment discrimination litigation. Yaffe had been general counsel for the Pennsylvania Human Relations Commission before going into private practice and had handled employment discrimination cases before, although not against a college. Michael Golden had been a Pennsylvania assistant attorney general and had represented the state in several employment discrimination cases as well as working on a higher education case involving student civil rights. Since they had joined forces only a few months before Kunda retained them they had no full-time secretary, no law clerks, no paralegals, and no associates. Furthermore, they agreed to take the case on a contingency basis, so that a loss would have had a serious financial impact on their young law firm. It was an indication of the attorneys' analysis of the strength of Kunda's legal claim that they agreed to take her case on such a basis, especially considering that the college had retained Morgan, Lewis, and Bockius, the largest firm in

Philadelphia, as its counsel for this case. It clearly would be a David and Goliath situation.

Kunda had decided that she would seek reinstatement as well as damages. She knew that such a remedy is unusual, even in employment discrimination cases, because courts are reluctant to return employees to professional employment situations where a determination has been made, even for illegal reasons, that the employee is inadequate in some respect. However, because she enjoyed teaching at Muhlenberg, she decided to ask for reinstatement. The college refused to discuss settlement, so Kunda never had to decide whether to accept a lump sum in lieu of reinstatement. The complaint filed by her attorneys in federal court asked for $350,000 in compensatory and punitive damages, attorney fees, and reinstatement at the rank of associate professor with tenure.[12]

The college's decision to defend the litigation rather than settle apparently was never in question. The president believed that because the FPPC had denied promotion to Kunda during her first review and no new evidence had been presented to suggest that that decision had been incorrect, the college's position was quite favorable. Furthermore, he viewed Kunda's lack of progress toward a master's degree as strong evidence of the merit of the college's position. In the president's view, the administration had handled the case properly, and he believed the college would prevail.

The college's decision to defend the litigation was also influenced by the outcome of an earlier allegation of sex discrimination by another faculty member. In that case, a female foreign language professor had been denied tenure by the college, and she had filed a claim of sex discrimination with the EEOC. This case differed from Kunda's in that although the department had recommended that the individual be tenured, the FPPC had voted against tenure because they questioned the equivalency of a degree awarded by the University of Havana and the level (collegiate or secondary) of her earlier employment experience. However, the negative FPPC vote was not unanimous, and the EEOC found probable cause to believe that the college had acted in a discriminatory manner. The faculty member, Ana Maria Diaz, sued the college in federal court. After two years of discovery, during which time several faculty agreed to testify on behalf of the college, the college decided to settle the case, and an estimated $75,000 was agreed to by the parties.[13]

In the opinion of several faculty members, the college had behaved properly in the tenure denial to Diaz, and the majority of the faculty supported its position (in direct contrast to their beliefs concerning the *Kunda* case). Many faculty speculate that other factors in addition to the merits of the case were involved in the college's decision to settle the litigation without going to trial. Faculty members believe that when the *Kunda* litigation was filed, the board determined to fight this case because the earlier case had been settled even though it was weak on the merits. In fact, a former professor reports that Morey said ''we're going to wrestle Connie Kunda to the mat'' (although Morey denies that he made such a statement), which suggests that the college was not inclined to settle a second discrimination claim.

Litigation Preparation

Academic employment discrimination cases are long and complicated, and the *Kunda* case was no exception. Discovery was arduous; the plaintiff was served with 103 interrogatories and the college with an initial set of 47 interrogatories and two additional sets when answers to the first were unresponsive. Depositions were taken from all relevant administrators, including the individual who was dean at the time of the Kunda decision but who had subsequently left to become the president of Cornell College in Iowa. Connie Kunda was also deposed (the questioning lasted one week), as were faculty members who had agreed to testify on her behalf, including the department head, Raymond Whispell, and faculty members of the FPPC and the FBA. The complaint was filed in June, 1977.

Kunda was actively engaged in the preparations for trial. She screened documents and witnesses and laid the groundwork for conferences between her attorneys and prospective faculty witnesses. She participated in all aspects of the preparation, and her attorneys deliberately involved her in the planning and implementation of their pretrial activities. They say that it was a good balance—she deferred to their legal judgment but was very helpful to them because she did so much of the legwork and because she was ''accurate in her assessment of the situation and the people and their willingness to help.''

Yaffe recalls that the numerous visits he and Golden made in order to interview and depose faculty created much emotion on campus and interest on the part of the local press. However, Yaffe and Golden did not want to try Kunda's case in the newspaper, and neither did she. Both the attorneys and the plaintiff were cautious in their dealings with the press and did not attempt to use publicity to pressure the college into a settlement.

Kunda also did much of the research required to answer the 103 interrogatories, and Yaffe and Golden did all of the legal research for and supervision of answers to the interrogatories themselves. The college refused to provide some of the material they requested, and Yaffe and Golden had to file a motion to compel discovery to obtain some of the data needed by their statistical expert, Bernard Siskin of Temple University. (The plaintiff had also filed an equal pay claim, which required analysis of salary practices at the college. In addition, the expert analyzed the pattern of tenure recommendations from the FPPC and the dean to see whether a trend emerged that suggested that the dean behaved differently in decisions on tenuring female faculty than in decisions concerning male faculty. The dean's decisions were important for two reasons: he was the first level of administrative [rather than faculty] review, and the president gave considerable weight to his recommendations.)

The administrators at Muhlenberg spent considerable time in preparation for the trial as well. In addition to giving depositions, they conferred at length with Roberta Staats, the attorney from Morgan, Lewis, and Bockius, in order to provide data on and explanations of the complicated process of peer review and evaluation at the college. The college had also been required to provide information to the EEOC, so it had been involved in discovery in some form since 1976. Although the dean's office was given the responsibility of collecting the documents needed for the defense, the president conferred frequently with defense counsel and was active in planning the college's defense.

Faculty at Muhlenberg state that there was never any communication about the litigation between the administration and the faculty—either before, during, or after the trial. Many of Kunda's former faculty colleagues cooperated fully with her attorneys and provided them with copies of records needed as evidence. All of the faculty that Golden and Yaffe believed were needed to mount the plaintiff's case agreed to testify in her behalf, although her attorneys decided to serve them all with subpoenas so that it would not be possible to identify those who had volunteered to testify. The college did not ask any faculty to testify on its behalf.[14]

Pretrial Impacts

Connie Kunda felt the difficulty of taking on the establishment in a decision to sue a college; the experience was draining both emotionally and physically. Some former colleagues would no longer speak to her and feared retaliation if they appeared to support her formally or informally. A clerk in the post office who had read about her case in the local paper remarked upon recognizing her name, "Oh, you're the troublemaker." She felt alone and exposed, and she was anxious about the impact of the litigation on her children and about how she would send her son to college. She worried about the difficulty of fighting an opponent that had money, staff, and an institutional defense and wondered whether there was any personal impact on the defendants, compared with the substantial personal impact on her. The contrast in resources available to the two parties concerned her; during the depositions, she and her attorneys ate brown-bag lunches while counsel for the defendants and defense witnesses dined out. She said that it was important to have absolute faith in her counsel and that that faith and the belief that she would be vindicated kept her going throughout the three-and-one-half-year litigation process.

Kunda's attorneys describe her as a person who was not litigious but who decided to litigate when it was apparent that she could get her job back in no other way. Roy Yaffe stated that she was not litigating for retribution and that she would have been willing to forgo the suit if relief had been available from another source. Nor did she try to build political support by pressuring people; according to her attorneys, people helped Kunda because they thought she deserved it. Yaffe noted that she grew stronger as the litigation progressed, despite the length and complexity of the discovery process, which surprised the attorneys as well as Kunda herself.

Administrators at the college were reluctant to discuss at length the impact of the litigation on either the institution or on themselves as individuals. The president remembers the long hours of pretrial preparation but only a few details of that preparation.

Trial Impacts

The nonjury trial began on May 10, 1978, and lasted four days (a relatively short trial for an academic discrimination case). The trial was held before Judge Daniel Huyett, who had a reputation for fairness and neutrality. Golden and Yaffe had decided to begin their case with Siskin, the statistical expert, who would demonstrate an inference of bias on the part of the dean that resulted in discriminatory tenure and promotion decisions for all women, supporting a legal theory of disparate impact as well as disparate treatment.

Siskin testified that the dean tended to vote negatively on tenure decisions for women faculty more often than he did for men, but the president consistently applied sex-neutral standards to decisions on promotion and tenure. Then the attorneys called Kunda to explain the promotion and tenure decision-making process at Muhlenberg and to tell her story. She testified about the lack of notice of the necessity for a master's degree. A difficult evidentiary dispute preceded this testimony, for Kunda's testimony was really hearsay— that is, she described conversations between herself and others about which those others (most importantly the former dean, Secor) could not testify and which they could not rebut. The defense counsel, Roberta Staats, objected to the hearsay testimony. However, Judge Huyett ruled that because the individuals with whom Kunda had had these conversations were agents of the college, the conversations were admissions by the defendant, which are exempt from the hearsay rule.

Kunda's testimony lasted nearly the entire first day of trial. Her attorneys report that she was an "excellent witness—sincere, credible" and was articulate in telling of the circumstances of her denial of promotion and tenure. After that, faculty witnesses were called to corroborate Kunda's testimony and expand on the issues involved. Her attorneys first called her department head, Whispell, who corroborated her testimony concerning his failure to notify her of the master's degree requirement. Whispell defended his failure to notify, saying that at the time she was hired, three faculty members had recently been promoted without such a degree. Whispell testified, ''I had no reason to expect that she would be treated any differently than any other person in the department. I was fully aware of what the handbook said [i.e., the terminal degree requirement], but I didn't feel that it was practiced.''[15]

The faculty members who testified for Kunda were an impressive array. John Reed, a faculty member at Muhlenberg for thirty years and head of the history department, testified as a member of the FPPC. He described its procedures and the reason why the FPPC voted positively on Kunda's case the second time it was presented. He noted that the committee had more information about her qualifications for the second vote, and stated that ''the Committee was convinced that she had the scholarly equivalent of a master's degree, based on the information which it acquired in the meantime, since the first split vote.''[16]

Other faculty testified as to the meaning of the scholarly equivalent terminology and the procedures for making decisions on promotion and tenure as well as on their evaluations of the plaintiff's qualifications for tenure and promotion. Of particular importance was the testimony of two male former faculty members who were denied tenure because they lacked a master's degree. They stated that they had been warned that the degree was necessary for tenure, thus corroborating Kunda's claim that male faculty had been advised of the requirement but that she had not.[17]

Thomas Lohr, a member of the psychology department for twenty-three years and its current head, also testified for Kunda. He was a member of the committee that had drafted the faculty handbook, and he testified about the committee's interpretation of the handbook requirement concerning time in rank. Lohr also had been a member of the faculty board of appeals that heard Kunda's appeal in 1974, and he described his and the other committee members' evaluation of her qualifications for tenure and promotion. After Lohr's testimony, Golden and Yaffe rested their case.

At this point in the trial, the defense attorneys moved to dismiss the complaint, a standard defense practice in civil litigation. The defense claimed that Kunda's attorneys had not established a prima facie case of sex discrimination and had not proven that the college had violated any of its own rules or policies. However, the judge disagreed, stating that the plaintiff *had* established a prima facie case and that the case would turn upon the credibility of the witnesses, some of whom he had not heard. He ruled that the trial must continue.

Since all the faculty witnesses testified on behalf of the plaintiff, the defense relied on the testimony of administrators and trustees. Morey testified concerning his attempts to upgrade the quality of the faculty at Muhlenberg and explained why earlier decisions to promote faculty members without master's degrees had been made. He admitted that he had not counseled the plaintiff concerning the need for a master's degree to obtain tenure. The chair of the trustee committee that had heard Kunda's appeal then testified and stated that the committee had determined, using its own expertise, that she did not have the scholarly equivalent of a master's degree and that the courses she had taken were continuing education, not graduate level work. The deposition of Secor, the former dean of the college, was read into the record. In the deposition, Secor said he could not remember many of the matters about which he was questioned—in particular, whether he had advised Kunda that a master's degree was required for tenure. He did, however, deflate the defense's argument that financial concerns influenced the Kunda tenure decision by saying that although there were some fiscal concerns about the physical education department, they were not substantial and that financial considerations were not involved in the denial of promotion or tenure to the plaintiff or to any other faculty member. He testified that although the plaintiff was an excellent teacher, she was not "fully qualified under the rules of our trade" for tenure.[18]

At the close of the trial, the judge complimented the attorneys for both parties, stating that "the trial was very competently tried." Kunda's attorneys reported that the relationship between the two parties' counsel was professional, and the many stipulations to facts and other pretrial cooperation simplified the conduct of the trial considerably. Yaffe characterizes the trial as "almost perfect," saying that it "went in like clockwork." All the witnesses they sought for the plaintiff cooperated fully, were supportive, and came to the trial even on days they didn't have to testify. The defense counsel did not use tricks or dilatory tactics but presented a straightforward argument. Furthermore, the attorneys were pleased that there were no surprises at the trial— no hostile faculty witnesses and no surprise testimony.

Although testifying in court often is difficult and stressful, no respondent indicated that enduring the trial itself was especially difficult. The president indicated that if he could advise other presidents in similar circumstances, he would advise against their attending the trial unless they had to be there to testify. He believes that his continued presence at the trial was unnecessary and that his visibility had a negative impact on campus relationships, because he became the symbol of the college's defense.

The faculty members who testified have mixed reactions to the impact of the trial on them personally. Whispell believes that his testimony in support of Kunda may have been a factor in the president's decision to remove him as department head and his subsequent replacement as athletic director, although Morey maintains that personnel decisions involving Whispell were related not to the litigation but to his performance in those positions. Other faculty members were not affected as directly but believe that the administration was displeased with their testimony.

For Kunda the trial was no more stressful than the entire experience of suing the college. The transcript shows virtually no evidence of browbeating witnesses or of arguments between counsel—it was quite a civilized trial. Its relative brevity and comparatively low-key nature may have been a result of the thoroughness with which both sides prepared their cases, so that at trial there were few surprises and few areas of disagreement (with the exception of the hearsay issue). But it was five months before the parties knew of the outcome.

Decision Impacts

In October, 1978, Judge Huyett ruled in favor of Connie Kunda. After reciting the history of Kunda's evaluation by the faculty committees and the board's decision to deny her tenure, the judge noted the strong concurrence among the faculty committees that Kunda was qualified for tenure and promotion. He reviewed the testimony of the two male physical education professors who had been counseled about the need to obtain their master's degree and found Kunda's testimony, combined with the lack of contradictory testimony, probative of the absence of such counseling in her case. The judge concluded that "the failure adequately to counsel plaintiff concerning the necessity of obtaining a masters degree constituted purposeful discrimination on the basis of sex."[19]

Furthermore, the judge found Kunda's belief that a master's degree was not required for tenure to be reasonable because of the college's inconsistent practice prior to Morey's arrival, even though under Morey's presidency the college did regularly refuse to tenure faculty who had not obtained terminal degrees.[20] Although the judge agreed that the requirement of a terminal degree was a neutral one, unrelated to gender, he wrote that because that requirement was not applied consistently, "the stated reason for denying plaintiff a promotion—the lack of a terminal degree—was pretextual."[21]

The judge ruled that Kunda had successfully made out a prima facie case of sex discrimination, saying that

> in the face of the virtually unanimous opinion of those in a position to examine Mrs. Kunda's performance most closely, the Muhlenberg College faculty, that the plaintiff was highly qualified for promotion and tenure, we are loathe [sic] to act as a "super-tenure review committee" and decide otherwise.[22]

The judge's ruling combined deference to academic judgments in general with a recognition of the importance of peer review rather than administrative review as the appropriate locus of academic judgment on the qualifications of an individual for promotion and tenure.

Judge Huyett concluded that the college had discriminated against Kunda in the negative promotion decision, because male faculty had been promoted without having obtained their terminal degrees. But the college *had* acted consistently in tenure decisions, the judge said, and thus had applied the terminal degree requirement consistently in Kunda's case. The judge ruled that the college had successfully rebutted the plaintiff's disparate impact claim in that it had demonstrated the rational relationship between the duties of a faculty member and the terminal degree requirement.[23] However, he wrote, the college's failure to warn her that a master's degree was required for tenure was proof that the college had treated Kunda differently from similarly situated male faculty, which resulted in a finding of discriminatory treatment in both the promotion and tenure decisions.

In fashioning a remedy, Judge Huyett used the traditional civil rights standard: determining "the position plaintiff would have been in had she not suffered the unlawful discrimination proven here."[24] The judge awarded Kunda promotion to assistant professor retroactive to September, 1973, but would not award her tenure outright because of his finding that the tenure decision had been made in a neutral manner. Because of the college's failure to warn her of the terminal degree requirement, however, the judge awarded her "tenure contingent upon obtaining her masters degree within two full school years"[25] of the date of the opinion; her tenure would be retroactive to September, 1975. He reasoned that since the president and the dean had testified that if Kunda had held a master's degree she would have been promoted, giving her an opportunity to obtain that degree did not violate academic principles, for both the faculty and the administration agreed that apart from the issue of the degree, Kunda was qualified for tenure. Judge Huyett also reinstated Kunda with full back pay.

Muhlenberg College appealed immediately and also filed a motion to stay judgment pending the outcome of the appeal. The trial judge, who ruled on the motion, refused to stay judgment but did agree to permit the college to escrow Kunda's back pay until the appeal had been decided. Thus, Connie Kunda returned to work at the beginning of the next semester, January, 1979, as an assistant professor of physical education.

Kunda and her attorneys believed that the unanimous support of her colleagues was key to the success of her litigation. In addition, the testimony of her former department head and a former faculty member that males had been counseled to obtain a master's degree but she had not and the determination of the FPPC that she had obtained the scholarly equivalent of a master's degree were the issues that were dispositive of the case.

Meanwhile, oral arguments for the appeal were held before the Third Circuit Court of Appeals on October 16, 1979. Despite the fact that this case concerned nothing more than one faculty member challenging the actions of one small liberal arts college, the decision by Judge Huyett to award Kunda "conditional tenure" created quite a stir in academic circles. Associations representing college administrators and trustees reacted with concern to the perceived intervention by a judge into matters more appropriately decided by academics. On the other hand, associations representing faculty employee interests welcomed the judge's remedy. The debate was over the very nature of a tenure decision: Is it primarily a judgment by peers that a faculty member is worthy, or do administrators and trustees have the right to make their own judgments of faculty qualifications? And if a court finds that discrimination has occurred, shouldn't the case be returned to the academic decision-making system rather than decided unilaterally by a judge?

The debate resulted in the preparation of amicus briefs by two powerful academic organizations, which took opposite views of the judge's action. An amicus brief in support of the college was filed by the American Council on Education (ACE) and affiliated organizations representing colleges and universities; amici for the plaintiff included the AAUP and the EEOC. The issue addressed by all amici was the award of conditional tenure, for the ACE believed that such an award was an inappropriate exercise of judicial discretion, while the AAUP and the EEOC supported the award because the plaintiff's peers had determined that she was qualified for tenure, and the denial had come from administrators, not peers. The Third Circuit, in a two-to-one vote, affirmed the ruling of the trial court, and ordered on February 19, 1980, that Connie Kunda receive the relief granted to her by the trial judge. The dissenting judge joined the portion of the opinion reinstating Kunda with promotion and back pay but believed that the award of contingent tenure was inappropriate and that the plaintiff should have to repeat the tenure review process (essentially the argument that the ACE had made).

The majority opinion, written by Judge Dolores Sloviter, strongly endorsed Judge Huyett's findings of fact and conclusions of law. Judge Sloviter is a former law professor at Temple University, and her opinion is strongly supportive of the faculty role in tenure and promotion decisions. The judges agreed that the college's failure to counsel Kunda on the importance of the terminal degree constituted purposeful sex discrimination and that the remedy of reinstatement and promotion was an appropriate one. With regard to the issue of the award of conditional tenure, the reviewing panel relied heavily on the determination of Kunda's peers that she merited an award of tenure. The opinion strongly supports the primacy of faculty rather than administrative determinations about faculty qualifications, stating:

> That decision [determination of faculty qualifications] is most effectively made within the university and although there may be tension between the faculty and the administration on their relative roles and respon-

sibilities, it is generally acknowledged that the faculty has at least the initial, if not the primary, responsibility for judging candidates.[26]

The panel noted that Kunda's qualifications were not in dispute, for the administration had testified that only the lack of a terminal degree stood between her and tenure. Therefore, the court said, the award of conditional tenure merely made operational a qualitative judgment already reached by both her faculty peers and the administration.

The majority demonstrated its particular concern that the remedy awarded Kunda be a meaningful one. They rejected the suggestion that she be afforded another tenure review after obtaining her master's degree, for the "intangible effect upon that decision because the candidate being considered was the successful party to a Title VII suit"[27] could result in a negative review, which would penalize Kunda once again. The panel noted the types of remedies used in nonacademic Title VII cases, including retroactive seniority and other employment perquisites, and said:

> The fact that the discrimination in this case took place in an academic rather than commercial setting does not permit the court to abdicate its responsibility to insure the award of a meaningful remedy. Congress did not intend that those institutions which employ persons who work primarily with their mental faculties should enjoy a different status under Title VII than those which employ persons who work primarily with their hands.[28]

Since Kunda had returned to work in January, 1979, the primary effect of the appellate court decision was the payment of back pay and attorney fees as well as a final determination of her employment status. As part of the final settlement, the college agreed to pay her attorney fees (an amount none of the individuals will disclose) and the back pay, less Kunda's earnings during the period of her separation from the college, as ordered by the district court. Because the college trustees decided not to appeal the case to the United States Supreme Court, Kunda's legal challenge had ended.

Most of the faculty were delighted with the outcome of Kunda's litigation against Muhlenberg. Morale had been low for years, and many faculty viewed Kunda's victory as a victory for the faculty as a whole. Despite the defeat endured by the administration, the new dean, Harold Stenger, welcomed her back, and she was permitted to return to work as though the litigation had never taken place. She earned her master's degree at East Stroudsberg State College in less than a year, having completed nine credits between the time she left the college and the time of the trial, and was awarded tenure and promotion to associate professor in August, 1980. Because the Muhlenberg

College bylaws require that tenured faculty be associate professors, Kunda received that promotion without a review. In 1987 she was promoted to full professor.

Posttrial Impacts

The effects of the *Kunda* litigation on Muhlenberg College are complex and subtle. As a small, private, liberal arts college, Muhlenberg is probably less susceptible to externally induced change than a state college or university would be. However, its very independence from outside funding sources means that the college must bear the costs of litigation out of its own funds, and one would expect the college to take steps to reduce or prevent costly legal disputes in response to the *Kunda* lawsuit.

Although some faculty at Muhlenberg believe that the decision itself had a limited impact on the Morey administration, changes implemented since the litigation began appear to be related to an effort to avoid future litigation. Those who perceive little change note that administrative decisions immediately after the conclusion of the lawsuit appeared to be made in the same way as they were prior to the litigation. Other faculty believe that the president retaliated personally against at least one of the faculty witnesses, but such an allegation is difficult to prove. Although the trustees continued to support Morey in his disputes with the faculty during the union campaign and the no-confidence vote, faculty report that the trustees became more cautious about making faculty promotion and tenure decisions and reviewed each case carefully instead of automatically accepting the president's recommendation. Indeed, after the *Kunda* case, the trustees reversed several of the president's recommendations, both positive and negative. Thus, in the view of some of the faculty, by the fall of 1983 the trustees were effectively making the promotion and tenure decisions at Muhlenberg College, an unusual practice in higher education.

Other consequences of the litigation are easier to trace. For example, although promotion and tenure decisions are still made through the same process, applicants for faculty positions are explicitly told that a terminal degree is required for promotion or tenure, and even "substantial progress" will not be sufficient for an individual to be promoted or tenured. The scholarly equivalent is no longer used, and the faculty handbook that listed such an alternative has been withdrawn by the administration. Faculty report that the administration never announced the outcome of the Kunda litigation to the faculty, nor was there ever a meeting of department heads, or other faculty, concerning implications of the litigation. Charles Bednar, head of the political science department, stated that "it's as though there was no lesson to be learned from the litigation, or recognition that chairs could benefit from earlier mistakes.'' The administration appeared simply to ignore the outcome of the case.

Others think, however, that the litigation did have an impact. Professor Thomas Lohr, former chair of the FPPC, believes that evaluation procedures are better structured as a result of the litigation and that the college is careful to develop a fuller record documenting the reasons for promotion and tenure recommendations. He notes the numerous changes in the promotion and tenure policies enacted by the trustees since the *Kunda* litigation and attributes these to administrative reluctance to defend another discrimination lawsuit.

At approximately the time that the trial was taking place, Joel Seigle, an assistant professor in the history department, was denied tenure. Seigle filed a claim of discrimination with the EEOC, asserting that he had been denied tenure because of his religion. The EEOC investigated and found probable cause to believe that anti-Semitism had indeed been a factor in Seigle's tenure denial. [29]

In denying Seigle tenure, the board of trustees had stated that his background was in European history but that the department needed an expert in American history. According to members of the department, the department head had argued that the department needed both Seigle and an expert in American history and had given Seigle a favorable recommendation. However, a senior member of the history department who also served on the FPPC had allegedly made numerous anti-Semitic remarks, and testimony obtained by the EEOC from faculty indicated that that person had influenced the decision by the FPPC. The EEOC found that Jewish persons were underrepresented on the faculty and that the proportion of Jewish students at Muhlenberg (18.7 percent) far exceeded the proportion of Jewish faculty, as Seigle was the only self-identified faculty member of the Jewish faith. [30]

Both students and faculty cooperated with the EEOC investigation, and their testimony apparently convinced the investigator that there was a connection between the faculty member's alleged anti-Semitism and the tenure denial. During the discovery process in the Seigle case, Seigle's wife was promoted and transferred to California; Seigle and the college negotiated a settlement of $12,000 in return for Seigle's agreement to drop the charges of discrimination and to decline the college's offer of reinstatement for one semester. [31] Because Seigle left the area, it is impossible to determine whether the college would have defended this third discrimination charge as vigorously as it did the *Kunda* litigation. Many faculty believe that the college would again have gone to court, but no conclusions can be drawn from the settlement.

A new system of nontenurable faculty positions was created in 1974 because the administration believed that this system was necessary because of the high percentage of tenured faculty at the college. A tenure cap of two-thirds tenured faculty has been established for each department. Although a few exceptions have been made to the nontenurable policy (for a new department head, for example), it is enforced for all new junior faculty, and the faculty report that the dim prospects for tenuring have made recruitment of new faculty most difficult. The policy was modified in 1981 to permit nontenurable faculty to transfer to a tenure track status, and they are allowed more than six years of probationary status as well.

It is difficult to trace other impacts of the litigation because of the long-standing tensions between the president and the faculty. Faculty respondents asserted that faculty-administrative relationships were strained at Muhlenberg throughout most of Morey's presidency, and the president confirmed that the relationship was stressed. The faculty's attempt to organize a union, their seventy-five-to-twenty-six vote of no confidence in the president, and the students' petition for Morey's resignation have already been described. In September, 1983, the president announced his retirement, effective at the end of the academic year. A search committee composed of three faculty members (one elected by the faculty, two appointed by the trustees), a student, the college's treasurer, and six trustees recommended that the president of Susquehanna College, Jonathan C. Messerli, be selected as Muhlenberg's new president.

Clearly the *Kunda* litigation complicated faculty-administrative relationships at Muhlenberg College under the Morey administration. In fact, one might question whether there was any institutional learning from the litigation, since a similar case was filed only a few years after *Kunda,* and the administration appeared willing to defend it. Faculty allege that decisions, when they were communicated to faculty at all, were very long in coming and were justified by some vague reference to policies that were unwritten and unknown to the faculty. On the other hand, Morey believes that the litigation has made the FPPC much more cautious in its documentation of recommendations concerning promotion and tenure; for example, the faculty is reluctant to record positive and negative votes or to associate names of committee members with certain viewpoints about the candidate under consideration. Furthermore, the college now makes explicit to faculty at the time of hiring the requirements for tenure, one of which is the terminal degree.

The litigation's impact on Connie Kunda has been substantial. She was successful in her suit, and she was promoted to associate and then full professor as well as appointed coordinator of athletics for women and director of the college's wellness program, both part-time administrative positions. However, she deplores the tensions on campus and admits that enduring the years of uncertainty regarding the litigation's outcome was extremely difficult. She asserts that an individual contemplating litigation must be very strong and must be aware of the emotional, physical, and financial drain it imposes. She said that a plaintiff must be willing to stand alone if necessary and to continue to believe that the outcome will be positive even though the process is lengthy and debilitating.

She attributes some of her problems with Muhlenberg to her own naïveté concerning how faculty are evaluated and how academic politics are played. She had assumed that "doing professional work" was enough; that it was unnecessary to "blow your own horn" about scholarly and professional accomplishments. She understands now the importance of documenting achievement and communicating with colleagues and superiors concerning expectations for promotion and evaluation standards.

The greatest impact of *Kunda v. Muhlenberg College* may be on the law itself. The case is the first example of a judicial award of conditional tenure, and, although no subsequent case has employed this unusual remedy, language in the case has been quoted frequently by courts that wish to reinforce the propriety of close scrutiny of the discrimination claims of individuals who work "with their mental faculties" instead of their hands. The judicial attention to the importance of peer evaluation and its primacy in promotion and tenure decisions has also been referred to by courts in more recent cases, although most academic discrimination cases do not contain the unusual circumstance of faculty groups *and* administrators agreeing that an individual is qualified, as was the situation in *Kunda*. Despite its unusual factual circumstances, the *Kunda* case made an important contribution to academic law because of its strong endorsement of peer review as the effective judgment on a candidate's qualifications for tenure.

Connie Kunda's life was unquestionably altered by the litigation, and, despite her present secure circumstances and success at the college, the experience is not easily forgotten. The litigation probably raised the level of conflict on the campus, although the conflict already present and the numerous other sources of administration-faculty tension again make it difficult to trace a direct cause-and-effect relationship between the *Kunda* litigation and the conditions on campus. Kunda's lawsuit and subsequent victory were a unifying force for a large portion of the Muhlenberg faculty, and that solidarity culminated in the no-confidence vote in May, 1983. Whether that vote influenced the president's decision to retire is unclear; it is probably fair to say, however, that the accumulation of conflict, of which the litigation was one segment, culminated in new leadership for Muhlenberg College. It remains to be seen whether that legacy of conflict will continue in the administration of the new president.

Muhlenberg faculty report a slow warming of relationships on campus with the arrival of Jonathan Messerli, the new president. Morale is improving, they note, and new attitudes are beginning to develop. At a recent faculty dinner, faculty who "hadn't attended college social functions in a long time" were present, and one faculty member who has avoided faculty meetings for years has become active again. As of the spring of 1985, it is much too early even to speculate about the future of faculty-administrative relationships at Muhlenberg College. The faculty hope that the difficult years at the college, in which the *Kunda* litigation played a significant role, are behind them.

NOTES

1. 463 F. Supp. 294 (E.D. Pa. 1978), *aff'd,* 621 F.2d 532 (3d Cir. 1980).
2. Walter P. Metzger, "Academic Tenure in America: A Historical Essay," in *Faculty Tenure,* ed. Commission on Academic Tenure (San Francisco: Jossey-Bass, 1973), pp. 93–159.
3. B. N. Shaw, *Academic Tenure in American Higher Education* (Chicago: Adams Press, 1971), p. 50.
4. Commission on Academic Tenure, *Faculty Tenure,* p. 256.
5. *Allentown Call Chronicle,* Dec. 23, 1979, p. B-1.
6. Commonwealth v. Tate, 432 A.2d 1382 (Pa. 1981).
7. Tate, 432 A.2d 1382.
8. John A. Deitrich, letter to Muhlenberg College faculty and staff, August 19, 1983.
9. Thomas Lohr, interview with author, September 21, 1983.
10. John Morey, interview with author, August 17, 1983.
11. Lohr, interview with author.
12. Complaint, p. 15.
13. *Allentown Morning Call,* October 4, 1979, p. B-1.
14. John Morey, tape-recorded comments, January 29, 1985.
15. Trial Transcript, p. 138.
16. Ibid., p. 176.
17. Ibid., pp. 223, 224, 232–33.
18. Ibid., p. 508.
19. Kunda, 463 F. Supp. at 305.
20. Kunda, 463 F. Supp. at 309.
21. Kunda, 463 F. Supp. at 305.
22. Kunda, 463 F. Supp. at 308.
23. Kunda, 463 F. Supp. at 312.
24. Kunda, 463 F. Supp. at 312.
25. Kunda, 463 F. Supp. at 313.
26. Kunda, 621 F.2d 532 (3d Cir. 1980).
27. Kunda, 621 F.2d at 549.
28. Kunda, 621 F.2d at 550.
29. *Allentown Morning Call,* Dec. 7, 1979, p. B-1.
30. Ibid.
31. Muhlenberg College Press Release, April 17, 1980.

Chapter 5
An "Average" Sociologist of Race Relations

Scott v. University of Delaware[1]

This case raised important legal and civil rights issues. A black sociologist challenged the traditional academic requirement of a Ph.D. degree because minorities are underrepresented among doctoral recipients, as well as the decentralized personnel decision-making process in universities, which makes accountability difficult. The remedy he sought was to require the university to hire blacks in proportion to their representation in the state's population.

The University of Delaware is an unusual institution for many reasons. It functions as a state university (although it is actually a private, state-assisted institution), attracting a high proportion of out-of-state students.

The state of Delaware is also an anomaly. It straddles the Mason-Dixon line, and "in spirit if not in law, Delaware was a Southern state, though it took the Union's side in the Civil War."[2] The state constitution required separate public schools for black and white children, and higher education was strictly segregated as well. Delaware State College was created for black students in 1891, and the University of Delaware, founded in 1867, was restricted to whites and was dejure segregated until 1950. Even today, the university still has a student body that is overwhelmingly white in a state whose population is 12 percent black.

Despite its relatively modest size (approximately 15,000 full-time and 5,000 part-time students) and its location in a state whose population is 594,000, the University of Delaware has been involved in litigation on several occasions. In the early 1970s, the university sued two Catholic priests to prevent them from using the common room of a university dormitory to hold religious services.[3] A state court ruled that the religious services were permissible. At least four faculty members have sued the university over negative employment decisions. One tenured faculty member won the right to a hearing before dismissal for cause,[4] and another won reinstatement and punitive damages against the university president when the court ruled that his contract had not been renewed because of the president's discomfort with the faculty member's views on homosexuality.[5] A third sued the university when he was denied tenure; however, he dropped the litigation after eighteen months of discovery and agreed to a dismissal of the case. Indeed, even the impetus to desegregate the university came as the result of a lawsuit in state court; ten black students asserted that the university's refusal to admit them violated their Fourteenth Amendment rights. The Delaware Court of Chancery agreed and ruled that the university had to admit black students.[6]

Before the case involving Nolvert Scott, a black sociologist, no faculty member had sued the university alleging racial discrimination in its decisions concerning hiring, promotion, and tenure. The filing of the lawsuit may have been inevitable, since the university employed very few black faculty as well as having only a small proportion of minority students on campus. In many ways, the university was on trial as much for its history of excluding blacks as for its allegedly unfair treatment of a particular faculty member. For example, the plaintiffs took every opportunity to note both the disparities between Delaware's black population and the proportions of minority students and faculty, and prior university practices, no longer followed, that had treated blacks unfairly. Even the opinion of the trial court mentioned that the university did not permit black students to room with white students in university dormitories until 1961[7] and noted as well that between 1951 and 1969, only thirty-seven black students received baccalaureate degrees and only fifty-two black students received graduate degrees. In the year of the trial (1976–77), the undergraduate student body was 3.4 percent black, and 1.8 percent of the graduate students were black.

Although the university's history of excluding blacks posed a special problem in the defense of Scott's case, the history of the sociology department with regard to race relations was quite different. In contrast to the seeming inevitability of a lawsuit against the university, the fact that the primary defendants in Scott's individual claim were the members of the sociology department was, in light of the department's history, ironic.

Frederick Parker, who joined the sociology department in 1946 and chaired it in the 1960s, wrote a history of the department that discusses the effect of the civil rights movement on the university and the sociology department.[8] In that document, Parker describes activities of departmental members in the 1950s and 1960s that assisted the desegregation of schools and communities in Delaware. Apparently the university was not willing to espouse the sociology department's views publicly, for Parker notes that the university administration "maintained a neutral or defensive stance on the issue" of racial integration,[9] especially in their refusal to release the results of a sociology department survey that indicated that university students viewed the admission of blacks to the university quite favorably. Parker also describes the attack on him by the head of the state legislature's budget committee for a speech he had given in Washington, D.C., about "fallacious racial beliefs." The legislator attempted to use the budgetary process to punish university faculty for views favorable to racial integration, but an editorial in the *Wilmington Morning News* on March 14, 1957, criticized the legislator (Senator Walter J. Hoey, a Democrat from Sussex County) for attempting to "abridge academic freedom and scientific truth" by linking the budget to social views.[10]

In 1968, Frank Scarpitti, who chaired the sociology department, was asked to chair a special university committee to study the status of black students at the university. The committee's report, "The Black Student and the University of Delaware," released in 1969, was critical of the university for its lack of efforts to improve the quality of life for its black students, noting that black students saw the university as "a cold, unconcerned, unwelcoming institution" with "a hostile environment where survival is contingent upon the black student's ability to endure psychological abuse of many sorts."[11] The report made several recommendations for improving the status and morale of black students on campus, one of which was hiring more black faculty members. In addition to chairing this special university committee, Scarpitti had been instrumental in defusing an emotional demonstration by black students over the university's failure to hire a black woman as director of the black studies department.

Frank Scarpitti, a young but already well-published scholar, had joined the sociology department in the fall of 1967. He was hired, along with several other faculty, to plan and implement a Ph.D. program in sociology. Concurrent with the initiation of the doctoral degree program was a shift in emphasis within the department. Teaching loads were reduced from twelve hours to six hours per semester, and the faculty were told that research and scholarship, including publications, would be important criteria for promotion and tenure decisions. Faculty hired before the shift in focus from teaching to both good teaching and high-quality research were told that the new standards applied to all alike. However, before deciding whether to renew the appointment of Nolvert Scott, the department did agree to renew the contracts of two faculty who had published little or nothing. The department decided to be lenient in these cases because they believed that these faculty were at a disadvantage, for they had been hired under an earlier value system and were now being expected to meet new and more demanding performance expectations.

When the context in which the case arose is understood, the merits of the particular plaintiff's case seem almost secondary to the numerous and important general issues at stake. The case itself is probably the most serious attack on the academic faculty personnel system that has been brought, for it challenged the theretofore sacrosanct union card for admission to the academic profession, the Ph.D. Although a Ph.D. has long been required of faculty by universities and selective colleges, such a requirement has an undeniably negative impact on the size of the pool of prospective black faculty members, for the proportion of Ph.D.'s who are black (just over 2 percent) is well below the proportion of blacks in the population (12 percent).

In addition to the debate between traditional academic hiring requirements and racial equity in academic hiring, a more fundamental issue added to the complexity of this case. The university had been de jure segregated until 1950 but was trying both to change its former image as a conservative, white institution and to recruit and hire black faculty. Unfortunately, since the maturation of the civil rights movement, the numbers of black academics holding Ph.D.'s has never been as great as the demand for credentialed black scholars, and the university's history and image discouraged prospective black faculty from considering Delaware. In fact, the combination of the university's historical stance and its poor record in hiring and keeping black faculty led some, including the EEOC, to question the university's claims that it was trying to comply with the civil rights laws. And so the claims of discrimination filed by Nolvert Scott attracted national attention far beyond the significance of the legal debate about Scott's individual competence.

Triggering Incident

In the fall of 1970, an assistant professor position became available in the sociology department, and the faculty decided to recruit an expert in the sociology of race relations. A national search was conducted, and three individuals were invited for on-campus interviews: Nolvert Scott, who was black, and two whites. Scott had taught for eight years at colleges and universities in Canada and had nearly completed his doctorate in sociology at the Pennsylvania State University. Scott recalled that approximately two dozen institutions were interested in hiring him at the time that he accepted the position at the University of Delaware. In recognition of the seller's market for black Ph.D.'s, the university, upon Scott's demand, agreed to pay him three thousand dollars more in starting salary than the normal rate for newly hired sociology faculty with Ph.D.'s. During the summer before he was to begin teaching at Delaware, Scott completed his dissertation and received his doctoral degree.

Scott's relationships with his students were difficult from time to time. Several students complained to Scarpitti, the department chair, about Scott's classes. They claimed that he brought his dogs to class, that he discussed his personal life in class, and that substantial portions of his lectures were irrelevant to the subject of the course or to the tests he gave. They also complained that he did not tolerate points of view that differed from his own. The course evaluations sponsored by the student government association rated Scott's courses as poor, and most of the students participating in the evaluations stated that they would not recommend Scott's courses. Furthermore, enrollment in the courses taught by Scott dropped precipitously during the years that he taught at the university; in the year before his arrival, enrollment in the race relations course (taught by a white faculty member) had been over one hundred, but it dropped to twenty-five or fewer after Scott began teaching the course. Scott blamed the enrollment drop on student bigotry rather than poor teaching.

Despite the new departmental emphasis on scholarship and research, an emphasis that began before Scott was hired, Scott produced no scholarly publications during his first two years at the university. In the spring of 1973, at the end of the second year of Scott's employment with the university, the department, under university policies, was required to recommend for or against contract renewal for Scott. The faculty examined Scott's publication record and his teaching. Although the importance of scholarship had risen since 1969, teaching was still considered very important within the department, and faculty members were reluctant to approve renewal or promotion if the candidate's teaching was not at least above average. Finding no record of scholarship and a mediocre teaching record at best, the department voted against recommending the renewal of Scott's contract. Unfortunately for the department, and for chairperson Scarpitti in particular, the department had never before in its history recommended against the contract renewal of one of its colleagues, and the first individual to receive a negative recommendation happened to be black.

According to Scarpitti, the departmental faculty placed great weight on Scott's teaching ability in evaluating him for contract renewal, because he had eight years of teaching experience before arriving at the university. Although Scott had written a newspaper article and a book review had been accepted for publication, he had no other publications. Scarpitti stated that had Scott produced some research, the department would have given him more time to prove himself rather than recommending against renewal at the end of his first contract term. However, the combination of poor teaching and the lack of scholarship convinced the department to recommend against renewal of Scott's contract for a second three-year term. This decision, when examined in light of earlier contract renewal decisions by the department, was a change of policy. In earlier cases, the department had recommended in favor of contract renewal of faculty who had published little or no research if their teaching was acceptable. For example, Shigeo Nohara, a Japanese-American who had been hired in 1965, was renewed in 1967 and again in 1970, despite the fact that he had published very little. However, Nohara had been hired before the shift in departmental emphasis from teaching to scholarship and had been given an especially heavy teaching load in comparison with Scott. Furthermore, Nohara's teaching had been rated higher than Scott's. The decision to give Nohara another two years to prove himself, made in 1970, reflected a departmental concern that Nohara had not been given enough time to comply with the new and higher standards. When Nohara failed to publish anything after his second contract renewal, his employment was terminated.

Perception of Alleged Discrimination

Scott's first two years at the university were marred by several incidents of racial harassment, which he perceived as evidence of the university's discriminatory attitude toward blacks. Probably the most serious incident was a student report that Scott had been seen lying on the ground on campus holding a liquor bottle, a report that was never verified by the administration. Nevertheless, the dean called Scott in and questioned him at length about the student's report but refused to identify the student or to attempt to verify the report. Although Scott hired a lawyer and eventually forced the dean and the president to write letters of apology, he continued to believe that he had been poorly treated by the administration because of this incident.

Two other incidents upset Scott and caused him to believe that faculty at the university were hostile to blacks. A university administrator stated in Scott's presence that Scott wasn't a "typical" black faculty member, that he didn't "look black" or "act black," suggesting that the speaker disapproved of Scott because, in that individual's opinion, Scott did not fit the stereotype of black faculty. In another incident, a member of the sociology department faculty made a statement during a faculty meeting that Scott had been hired as "window dressing" and that departmental attempts to recruit a woman faculty member would be similarly insincere. Although the department chair and the rest of the departmental faculty wrote Scott letters of apology for the incident, no action was taken to censure the individual who made the statement.

The department's decision to recommend against renewing Scott's contract surprised and angered him. The nonrenewal, coupled with the earlier incidents of harassment and the bigotry he perceived behind the dwindling enrollments in his courses, appeared to him to be based on race discrimination rather than on his performance. With one year of his three-year contract yet to be completed, Scott underwent open-heart surgery in the fall of 1973 (his second such operation) and taught only during the spring semester of 1974.

Use of Internal Remedies

The faculty at the University of Delaware are represented by a bargaining agent, their local AAUP chapter. The AAUP became the bargaining agent in the early 1970s, and the first contract between it and the administration was signed in 1973. The contract contained a grievance system through which faculty who had been denied reappointment, promotion, or tenure could appeal. However, Scott did not use the contractual grievance system, apparently believing it could not provide him relief, since it permitted only appeals of procedural violations rather than challenges to the accuracy or fairness of the substantive decision to deny reappointment. Instead, he filed a complaint of race discrimination with the EEOC, the first step in employment discrimination litigation.

Litigation Decision

Upon Scott's filing of a complaint with the EEOC, the commission decided to conduct an on-site investigation of his claim. In addition to his claim of individual discrimination, Scott had alleged that the university's hiring and promotion practices discriminated against blacks as a class and that the requirement that candidates for faculty positions hold a Ph.D. had a discriminatory impact on blacks, because only a very small proportion of the holders of doctoral degrees were black. The EEOC agreed with Scott's contentions concerning classwide discrimination at the university and issued a finding of probable cause to believe that the university was discriminating against blacks in its hiring requirements. Although the EEOC investigator, Leo Sanchez, admitted that the commission found no actual policies or practices that discriminated against blacks in the hiring process, the commission made extensive use of statistical data that showed that blacks were underrepresented at the university despite the relatively small number of blacks with Ph.D.'s. Furthermore, the commission found reasonable cause to believe that the nonrenewal decision about Scott had been tainted by discrimination and issued him a right-to-sue letter on April 17, 1974.

Litigation Preparation

To represent him in court, Scott chose Bader, Dorsey and Kreshtool, a firm well known in Delaware for its civil rights and labor law expertise. The firm was familiar to the administration at the university, for it had represented faculty litigants Aumiller, Anapol, and Gordenstein,[12] as well as the priests in the *Keegan* case.[13] Except for Gordenstein, all of them had prevailed against the university. The firm (since disbanded) was viewed as liberal and committed to social justice; indeed, all of the senior partners were on the board of the Delaware chapter of the American Civil Liberties Union. Scott's attorneys reported that firm members were outraged at Scott's treatment by the university and agreed to take the case on a contingent fee basis.

The case was assigned to two of the firm's younger members, John Grady and Thomas Neuberger, both of whom routinely handled employment litigation. Upon receipt of Scott's right-to-sue letter, they filed an individual claim of discriminatory treatment and a class claim of discriminatory impact against the university.

Scott's individual claim was filed under three federal laws: Title VII of the Civil Rights Act of 1964, which forbids discrimination in hiring or employment; section 1981 of the post–Civil War Civil Rights Act, which protects the right of individuals to make and enforce contracts without discrimination; and section 1983 of the same act, which prohibits state agents (here, the university) from taking actions that deny individuals the "rights, privileges, or immunities secured by the Constitution and laws" and provides for individual liability of state agents should a court find that such illegal conduct has in fact occurred. He also claimed that university agents conspired to deprive him of his civil rights, a violation of section 1985 of the same law. The relief requested was reinstatement and back pay for Scott, as well as damages for suffering and embarrassment.

Although Scott's attorneys believed that the university had treated Scott differently from other, similar faculty in its decision not to renew his contract and thus that Scott's individual claim of discrimination was valid and legitimate, they also believed that the university's hiring and promotion practices resulted in a disproportionately small number of black faculty and so appended a class action claim of disparate impact, often called a pattern and practice claim. It appears that although Scott agreed with the filing of the class action claim and assisted the attorneys if he was able to with the information needed for the class claim, the primary responsibility for filing and prosecuting the class action belonged to the attorneys, Grady and Neuberger. The relief sought for the class was an order that the university hire one black for every two white faculty members hired until the proportion of black faculty reached 12.5 percent. No financial damages were sought for class members.

There was no group of black faculty at the university or blacks denied faculty positions at the university who actively and visibly supported the class claim. In fact, Scott's attorneys were only able to find two black faculty members (neither of whom provided evidence of discrimination) to testify on behalf of the class plaintiffs and could locate no blacks willing to testify that they had been denied positions at the university or discriminated against in promotion, tenure, or renewal on account of their race. Despite the fact that it is possible to win a pattern and practice case on the basis of statistics alone, the dearth of witnesses willing to testify to the harm caused them by the university's employment policies was probably responsible, in large part, for the failure of the class claim.

The EEOC had found probable cause to believe that the university's employment practices were responsible for the low number of minority faculty, and thus the commission agreed to assist Scott's attorneys in the class action portion of the litigation. This assistance amounted primarily to an amicus curiae brief at the trial level, posttrial argument by an EEOC attorney at the trial level, and the testimony of the EEOC investigator, Leo Sanchez, concerning the underutilization of blacks on the Delaware campus. According to Scott's attorneys, the EEOC provided no further support, either financial or legal, to the plaintiff in the class claim.

Nor was visible support forthcoming from the black community. Scott had been active in the local NAACP, and it is widely believed at the university that the NAACP financed the class action portion of Scott's lawsuit. However, although the NAACP filed an amicus brief in Scott's appeal of the negative trial court decision, it did not participate in the conduct of the litigation, nor did it contribute more than perhaps a token financial amount to the case.

The university had traditionally retained the Wilmington law firm of Potter Anderson and Corroon to handle its legal business (with the exception of its negotiations with the faculty union, which were handled by a Philadelphia law firm). The same firm had defended the university in the *Aumiller, Anapol, Gordenstein,* and *Keegan* cases, and the university turned to it again when Scott initiated his lawsuit. John Sinclair took the lead in the university's defense of the Scott case. Sinclair had worked with administrators at the university for some years, though primarily in matters of corporate law and real estate. His handling of the university's defense of the *Scott* case was excellent, according to Scott's attorneys, and he proved to be a formidable opponent.

Pretrial Impacts

Sinclair's first strategy was to try to avoid bringing the case to trial at all, while maintaining the university's innocence. He first filed a motion to dismiss the case, arguing that Scott's claim did not state a cause of action under any of the three laws under which it was filed. The federal district court ruled on November 20, 1974, that Scott's individual claim did indeed state a cause of action under Title VII, although the judge dismissed Scott's claims against the individual defendants (leaving only the university as a defendant, since Scott's EEOC claim had only named the university). He also dismissed Scott's individual section 1981, 1983, and 1985 claims for failure to plead specific wrongs by specific defendants.[14]

In class action litigation, it is necessary for the plaintiff to obtain a legal ruling that the class is appropriate, a process termed certification of the class. Federal Rule of Civil Procedure 23(a) requires that the plaintiff establish to the satisfaction of the judge that (1) the class is so numerous that joinder of all members is impracticable (the numerosity requirement); (2) there are questions of law or fact common to the class (the commonality requirement); (3) the claims or defenses of the representative party are typical of the claims or defenses of the class (the typicality requirement); and (4) the representative party will fairly and adequately protect the interests of the class. Defendants in class action claims will routinely attempt to block certification of the class, claiming that it does not meet one or more of the requirements of rule 23(a). Sinclair was no exception, and he challenged Scott's attorneys' motion to certify the class. He argued that Scott was not a member of the class he was attempting to represent, because he had not been discriminated against in recruitment or hiring (since he *had* been hired), and thus he could not represent the interests of those individuals against whom the university had allegedly discriminated in hiring. Furthermore, Sinclair argued that Scott was the only black ever to have been terminated by the university; he constituted a class of one, thereby failing to satisfy the numerosity requirement. However, the judge stated that Scott was alleging a series of continuing violations and was an appropriate representative of the class. On September 11, 1975, Judge Walter Stapleton certified the class.[15]

Less than a year later, the parties were in court again. Sinclair was once more challenging the appropriateness of the class, and he filed a motion to decertify. He argued that during the discovery process, the plaintiff had not been able to identify any black faculty members who had been discriminated against by the university. Scott's attorneys disagreed, noting that in answers to depositions, Scott had provided information about several individuals against whom the university had allegedly discriminated, as well as statistical information showing a substantial discrepancy between the proportion of blacks at the university and the proportion of blacks holding Ph.D.'s. Judge Stapleton again ruled in favor of the plaintiffs, stating that to decertify the class would require a finding that neither Scott nor other plaintiffs had been discriminated against, a ruling that could not be made until a trial on the merits had been held.[16]

While the legal jousting was occurring in court, administrators at the university were busy gathering data, both to respond to Scott's attorneys' requests for documents and to prepare the university's defense. The data-gathering effort was coordinated by the provost, L. Leon Campbell, and his staff assistant, Virginia Lussier. John Sinclair needed information on the efforts of the university to recruit and hire minority faculty, which required every department chair and dean to sort through their records and produce the data. The data compiled by the provost's office fill three file drawers.

Trial Impacts

The trial in the Scott case began on April 4 and concluded on April 26, 1977, totaling sixteen full days of trial. It was the fourth time that the attorneys had been before Judge Stapleton, and over four years had elapsed since Scott had first filed his complaint with the EEOC.

Scott's Individual Claim

In his claim of discriminatory treatment, Scott asserted that two sets of circumstances showed that the sociology department's decision to recommend against renewal was infected with bias: first, the incidents of racial harassment noted earlier, and second, the more favorable treatment given nonblacks whose contracts were renewed by the department. Furthermore, he asserted that the evidence used by the department to judge his teaching (student evaluations) was defective and unfairly biased against him because the students themselves were guilty of racial bias.

Although Scott's attorneys presented several witnesses who testified about the incidents of racial harassment, Judge Stapleton found them of little importance. Although the judge noted that the evidence was indicative of "racial prejudice on the University campus,"[17] he did not believe that these incidents could fairly be connected to the university's decision not to renew Scott's contract. However, the allegation that similarly situated nonblack faculty had been treated more favorably than had Scott was a serious charge, and the judge examined the evidence on that point with some care.

Scott selected four faculty members for comparison purposes, all of whom had been granted contract renewal or promotion at about the same time that the negative decision was made about Scott. Only one comparable faculty member was from the sociology department, two were from the English department, and the fourth was from the educational foundations department. In essence, Scott argued that these four faculty members had received departmental performance evaluations similar to his but that each of the four had been given more time to prove himself, while Scott had not. The circumstances surrounding the reappointment of the sociology department's Nohara have been described; the judge found sufficient evidence to demonstrate that Nohara was not comparable to Scott because he had been hired under a different set of requirements (teaching only), had been given a substantially heavier teaching load than had Scott (twelve hours per semester rather than six), and had a sizable research project in progress at the time that the challenged renewal decision was made (1970). In contrast, Scott was unable to demonstrate evidence of any serious research in progress at the time of his renewal and had even told a new faculty member that "he did not feel his interests matched the University's and the Department's interests and that he did not perceive himself as writing the kind of scholarly journal articles that were required."[18] This testimony suggested that Scott was aware of the publication requirement and also was aware that his performance fell short of the department's expectations before the negative renewal decision was made.

The two comparable faculty in the English department had been approved for renewal even though they had produced little scholarship. The university provided testimony to the effect that renewal was automatic in the English department and demonstrated that both of these individuals had received terminal contracts after their second three-year terms because of their lack of scholarly productivity. This admission of automatic renewal supported the plaintiff's claim that decentralized employment policies and procedures resulted in differential treatment among departments; however, the judge did not agree that decentralized employment policies were necessarily discriminatory.

The fourth comparable faculty member, employed in the educational foundations department, was also denied contract renewal at the end of his second year (the same year in which Scott was denied renewal). However, he was evaluated at the end of his third year (which should have been his terminal year) and was given an extra year as his terminal year. He was offered a third opportunity for evaluation, with the potential for being retained, but declined the offer and left the university. Scott claimed that these extra opportunities for evaluation and renewal resulted in treatment more favorable than the treatment he had received at the hands of the sociology department, and thus the university's tolerance of nonstandard departmental policies was, in effect, discriminatory. Although Judge Stapleton did not disagree, he ruled that

> there are rational explanations for this which are unrelated to race. The practices in the English Department and in the Department of Educational Foundations at the times of their renewals were simply different than the practice of the Sociology Department in 1973. There is nothing in the record to suggest that the differences in procedures between departments were somehow a mask for discrimination, and nothing in Title VII nor the Civil Rights Acts requires that all academic departments of a university operate in the same manner.[19]

The EEOC had found cause to believe that the negative renewal decision was discriminatory and noted the unreliability of the student evaluations used by the department as evidence of Scott's poor teaching ability. The EEOC investigator testified that only 23 percent of Scott's class had participated in the teaching evaluation and that no peer evaluations of his teaching had been done. However, Scarpitti testified about numerous student complaints concerning Scott's teaching, as well as the declining student enrollments in the courses assigned to Scott. After analyzing the evidence of Scott's lack of scholarship and his record of poor teaching, Judge Stapleton concluded that

> the failure of the University to renew Scott's contract resulted from the opinion of nine members of the Sociology Department that he was not, and would not develop into, an acceptable permanent professional col-

league. This opinion was based primarily on what they considered to be a demonstrated lack of interest in pursuing the kind of scholarship, research and writing which they thought to be significant, and secondarily, on the view that one with the teaching experience which Scott had should have developed greater effectiveness in relating with students. . . . Scott was not the kind of "sociologist's sociologist" the department was looking for. He appeared to lack either the interest or discipline necessary to do the kind of research and publication that they were interested in. . . .[20]

The judge went on to cite the good faith of the members of the department, noting that "a number of these men had backgrounds in the civil rights movement and elsewhere which vouch for their concerns about equal rights."[21] Thus, he ruled, "Dr. Scott's disparate treatment claim is without merit."[22]

The trial court opinion in Scott's individual claim is interesting in that Judge Stapleton did not use the three-part order of proof described in the *McDonnell-Douglas* case (and outlined in chapter 2). The judge did not rule on whether Scott had made out a prima facie case of racial discrimination but appeared to concentrate on the rebuttal portion of the test. His ruling that the nonrenewal decision was made for legitimate, nondiscriminatory reasons appears to satisfy the *McDonnell-Douglas* test, but the absence of the familiar model for judicial analysis is surprising.

The Class Claim

Scott alleged that university practices with regard to recruitment, hiring, renewal, promotion, tenure, and salary had a discriminatory impact on blacks and thus violated each of the laws used for his claim of individual discrimination. Two basic arguments supported this claim: first, that requiring a Ph.D. for employment resulted in an underrepresentation of blacks on the faculty; and second, that the decentralized and subjective employment decision-making system used by the university was disadvantageous to blacks. The EEOC joined this portion of the litigation as amicus curiae. Although their arguments were unsuccessful, they are important in demonstrating the difference in judicial attitude toward hiring requirements in higher education as compared with employment practices in business and industry.

Under the teachings of the Supreme Court in the landmark case of *Griggs v. Duke Power Co.*,[23] if an employer requires that candidates for employment have a certain level of education or training or insists on other qualifications that result in excluding a disproportionately large number of minorities or women from obtaining employment, the employer must demonstrate that the job qualifications are related to the actual work to be performed, a doctrine known as the business necessity defense. Furthermore, the EEOC has published "Uniform Guidelines on Employee Selection Procedures,"[24] which mandate that all employment practices that have a disparate impact on minorities be validated by the employer as job related. However, the Supreme Court has not always enforced the requirements of the EEOC guidelines, and Judge Stapleton did not require the university to validate the relationship between a Ph.D. and the job content of a faculty member. Instead, he required the university to demonstrate that the Ph.D. bore a "manifest relationship" to the responsibilities of a full-time faculty member and then required the plaintiff to show that "some other criterion or selection procedure with less of a disparate impact upon blacks would serve the University's legitimate interests as well" as the Ph.D.[25]

The judge noted that although "the evidence on the question of justification is surprisingly sparse," the university had provided two rationales for requiring faculty members to hold a Ph.D. He asserted that the record demonstrated that "the experience, knowledge and skill acquired in obtaining a Ph.D. are reasonably related to the ability to do research, think creatively, and add to the existing fund of knowledge through publication and other communication in one's chosen field."[26] The university had produced testimony by both Scarpitti and the university president, E. Arthur Trabant (neither of whom had been qualified as expert witnesses on the issue of industrywide practices with regard to the requirements of candidates for faculty positions), to the effect that the university was "in the business of creating knowledge as well as in the business of disseminating knowledge," and thus training in research and advanced scholarship was important to the furtherance of the university's mission.[27] Second, the judge viewed graduate teaching as an important component of a faculty member's responsibilities; the university had presented testimony that a Ph.D. was "reasonably related to an ability to teach graduate students."[28]

The plaintiff and the EEOC argued that the majority of faculty time was spent in teaching undergraduate students and that a master's degree was sufficient for most undergraduate teaching. Furthermore, the plaintiff noted, other kinds of experiences were often at least as valuable as doctoral study, and the Ph.D. requirement should not be applied consistently, especially to minority candidates for faculty positions. The judge, however, noted that the plaintiff's emphasis on undergraduate teaching "ignores a substantial part of the responsibility of a member of the University faculty" to conduct research and produce publications and stated that "the University's choice of mission is not a subject for judicial review."[29] Furthermore, the university *had* made numerous exceptions to the Ph.D. requirement and in fact had hired several blacks who did not hold the Ph.D. Therefore, the judge concluded that the university had successfully demonstrated the legitimacy of requiring a doctoral degree of faculty and that although the plaintiff's suggested alternative of requiring only a master's degree would have a less adverse effect on blacks, such a requirement would not serve the university's legitimate interest as well as the doctoral degree requirement did.

The second claim, that the decentralized and subjective decision-making policies endorsed by the university permitted classwide discrimination against blacks, was the heart of the class claim. The plaintiff employed Bernard Siskin, who also served as an expert witness in the *Kunda* litigation. Siskin analyzed the racial composition of the university's faculty, compared it with the pool of available black Ph.D.'s, and concluded that "there is something in the process of selecting new full time faculty which relates to race."[30] The plaintiff supplemented his statistical case with the testimony of two other expert witnesses, both of whom were distinguished sociologists, one black and one white. Alfred Lee, a former president of the American Sociological Association, criticized the university for its low proportion of black faculty and testified about recruitment strategies to increase the number of blacks. James Blackwell, a black sociologist who had written books about blacks in higher education, provided similar testimony. But neither expert addressed the issue of Scott's individual claim. Lee, however, testified that Scott was an "average sociologist with an average reputation [working in] an average institution" and should have been given more time to produce research.[31]

The judge apparently agreed with the experts, at least to the extent of determining the plaintiff's prima facie case. Using Siskin's figures, which the university had disputed, Judge Stapleton found that the disparity between the hiring pool (2.55 percent black) and the proportion of blacks on the faculty (1.46 percent) was statistically significant, using EEOC guidelines that stated that any probability of less than 5 percent is statistically significant—here, the calculated probability of finding only 12 black faculty members in a faculty of 818 was only 3 percent.[32] Despite the fact that the proportions involved were so small, the judge used a method of statistical analysis employed by the Supreme Court in *Castaneda v. Partida*,[33] which states that if the difference between the expected proportion of blacks exceeds the observed proportion of blacks in an employer's workforce by 3 or more standard deviations, then a finding of discrimination is warranted. In this case, the difference was 1.97 standard deviations; however, the judge noted that the EEOC's 5 percent guideline was roughly equivalent to 1.65 standard deviations and decided that the difference was significant. Therefore, Judge Stapleton ruled that based upon statistical evidence alone, the class plaintiff had established a prima facie case of racial discrimination by the university. However, the judge noted that all of the evidence, both statistical and nonstatistical, had to be sufficiently persuasive in order for the plaintiff to demonstrate race discrimination on the part of the university.

Other evidence examined by the judge, however, weakened the impact of the plaintiff's statistical case. First, when the judge excluded the faculty hired before 1965, the year in which Title VII took effect, the proportion of blacks on the faculty, not surprisingly, rose, and the difference between the observed and expected proportions of blacks on the faculty dropped to a level below statistical significance. It is interesting that Judge Stapleton selected 1965 as the date before which to exclude evidence of hiring: Title VII was not made applicable to colleges and universities until 1972—the year after Scott was hired and the year before he was denied renewal. Had Judge Stapleton used 1972, the plaintiffs would have had no statistical case at all. However, since the judge had already ruled that the plaintiff had successfully made his prima facie case, the problem of which date to use to exclude an "irrelevant portion of plaintiff's sample"[34] is not legally important.

Finally, the judge turned his attention to data presented by the plaintiff on the proportion of minorities in the university's applicant pool for faculty positions. The data were somewhat suspect, because only 75 percent of the applicants for faculty positions at the university had returned a form indicating their race. However, of those who did indicate their race, only 1.78 percent of the applicants for faculty positions at the university between 1974 and 1977 were black. Because the plaintiff was unable to demonstrate that the 75 percent of the applicants who returned the form were unrepresentative of the total pool of applicants, the judge ruled that the data were sufficiently probative to indicate that a substantially smaller percentage of blacks applied for faculty positions at the university than was available in the national Ph.D. labor pool (2.55 percent). However, the 1.78 percent proportion of blacks in the applicant pool corresponded closely with the hiring rate of blacks (1.46 percent), and thus the judge refused to find the university guilty of discrimination—intentional or unintentional—against blacks.

Evidence presented by the university also contributed to the trial court's finding that the university had operated within the law. John Sinclair, the university's attorney, collected and presented a substantial amount of evidence, first as to the fairness of the university's decentralized system and second as to the numerous unsuccessful efforts of department chairs and deans to attract blacks to the university. Furthermore, the defense presented, and the judge analyzed, the career developments of each of the twenty-six black faculty members who had been employed by the university, whether or not that individual was currently at the university. And finally, the plaintiff was unable to locate, or to persuade to testify, any blacks who had not been hired or whose employment had been terminated on a discriminatory basis.

Sinclair conducted four and one-half days of testimony by department chairs and deans, who described the recruitment and hiring processes used in their departments as well as the evaluation system used to make renewal, promotion, and tenure decisions. Most significant to the judge's ruling was the testimony of fourteen chairpersons and deans about the lengthy and almost always unsuccessful attempts they had made to hire black faculty. These witnesses described the promises made to black candidates, the relaxing of the Ph.D. requirement in some cases, and offers of salary higher than comparably or better qualified whites could command at the university. In most of these instances, black candidates accepted jobs elsewhere or left the university within a year or two. At the time of the trial, only two black faculty members were tenured, and only two more had reached the tenure decision stage (normally, six years after the initial hiring); the others had left before a renewal or tenure decision was made. Furthermore, Trabant, the university president, testified that he had refused to approve new faculty positions in some departments until the department hired a black faculty member; indeed, the sociology department was under pressure to hire a black faculty member during the time that Scott was recruited and hired.

Judge Stapleton analyzed the career progression of each black faculty member employed at the university since 1965. Of the twenty-six such faculty members, only Scott had left the university involuntarily. Four blacks were tenured or close to the tenure decision point at the time of the trial; one had left, just after being recommended for promotion, to teach at Lincoln University, a predominantly black college in Pennsylvania. Three blacks had been visiting faculty members who had stayed only one year, although the various departments had attempted to hire two of the three permanently. Nine black faculty members had left voluntarily before even a decision to renew their contract had been made, and the remaining eight untenured faculty members had not been at the university long enough to receive tenure.

The university's evidence of apparent good faith and what the judge characterized as "extraordinary efforts" made to recruit and hire black faculty, when combined with the inability of the plaintiffs to present testimony by any individual "who claims to have been discriminated against" in the hiring or promotion process,[35] apparently convinced the judge that although the proportion of black faculty was very low at the university, the university's decentralized and subjective hiring and promotion policies were not responsible for the underrepresentation of blacks. Rather, he found, the university's reputation as "ultra conservative" and its characterization as an unappealing employment location for blacks was responsible for the low numbers of blacks attracted to faculty positions there. The judge concluded that "black preference," rather than discrimination, was responsible for the low numbers of black faculty at the university. Thus, the class plaintiffs fared no better than had Nolvert Scott in his individual claim.

Decision Impacts

Scott and his attorneys were disappointed by the trial court outcome and decided that an appeal to the Third Circuit had a good chance of succeeding.

With regard to Scott's individual claim, the attorneys thought that the examples of comparable faculty were well chosen and convincing, that the substantial evidence of harassment was compelling, and that the expert testimony had been weighed too lightly. In the class claim, the plaintiffs viewed the judge's refusal to follow the EEOC guidelines and/or the business necessity requirement as reversible error. Furthermore, they believed that their statistics standing alone proved that the Ph.D. requirement and the decentralized decision-making structure impermissibly excluded blacks and that independent evidence of discrimination against individuals was not necessary.

Therefore, Grady and Neuberger agreed to appeal Scott's case to the Third Circuit. They were joined by the NAACP and the EEOC as amici; no amici filed on behalf of the university at the circuit court level.

After the end of his terminal year at the university (1973–74), Scott took a job with the Eastern Pennsylvania Psychiatric Institute as a researcher. However, he was laid off in August, 1976, for financial reasons and was later appointed intergroup education advisor for the Pennsylvania Department of Education. Two days before the oral arguments were held in his appeal, Nolvert Scott died of a heart attack, at the age of forty-five.

Despite Scott's death, some of his individual claims survived and were presented to the Third Circuit by his attorneys. Scott's back pay claim belonged to his estate, although reinstatement claims and claims for punitive damages were extinguished. And, of course, the class claim survived Scott.

The manner in which the parties presented the issues on appeal demonstrates not only the difference in their philosophies but also dramatizes their contrasting interpretations of the facts in the case. Scott's attorneys repeatedly cited the university's historically poor treatment of blacks and attempted to convince the appellate panel that the disparity between the labor pool of black Ph.D.'s and the university's proportion of black faculty was in itself sufficient evidence of discriminatory practices. On the other hand, the defense argued that the plaintiff was concentrating on the past and ignoring the present. It pointed out the district court's finding that in recent years there had been a substantial commitment of resources by the university for the benefit of blacks. Furthermore, the university argued that liability could not be established by the extent to which its efforts to attract black faculty had fallen short of its own goals, saying that "liability for violation of the constitutional and statutory rights of blacks is not measured by the University's degree of success in recruiting, hiring and retaining black faculty members."[36]

The parties also placed differing interpretations on the failure of Scott's attorneys to find any black faculty or applicants who would testify that the university had discriminated against them. The university asserted that such individuals did not exist, while the plaintiff maintained that blacks were intimidated and unwilling to testify in Scott's behalf for fear of retaliation by the university. Furthermore, Scott's attorneys asserted, blacks didn't even bother applying to the university, because of its reputation among the community of black academics for being conservative and unwelcoming to blacks.

The appeal was argued before a three-judge panel of the Third Circuit: Judge Arlin M. Adams, Judge James Hunter, and Judge Leonard I. Garth. Judge Garth wrote the opinion, with which the other judges concurred. However, Judge Adams wrote a special concurring opinion, agreeing with the outcome of the appeal but presenting interpretations of legal doctrine regarding class action litigation that differed somewhat from the interpretation put forth in the majority opinion.

Judge Garth made short work of Scott's individual claim, affirming the findings of the district court in little more than two pages of text. Scott's argument was that the holding of the trial court was against the weight of the evidence, which requires a reviewing court to use a "clearly erroneous" standard of review. In other words, the appellate judges could overturn the findings of the trial court only if those findings were manifestly against the weight of the evidence, a very difficult standard to meet. Garth first reviewed the Title VII order of proof (the *McDonnell-Douglas* standard), but did not criticize the trial court for failing to structure its opinion using this order of proof. Nor did the appellate opinion explicitly follow the *McDonnell-Douglas* standard: there was no discussion of whether or not Scott had made out a prima facie case in his individual claim, nor whether the sociology department had established a legitimate nondiscriminatory reason for nonrenewal. The judge simply summarized the trial court findings that the reasons for Scott's nonrenewal were related to his performance and not to racial discrimination and affirmed the trial court's judgment against him.

The treatment of the class action aspect of the appeal was complicated by the interjection of a procedural issue concerning the reviewability of the class certification. In Sinclair's view, the trial court should never have certified the class, because the plaintiff had failed to satisfy the commonality, typicality, and numerosity requirements of rule 23. Consequently, his brief in the Third Circuit defended the trial court judgment not only on the ground that it was justified by the law and the facts, but on the additional ground that the class should not have been certified because Scott had not satisfied rule 23. When the appeal was filed, Sinclair concluded that a cross-appeal was unnecessary, relying on Supreme Court precedent. Furthermore, a determination by the court of appeals that the class had been improperly certified would neither enlarge the university's rights nor lessen the plaintiff's. In fact, such a determination would lessen the university's rights by depriving it of the res judicata effect of the judgment (which would have foreclosed future suits by the members of the class against the university). In the opinion of the university's counsel this was too minimal a consideration to outweigh the advantages of defending the judgment on an additional ground and of sending to the district court a message that it had acted improperly in certifying the class and refusing to decertify it. Grady and Neuberger came to a different conclusion concerning the necessity of a cross-appeal, and in their answering brief they urged the court of appeals not to consider the correctness of the class certification because of the absence of a cross-appeal by the university.[37]

The court of appeals decided to address the issue of class certification, following the argument made by the university that doing so was within the court's discretion.[38] Judge Garth, writing for himself and Judge Hunter, expressed the view that review was important and necessary because the interests of the absent class members (i.e., all except Scott) were harmed by the negative ruling at the trial level. Judge Garth wrote that the interests of the class plaintiffs would be better served by having the class decertified than by foreclosing their opportunity to sue the university at some future time for race discrimination.

During the pretrial motions and arguments, the university had argued against certification of the class because Scott, having been hired and holding a Ph.D., was not typical of the plaintiffs he sought to represent (individuals not hired and not holding Ph.D.'s). The appellate court agreed and furthermore stated that Scott's interests as a plaintiff conflicted with the interests of those whom he sought to represent, since his hiring worked against other individuals who would have desired to become faculty members in the sociology department. Ruling that Scott was not typical of the class, Judge Garth noted that Scott had been hired by the university, held a doctoral degree, and was paid a salary premium by the university. The judge observed:

> Understandably, in view of these facts, he could not, and does not, claim that he was discriminated against by the University's hiring policies which resulted in his employment. Moreover, in so doing, he disputes the validity of the University's requirement of a doctoral degree as a primary hiring criterion. He thus attacks, via the applicant class, the very degree which he possesses and which he asserts in his own favor in seeking relief on his individual disparate treatment claim. The assertion of these inconsistent positions necessarily forecloses any contention that Scott's claims are typical of the claims of those applying for faculty positions.[39]

The defendants had also argued earlier that the class did not satisfy the numerosity requirement in that the only identified class member was Scott himself (and even Scott was not an appropriate class member, according to the appellate court). The university argued that the class was hypothetical because no individual had been identified who claimed that the university had discriminated against him or her. Quoting the opinion of the trial court on the issue of the university's treatment of its black faculty, Judge Garth agreed that the numerosity requirement had not been satisfied, in that "Scott has not identified a single past or present faculty member, other than himself, who was arguably discriminated against by the University's contract renewal, promotion, and tenure practices."[40] Furthermore, the judge noted, any individuals who believed themselves so injured could maintain their own actions against the university, and Scott's championship of their purported cause was unnecessary.

The appellate court vacated the portion of the trial court's judgment that pertained to the merits of the class claim, which meant that only the denial of Scott's individual claim had been affirmed on the merits, and that from the perspective of legal precedent, the issue of whether the university's employment practices discriminated against blacks as a class remained unanswered.

Because the appellate court decertified the class, it did not address the plaintiff's assertion that the trial judge committed reversible error by not requiring the university either to demonstrate the business necessity of the Ph.D. requirement or to validate the Ph.D. requirement against the content of the job of a faculty member. The EEOC, in its amicus brief, had argued these points vigorously in addition to its assertion that the statistical evidence of disparity was sufficient for the court to reach a finding that the university's employment practices were discriminatory.[41]

In his special concurrence, Judge Adams wrote in support of the panel's decision to review the class certification issue despite the absence of a cross-appeal by the defendants.[42] However, Adams was concerned that the majority's language describing Scott's atypicality when compared with other class members might be overinterpreted to foreclose other potential plaintiffs whose circumstances were somewhat different from those of other potential class members. The judge noted that plaintiffs whose interests diverged from but did not conflict with the interests of other class members were still appropriate representatives of a class but agreed with the majority that Scott's interests had conflicted with other class plaintiffs. With regard to Judge Garth's discussion of the numerosity problem, Judge Adams agreed that because of Scott's inability to identify other faculty members against whom the university had allegedly discriminated, "it would be improper to bootstrap an individual complaint into a class action by hypothesizing a class of aggrieved individuals on the basis of speculative future members."[43]

Although Scott's attorneys petitioned the Third Circuit for a rehearing, the court refused, and the attorneys, dismayed at the decertification of the class claim in particular, decided to appeal to the Supreme Court. They presented three issues in their petition for a writ of certiorari: (1) whether the appellate court misconstrued the plaintiff's burden in its finding that he did not make out a prima facie case of race discrimination in the individual claim; (2) whether the appellate court's review of the class certification issue was proper; and (3) whether the appellate court's decision that Scott's interests and those of the other class members were inherently in conflict was correct.

Grady and Neuberger asserted in their petition that Scott had at least made a prima facie case of race discrimination, because he had demonstrated that similarly situated faculty members were treated more favorably than he. However, the trial court had found, as an issue of fact, that these four comparable faculty's situations were not similar to Scott's, and thus Scott's attorneys were actually challenging a finding of fact. They also argued that the appellate court's decision to review the propriety of the class *sua sponte* (on the court's own initiative) was contrary to settled law and thus reversible error.

The university was assisted by an amicus brief filed by the Equal Employment Advisory Council (EEAC), an organization of employers working against an expansive interpretation of the civil rights laws. The EEAC appeared to be especially concerned about the dispute between the plaintiff and the defendant concerning proof of discrimination using statistics alone. The EEOC had argued at the trial and appellate levels that the statistical evidence against the university was sufficient to reach a finding of discrimination; the EEAC took an opposing position.

> In the "seller's market" context, the court properly recognized that it could not simply rely on a presumption that any statistical disparity was the result of discrimination by the employer. For when the overall demand for qualified minority workers exceeds the supply, a proportionate shortage in one employer's work force is not a reliable indication that the employer's hiring practices are discriminatory. Instead, it more probably signifies only that other employers' minority recruitment efforts have been more effective. This may reflect problems of management, or it may result from factors wholly beyond the employer's control. It does not, however, establish a violation of the law.[44]

Despite the care with which Grady and Neuberger constructed their petition and despite their continued belief that the class claim in particular was meritorious and that Scott had been wronged by the university, the Supreme Court denied the attorneys' petition on October 29, 1979,[45] and the litigation was finally over.

Posttrial Impacts

Because Scott died of a heart attack two days before his attorneys argued his appeal before the Third Circuit, it is not possible to document the personal impact of the litigation on Scott. However, his loss at the trial level, the necessity of leaving the university, his difficulty securing employment in a related field, and the loss of a second position (through layoff) after only one year may have combined to produce Scott's fatal heart attack, given his history of heart disease.

Scott had a devastating impact on his attorneys, who had taken the case on a contingent fee basis. Both Neuberger and Grady spoke of the sharp disappointment of working hard and long (over two thousand hours) and incurring legal fees of two hundred thousand dollars plus many thousands more in related expenses in a case in which they believed but for which they never received payment. Both attorneys stated that it is especially difficult for women and minorities in academic positions to succeed in a claim of discrimination, because judges are reluctant to scrutinize or to criticize the actions of college and university administrators. Both thought that an average or mediocre minority plaintiff cannot prevail, even if he or she is treated more severely than similarly average or mediocre white male faculty. And both attorneys, now in solo practice, have concluded that they can no longer accept individual or class employment discrimination claims by college faculty unless a retainer is paid in advance, for, as Neuberger stated, ''even in the best case, the plaintiff still only has a fifty-fifty chance of winning.''

Grady agreed and noted that universities are better educated about employment discrimination now, and either have improved their practices or have learned more sophisticated and less discernible ways of discriminating against women and minority employees. He believes that cases in which plaintiffs have a reasonably good chance of prevailing are now being settled by employers anxious to avoid a losing court battle, and thus only the marginal cases are going to court. He also cited an apparently prevailing belief that underrepresented employees have received ''too much of a good thing,'' noting the Supreme Court decision upholding seniority against the affirmative action claims of black firefighters in Memphis.[46] If other attorneys who represented plaintiffs in unsuccessful academic discrimination litigation decide to avoid such cases in the future, prospective plaintiffs who seek remedies against actual or apparent employer discrimination may have difficulty finding competent, experienced counsel to represent them.

As noted earlier, the University of Delaware has been sued by at least four faculty members attempting to overturn negative employment decisions, so it is neither possible nor sensible to attempt to trace a cause-and-effect relationship between the Scott litigation and changes in university employment policy. However, each of these cases has had an impact on administrator attitude and behavior in faculty employment decision-making situations, and such impacts are useful to analyze.

Helen Gouldner, who chaired the sociology department during the terminal year of Scott's contract, became dean of the College of Arts and Science the following year. She, then, has been a defendant in each of the four cases filed by faculty against the university in the early and mid-1970s, as has L. Leon Campbell, provost of the university. Both believe that the litigation has resulted in clearer, tighter faculty employment policies and practices and has also contributed to an emphasis on greater accountability in the decision-making processes. However, the administrators attribute much of the emphasis on accountability and procedural clarity to the presence on campus of a faculty union whose grievance system is designed to address procedural weaknesses and failures.

The procedures for reaching decisions on renewal, promotion, and tenure are still decentralized to some degree. Each department is required to draw up its own set of procedures, just as they did at the time of Scott's nonrenewal in 1973. However, the university senate has created a set of guidelines with which these procedures must comply, and the universitywide promotion and tenure committee will not approve a department's procedures until they comply with universitywide standards. Differences in departmental policies lie basically in the weighting of certain criteria for promotion or tenure (e.g., whether service is emphasized equally with research and teaching or carries less weight). A department also has some flexibility as to whether the entire department votes on a promotion or tenure recommendation or whether the faculty elects or appoints a committee to make such a recommendation. Department chairs are not members of the faculty bargaining unit at the university and thus make an independent recommendation on a candidate's application for promotion or tenure.

The present promotion and tenure review process at the university requires that the candidate be given reasons for any negative recommendation at each step of the process. After the department faculty and the department chair each make a recommendation for or against promotion or tenure, an elected, collegewide promotion and tenure committee considers the candidate's dossier. After the college committee makes a recommendation for or against promotion and/or tenure, the dean reviews the dossier and makes an independent recommendation. At each of these decision levels, the decision maker must notify the candidate in writing of the decison and, if the decision is negative, of the reasons for the decision.

The dossier then goes to the university committee on promotions and tenure, where it is reviewed and a recommendation is made. The standard of review for this committee is the "relevance and appropriateness of the credentials offered to support the request for promotion. . . . [T]he Committee exercises its best judgment as to the adequacy of the evidence in meeting the unit's published criteria."[47] The committee reviews the quality of the candidate's dossier independently, as well as the adequacy of the support for the recommendation at each level of the review process, measured against that department's own criteria for promotion or tenure. Following the committee's review, the provost reviews the dossier and makes a recommendation to the president, who forwards the recommendation to the trustees for action. The president does not formally take part in the review process, although the provost reviews each recommendation with the president before the trustees vote on each candidate.

At each step of the process, two important accountability checks are mandatory. First, as noted earlier, each decision maker or group must notify the candidate of the recommendation and must give reasons for any negative recommendation. Furthermore, if an administrator (department chair, dean, or provost) does not concur with the recommendation of the faculty committee just below that administrator in the decision chain (i.e., faculty, college committee, or universitywide committee), the administrator explains to that committee the reasons for the administrator's inability to concur with the committee. In addition, the standard of review beyond the college is primarily the adequacy of the evidence supporting the recommendation for or against promotion or tenure. And the candidate may appeal a negative decision at any step of the promotion or tenure process and request a hearing before the individual or committee making the negative recommendation, as well as requesting a reconsideration of the negative recommendation. The chair and dean, as well, can ask for reconsideration of a negative recommendation by the provost, although formal appeals by candidates are heard by the university committee on promotions and tenure, according to Campbell.

The contractual grievance procedure negotiated by the union is limited to procedural violations of the contract and culminates in binding arbitration. Although several administrators note that in the early years of unionization at the university many grievances were filed, fewer have been filed in the past few years, and most of those have concerned merit pay. Gouldner attributes this downturn in the rate of grievances to several factors: the improved ability of department chairs to either avoid committing procedural errors leading to grievances (or improved handling of grievances at the first level should an alleged procedural violation occur), the union's decision, on occasion, to counsel faculty against pursuing grievances because of the time and expense involved for a few hundred dollars of merit pay, and the determination by the university as a whole to follow its own procedures and to clarify and improve the procedures so that violations can be avoided more easily.

A performance evaluation system independent of the promotion and tenure review system has been implemented at the university. The faculty senate voted to develop a system of peer review for all faculty, tenured and untenured, at regular intervals. Gouldner suggests that one reason for the faculty's decision to implement such a system was to "protect the tenure system for a very visible state university'' by creating an accountability system for faculty performance. Assistant professors are evaluated every two years, associates every three to five years, and full professors every five to seven years. A peer review system is used, and the dean receives a summary of the evaluations. In addition to the peer review system, the department chair evaluates faculty every year for merit pay decisions. Although some faculty believe that faculty are reviewed too frequently, Gouldner pointed out several advantages of the peer review system. She noted that critical peer reviews had, in a few cases, convinced unproductive faculty to accept offers of early retirement or to seek positions outside academe. In other cases, faculty who were doing high-quality work but had been overlooked by their department chairs were promoted, and others who had been drifting were woken up and began producing scholarship again. Furthermore, the dean's perusal of the peer reviews and the annual chairpersons' reviews reveals the degree to which the faculty member's record supports the recommendation made; the dean makes a point of talking to chairs or heads of departmental peer review committees if reviews are glowing but unsupported by evidence of high-quality performance.

The amount of faculty evaluation at the university is substantial, and the provost believes that the frequency and thoroughness of the review procedures help guard against decisions based on illegal criteria such as race, sex, or national origin. The scrutiny is so thorough, he believes, that "aberrations would be caught" should discrimination be a factor in an individual's decision or the decision of a committee.

Other administrators, however, are not as sanguine about the annual evaluations by chairs and the regular peer reviews. The current chair of the sociology department, Russell Dynes, believes that evaluations are conducted too frequently and that they create an antagonistic relationship between the chair and the departmental faculty. Because the university uses a numerical ranking system within each department, the chair is forced to make comparisons among faculty and to award numerical values to certain kinds and degrees of faculty performance. Dynes maintains that such a system encourages faculty to "seek credit for what they should do anyway," in that they press the chair to rate certain kinds of activities (public service, for example) more highly so that their overall ranking will improve. He believes that the system isolates the chair from his or her departmental colleagues because it fosters conflict among faculty and between faculty and the chair. He believes that the annual evaluations, as well as the peer evaluation system, are a way in which chairs are required to "deliver the administration's bad news" to the faculty.

With regard to the impact of *Scott* itself, both the dean and the provost believe it had very little impact on the university. It was the third faculty case to come to trial. (Although *Aumiller* was filed two years after *Scott*, it was decided a year earlier b∂cause of all the time required for the *Scott* pretrial motions.) Furthermore, the university believed that the department had acted properly in this case and was convinced that it would prevail. The trial court opinion did not criticize university employment practices but essentially supported the university's attempts to hire black faculty without penalizing the university for its lack of success. It is possible that the university may have had and still may have more difficulty in recruiting black faculty than it would have if *Scott* had not been litigated, but it is impossible to be sure. Both the dean and the provost believe that the biggest impact of *Scott* was the time and energy that it required of the defendants and the lowered morale of the faculty in the sociology department, who believed that they had been wronged by Scott's accusations of racism.

Frank Scarpitti, in particular, was affected by the litigation. He maintains that his scholarly productivity did not suffer (in contrast to that of the department chair in the *Lieberman* case against the University of Connecticut, who said that the litigation cost him at least one book) but that his "stomach" suffered. Scarpitti and his wife had been friendly with Scott and his wife, and they had visited each other's homes frequently during Scott's employment at the university. Even during the litigation, according to Scarpitti, he and Scott would talk by telephone and remained on friendly terms. But Scarpitti had a reputation as an empathetic and unbiased individual, and Scott's generalized accusations of racism and bigotry against the departmental faculty troubled Scarpitti greatly.

The impact of *Scott* on the sociology department's standing in the discipline was not substantial, in Scarpitti's view. Although Scott was able to secure the expert testimony of two distinguished sociologists, Scarpitti does not view *Scott* as a cause célèbre among either sociologists in general or black sociologists in particular. He believes that Scott was not well integrated into the professional community of black sociologists, perhaps because of the small amount of publishing he had done.

Scarpitti also believed that the impact of *Scott* was limited within the sociology department. The majority of the departmental faculty had agreed with the decision not to renew Scott's contract, and they supported the chair during the litigation. In fact, seven of the departmental faculty testified on behalf of the university at trial. Scarpitti believes that the litigation unified the departmental faculty and had no impact on interpersonal relationships. He agrees, however, that informally the faculty are more sensitive and more careful about documenting their recommendations. He also sees more care taken across the university in the promotion and tenure review process. He believes, however, that the major sources of influence are not the *Scott* case, but faculty unionization at the university and the general litigiousness in higher education throughout the country.

One issue that arose in *Scott* and has arisen in other cases as well is the amount of support given by the university to the department chair. If the decision at the department level is negative, the primary defendant may be the department chair. In some cases, according to Dynes and Scarpitti, department chairs at other universities have had difficulty persuading their institutions to assist them with the defense of the case, and in one case, a department chair was initially required to pay his own legal bills. In another case, a biology professor sued by a student for whom he had written a letter of recommendation had to spend two thousand dollars of his own funds to defend a libel suit before the university agreed to underwrite his defense. Moral support is nearly as important as financial support, according to these individuals, and such support is not always forthcoming from higher-level university administrators who must defend the decisions made by departmental faculty and chairs.

Campbell and Gouldner did not hesitate when asked what advice they would give to administrators facing employment discrimination litigation by faculty. Both said that such litigation is part of the job and should be viewed that way rather than as a personal attack. Gouldner stated that administrators or faculty sued for the first time often experience a feeling of moral outrage that makes preparing for and defending the litigation more difficult. However, increasing familiarity with litigation results in a change of attitude, she noted, and administrators learn to see it as part of the process of managing a large, complex organization.

Campbell believes that the most successful way to avoid litigation is to "make sure policies and procedures are in place and make sure they're followed." The "old collegial ways" of making decisions are no longer appropriate, Campbell believes, in the current atmosphere of unionization and litigation. Although developing and following procedures cannot eliminate litigation, it can increase an institution's chances of prevailing in court.

Gouldner agreed with this advice and added some views on measures that may prevent litigation. She noted that administrators at all levels have a propensity, when they hear negative information, to tune it out until the problem becomes so large that it cannot be ignored. The wise course, she believes, is to deal with even small problems immediately and resolve them informally, especially in an institution that is unionized. Once the grievance process begins, she warns, informal resolution is impossible, because the sides are polarized.

The administrators also viewed careful documentation as crucial to the successful defense of employment discrimination litigation. Campbell stated that in *Scott,* the department chair had followed the procedures and had documented the decisions properly, which went a long way, in his opinion, toward the university's success in the case. Even if a department, committee, or individual behaves properly and follows the correct procedures, the appropriate behavior needs to be proven in court, and careful documentation is the mechanism through which cases are successfully defended. The provost and dean also praised the frequent evaluation of probationary faculty and the subsequent decisions, based on these evaluations, not to renew the contracts of junior faculty who were not performing up to university expectations. Nonrenewals backed by sufficient evidence of unsatisfactory performance also lessen the opportunity for successful challenges of negative promotion and tenure decisions.

Despite Scott's lack of success in either his individual claim of disparate treatment or his class claim of disparate impact, the case is important for several reasons. The stakes were high, for the plaintiff was challenging one of the tenets of academic tradition: that a research university can require its faculty to hold the doctorate and to produce scholarship, whether or not such scholarship is directly related to what happens in the classroom. Furthermore, the case had the potential to bring explicit affirmative action requirements, much like the goals and quotas required of police and fire departments in urban areas, to research universities, where employment and promotion decisions are subjective, confidential, and virtually unreviewed by external agents. And the litigation also challenged the decentralized, subjective process of evaluating faculty for renewal, promotion, and tenure.

The *Scott* case can be viewed as affirming the traditional norms of academe, but it also raises other, unanswered questions. To what degree, for example, should a university be held responsible for the racism of its students and faculty, especially when high-level administrators are aware of these problems? If a university recruits members of formerly underrepresented groups, is its responsibility to them over when the hiring is completed, or does some responsibility remain to nurture those individuals in a potentially hostile environment? These are ethical questions rather than legal issues and remain to be addressed by other institutions facing similar problems.

The *Scott* case, then, may not have affected the university deeply, but it is important in the history of academic discrimination litigation. Challenged by a team of competent civil rights lawyers with assistance from the EEOC, a historically de jure segregated state university with very few black faculty or students, in an environment that still is viewed by black students as inhospitable,[48] succeeded in convincing both a federal trial court judge and a panel of three federal appellate judges that its employment practices, although admittedly resulting in few black faculty, were neutral in intent and justified in practice.

This precedent and others have produced an ironic result. Like elementary and secondary schools, border state and southern public universities and colleges were de jure segregated prior to *Brown v. Board of Education*. Yet, as chapter 2 points out, though white faculty have won many lawsuits against formerly black institutions, black faculty have not been successful in suing white institutions in the federal courts. No one would have predicted that result. Is it that white institutions have been more successful in curing the defects of segregation? Or that the particular black plaintiffs who sued have not had good cases? Or that the courts have created a very high threshold for proving discrimination in the academic environment, which falls more heavily on blacks than whites? The *Scott* case suggests that all three of these explanations may be valid.

NOTES

1. 385 F. Supp. 937 (D. Del. 1974), 68 F.R.D. 606 (D. Del. 1975), 16 Fair Employment Practices Cases 737 (D. Del. 1976), 455 F. Supp. 1102 (D. Del. 1978), *modified,* 601 F.2d 76 (3d Cir. 1979), *cert. denied,* 444 U.S. 931 (1979).
2. Richard Kluger, *Simple Justice* (New York: Alfred A. Knopf, 1975), p. 426.
3. Keegan v. University of Delaware, 349 A.2d 14 (Del. Super. Ct. 1975).
4. Anapol v. University of Delaware, 412 F. Supp. 675 (D. Del. 1976).
5. Aumiller v. University of Delaware, 434 F. Supp. 1273 (D. Del. 1977).
6. Parker v. University of Delaware, 75 A.2d 225 (Del. Ch. 1950).
7. Scott, 455 F. Supp. at 1104.
8. Frederick Parker, "Outline of the History of Sociology at the University of Delaware—1913–1966" (University of Delaware, Newark, Del., 1973).
9. Ibid., p. 23.
10. Ibid., p. 24.
11. Frank Scarpitti, "The Black Student and the University of Delaware" (University of Delaware, Newark, Del., 1969), pp. 2–3.
12. Aumiller, 434 F. Supp. 1273, Anapol, 412 F. Supp. 675. Gordenstein's case was dismissed.
13. Keegan, 349 A.2d 14.
14. In order to prevail in these claims, Scott had to assert that specific individuals denied his civil rights and deliberately conspired to do so. The judge ruled that Scott had not made allegations of specific wrongdoing by particular individuals, and thus relief under these laws was not available to him.
15. Scott, 68 F.R.D. 606.
16. Scott, 16 Fair Employment Practices Cases 737.
17. Scott, 455 F. Supp. at 1123.
18. Scott, 455 F. Supp. at 1119.
19. Scott, 455 F. Supp. at 1120.
20. Scott, 455 F. Supp. at 1121.
21. Scott, 455 F. Supp. at 1122.
22. Scott, 455 F. Supp. at 1123.
23. 401 U.S. 424 (1971).
24. 29 C.F.R. § 1607.1 et seq.

25. Scott, 455 F. Supp. at 1124.
26. Scott, 455 F. Supp. at 1124–25.
27. Scott, 455 F. Supp. at 1125.
28. Scott, 455 F. Supp. at 1125.
29. Scott, 455 F. Supp. at 1126.
30. Scott, 455 F. Supp. at 1128.
31. Trial Transcript.
32. Scott, 455 F. Supp. at 1127.
33. 430 U.S. 482 (1977).
34. Scott, 455 F. Supp. at 1128.
35. Scott, 455 F. Supp. at 1129.
36. Defendant's Appellate Brief, p. 9.
37. Scott's attorneys cited the case of *Joseph v. Norman's Health Club, Inc.*, 582 F.2d 86 (8th Cir. 1976), which held that an appellee could not challenge the class certification of a truth-in-lending claim when it did not file a cross-appeal. Under appellate rules, this was the last brief, and counsel for the university had no opportunity to rebut the arguments of Grady and Neuberger.
38. Scott, 601 F.2d at 83.
39. Scott, 601 F.2d at 86.
40. Scott, 601 F.2d at 89.
41. The Third Circuit's decision to vacate the class action portion of the lower court judgment and the subsequent Supreme Court refusal to review the case mean that this issue is still an open one for higher education employment discrimination litigation. However, a similar case in the Second Circuit Court of Appeals may provide guidance. The court ruled that it was not discriminatory for a medical center to require a college degree for certain health care jobs, despite the fact that proportionately fewer blacks than whites possess such degrees. Townsend v. Nassau County Medical Center, 558 F.2d 117 (2d Cir. 1977), *cert. denied*, 434 U.S. 1015 (1977).
42. Scott, 601 F.2d at 90–91.
43. Scott, 601 F.2d at 94.
44. Brief Amicus Curiae of the Equal Employment Advisory Commission, p. 7.
45. 444 U.S. 931 (1979).
46. Firefighters Local Union No. 1784 v. Stotts, 467 U.S. 561 (1984).
47. Faculty Handbook, University of Delaware, III-K-6.
48. Charles S. Farrell, "University of Delaware Tries to Live Down 'Racist' Image," *Chronicle of Higher Education*, November 9, 1983, p. 17.

Chapter 6
The Feminist Implosion

Mecklenberg v. Montana State University[1]

This case is the first successful class action ever brought by women faculty. That makes the lawsuit historically noteworthy, but the case is even more important because of the process used in implementing the judge's far-reaching decision. *Mecklenberg* stands as a model for implementing sex equity by balancing plaintiff, administration, and other faculty participation.

Nestled in Montana's Gallatin Valley, near the confluence of the Jefferson, Madison, and Gallatin rivers, the city of Bozeman surely would have survived over the years to serve surrounding ranching, farming, and forestry interests. But since Montana State University (MSU) was founded in the nineteenth century, Bozeman has grown principally to serve that expanding academic center. By 1980, the university's eleven thousand students and two thousand employees constituted almost 40 percent of the population of the community.

MSU is part of the University of Montana state system, whose six campuses barely stretch into the vast reaches of the nation's fourth largest state. There are four regional campuses—Eastern Montana College at Billings, Western Montana College at Dillon, Northern Montana College at Havre, Montana College of Mineral Science and Technology at Butte—the University of Montana at Missoula, and MSU. Only two tiny private colleges exist in Big Sky country.

Montana has the classic system of two main campuses with the liberal arts and professional schools at Missoula and the land grant engineering, agricultural, and physical sciences schools at Bozeman. MSU was established as the Agricultural College of the State of Montana four years after statehood in 1893. Just before World War I, it became the Montana College of Agriculture and Mechanic Arts. It did not change its name to Montana State College until 1935 and did not acquire university status until 1965. As it expanded in size and mission, it encountered opposition from the older University of Montana. But today rivalry between the "granola people" at Missoula and the "cowboys" at Bozeman is generally good-natured.[2] Since there are only 750,000 people in the state, the leadership elite is small and everybody knows everybody else.

Given the temper of the times and MSU's subject matter focus, it seemed only natural that the Bozeman campus attracted many more males (students and faculty) than females. In the early seventies, MSU's student body was 60 percent male and its faculty 80 percent male, with the females mostly in home economics, elementary education, and nursing. That hadn't seemed like much of a problem to anybody. In the Montana tradition, mining, cattle, and forestry were a man's world and women came along afterward.[3] As one Montana historian put it, the frontier ethic was to ''trap it, to shoot it, to mine it, and get out.''[4] If any place was Marlboro country, it was Montana.

What seemed like the natural order of things began to change in Montana as everywhere else. The state's new 1972 constitution contains an equal rights provision, and Montana also ratified the federal Equal Rights Amendment. After the amendment of the Civil Rights Act and the Equal Pay Act in 1972, and under increasing pressure from HEW's Office of Civil Rights, MSU began its first affirmative action plan in 1973.[5] But it took a conservative view of the whole process. In the plan's preface, President Carl M. McIntosh wrote,

Montana State University takes the position that affirmative action means that we must make a diligent search for qualified women and minorities. This does not mean substituting either sex or ethnic culture for merit. Everyone deserves to know that he or she was selected on the basis of having the best qualifications among those available for the position.
. . . Departments have the obligation of making a determined search for women and minority group candidates. They have no obligation and should not waive merit criteria in order to achieve ''quotas.'' Competence is absolutely essential and no long-term solution of the perplexing problems of redressing past discrimination or imbalances can be achieved by a different kind of discrimination.[6]

In explaining why there were relatively few women at the university, the plan suggested,

Montana State University is located in a small agriculturally-oriented community in the northern Rocky Mountains. This geographically isolated location, combined with budget restrictions resulting in less than competitive salaries, makes it difficult to attract qualified female candidates for professional positions.[7]

Still, the affirmative action plan was the first official analysis of the problem of women and the university.[8] The document is about four inches thick, partially filled with the standard boilerplate of printouts, computer forms, and lists, but in its analytical sections it is remarkably candid. The information in it was indeed a legal time bomb. For example, the plan portrayed the underrepresentation of women in promotions. The MSU faculty profile by rank and sex in 1973–74 was as follows:[9]

	Male	Female
Professors	138	6
Associate Professors	144	23
Assistant Professors	114	33
Instructors	27	47

Moreover, the data documented that among faculty who held doctorates, women waited seventeen years to be promoted to full professor and men only seven. Finally, by using a regression analysis to predict sex-neutral, bias-free salaries, the university's study showed that 70 percent of the faculty women were below the predicted level.

Clearly, given the right plaintiffs, the right court, and the right judge, the university had a problem on its hands.

Triggering Incidents

The affirmative action plan was written by Mollie Hatch, a member of the physical education department and from 1973 the university's first affirmative action officer (on a part-time basis). Hatch had been concerned about problems of women on the MSU campus for several years.[10]

In the fall of 1972, she called together a group of departmental women (faculty and blue-collar workers) to talk about some salary data she had been examining. Since MSU was a public institution, its salary figures were published and stored in the library, but little collective use had been made of that information. The figures seemed shocking to the group. Some of the differences in salaries of women and men doing similar jobs appeared to be of the magnitude of 25 percent or more. For example, Ellen Kreighbaum and Bette Lowry, who later became plaintiffs, were paid about four thousand dollars less than each of three males they regarded as comparable. Seeing those numbers was an energizing, if not radicalizing, experience. Gradually, information about salary discrepancies began to spread around the campus, and that raised questions about other personnel practices at MSU and about the role of women there generally.

But during the 1972–73 academic year one of the catalysts of the MSU women's movement was about as far away from the campus as you can get. Helen Mecklenberg, of Scottish immigrant stock and a rancher's daughter, came to Bozeman to take her bachelor's degree in chemistry in 1951. After graduation, she married and bore four children, but she wanted to continue as a scientist. When the youngest child was two, she decided to begin pursuing a doctorate. Her family responsibilities restricted her to MSU, but she had heard that her old chemistry department refused to take women Ph.D. students. So she enrolled in the plant genetics program in the School of Agriculture, obtaining her doctorate in 1969. Since she had to stay in Bozeman, the university was her only potential employer. Administrators in the agriculture school said they wouldn't hire a woman, but she obtained a three year post-doctoral appointment with a friend in the chemistry department. When that ran out, she obtained a one-year instructorship in the Department of Zoology and Entomology. After signing that contract, she realized that nobody else with a Ph.D. and three years of post-doctoral experience would have been given less than an assistant professorship. She protested, and her contract was rewritten to give her that rank. From then on, she felt, the university administration was aware she might be a problem.

Moving to the biology department with a series of one-year contracts, she began to apply for promotion to associate professor. In 1971 she was told that her all-MSU experience was too parochial and that she couldn't be promoted until she had spent time on some other campus. Against her better judgment, she took a year's leave of absence to do research at the University of Miami Medical School. She applied for promotion that year but was turned down because she was away. In 1973 she applied again and first was told that she couldn't be promoted because she had just gotten back. When she pressed, she was told that her promotion had been discussed with someone at central administration and that "somebody up there doesn't like you." The Scottish rancher's daughter began to have reciprocal feelings, and she was determined to do something about it.

Perception of Alleged Discrimination

In those days at Montana State, as was common elsewhere, the salary decision-making process was informal and centered almost all the power in the department head. Faculty received form letters every year with a new salary typed in, but no reasons were given for changes. Nor were there any formal pre–salary decision evaluations or post–salary decision discussions. If you didn't like your raise, you could talk to the head who had made the decision or the dean who had approved it. Few faculty bothered.

One reason was that challenging a department head's salary decision might create problems later, when the more important promotion and tenure decisions had to be made. MSU did not follow the AAUP's seven-year up (tenure) or out rule. Faculty remained as full-time instructors or assistant professors for much longer periods. In theory, only after being promoted to associate professor and holding that rank for three years could a person be tenured. In fact, for men the rule was often breached.

Like salaries, promotion depended on the goodwill of the department head. If he (thirty-three out of thirty-five heads were male) was not willing to champion a case, promotion was extremely unlikely. In 1972, promotion and tenure decisions were handled by a standing committee of the president's forum, which included the top MSU administration. But the faculty handbook stated clearly, "The departmental head concerned shall always be invited to attend meetings of the Tenure and Promotion Committee when a staff member in his department is being reviewed."[11] There was no requirement of any peer review of candidates, and direct communication between the candidate and the reviewing committee was not thought appropriate. So the head dominated the evaluation process by controlling information. In return the head was appointed by and served at the pleasure of his administrative superiors. The tradition at MSU was for long tenure as head, with freedom to run the department.

By the fall of 1973, a women's faculty group had begun to hold regular meetings on campus problems. The attendance averaged thirty to forty, almost half the women on campus. To reach the many faculty scattered around teaching sites in Butte, Billings, and Great Falls, meetings often were held in the Bozeman School of Nursing facility so that others more distant could participate through its special communication system. The first stage was seeing that the problems the women faced as individuals had some common origin within the governance system and in the attitudes of those who ran it. The second stage was a debate over whether to dare to challenge it and how. As an initial step, the group elected Helen Mecklenberg chairperson.

From the university administration's perspective, what appeared to the women as an unsympathetic, old boy's network seemed to be an appropriate combination of academic tradition and Montana lifestyle. Putting authority in the hands of a departmental head, after all, can be traced to the model of the professor in the nineteenth-century German university, after which so many American institutions patterned themselves. In this tradition, academic power rests with the most senior, most productive member of the department, not with the person who might emerge from an election by those seeking to minimize demands placed on them. In this model, the university is seen as a meritocracy, not a democracy.

President McIntosh also thought there was a special Montana character to the MSU governance policies. Born in the Northwest, he had been president of Idaho State for twelve years and of Long Beach State for another ten years before coming to Bozeman in 1970. One of the first things he noticed in leaving the California State University and College system (which is very large, bureaucratic, and hierarchical), was that Montana State had no formal organization chart. The previous president knew who could do which jobs best and pretty much kept that information in his head. Coming to Montana State, McIntosh remembers, was like experiencing "the last of the free range." There was a sense of community and trust; handshakes were more important than legal agreements.[12] Elaborate procedures were unnecessary and inappropriate.

But the world was changing. The free range was no more, and McIntosh began to create a more formal organization and institute new procedures.[13] A system for determining whether women faculty suffered discrimination, however, was not on the agenda.

Problem Evaluation and Informal Consultation

As the evidence piled up and the magnitude of the problem became apparent, the women began to think about ways of obtaining assistance. Montana was not a state with strong women's groups or civil rights organizations. The HEW Office of Civil Rights had sent a team to MSU prior to 1972. After an investigation, they worked out a statewide agreement that equalized the position of housekeepers (female) and custodians (male), but they thought the data about faculty were too chaotic to support a decision. The regional offices of HEW and EEOC were in Denver, more than seven hundred miles away, and seemed too geographically and psychologically distant to help. Also, the administrative approach did not seem very promising.

One plaintiff later complained:

> There is an administrative route through HEW. We get awfully tired of waiting for them to do something. . . . Under HEW guidelines, they have to make the settlement, but you have to force them to follow the law. Women's Equity Action League reported only one university has settled these problems without some kind of suit. . . . Every year that goes by, you lose another year's back pay.[14]

So they decided to do what Bozeman residents usually do when faced with a problem. They turned to their neighborhood for help. Locating lawyers in Bozeman is not a difficult task. Attorneys have apparently been attracted by the vigorous outdoor lifestyle, and there is one for about every five hundred inhabitants. Ellen Kreighbaum and Bette Lowry found an attorney who began to meet with the women's group to explain the law. But before he could really begin the case, he moved to Washington, leaving the case to his partner, whom the two women found not energetic enough in pursuing the case. Helen Mecklenberg had been working with a well-established plaintiff's lawyer in town, but he taught constitutional law part-time at MSU and declined to take the case.

Consequently, all three of the women turned to a much younger attorney, Gregory Morgan, who was a virtual novice but well connected. Morgan's family was one of the first hundred families to settle in the Gallatin Valley, and that made him a rare fifth-generation Montanan. He had left the valley to join the Marine Corps and ended up at Quantico. Seeking work in nearby Washington, he had found a job on Senator Mike Mansfield's staff. After finishing his undergraduate and legal education at George Washington University, Morgan had returned to Montana to become law clerk for Judge W. D. Murray, the state's senior federal district judge.

Morgan knew he had a good case as soon as he talked to the plaintiffs. They already had "many of numbers" (the evidence necessary for proof), and they had access to key MSU internal documents.

Morgan saw his first responsibility as helping the plaintiffs to see the case in long-range perspective. He told the women that

> after all was said and done, he would be gone and they would remain with the faculty and the administration at MSU. Whenever possible, he directed their interests beyond redress to include procedural correction, so that in the future, cases like theirs simply would not become cases like theirs.[15]

In the meantime there were some practical steps to be taken. More information had to be acquired. Money had to be raised. (Morgan was nearly certain an appeal to the Ninth Circuit would be necessary.) An expert had to be found. The class had to be properly set. Two additional faculty types were necessary; Morgan wanted a plaintiff to represent part-time faculty and a plaintiff who was a nurse (half of all MSU women faculty were nurses) to round out the class. Elaine Pratt was easy to convince. She had a Ph.D., but year after year she could get nothing but part-time work. Since her husband taught at the university, she had little bargaining power. Jeanne Claus was a harder case. The idea of a lawsuit made her uncomfortable. As she put it, "[N]ursing did not train me to challenge authority." But her daughter had just been through the battle in the airline industry to give stewardesses the status and pay of flight attendants. Prodded by her daughter, Claus signed aboard.

Finally, the salary issues Kreighbaum and Lowry first raised had to be expanded to cover the interests of the class that was forming. Their original complaint of March 9, 1973, charged "unequal pay for equal education and equal work." Fifteen months later, after working with Morgan and the larger women's group, they amended their charge to include "retaliation, discrimination in promotion, underutilization of women on the university faculty, and underrepresentation by females as deans, vice presidents, and on faculty committees."

By 1973 Mollie Hatch had enough data and enough frustration to nearly decide to make the information public. This was, as she called it, a publish and perish strategy. But rumblings of her work had begun to reach the administration, and they decided to respond by making Hatch MSU's first affirmative action officer, a part-time one. From McIntosh's viewpoint the appointment was ideal, because Hatch was knowledgeable about the problems, and she could "bridge any doctrinaire gaps" and wouldn't maintain an adversarial relationship. From the plaintiffs' perspective, at least in hindsight, Hatch was given an office, table, and chairs, but no real mandate or authority, and was effectively removed from the struggle for women's rights. As one plaintiff said,

> The Affirmative Action Officer (at MSU) is only half-time and doesn't have the kind of authority or push needed. She has no autonomy and can't be what an Affirmative Action officer is supposed to be. It should be a full-time, 12-month job with better pay.[16]

Like most affirmative action officers, Hatch found herself in a complex situation. She was now a member of the administration with certain obligations, but she was also committed to equal pay and other causes. To add to the difficulty, the applicability of civil rights law to higher education was not at all clear, and the task of affirmative action officers (most of whom were just being appointed) was not well defined. Hatch saw her first major task as the production of an affirmative action plan, which was then a new requirement of the HEW Office of Civil Rights.

Use of Internal Remedies

In 1972, the MSU faculty handbook listed some fifty-five committees. There was a mysterious feasibility studies coordinating committee as well as the ever-popular traffic appeals committee. But there was no committee concerned with equal opportunity or any general grievance committee. The custom was that if you had a problem you discussed it with your department head, who would take it up with the dean, and so on. The difficulty was that most likely the problem was caused by a decision the head had made in the first place, which had already been confirmed by the dean, and so on. Nevertheless, several of the women decided to present the issue to their administrative superiors. Ellen Kreighbaum approached her department head, but he just said she didn't have a case and that pushing it was not a good idea. Eleanor Pratt, the part-timer, was even more vulnerable. When she talked to her department director, she was told to keep her mouth shut or risk angering him and losing her job in the fall. Not surprisingly, she said, "I see that as a threat."

Still, bringing a lawsuit against the university was psychologically a hard thing to do in Bozeman, Montana in 1974, particularly since several of the plaintiffs had a genuine feeling of loyalty toward the university. Some of the plaintiffs talked anonymously about their attitudes to the women's editor of the *Bozeman Daily Chronicle* at this time. One of the plaintiffs noted:

> It's not just salary, though, it's a voice. . . . People who are not so under-paid are still bitterly resentful of the fact they have no voice in university governance. We have no female top administrators. We have only two female department heads (heading nursing and home economics), so there are almost no lower-ranking administrators to draw from (for university administration jobs). . . .
>
> . . . One of the first things to correct is under-utilization of minorities and women. Departmental duties are not just duties; they're also privileges. Those are exactly the responsibilities I want. And I'm denied them on the basis of my sex. College and departmental responsibilities are extremely important when it comes time to eliminate discrimination: who is admitted to graduate school, hiring of new staff, departmental policies, university goals and standards. Most of us are denied having responsibilities given to us. . . .
>
> . . . There is an enormous psychological impact on how you perform if you don't have role-models . . . when you recognize that because of circumstances of your birth and not training or ability, you're never going to get beyond a certain point. It makes it awfully difficult to be gung-ho about anything. After so many times of beating your head against the brick wall, it gets depressing.[17]

Another plaintiff said,

> It took us three months to get our way into the president's office. They [the administration] have attempted to handle it completely unilaterally, accepting no input from the women faculty. . . .
>
> . . . No one will pay attention until their cage has been rattled.[18]

By July, 1974, Kreighbaum and Lowry had received the right-to-sue letter from EEOC. The way was clear for a lawsuit. The question was whether a lawsuit would rattle any cages at MSU.

Settlement or Litigation Decision

Montana State had been sued rarely in the past. Earlier in McIntosh's administration, the university was challenged by a group of students who wanted to change a commitment previous student leaders had made to fund a football stadium. Their lawsuit did not alarm the university much. The students were sure to lose, and they did. Furthermore, McIntosh thought himself lucky that the issue was a football stadium rather than Vietnam and that a lawsuit rather than a sit-in was the means of protest. So when the notice of the sex discrimination case came to the attention of university officials, they were not very experienced in or prepared for handling it. MSU had no in-house counsel and no relations with outside counsel except for routine contract work.

By March, 1974, the university was aware that it might be sued for sex discrimination and that it had to obtain legal representation. Under Montana law, state agencies had to be represented by the state attorney general's office, but that office had recently made an agreement with the commissioner of education to delegate education cases. The commissioner's office, newly established, had just created a legal staff by hiring two freshly minted lawyers. Barry Hjort, on whose desk this case and seven others fell, had graduated from the University of Montana Law School in 1973. After spending six months in Washington, D.C., with the Department of Justice's Division of Land and Natural Resources, Hjort responded eagerly to the idea of returning to Montana to work in the commissioner's office.

In confronting the discrimination charge, Hjort faced a formidable internal problem.[19] Such cases are inherently complicated. Little law existed at the time. He was very inexperienced, having tried only one case previously. To make matters worse, his clients were equally inexperienced and saw the case as a challenge to their integrity.

McIntosh decided that the principal administrative liaison for the case should be Vice-president Bill Johnstone, but there was never a formal designation and no sense that a specific strategy had to be formulated. Johnstone was the logical choice, although he was widely perceived as the most conservative member of the administration.

Johnstone's roots in Montana and at MSU were very deep. After receiving his bachelor's degree from Bozeman, he became superintendent of a small Montana school system. He then picked up a master's degree at Missoula, so he could prove "he knew how to do what he already was doing." He came back to Bozeman in 1958 to teach, and the next year he was acting dean of education. During his career he also served as director of institutional research, acting vice-president for academic affairs, and even acting president. In 1974 his position as vice-president for administration made him the senior vice-president.

Johnstone remembers that the administrative style then was program- rather than procedure-oriented.[20] Get the job done! Records and rules were comparatively unimportant. The Northwest Association of Colleges and Schools had commented in 1970 that MSU was run like a big family and that that could not go on much longer, but Johnstone has fond memories of this style. During that period, MSU doubled its enrollment and achieved university status and a parity with the Missoula campus. The job, as he saw it, had been done.

From the plaintiffs' perspective, a settlement was still more attractive than a trial. They all intended to remain working at MSU, and it is Morgan's philosophy always to seek a settlement. After the data had been analyzed, Morgan sent an emissary to see Mollie Hatch. His mission was to show Hatch enough of the prospective evidence to convince her to persuade the university administration that settlement was in its best interest. He failed. The evidence was complicated. Moreover, Hatch was convinced that the plaintiffs' threat of lawsuit was wrong. Still the plaintiffs sought to avoid a showdown. Twice before the trial, Morgan, Hjort, and Johnstone met to talk settlement. Morgan remembers that $90,000 was the figure discussed. But the university was not prepared to concede anything. Since the facts in its own affirmative action plan made the defense difficult, why was there no serious settlement attempt? It is Morgan's theory that public agencies generally are reluctant to settle since the costs of trial and possible penalties, should the case be lost, are shifted to other agencies' budgets. Unlike private corporations, he noted, public agencies can afford to regard litigation's financial costs as "Monopoly money." Furthermore, Morgan thinks public agencies know that judges will identify with them as part of the established order of things and will have at least an initial predisposition favorable to them. With regard to the possible ethical reasons for settling with its female faculty, Morgan believed the university just did not care.

Not surprisingly, the university officials saw the settlement problem differently. Johnstone was ideologically convinced that the plaintiffs didn't have a case, but McIntosh approached the problem more pragmatically. He remembered a lawsuit at the University of Montana in which, when the university lost, the legislature provided a special appropriation to pay for the damages. McIntosh thought that was a good precedent, and he worried that any pretrial settlement costs would have to come out of the regular MSU budget. That would not only constrict university development but would damage the morale of faculty whose own paychecks were being reduced and undermine support for the other goals of the settlement. Even when a member of the board of regents called McIntosh to urge settlement, he decided against it. Too many actors in the board and the legislature would have to be in agreement about that strategy before the university could feel secure that its regular budget would not be reduced.

There were additional factors that made the situation uncertain. In 1972, Montana's new constitution altered the governing board for higher education and created a new commissioner of higher education. As it turned out, the first commissioner, Larry Pettit, was the new governor's campaign manager and brother-in-law. More important, he had been an associate professor of political science at MSU and had had some personal disagreements with the university administration. It was not at all certain what kind of support the university could expect from the commissioner's office.

Litigation Preparation

The plaintiffs' amended complaint was filed on July 30, 1974, twelve days after the Department of Justice had issued right-to-sue letters to Kreighbaum and Lowry. The complaint was filed on behalf of "Jane Doe, as a woman employed on the faculty at Montana State University and on behalf of a class similarly situated." The reason for use of a Jane Doe complaint was that "plaintiffs feared retaliatory action."

The complaint named as defendants the Montana State Board of Education as well as the university. The class was defined as "female persons who are employed, or might be employed, by Montana State University and its various facilities located in the State of Montana."

The substance of the charge was that the defendants had established an employment system that limited the opportunities of female employees. Specifically, it argued that women were excluded from top administrative positions and leadership roles in faculty committees, discriminated against in promotion, salaries, and hiring, and subjected to discriminatory retaliation if they were "active in or in sympathy with civil rights for women." The charges were brought under Title VII of the Civil Rights Act of 1964, the equal pay provisions of the federal Fair Labor Standards Act, and the equal pay provisions of Montana state law. The plaintiffs sought an injunction against further discrimination, monetary relief for previous discrimination, a requirement that an approved affirmative action plan be developed, and, of course, attorney fees.

Within the university a substantial debate took place over how to respond. No one had any experience in such matters. Civil rights lawsuits of any kind were uncommon in Montana. Not only had Montana State not been subject to a lawsuit like this before, a faculty class action based on sex was unprecedented nationally.

The debate took place over two issues. How much data should be shared with the plaintiffs? What kind of trial preparation should take place?

The administration's first inclination was not to share any information at all. Hjort tried to explain that under civil rights law, plaintiffs had the right to certain data. But the rules of discovery were foreign to McIntosh and Johnstone and to the ethos of Montana State, so the decision was to resist. Second, there was a debate about whether to bring in a national expert. Hjort thought that given everybody's inexperience one was necessary, but the administration balked at the cost. Further, they were content with a study done for the 1975 affirmative action plan by Kenneth Tiahrt, a professor of statistics at MSU. Although he was available as an expert and was an able statistician, Hjort was concerned because Tiahrt knew nothing about discrimination theory and had no trial experience. Nevertheless, it was the client's decision to make.

The university's attempt to deny the plaintiffs information was not very successful. Initially, as is common, it tried to avoid complying with requests for information by arguing that the data were private. But the university's constitutional status required that even its salaries be publicly reported. Therefore, the judge ruled at a discovery hearing that faculty personnel computer printouts had to be turned over to the plaintiffs, although they would have to pay for the necessary computer time. After that skirmish, the university decided to be cooperative and two months after the interrogatories were presented provided virtually everything needed to complete the plaintiffs' analysis.

Although the plaintiffs could use the affirmative action plan for some of their data, they still needed to do further analysis. Lawyers are plentiful in Bozeman, but statistical experts unrelated to the university are not. Tiahrt, the most experienced statistician at Montana State, was testifying for the defense. The plaintiffs turned to Jack Gilchrist, an MSU sociologist who had the needed statistical capabilities. Accepting the plaintiffs' invitation was a difficult decision for him. In fact, he turned it down twice. He believed in the plaintiffs' case. The problem was interesting, and the fee was attractive, but he was an untenured assistant professor at MSU. Only after Morgan convinced him that the case would never get to trial did Gilchrist finally accept. Even then, he went to Johnstone to ask for permission to take on the assignment, in order to avoid any charge of conflict of interest and decrease his chance of subsequent retaliation.

Although the university decided to provide the information plaintiffs requested, it moved ahead with the standard defensive tasks. It responded to the complaint by challenging the jurisdiction of a federal court to enforce any rights granted under Montana law, by pointing out that the Montana Board of Regents was the proper defendant, not the Montana State Board of Education (whose jurisdiction was now elementary and secondary schools), by arguing that any wage disputes were the result of differences in the quality and quantity of faculty members' productivity, by denying all other forms of discrimination, by attacking the notion that a proper class existed, and by objecting (most vigorously) to proceeding with the case without an identified group of plaintiffs.

The judge responded by holding a pretrial conference in which Morgan submitted the name of one plaintiff and accompanying documents *in camera* in order to prove that a class existed. In addition to the rank data noted earlier, Morgan noted that women comprised only 11 percent of the membership of appointed boards, committees, and councils although they were 20 percent of the total faculty. Finally, plaintiffs argued that since there were 105 MSU female faculty, the class was so numerous as to render individual suits impractical. Morgan sought to preserve the Jane Doe status of his clients by suggesting in the plaintiffs' pretrial brief that "discrimination on the basis of sex is a matter of sensitive and highly personal nature to males and females alike and one in which the interests of the public can best be served by downplaying confrontations between individuals."

The university responded first that it could not make appropriate counterarguments if it did not know who the plaintiffs actually were and second that the class could not include all 105 female faculty, since at least some of them had been promoted to full professor, served on committees, or did not share other class characteristics. Furthermore, the defendants submitted that in the context of higher education, where initial employment and subsequent work and salary promotions depend in large measure on qualitative factors and merit, simple comparisons on a purely male versus female percentage are neither warranted nor appropriate. Finally, Hjort noted that at that stage of the litigation it would be foolhardy to engage in retaliation against any plaintiff.

On February 24, 1975, almost eight months after the complaint was filed, Morgan decided to waive anonymity. He knew the precedents were against him on this point. In return, Judge W. D. Murray granted a comprehensive class action order six weeks later.

By now the university was in an even more difficult situation. The five plaintiffs had expanded into a comprehensive class representing all female faculty, and they had data that suggested there were substantial problems of discrimination. Gradually, another factor entered the internal debate. Don Clark had come to MSU the year the lawsuit began, after retiring from an Air Force career.[21] During his military service, he had worked with or served on delegations that negotiated the Strategic Arms Limitation Treaty (SALT), the Law of the Seas, and other high-level treaties. His job at MSU was to teach international affairs and to work with the president as his personal assistant. The lawsuit was not particularly in his portfolio, but he began to learn more about it when he became Barry Hjort's handball partner. As they talked about the case, Clark could tell that Hjort thought it was a loser. But just two years out of law school and managing several other cases for the commissioner, Hjort was not in a position to be a powerful influence for settlement. Although Clark had begun to explain to the president the precarious legal position the university was in, he was still the new boy on the block compared to Johnstone. The university was committed to seeing the lawsuit through, even though McIntosh had begun to believe that the chances of winning were no better than fifty-fifty.

In the meantime, the plaintiffs pressed their attack, and an initial trial date was set for June 18, 1975. The defense succeeded in getting one postponement, but a firm date was set for August 11.

Pretrial Impacts

As the nature of the issues the women were raising and the particular plaintiffs became known, the administration sought ways to defuse the situation. Externally it did not have much of a public relations problem. There was little publicity in newspapers around the state about the filing of the lawsuit, and the campus newspaper virtually ignored it. Since there were no civil rights organizations of consequence in Montana that could draw attention to the trial, there was no public pressure on the university to settle.

Still, it was apparent that the women on the campus were increasingly united behind the plaintiffs. When campus authorities refused to recognize Helen Mecklenberg as the women's leader, she put together a petition supporting the suit that eventually contained the signatures of 105 of the 135 eligible women. The petition was presented to Judge Murray in one of the pretrial hearings.

Failing to discredit Mecklenberg, the administration tried another tactic with Ellen Kreighbaum. After the discrimination charge had been filed, she was approached by a member of the administration and informally offered the position of dean of students. There was a desire to get women into the administration, it was said. But Kreighbaum knew that she was not qualified for that particular position and regarded it as a dead-end job anyway. Also, Kreighbaum believed the offer was an attempt to coopt her, so she politely declined.

Elsewhere, the women's cohesion was not quite so solid. Two female scientists who believed their promotions were overdue decided not to join the plaintiffs. They thought the risks, either for themselves or their faculty husbands, were too great. Kreighbaum and Mecklenberg saw it differently. The former was an optimist and believed that law and justice would prevail in the end, and the latter was a realist who realized that her very visibility in the lawsuit gave her protection from retaliation.

The pretrial impact on the university is much harder to gauge. During McIntosh's administration, a number of organizational changes were made that were related to avoiding sex discrimination. But they might have been made anyway, since HEW's affirmative action program was beginning to affect all campuses that had federal contracts. It probably would have been difficult for the participants to sort out their motives at the time. A decade later it was impossible. Still, some of the changes are worth noting.

By 1974, the university had begun to alter its personnel policies. One change was an attempt to clarify MSU's ambiguous tenure policy. Although early handbooks had made reference to AAUP guidelines that require that a tenure decision be made before the seventh year, MSU really didn't follow such a policy and frequently waited much longer to tenure a professor. Consequently, the faculty talked about possessing legal tenure or AAUP tenure on the assumption that after seven years they could at least appeal to the national organization for tenure if not to Montana law. That, at least, was the theory, though no one ever tried it until the late seventies. A professor of English who had passed the AAUP specified period of probation was denied a contract renewal. He appealed to the local AAUP group, which happened to be led by Mecklenberg. The administration backed down and reinstated the professor, but the following year the faculty handbook contained the following clarification.

> Tenure at Montana State University as defined by statutes and the Board of Regents is given in Section 412, Tenure (Faculty Handbook). The tenure status shown in each individual contract is as defined by these regulations. In addition, the University endeavors to observe the recommendations of AAUP with regard to tenure as being indicative of good administrative practice and a general consensus in the higher education community. However, it must be noted that the AAUP criteria for tenure are not recognized by the Board of Regents or the Legislature.[22]

The national requirements of nondiscrimination had begun to be felt in Bozeman, particularly those promulgated by the Department of Agriculture. An affirmative action officer and a faculty committee were appointed and a draft of a plan completed. In the 1972–74 faculty handbook a new section on equal employment was added. In addition to the standard nondiscrimination disclaimers, the statement said, under the goals and timetables section:

> The University is a complex and diversified institution, therefore attainment of the ultimate goal—full utilization of qualified female and minority group persons in each position category in numbers reasonably expected by their availability—is a long-range undertaking. Nevertheless, the University will continue to direct its efforts in good faith toward attainment of the objectives of its policy. Results achieved under this program will be evaluated annually and the program revised as required.[23]

Trial Impacts

Although the case raised novel issues concerning the application of federal law and by Montana standards was a fairly complicated lawsuit, Judge Murray set aside but one week to try it. The site of the trial was a marvelous anachronism for the first major sex discrimination class action in higher education. Bloody, bawdy Butte, perched on the richest hill on earth, was the center of the war of the copper kings in the nineteenth century and also the center of intense labor strife.[24] Today, its mines closed and its population reduced from one hundred thousand to about twenty thousand, Butte still lives in the past. Its federal courthouse, built in the neoclassical style around the turn of the century, reflects the pretensions the city once had, but its raucous history is not out of sight either. In front of the judge's chair is a carved wood panel in which a .45 slug is embedded. It was fired years ago by an enraged bootlegger who sought to right an injustice and almost ended up leveling a justice.

By 1975, Judge Murray had presided over the Butte Federal Courthouse for twenty-six years.[25] Indeed, he had formally retired in 1965, but he still carried nearly a full load of cases just because he loved the law. Even when his health forced him to warmer climates in the winter, he heard cases at his vacation sites. Not surprisingly, Judge Murray is a bit of a legend in Montana. His father, the late Senator James Murray, was a "Butte Democrat," a phrase dating to the period when that city's booming economy made it dominant in the state. The phrase also reflects a style of politics, an intense liberalism that has wrestled with Anaconda and other corporations for control of Montana over the decades. James Murray served in the U.S. Senate from 1935 to 1961, the longest term of any Montana senator. Certainly one of the proudest moments of his public life was when his Senate colleagues confirmed President Truman's nomination of his son to the federal bench without a dissenting vote in 1949.

As the son of a powerful politician, William Daniel Murray had a rather privileged life compared to his Butte peers. He grew up in a twenty-six-room mansion modeled after a French chateau, and he is remembered as the "Silk Stocking Boy," the only nonminer on one of Butte's championship semi-professional football teams.[26] He received his B.S. from Georgetown University and an M.S. from Columbia, though he returned to the University of Montana for his law degree. On the judicial bench, he has the reputation of a gruff, no-nonsense judge who is not above dressing down an errant lawyer. Murray is an egalitarian in a fairly literal way. He is opposed to the ERA, but he once struck down a draft law because it did not treat men and women alike.

Morgan began the plaintiffs' case by examining Mollie Hatch, who had written the MSU affirmative action plan. After Hatch's testimony, Morgan put each of the plaintiffs on the witness stand except, ironically, Helen Mecklenberg, who was vacationing in Europe.

Then he called James Pickett, head of the biology department, and also McIntosh. It is commonplace for the plaintiffs' attorney to put the chief defense witnesses on the stand. The tactic is called "pulling the teeth." Its logic is that it is best to have the most damaging evidence against the plaintiffs come out under examination by the plaintiffs' attorney, where it can immediately be minimized and challenged. And in this instance Morgan also thought he could catch Pickett and McIntosh in some inconsistency that would prove Mecklenberg's retaliation charge.

Pickett testified that Mecklenberg's failure to be promoted was due to her "meager research productivity" and "average" teaching. But Pickett's credibility was undermined by three factors. One, he had recommended Mecklenberg for a promotion, though perhaps not with great enthusiasm. Two, he had approved an unusual $3,000 raise for her without a promotion. Three, she had not been given a written statement of the reasons for her denied promotion even though the revised faculty handbook appeared to require it.

McIntosh faced intense questioning about whether the university knew Mecklenberg had filed a charge with EEOC when it denied her a promotion in 1974. Although he insisted it did not and that retaliation was not a motive, cross-examination showed that the university had received a copy of her complaint about six weeks before it made the negative promotion decision.

Finally, on the third day of trial, Morgan brought Jack Gilchrist to the witness stand to testify about his statistical analysis. It was the assistant professor's first time on the witness stand—and he had been promised that there would never be a trial. He remembers being so nervous that the attendant had to carry his briefcase. When it was all over, he had been on the stand for seven hours, five of them under cross-examination. Nevertheless, his data and his testimony stood up. Gilchrist's data showed that of all MSU faculty with Ph.D.'s and sixteen years of experience, 70 percent of the males were full professors, but only 42 percent of the females had achieved that rank. Of the males with that amount of experience and master's degrees, 41 percent were full professors, but only 5 percent of comparable women had been awarded that title. Even though the faculty handbook specified that the normal minimum time required in rank before promotion was three years for instructor and five years each for assistant and associate professors, males consistently spent less than the minimal time and women spent more. But the most important part of Gilchrist's analysis was his salary study. He believed that although it was appropriate to control for department, years of experience, and type of degree held, he did not include rank, tenure, or the number of promotions in making salary comparisons because he held that those variables might be both sex dependent and tainted by discrimination. Using this approach, Gilchrist calculated that it would take $222,776 to bring females up to the salary level of comparable males. Gilchrist believed he was making an impact on the judge, but he couldn't be sure.

Ellen Kreighbaum was annoyed with one aspect of Morgan's presentation. At dinner, after the court closed, she pointed out that he had consistently addressed male faculty and administrators as professor and doctor, even when they didn't possess that rank or degree. Women faculty, on the other hand, were called Miss or Mrs. or even by their first name. Morgan was embarrassed, but he and Gilchrist decided to turn it into an advantage by playing a scene for the judge when testimony resumed. After Gilchrist took the stand the next day, Morgan asked him how, in a university atmosphere, sex discrimination could exist. Gilchrist replied that much of it was subtle and unintentional. When asked for an example, the sociologist chastised the attorney for his invidious use of nomenclature in dealing with previous male and female witnesses. At first Judge Murray appeared not to understand, but after informal colloquy on the matter, he nodded and turned to Gilchrist and thanked him for very instructional testimony.

The university countered by calling Tiahrt, the MSU statistics professor who had done the original affirmative action plan studies, as its first witness. Tiahrt could do little but repeat his findings of several years before. That study did find that inequities existed in certain ranks and in particular years, but he asserted that there was not a systematic problem of salary differences related to sex at Montana State. His conclusion about the lack of a pattern depended, however, on his use of rank as a controlling variable. Otherwise, the difference in salaries for males and females was hard to refute. Rank, of course, might be an independent surrogate for merit or productivity. Or it might be a result of a sex-biased personnel process.

Other defense witnesses had to explain the statistics that showed women comparatively underrepresented and unrewarded. The hostile climate and the geographical isolation of Montana were mentioned as reasons the university had trouble recruiting women. There were assertions that women's careers were more limited by family obligations and that women were less professionally ambitious. Since promotions and salary increases are to some extent based on ability to garner grant money from federal or state sources, evidence was introduced that many more men than women had received grants. All in all, in a five-day trial the defense used less than a day and a half to present its case. By the end of the week, McIntosh was sure the university had lost.

A month after the trial was over the plaintiffs had submitted, as is customary, a posttrial brief in the form of a memorandum of proposed findings of facts and conclusions of law. After a cursory restatement of the grievances of the individual plaintiffs, Morgan focused on what he saw as the systemic problems at MSU. He noted that not only were there no women deans or vice-presidents but no women sat on any of the committees with decision-making authority, such as the promotion and tenure committee, which reviewed salaries and promotions. Then Morgan borrowed from four decisions in which courts had invalidated employment systems that discriminated against blacks: *Griggs vs. Duke Power Co., United States v. Ironworkers Local 86, Rowe v. General Motors,* and *Baxter v. Savannah Sugar Refining Corp. Griggs,*[27] he noted, stood for the proposition that employment criteria, even if neutral on their face, are illegal if they have an adverse effect on a protected class and are not a business necessity. Without naming any specific criteria, Morgan suggested that Montana State's system had an adverse affect on women. From *Ironworkers,* he cited the famous dictum in Title VII cases that "statistics often tell much and courts listen because the only available avenue of proof is the use of statistics to uncover clandestine and covert discrimination by the employer or union involved."[28] Finally, Morgan used *Rowe*[29] and *Baxter,*[30] both cases in which blacks had fared poorly in promotion systems where white supervisors had unfettered discretion, to draw the analogy with women at MSU whose salaries and promotions were heavily influenced by male department heads who acted without written rules or standard procedures.

The defense memorandum of proposed findings and conclusions of law, after attacking the plaintiffs' definitions of two appropriate classes, moved to discussing the plaintiffs' statistical argument. The defense's difficulty was that even the numbers it produced were not very helpful to its cause, so in fact that section of the memorandum contained no statistics. Instead, Hjort argued that evidence of underutilization is not the same thing as proof of discrimination and used a quotation from the Fifth Circuit: "We recognize that statistics are a powerful tool in the hands of a Title VII plaintiff, but we are also aware that undue emphasis on their use may obscure rather than advance the judicial process."[31] Nor, the defense argued, could it be held responsible for the "mores of our society which place more personal obligations" on women than men. The memorandum suggested that these "obligations" might be the reason that during the previous years, women obtained only 3 of the 126 research grants awarded to MSU faculty.

Above all, Hjort challenged the plaintiffs' egalitarian assumptions. He declared that

> salary and rank discrepancies are natural to an institution of higher education where faculty members are evaluated for promotion and salary increases on the basis of their instructional ability, research endeavors, and contributions to the public, the institution and their academic fields.

Such evaluations, he argued, should not be second guessed by courts. He quoted the conclusion of the Second Circuit in turning down a female plaintiff. In rejecting her attempt to get the court to overturn a negative tenure decision, the decision states:

> [Plaintiff] would remove any subjective judgments by her faculty colleagues in the decision-making process by having the courts examine "the university's recruitment, compensation, promotion and termination [procedures] and by analyzing the way these procedures are applied to the claimant personally." . . . Such a procedure in effect would require a faculty committee charged with recommending or withholding advancements or tenure appointments to subject itself to a court inquiry at the behest of unsuccessful and disgruntled candidates as to why the unsuccessful was not as well qualified as the successful.[32]

Decision Impacts

Judge Murray's decision was not long in coming, and it was not very surprising. The university had lost and lost conclusively.

The judge found that the class of female faculty was appropriate and that women were underutilized in the faculty and then proportionately underrepresented in the governance structure. The decision noted that the affirmative action plan was a conservative statement of the problem, since it calculated availability of qualified women based on those holding the doctorate, while in fact more than a third of the MSU faculty did not possess the doctorate.

In the Gilchrist/Tiahrt debate, the judge sided with the junior sociologist rather than the senior statistician. Rank, the judge agreed, might be a sexually tainted variable and could not be used in comparing salaries. Three things led him to that conviction. First, there was a great disparity in the number of men and women who had senior rank. Second, the promotion decisions at MSU reflected what were called a "non-merit system." According to Judge Murray:

> There are a great number of variables which those in the promotion review process are allowed to consider. In addition, the various academic departments at the University may weigh these factors differently. Thus those who play a role in the promotion process may apply a number of vague and subjective standards, and there are no safeguards in the procedure to avert sex discriminatory practices.[33]

Third, women were almost wholly excluded from the personnel decision-making process. Unless the female candidate happened to come from one of the two female-headed departments (out of thirty-five), no person of her sex would play a role in the decision. Although Judge Murray did not cite the *Rowe* or *Baxter* decisions, he apparently accepted their philosophy that when one class is permitted to judge another class using subjective measures and a disproportionate statistical outcome occurs, a prima facie case of discrimination exists. Decentralized decision making and subjective measures are characteristic of the university faculty personnel process everywhere in the United States. MSU's outcomes may have weighed more heavily against women, but its structure was close to the norm. Consequently, what is implicit in Judge Murray's decision was potentially of considerable national significance. His opinion comes closer to stating the criteria for determining a sexually discriminatory academic personnel pattern than any other decision yet written. The elements Judge Murray used were:

1. Women are concentrated disproportionately at lower ranks.
2. Women are paid less even in the same rank.
3. Women are relatively excluded from personnel decision-making positions.
4. The criteria and standards for personnel decisions are diverse and subjective.
5. There are no checks and balances or appeal procedures to protect against arbitrary decisions.

Still, it is possible to argue that these conditions are not caused by discrimination. But the judge found the university's argument about climate and geography deterring women "totally speculative" and the contention that women were relatively less ambitious and more hampered by family obligations "wholly conjectural." The university's most objective defense was that grants were a legitimate factor in salaries and promotions and men overwhelmingly won more grants. But the judge responded obliquely that although that was true, "the grants were concentrated primarily in the physical, biological and agricultural sciences—all fields which are heavily dominated by men at Montana State University." That is the end of the judge's statement on the matter. When asked eight years later why he said that, the judge could not remember, and it is not clear why he thought promotion and salaries should not be related to successful grantsmanship even if males dominated the best-funded disciplines.

As for the specific plaintiffs, the outcome was more mixed. The judge agreed that Ellen Kreighbaum and Bette Lowry had been the victims of salary discrimination. He also found that Helen Mecklenburg (promotion) and Eleanor Pratt (hiring) had suffered retaliation for their activities on behalf of women. Jeanne Claus, however, the judge believed, should have known about the degree requirements for promotion and had not been discriminated against. Perhaps most important, Judge Murray ruled:

> The evidence shows discrimination against women as a class by the defendants at Montana State University in that females are underutilized

as deans, vice presidents, department heads and as instructional faculty in many departments of the University. Women have also been discriminated against as a class in the areas of promotion, tenure, salary, and appointment to important university committees.[34]

He then added the boilerplate sentence, "More particularized, equitable relief may be ordered by the Court at the time the questions regarding damages are resolved." The language the judge used was conventional, but the process actually employed was unusually creative.

Posttrial Impacts

The legal implications of the Mecklenberg decision were potentially of considerable consequence. In their first class action women had not only won, but a federal judge had determined that rank could not be used in establishing salaries and had suggested what the elements of a discriminatory academic personnel system were. Since these elements were commonplace in higher education and since women were almost everywhere paid lower salaries than men, even within the same rank, Judge Murray's decision might, if followed, have changed the character of American academic personnel practices. Ray J. Aiken, a professor of law and university legal counsel at Marquette University, recognized that possibility, and was alarmed by it. Writing in the *Journal of College and University Law,* which is published by the National Association of College and University Attorneys, he commented:

> Mecklenberg is a fundamentally bad decision, and one which is virtually unprecedented in its unrestrained invasion of the universally-accepted academic selection process at all of the faculty and administrative levels of the institution. . . . What, if any, alternatives are available to the institution? The most obvious is to appeal the decision, staking whatever resources can be allocated to the effort upon the likelihood that a more tolerable result can be achieved. Less acceptable alternatives would be to attempt to achieve a measure of detente by compromise with the claimants, or to simply surrender the affairs of the institution entirely into their hands and those of the district court. So long as the costs of the institution's response can be counted simply in terms of its own (the state's) funds, a cash settlement with the claimants and their counsel would seem to suggest a practical, if not palatable solution. But when the cost of settlement implicates the financial position of the institution's associated personnel, or the academic integrity of the institution, it becomes unthinkable and intolerable to consider detente or compromise. The invasion must be resisted at any cost.[35]

Back in Bozeman an appeal was being considered, but not on the basis of the lofty national principles Aiken had invoked. As before, the case was considered as a local matter influenced mainly by Montana politics and the personalities at MSU. To protect the appeal option, Hjort filed a notice of appeal a month after the decision and set in motion the steps to bring the matter to the Ninth Circuit in San Francisco. But six months later the appeal was dead. What had happened?

The appeal was discussed in the inner circle of Montana higher education. Mecklenberg went personally to see the commissioner of education and the chairman of the board of regents to argue against an appeal. She remembers that they seemed sympathetic and opposed to an appeal, but Barry Hjort affirms that he received no outside pressure for or against one. Others are certain that the regents saw no profit in becoming involved in the controversy. So the issue went back to the campus. Johnstone was, as ever, certain that MSU had done no wrong and wanted to appeal. But for McIntosh, sitting through the five days of the trial had been an eye-opening experience. Although he thought the judge had not credited certain of the university's defenses, on other points he had become convinced the university was wrong. He decided to settle and concluded that Don Clark, former Air Force treaty negotiator and a person new to the campus, should be his representative. His instructions were simple: Get the best deal possible that is fair to the campus and the plaintiffs.

If the judge believed Montana State females were discriminated against as individuals and as a class in the areas of promotion, tenure, salary, participation in university governance, and administrative appointments, how should the remedy be fashioned? The problem was an unprecedented one for the courts in 1976. Judge Murray knew little about universities and, in any event, did not have the activist temperament of some of his judicial brethren on the federal bench such as Frank Johnson (Alabama), W. Arthur Garrity[36] (Massachusetts), or Miles Lord[37] (Minnesota). Nor was the problem one the lawyers could settle in detail. Neither Morgan nor Hjort had the time or, more important, the knowledge to attempt the task by themselves. Involving the plaintiffs and their administrative adversaries might only exacerbate and prolong the conflict.

So with McIntosh's blessing "The Court says we lost, so it's a dead issue. Now let's get on with it and correct it,"[38] the decision was made to implement a settlement in a two-step plan. First, the lawyers met with Don Clark, who managed to serve both as the president's representative and honest broker in the creation of a master plan; second, faculty panels were convened to make individual promotion and salary decisions.[39] Among the highlights of the master plan were revisions in the affirmative action plan, and the establishment of a new affirmative action advisory committee with membership in the university council. The new committee was to be at least 25 percent female (their percentage in the faculty overall) and to include one plaintiff. The director of the School of Nursing was made a dean, the first female administrator of that rank at Montana State. Quotas for female representatives were established for university governance committees. Particularly important were the hiring rules. Females were to be 25 percent of all faculty and administrative search committees, and they had the right to submit a minority report to the president if the committee recommended a male rather than a female applicant.

These adjustments were fairly easy, but determining the proper rank and salary for existing female faculty was complex and potentially expensive. First, the university affirmed that it would accept the AAUP seven-year up-or-out rule, thus standardizing the process. Then an ad hoc promotion review committee was set up to consider retroactive promotions as far back as 1973–74. Males as well as females could apply, but the process was designed to rectify inequities in the promotion of women. Females were to have at least three of the seven positions on the committee, which was charged to review all women automatically who had been in rank longer than the minimum time. Altogether, thirty-eight faculty (thirty women and eight men) applied for retroactive promotions. After hearing from department heads and candidates, the committee recommended seven women and two men for promotions that were in some cases three years overdue.[40]

The salary equity question was the most difficult, because it potentially affected over 138 women. Two choices existed. The problem could have been turned over to a statistician who could have developed a regression formula that would have dictated salaries. But any such formula would have also turned up some male faculty who were not receiving their predicted salaries, thus increasing the university's fiscal liability. So the decision was made to use a system of pairing each female faculty member to the male who most closely approximated her field, educational level, and experience. Merit factors (quality of teaching and research) were not considered because "Judge Murray ruled the present merit system to be non-standardized."

Identifying the appropriate pairs and calculating a new salary figure was a complex task. During the summer of 1976, a faculty equity team was formed. Each of the parties selected two members of the team and agreed to the two selected by the other party. The two males and females then recruited an outsider, Fred Harcleroad, professor of higher education at the University of Arizona, to serve as a consultant and mediator. The most difficult problem occurred in finding pairs for faculty in the library and the School of Nursing, where there were few comparable males. After finding there were no internal inequities among male and female librarians, the equity team compared MSU library salaries with those at other Rocky Mountain region institutions. These internal and external comparisons led to the conclusion that no discrimination existed. For nurses this methodology could not work, because there were no males in the MSU school and almost none in other nursing schools. Consequently, the team created a hypothetical male nurse by using males without doctorates in other MSU professional schools to construct salary patterns. The results, which were approved unanimously by nursing faculty, gave increases to all but two of the thirty-four nurses, the largest cumulative adjustment being $14,470. Altogether, seventy female faculty received both pay and benefits amounting to $403,000.[41]

By the fall, the parties submitted the package of governance changes, promotions, and salary adjustments and $47,500 in attorney fees for Greg Morgan to the judge for his approval. Nothing like this settlement process or outcome had ever before occurred in Montana or, for that matter, anywhere else in higher education. Judge Murray was pleased and signed the judgment on November 12, 1976, enjoining the defendants permanently from discriminating against women as individuals and as a class and ordering compliance with the master plan.

In his report to McIntosh, Harcleroad commented:

> The cooperative spirit in which this difficult and unprecedented task has been approached has been basic to its acomplishment thus far. . . .
> Further development of collegial relationships on the MSU campus will be greatly affected by this suit and the widespread adjustments taking place in faculty personnel and governance which have accompanied it. The way in which this potentially explosive part of the activity has been carried out can serve as a fine example for other groups in the future.[42]

What have been the long-term consequences of the litigation process and the unusual procedures for implementing the decision at Montana State University? Some impacts can be documented concretely. Others are more speculative. First, there was an obvious change in the governance system. The administrative council and president's forum were dissolved and replaced with a new operations council with a guaranteed female representation. The university hired its own in-house counsel[43] as well as a full-time affirmative action officer. A women's athletic directorship was created. Standards for hiring, promotion, and tenure became more clearly articulated, and particularly important to women was the effort "to eliminate unnecessary criteria which inhibit the ability of current staff to be promoted."

Other possible impacts are more subtle. A month after Judge Murray's decision, McIntosh found himself before a closed-door meeting of the Montana board of regents, accused of concealing $1 million in student fees so as to increase MSU's state appropriation. The motion asking for his resignation failed four-to-three, but that damaging tally was leaked to the press.[44] Three months later, McIntosh was the subject of a rare vote-of-confidence poll on the campus. With almost half of the faculty participating, 60 percent of the ballots said he should not be retained as president.[45] Lacking both external and internal support, McIntosh resigned the following fall. Many issues were involved in the erosion of his popularity and even his zest for the job, but his own explanation suggests that the *Mecklenberg* case was a factor. He told the *Bozeman Chronicle,*

> We still have the same set of problems, but today we have less choice in identifying solutions to problems. There are more external constraints, more laws on how the University may conduct its business and an unfortunate tendency for overreliance on the courts.[46]

With McIntosh gone, Johnstone left administration to return to the classroom. He said he found it difficult to adjust to the new administrative style and "federal involvement" in education.

The litigation did not fulfill all the women's expectations. After an initial giddy period when the impact of higher salaries and increased acceptance in campus governance was first felt, some women became disillusioned with some of the results of the process. One consequence of the master plan was that women who were considered by their male counterparts as the most talented and/or as team players were overwhelmed with committee assignments, while their less well regarded or more radical sisters were still excluded. Also, whenever a personnel action regarding a woman was negative, there was the natural question about whether that action was a continuation of discrimination or, at least, inconsistent with the spirit of the master plan. Several sought out Greg Morgan to represent them, and some settlements were negotiated. Some males felt they were damned if they did (if they bent over backward to favor female colleagues) or damned if they didn't (if they upheld traditional merit standards). Other males felt their salaries or promotions were held back to let women advance. Sara Lee Visscher, professor of entomology and chair of the ad hoc committee on retroactive promotions, said to a reporter, "Some men viewed women after that lawsuit with fear, resentment, and overt hostility."[47] Efforts to recruit new women faculty in senior ranks proved generally ineffective, and even the most committed feminists would concede privately that Bozeman was not a very hospitable place (particularly for a single woman).[48] On the other hand, salaries for senior women, counter to the national pattern, remained almost equivalent to those of senior males in ensuing years.[49] This clash of expectations often focused in the work of the affirmative action officer. In 1984, there was a long, bitter, and public fight between the latest affirmative action officer (there have been several since the litigation) and the president over her role. The affirmative action officer was terminated and retained Greg Morgan as her attorney. When lengthy negotiations broke down, she fired Morgan, hired a new lawyer, and finally settled for $14,000 before leaving for a better job in Wisconsin.

On balance, has the litigation and the settlement process left MSU a better campus for women, with clearer personnel procedures for all? The answer is certainly yes. Has discrimination been eradicated and is MSU a model of "cooperative spirit" between men and women?[50] The answer is a firm no. The rise in consciousness of discrimination and the extent of faculty involvement in the settlement mandated by the master plan would almost guarantee lingering disharmony. Would the outcome have been better if either the court or the administration had dictated the settlement? Probably not.

The litigation process also had mixed results for the individual plaintiffs and other participants. Eleanor Pratt was given the part-time position in French she had been denied and some back pay. She became MSU's acting affirmative action officer for a time and then left the university to do the same job in the federal government. After the lawsuit, Bette Lowry and Ellen Kreighbaum received more than thirteen thousand dollars each in back pay and were fully reintegrated into the MSU community, both eventually serving as chair of the Department of Health, Physical Education and Recreation. Lowry subsequently left to become chair at Humboldt State, but Kreighbaum has remained to become a member of the establishment and looks at the litigation as a positive step for women. The results for Helen Mecklenberg were more paradoxical. She got her promotion and over five thousand dollars in back pay, but the process has made her bitter. As soon as the case was over, leadership in the women's movement passed her by. She resented being excluded from the settlement process and is critical of the results. She became dissatisfied with Greg Morgan and in 1978 approached another attorney to try to reopen the case to go back to court to get the master plan "implemented."[51] Kreighbaum and Lowry would not join in this attempt, and it failed. Mecklenberg believes her salary has fallen substantially behind those of her peers, and she knows she never will make full professor. For some time after the litigation, many of her male colleagues made snide remarks and refused to attend department meetings with her. When asked whether she would do anything differently, she replied, "I would not be an academic. Although I love this way of life, you have to cope with arbitrary, capricious decisions. Why not be in industry and make money!"

Jack Gilchrist got his promotion and felt some administrators were deferential because of his involvement in the litigation. Barry Hjort, in the normal course of events, left state service to join a private practice, where he obtained some clients in discrimination cases because of his previous involvement in the *Mecklenberg* suit. Although he won a substantial amount in attorney fees,

Greg Morgan's intense efforts in the *Mecklenberg* case were not fully appreci-
ated by his law firm, and he soon left it. For a time there was a flurry of
national interest in his trial strategy, and he was invited to speak in New York,
New Orleans, and San Francisco for the Practising Law Institute. But that has
now died down, and he operates a one-man office, serving, among other
clients, MSU employees who think their legal rights have been violated.
Every year at tenure time, he sees five to ten faculty. But after working on
several additional discrimination cases, Morgan has decided he will take no
more. In his opinion the courts have made the cases so protracted and difficult
to win that the client too often ends up a martyr, hostile to her attorney.

Judge Murray, at age seventy-seven at the time of this writing, still takes
his turn on the bench in the Butte courthouse. *Mecklenberg* is just one of the
hundreds of cases he has decided, and he doesn't think about the ironic fact
that although his decision created considerable discussion among scholars, it
has had very little influence on the law. It has been cited in other decisions
very few times. Since it was the first class action litigation and one of the few
cases women have won against a university, its lack of impact on the law is,
on the surface, hard to understand. But there is a simple explanation. Judge
Murray decided not to publish the decision. Indeed, if Greg Morgan had not
responded to the invitation of the Commerce Clearing House to have the
decision published in its *Employment Practices Decisions,* the *Mecklenberg*
opinion might have been the legal equivalent to the Zen riddle of whether a
tree makes a noise when it falls deep in the forest where no one can hear it.
Since Judge Murray did not submit his decision for publication in the standard
reporter systems, its influence has been limited. Sometimes a judge will not
send in a decision for publication because he thinks the facts are unique, so
that his opinion is not applicable elsewhere. Occasionally, a judge will feel a
particular opinion is not the best example of his (or more practically, his
clerk's) legal craftsmanship and will happily leave the decision to be buried.
But aside from those laudable motivations to reduce printed legal trivia,
attitudes toward publication may reflect profound differences in judicial philosophy. Some judges see themselves in a scholarly or activist role and view
their individual decisions as appropriate occasions for making law and publication as a necessity to achieve that purpose. Other judges see their proper
role as that of deciding only the case before them and not that of making more
general laws if that can be avoided. Judge Murray believes his task is to apply
the law to the particulars in the suits Montanans bring before him and not to
influence the national scene. He thinks too many decisions are printed and
rarely submits his for publication.

Consequently, like the implosions that used to rock the now quiet Butte
copper pits, the impacts of the *Mecklenberg* litigation process have generally
been confined to the local participants. The Montana case has not created the

legal precedent faculty women needed to challenge the fundamental personnel arrangements in American higher education.

NOTES

1. 13 Employment Practices Decisions ¶ 11,438 (D. Mont. 1976).
2. Richard Roeder, the university's specialist in Montana history, remembers Cowboy Day, when the undergraduate males wore holsters and fired blanks at each other with .357 Magnums. That tradition lasted until the sixties. But MSU's image as "Moo U, the Udder University" is changing as it moves more into science and technology, although its School of Agriculture and extension services are very important to the state.
3. In 1900 the ratio of men to women in the state was twice the national average. Among males, the percentage of unmarried men was 13 percent higher than the national average. In those days there were only 1.7 persons to the square mile in Montana. K. Ross Toole, *Twentieth Century Montana: A State of Extremes* (Norman, Okla.: University of Oklahoma Press, 1972), p. 16.
4. Merril G. Burlingame, *A History of Montana State University* (Bozeman, Mont.: Office of Information Publications, 1968), p. xii.
5. The first draft of the plan was completed in August, 1973, but it was revised in 1975 because HEW had not yet approved it. During that year, most institutions experienced delays in getting approvals. HEW was short of personnel and did not have policies about many questions.
6. Letter dated March 3, 1975, used as a preface to the affirmative action plan.
7. Montana State University Affirmative Action Plan, 1975, p. 38.
8. There are very few blacks, hispanics, or Asians in Montana, but Indians are about 5 percent of the state's population. MSU had not traditionally developed many programs for Indians. Minorities of all types constituted only 7 of the 569 faculty in 1975.
9. Montana State University Affirmative Action Plan, 1975.
10. This section is based on information obtained in author's interviews with Ellen Kreighbaum, Bette Lowry, and Helen Mecklenberg in June, 1984.
11. Montana State University Faculty Handbook, p. 21.
12. Carl McIntosh, interview with author, June, 1984. McIntosh himself agreed to move from Long Beach State on the basis of a handshake and never had a written contract.
13. McIntosh remembers reading an auditors' report shortly after he arrived about a "problem" in an MSU agricultural extension center in northern Montana. The auditors were horrified to discover that when unbudgeted overtime work was called for, the extension head would sometimes pay the men with a side of beef from the university herd. A practical solution, perhaps, but in the era of witholding and Social Security taxes, it had to go.
14. Florence Trout, "MSU Women Seek Better Breaks in Job," *Bozeman Daily Chronicle,* July 30, 1974.

15. Donald L. Clark, "Discrimination Suits: A Unique Settlement," *Educational Record* 58 (Summer, 1977): 234.
16. Trout, "MSU Women Seek Better Breaks."
17. Ibid.
18. Ibid.
19. Barry Hjort, telephone interview with author, June, 1984.
20. Ed Johnstone, interview with author, June, 1984.
21. Donald Clark, interview with author, March, 1983, and June, 1984.
22. Montana State University Faculty Handbook, p. 41.
23. Ibid., p. 47.
24. Carl B. Glasscock, *The War of the Copper Kings: Builders of Butte and Wolves of Wall Street* (New York: Grosset and Dunlap, 1966).
25. Judge W. D. Murray, interview with author, June, 1984.
26. After noting that his boyhood home looked more suitable for a Republican (actually a monarchist), the judge was asked how he turned out to be a liberal Democrat. "Good conscience" was his reply. Interview with author, June, 1984.
27. 401 U.S. 424 (1971).
28. 3 Employment Practices Decisions ¶¶ 8213, 6717 (9th Cir. 1971).
29. 457 F.2d 348 (5th Cir. 1972).
30. 495 F.2d 437 (5th Cir. 1974).
31. Hester v. Southern Ry., 497 F.2d 1374, 1381 (5th Cir. 1974).
32. Faro v. New York University, 502 F.2d 1229, 1232 (2d Cir. 1974).
33. Mecklenberg, 13 Employment Practices Decisions at 6494.
34. Mecklenberg, 13 Employment Practices Decisions at 6499.
35. Ray J. Aiken, "Legal Liabilities in Higher Education: Their Scope and Management," *Journal of College and University Law* 3 (November, 1977): 225.
36. Robert Wood, "Professionals at Bay: Managing Boston's Public Schools," *Journal of Policy Analysis and Management* 1, no. 4 (Summer, 1982): 454–68.
37. See chapter 8.
38. Clark, "Discrimination Suits," p. 235.
39. Clark has written a very useful participant observer description of the settlement process, which is summarized in the following pages. Although he did not have a traditional faculty background, Clark had a very strong commitment to faculty involvement. He wrote:

    [I]f collegiality is not to suffer—and my theme here is that such cases can be resolved with collegiality intact—then outsiders, particularly the typical labor-management arbitrator, certainly cannot come in and take over. So the solution is to find people who can represent the sides, but they must understand the university structure and the peculiarities of the university environment. ("Discrimination Suits," p. 235)

40. Report of the Ad Hoc Committee on Retroactive Promotion for Compliance with the Court Orders Concerning Sex Discrimination at Montana State University, May, 1977.
41. Report of the "equity team" for MSU compliance with court orders concerning

sex discrimination, September 1, 1976. As McIntosh had hoped, the money came from a special state appropriation and not from the regular university budget.

42. Fred Harcleroad, letter to Carl McIntosh, August 13, 1976, p. 2.

43. In part, this move was aimed at reducing the university's legal liability, but Don Clark, in a letter to Greg Morgan written a month after the decision, put another face on it: "[I]f there is one thing Mollie [Hatch, the affirmative action officer] has said would help her do her job, it was a Legal Counsel with Affirmative Action and Title IX experience. Thus, we set out to get one—not to hinder, but to help the affirmative action concept." March 17, 1976.

44. Charles S. Johnson and Arthur Hutchinson, "MSU Squabble Gives Rare Glimpse in System," *Sunday Missoulan,* March 28, 1976, p. 18.

45. *Bozeman Chronicle,* June 6, 1976, p. 1.

46. *Bozeman Chronicle,* July 7, 1977, p. 1.

47. Peter Caughey, "MSU Jobs Record Criticized," *Bozeman Chronicle,* November 15, 1981, p. 1.

48. Eric Wiltse, "MSU Female Faculty Lags," *Bozeman Chronicle,* January 29, 1981, p. 1.

49. *Bozeman Chronicle,* February 9, 1984, p. 13.

50. The only systematic data on this subject (and it covers only perceptions) can be found in the report of the Faculty Council Ad Hoc Committee on Sex Discrimination, June 1, 1982. Another commentator on the Mecklenberg case states that "the 'winners' . . . have received something short of equity." Joan Abramson, *Old Boys, New Women* (New York: Praeger Publishers, 1979), p. 120.

51. William Conklin, letter to William J. Tietz, August 29, 1978. Conklin detailed a series of instances in which the letter of the master plan requirements had not been carried out. One of the ambiguities of Judge Murray's order is that in addition to permanently enjoining the university from discrimination, it can be read as permanently requiring adherence to the stipulations of the master plan, which was aimed at creating a new governance system and solving other problems at a particular period in time.

Chapter 7
Rah Rah Rajender—Rah for the U of M

Rajender v. University of Minnesota[1]

This lawsuit began in 1971, but its direct effects will last until at least 1989. The incident that sparked the litigation was one of the scores of mundane personnel actions that occur annually in every large university. Yet when the case is finally concluded, the amount of money involved, the number of personnel decisions affected, and the scope of judicial intervention required will be unprecedented in academia.

The "Minnesota Rouser," whose climax is the last half of this chapter's title, is one of the handful of college songs with national recognition. Not only does its driving beat herald the university's teams in athletic contests, but it is used to salute Minnesota's many national politicians wherever they go.[2] Recently, however, the most rousing activity on the Minnesota campus has been not the victories of the Golden Gophers, but the legal triumph of Shyamala Rajender. Her lawsuit has had more impact on a university's personnel practices than any other case in the nation's history. But for Rajender herself, the outcome has had a strange and bitter meaning.

That the University of Minnesota (UM) could be challenged so effectively from within was unlikely. UM is not only the nation's seventh largest university system, but in many evaluations one of the best. With almost eighty thousand students, forty-five hundred faculty, and $100 million in federal research funding, the university is usually ranked about fifteenth to twentieth nationally in quality and prestige. Still, at that level of competition, positions are not secure, and some believe UM may be slipping.[3]

But although Minnesota may lose some of its academic stars to rising Sun Belt institutions[4] and more than its share of athletic contests to Big Ten foes, within the Land of Ten Thousand Lakes it is unrivaled. Unlike other states that separate land grant and liberal arts universities into competing systems or have spawned strong regional or urban campuses to challenge the traditional flagship campus or have old or prestigious private universities, there are no real competitors to the University of Minnesota in the state. Although there are fifty-seven other colleges in Minnesota, UM enrolls a majority of the state's undergraduate students and gives all the state's M.D. and Ph.D. degrees. The university sprawls across the Twin Cities of Minneapolis and St. Paul in two campuses covering over a thousand acres and encompassing half a billion dollars worth of buildings, but it also includes four other campuses

(Duluth, Morris, Crookston, and Waseca) and operates six agricultural extension stations.[5] Its annual budget approaches $800 million.

The symbiosis of university and state is more than a matter of size and scope; it reaches the spirit of what it means to be a Minnesotan. The university's charter in 1851 preceded statehood by six years. Though the Minnesota Territory was then on "the edge of civilization, the frontier rim of mid-America," the university's founders saw that "The children of the present are the citizens and rulers of the future, and upon their education depend the character and the destiny of our infant commonwealth."[6] To secure the institution's financial base, Congress provided a land grant of forty-six thousand acres. But after the panic of 1857, the university's status declined, and there were more cattle and turkeys than students housed in Old Main. Even worse, competitors in the private sector were created, and another public agricultural campus threatened to receive the Morrill Act designation. The university's friends in the legislature succeeded, however, in adding the Morrill grant to the previous land grant, and its public rival withered. A decade later the university had mapped out its mission as

> a federation of schools . . . embracing potentially all subjects of human practical interest; teaching always with reference to principle, occupying ever an attitude of investigation, knowing no favorite studies, at all times imbued with the scientific spirit.[7]

The cost might be expensive. The university's first president, William Watts Folwell, was clear about that, speaking in 1869 of the need for "millions" if the state would have "the University in its full proportions." But he noted that in the land grant tradition, "if the expenditure of say $20,000 could result in discovering but one species of apple, sure to thrive in Minnesota, no one would call that money ill-spent." Decades later UM horticulturalists gave us the Haraldsen apple.

As alma mater, she has nurtured the state's growth in other ways. In addition to fostering agricultural prosperity, the university has made considerable contributions to Minnesota's developing high-tech industries, its excellent health care system, and its burgeoning cultural reputation.[8] In return, it receives substantial state and corporate support, ranking consistently in the top five among all public institutions in private giving. Therefore, it is no surprise that few of the state's major political, business, or cultural leaders have been untouched by UM.

The university's state is a distinctive blend of conservative people and liberal attitudes. As adopted son Hubert Humphrey once said,

> There's a really great thing about Minnesotans. If you try to maintain the kind of honesty and morality they stand for—and it's pretty rigid—

they'll forgive any crazy ideas you may have. No matter how liberal. Most of the great liberal ideas of this nation came from Minnesotans.[9]

From the state's Red River valleys and Blue Earth counties farmers gave birth to the Grange in the nineteenth century, while their more urban neighbors spawned the Populist movement and the People's party. During World War I, Minnesotan Charles A. Lindbergh, father of the aviator, was a leading spokesman for the Progressives. About the same time, Arthur C. Townsley organized the nonpartisan League of Anti-War Socialists. From this fertile soil of Minnesota liberalism came the Farmer-Labor party, which in 1944 merged with the state's Democratic party. That union has produced a steady stream of liberal ideas and politicians.[10]

Still, the lifestyle of Minnesotans is not particularly liberal, say in the sense of Californians or New Yorkers. It is not really true that the Norwegian bachelor farmer of Garrison Keillor's "Prairie Home Companion" is the state's archetypal citizen (any more than Lake Woebegon reflects the dynamic Twin Cities), but Minnesota's ethnic and religious heritage is still very strong. This balance between conservative life-style and liberal politics is important. Although the university shapes the state in powerful ways, it cannot go very much beyond the existing social and political consensus, and it could not survive in a posture of antagonism.

Triggering Incident

Of all the 4 million persons living within Minnesota's borders in 1972, one of the least likely to disrupt university-state relations was Shyamala Rajender. It was even unlikely that she would be there. Rajender was born in Madras, a lovely tropical city nestled against the Bay of Bengal. Her family was upper class. Several uncles were lawyers, one was a judge, and her father was a magistrate. Rajender set out to become a chemist and graduated with a B.S. in that subject from Pachaippas College in 1949.

She wanted more training, however, and began considering graduate education in the United States. But where to go? She had a friend at the University of Wyoming and was offered some financial aid there; so she set out alone, landing in Laramie in January, 1960; the temperature was thirty-two degrees below zero. In the spring, her husband, a colonel in the Madras special constabulatory, and her son and daughter joined her.

At Wyoming she finished her master's degree in 1961 and her Ph.D. in 1965. The university then offered her a job as assistant professor, which she accepted. But there were problems in Laramie. It was too cold. There were few opportunities for her husband, who had also obtained a Ph.D.; and, as a scientist, she was ambitious to be in a larger institution. In 1966, she took a year's leave from Wyoming and accepted a one-year post-doctoral fellowship at the University of Minnesota. Her sponsor was Rufus Lumry, a distinguished chemist whose research was in the area of molecular descriptions of protein. After the first year, Lumry asked her to stay a second. It was a serious decision. In order to accept, she resigned from Wyoming, and her husband found a job teaching business administration at St. Cloud State. Another year went by, and a third post-doc was offered. Although she had to take it, she was beginning to be anxious about finding a permanent position. She was now appearing as second author on some of Lumry's scientific papers, but she was not being interviewed for regular faculty positions at the University of Minnesota. Nor did Lumry's attempts to place her at other reputable institutions bear fruit, despite his enthusiastic reference letters. In 1969, Rajender was hired as a temporary (non–tenure track) assistant professor, but the following year that position was lost due to retrenchment. Again, she was not interviewed for any of the permanent positions available.

The UM chemistry department Rajender sought to join was a very substantial enterprise. It was created in 1870, and at one point it was a separate school, including pharmacy as well as chemical engineering. Although today it has only departmental status, chemistry's size, status, and wealth give it a certain feudal independence among university fiefdoms. Its current glossy, sixty-two-page recruiting brochure for graduate students contains the statement "Our department has a long and illustrious history and a distinguished faculty." Self-conferred or not, the accolade is true. Among the many prominent scientists connected with the department are two Nobel Prize winners, one a faculty member and one an alumnus. Currently, its forty-one members obtain federal and commercial grants of almost $4 million a year and award about twenty Ph.D. degrees annually.

Of the 180 graduate chemistry departments in the United States, how does one such as Minnesota's achieve such prominence? There are probably three keys. The first is to hire and tenure carefully. Since every person is expected to be competitive in obtaining external research grants, the screening process is very rigorous. The second is to use that external income to fund the best graduate and post-doctoral students and the finest state-of-the-art instrumentation. Combining professorial imagination with such students and equipment can create a series of laboratories competitive with the most productive in the world. The third step is to place one's graduates in the best schools and laboratories, thus ensuring the reputation of the department and the continuing cycle of dollars and students. It was calculated in 1984 that one of the most distinguished members of the department, Izaak Maurits Kolthoff, author of 1,000 papers in analytical chemistry, had directed 51 Minnesota chemistry Ph.D.'s, who had then produced some 1,073 Ph.D. descendants.[11]

Maintaining a department of this quality and magnitude is by no means a sure thing. Other academic institutions and industrial firms are constantly poised to pick off a dissatisfied professor. On the other hand, if the department makes one or two poor tenure decisions, an entire field can go dim for a decade or more. Always there has to be concern for the intangibles of status and reputation.

Perception of Alleged Discrimination

The department was not exactly in trouble in the late sixties, but it was worried. After World War II, chemistry at UM was ranked ninth in the country, but by 1968, a new survey showed it to be only twentieth. A common response to such slippage is to go outside the university to pick a strong new chair. In this instance, the university chose Robert Hexter, who was recruited from Carnegie-Mellon. Hexter's principal task was to centralize and upgrade the department and to enforce other university policies, one of which was affirmative action. Hexter appointed himself affirmative action officer, but it is fair to say he was not an enthusiast. Shortly after his arrival, he received a letter from Dartmouth inquiring whether UM had any candidates for a position the college had available. As was conventional for the period, the letter was worded only in the masculine pronoun and ended with "Thank you for helping us find the right man." Hexter wrote back to Dartmouth commenting on what happened after its recruitment letter was posted.

> Your letter of December 17, 1969 has attracted considerable attention in these parts. In these days of protest, it will probably come as no surprise to you that the distribution of your letter within this Department precipitated the visit to my office of three female post-doctoral fellows (sic), as self-appointed defenders of their sex.
>
> After rising to the defense of your use of the English language (Webster: "1. A member of the human race."), I promised the local ladies that I would write to you in their behalf for a clarification, even though I consider it to be unnecessary.[12]

One of the "local ladies" was Shyamala Rajender.

Among Hexter's early tasks was recruiting for nine positions. Letters were sent to more than 100 "distinguished institutions at home and abroad." Open advertisement for academic jobs was not a common practice in those days. The letters produced 150 applications. Thirteen persons were interviewed "two days each by the entire faculty"; 5 persons were eventually hired. Only 2 of the 150 applicants were women; a black male was appointed. One of 2 female applicants was Rajender, but the recruitment committee ranked her as suitable only for a temporary position.

In seeking permanent appointment, Rajender had several liabilities. First,

UM would not ordinarily turn to the University of Wyoming chemistry program for its tenure track positions. Second, although Lumry was willing to recommend her to such places as MIT, universities are reluctant to hire their own graduates or post-docs. Finally, the department had strong status needs in filling those appointments, and in that era few female academics could supply those needs. In 1965, Theodore Caplow and Reese McGee wrote their classic study, *The Academic Marketplace*. The major departments, they found, were very status driven in making employment decisions, and "[w]omen tend to be discriminated against in the academic profession not because they have low prestige but because they are outside the prestige system altogether."[13]

In this environment, Rajender continued to press for a tenure track appointment, but without success. When the department came up short in its 1969 recruiting efforts, they turned to her to fill the teaching gap as a temporary assistant professor. In 1970, a similar situation arose. Of the 272 outside applicants, none was a woman. At the close of recruiting, the department still had teaching needs, and Rajender was given another one-year appointment. In April, 1971, she applied again for a regular appointment in bioanalytical chemistry but again she was not successful.

In the meantime, other difficulties had arisen. Although she continued to work in Lumry's lab, as her attention moved toward teaching, other post-docs began to have a more central place in its work. Her role as a researcher seemed in jeopardy. Nor was her future even as a temporary faculty secure: questions had been raised about her teaching ability.

The idea that she might be a victim of discrimination was not immediately apparent to Rajender. She did not consider herself a feminist or a political person of any kind. At Wyoming, she had never encountered anything that seemed to be sex discrimination. But at Minnesota, she began to be bumped around a lot, was moved involuntarily to four different offices in two years, and was not getting what she perceived as adequate laboratory space, summer research support, or secretarial services. Was it discrimination or just that she was the low person on a very elite totem pole?

After a time the answer seemed clear. One of her earliest memories was of male faculty frequently lunching with male post-docs at the Campus Club (itself not open to females as full members until 1968) but never inviting female post-docs. To force the issue, one day she and the other two female post-docs invited themselves to a lunch table of male faculty. As she remembers it, an absolute silence came over the table, and one by one the males drifted away without any meaningful conversation. Later, when she had the temporary assistant professor's position and could attend faculty gatherings, she remembers meetings where males said openly that hiring a woman would "ruin the department's image," because her inevitable inability to attract grants and graduate students would lower the department's quality.

The department had apparently acted on that premise. In its 102-year history, it had had only one female tenured member. She had been hired during World War I, when few men were available, and kept on in a temporary basis until World War II, when the shortage arose again. Seizing the advantage, she insisted that if she was going to do the work, she should be tenured. The department complied in 1942. Four years later she retired, after a career of more than three decades at the university.

The more Rajender investigated the situation, the more she became convinced that her problem was sex discrimination. She was on good personal terms with everyone in the department. Her mentor, Lumry, had assured her when she complained about her (and his) inability to find a full-time position for her that he was willing to support her in his laboratory "forever." But after surveying the situation, she concluded that although nationally 8 percent of the new chemistry Ph.D.'s in 1970 went to females, when it came to regular faculty positions "there is little doubt that women were kept out of the academic segment of the profession deliberately."[14]

There was one final incident. Rajender had applied to the Research Foundation in Minnesota for a grant to do some investigation on her own. The foundation liked the proposal but said that it was not its policy to fund research by persons only temporarily employed at the university. At that point, Lumry wrote a letter for her assuring the foundation that Rajender was a good researcher and would be at the University for a long time in his laboratory. But he conceded that

> the problem in providing much deserved research support for her is that she does not now and is not likely to fall into a regular teaching position at the University. In ability, she competes well with others whom we have interviewed in recent years. Nor is her age important since she already has as much research production behind her as many men whose careers have been devoted to research and teaching. If she were an obvious star, I think we could avoid male prejudice, but under the circumstances she is really disadvantaged—as a woman—at this University.[15]

The problem now seemed clear to Rajender. But what to do? She had no experience in women's rights or advocacy or the university bureaucracy. She was not even a citizen.[16]

Problem Evaluation and Informal Consultation

Even before the faculty amendments to the Civil Rights Act and the Equal Pay Act and the passage of Title IX had been enacted, the University of Minnesota had begun to respond to its own liberal instincts and those of the state it served. In 1968, the regents' new policy on equal employment opportunity declared, "The University's Civil Service policy commitment is to take affirmative action to hire and promote disadvantaged persons wherever there is a reasonable possibility of competent performance."[17] Taking risks to hire "qualifiable persons" is one thing at the civil service level but another in faculty positions. Even so, in 1971 the University Senate Committee on Faculty Affairs reported that

> if a unit of the University persistently fails to correct existing inequities in regard to women or ethnic minorities and is unable to demonstrate that the reasons for its failure are beyond its control, all of its personnel decisions should become subject to college level or central administration review until such time as the unit appears capable of eliminating discrimination by itself.[18]

That same year the UM administration informed all departments that

> in the absence of evidence that the hiring unit already had achieved a reasonable balance in its minorities and women's employment pattern, vacancies should be opened first to qualified minorities or women's candidates. . . . If good faith efforts to recruit qualified minority or women applicants fail, the position may be filled in the normal manner. Without such consideration and efforts, vacancies may not be filled.[19]

Chemistry was not convinced. Hexter wrote to his dean in February, 1971,

> In the face of the situation in Chemistry where so few applications [2 out of 422 in 1971 and 1972] are received from women, after wide broadcasting of the existence of these positions, we do not see where we can take any further affirmative action.[20]

But the situation of women on the UM campus was beginning to receive more and more attention. A women's advisory group, the Committee for University Women's Progress, had been formed. Rajender had not been involved initially, but in 1971 she began to talk to members about her problem and joined the group. In addition, the university president had appointed a task force on the status of women. Rajender consulted the chair of the task force, who advised her to talk to a female administrative assistant to the vice-president for academic affairs, since there was not yet an equal employment opportunity officer at Minnesota at that time. The assistant was shocked at the content of Lumry's letter to the research foundation and suggested that she would like to take Rajender's complaint to the Ad Hoc Committee on Discrimination, which had just been created. It would be a case of first impression for the new committee, but a very good test. Rajender was still reluctant. Her one-year contract for 1971–72 had not yet been offered, and she feared retaliation. But the administrative assistant assured her that if she filed a charge she would be protected for at least one more year, while the grievance was processed. Rajender agreed. The assistant then asked the vice-president to call the chemistry department and tell chairman Hexter to renew Rajender's contract for another year and to give her every consideration for any permanent position.

Putting her fate in the hands of the newly formed ad hoc committee was an uncertain business, so to protect herself further, Rajender also filed a sex and ethnic discrimination complaint with HEW. She did not intend to let the matter die.

Use of Internal Remedies

Like most universities in that era, UM did not have a specific structure for responding to discrimination charges. The existing faculty grievance committees were traditionally oriented toward academic freedom and protection of tenure issues. Nevertheless, the number of discrimination complaints was increasing, and the university had to respond. There were generally two choices. The mandates of the traditional grievance committee could be expanded to take advantage of their experience and status, or a new structure could be set up that was particularly concerned with discrimination. The choice was more than a matter of workload. The traditional committees were usually dominated by senior, AAUP-type white males, while discrimination committees were often chosen to reflect the needs of the newer and more junior female and minority constituencies. In handling complaints of bias, moreover, the traditional committees usually saw themselves as guardians of due process, which, if too rigidly observed, tends to protect the status quo, while the discrimination committees often viewed themselves as advocates of equality, which, if too zealously pursued, undermines merit. Minnesota decided on the latter alternative, and its committee contained five women and five men, also carefully balanced between faculty and civil service.

The ad hoc committee began its proceedings in November, 1971, by interviewing Rajender and several chemistry department faculty. A month later they gave the university president, Malcolm Moos a unanimous report. It affirmed that Rajender had been discriminated against on the basis of sex and possibly national origin. Regarding the issue of scholarship, the committee noted the excellent references Lumry had written for her. Although it found quality of teaching more difficult to establish, it discounted critical materials because there appeared to be some evidence of prejudice against Indians as chemistry teachers and because she had never been formally evaluated.

The chemistry department had a meeting about the response it should make.[21] One professor sympathetic to Rajender urged the department to give her the tenure track position and then judge her performance on the merits at tenure time. But the consensus was that that would be giving in to pressure and that the department could get administration support if it held firm.

Chemistry then began to use its formidable political clout on campus to reverse the decision. A student who had previously complained about Rajender's teaching was asked to put his comments into writing. The student responded by creating a hostile petition eventually signed by many of his colleagues. The senior faculty member who had been in charge of the general chemistry section for twenty years and who had earned a national reputation for that work was asked to state in written form the criticism of Rajender's teaching he had previously voiced. Her mentor, Lumry, began to back away from his previous glowing endorsement of her research skills.

But the central rebuttal was Hexter's nine-page, single-spaced letter to the administration summarizing the department's position. In the letter, he criticized the ad hoc committee's findings and Rajender's performance, defended the quality of the department's new hires, and discussed its attitude toward affirmative action. Hexter challenged the committee's findings that Rajender had been treated unfairly or irregularly in any way with regard to lab space or funding. He also denied any unfair treatment in her relationship to her mentor. The committee had found that the chemistry department "permitted Dr. Rajender's sponsor to be unduly proprietary of her time and professional aspirations." But the department saw the mentor–post-doc relationship as a part of the tradition of academic freedom. Hexter wrote, "While the system has obvious dangers, to do less would seriously restrict freedom, including that of inquiry. It is this freedom that has enabled American chemistry departments to surpass those of Europe and we are certainly not inclined to relinquish it."[22]

With regard to teaching, he described classroom visitations and discussions about teaching improvement with her and concluded: "While senior faculty who have had some exposure to Indian English may find hers clear, this is not necessarily true for the University of Minnesota freshman meeting his first Indian instructor."[23]

Particularly irritating to Hexter, since no chemists were members, was the committee's assertion that "some of the recent male appointees in the department, although competent and showing promise, are not necessarily outstandingly superior."[24]

Those were his recruits. He noted that the eleven men he hired had published about one hundred papers in three years and concluded, "Dr. Rajender is simply not in this league."

The end of the rebuttal contained the chair's view of the role of affirmative action in the Rajender case.

> Dr. Rajender hasn't been discriminated against. She was judged and found not qualified. If, as you say, quality is to be maintained, it must be left to the peers within each field to be judged. There is no question that women have been discriminated against by society, in general. But we at the University must make an important decision. If our prime goal is to be excellent (which was my assumption as well as instruction), we must insist on that and only that. If instead, we seek immediate redress of past injustice, we then require affirmative action with its necessary sacrifice of excellence, at least for the immediate future. We cannot have both.[25]

He then concluded that in the face of the chemistry department's perception of Rajender's inadequate qualifications, "I predict a most serious lack of collegiability—*toward her*—if she is appointed."[26]

In this exchange, Rajender was a spectator. She was not shown a copy of the committee response nor asked to comment.

The problem then landed on Malcolm Moos's desk. Moos had been UM president for four years, after a career as a political scientist and presidential speech writer. He was a Republican, but in the liberal Harold Stassen Minnesota tradition, and a believer in civil rights.

The conflict placed the president in a difficult position. On the one hand, a committee he had appointed had found that the rights of a lowly temporary assistant professor had been violated by a department with a very poor affirmative action record. On the other hand, a strong new department chairman, whom Moos had also appointed with the charge to reenergize one of the university's major departments, was insisting that his action in the Rajender case was defensible in the interests of preserving academic quality. Moos decided not to support either side. According to the university's press release on the matter,

> Moos overruled the charge of individual discrimination, stating that the department appeared to look only at candidates' qualifications when filling positions. He did agree, however, that the department, which has not hired a woman for a permanent teaching appointment in thirty years, did show a pattern of discrimination against women.[27]

It was a statement that would come back to haunt Moos. By denying the specific claims of a potential plaintiff but affirming the general validity of her charge, he had sown the seeds of the lawsuit.

The president's position caused a considerable controversy on the campus. For the first time, the campus newspaper, the *Minnesota Daily,* began to write about the case, causing a flurry of letters from women about sex discrimination at UM. The ad hoc committee went as a group to see Moos, complaining that while he had seen fit to consult with the chemistry department before overturning their decision, he had not consulted them. When the president stood firm, the committee's chair resigned. Moos then decided to turn the matter over to the senate judicial committee, UM's traditional faculty grievance body. The ad hoc committee decision, which was not based on a full evidentiary hearing, was to be regarded only as a finding of probable cause. The final determination would be by the judicial committee.

The judicial committee used a formal adversary process, and the university offered to provide Rajender with an attorney (as she understood it, at their expense). She did not meet with the lawyer until two days before the hearing. The committee normally had five members, but its female chair had been a member of the ad hoc committee and therefore disqualified herself. After two days of examining witnesses and consulting with the academic vice-president who attended the sessions, the committee split in half. Two members found the department's explanation for its decision persuasive and believed its Rajender decisions to have been made on the merits. Two others were disturbed about some of the discriminatory implications in the departmental letter and other documents. But both sides agreed on the finding that Rajender did not prove that discrimination was the *only* basis for refusing her a tenure track position. Unlike the civil rights tradition, where once a prima facie case is established the burden shifts to the defense, this proceeding, following common practice for tenure issues, placed the burden at all times on the claimant.[28]

Under those circumstances, Moos wrote Rajender that he was agreeing with the judicial committee. Her contract would expire in June, 1972. Rajender's situation was becoming increasingly difficult. She had obtained United States citizenship in 1971, and there was no thought of going back to India. No offers from other universities to teach chemistry were forthcoming. Despite all this controversy, Lumry had offered her another year as a postdoc, but she was now forty-five, and she wanted a more independent career. She decided she had to broaden the controversy.

In June, 1972, she filed formal complaints with the Minnesota Human Rights Department, the regional office of HEW, and EEOC. But she had one last chance within the university—the regents. In July, she wrote Moos to request a hearing before the board of regents. Since Minnesota's constitution gives the university autonomy in the management of its internal affairs, the regents are the link between the public and the academy. The legislature chooses twelve regents, one from each of the state's congressional districts and four at large. The job is a prestigious and occasionally time-consuming, unpaid avocation.

Although a last resort appeal to an institution's governing board is commonplace in American higher education, it is rarely effective. Regents are most comfortable with ceremonial occasions, long-range planning, major budget reviews, and top administrative appointments. Personnel conflicts involving temporary assistant professors are ordinarily beneath their purview. Since the president had already ruled on the matter, a contrary decision by the regents would be tantamount to a no-confidence vote. Further, the significance of a sex discrimination charge in a university was not fully apparent in 1972. So, not very surprisingly, the regents decided not to give Rajender the hearing she had requested. A committee did, however, review the papers given to them and voted to affirm Moos's decision. No more appeals were available within the university.

Rajender continued to seek a forum outside. She began to correspond frequently with HEW and EEOC. She sent letters to all major Minnesota politicians and HEW Secretary Caspar Weinberger. But that was all symbolic activity. What she wanted to do was to begin a formal legal action against the university. Then in March, 1973, the Minnesota Human Rights Department, after investigating, issued a formal finding of probable cause that she had been a victim of discrimination. The matter would no longer stay within the university.

Settlement or Litigation Decision

The Human Rights Department letter was the good news. The bad news was that the department had a two-year backlog and was not likely to take any action before then. With no academic job in sight, Rajender couldn't wait. What she wanted was a right-to-sue letter from EEOC to move the issue into a federal court. For that she realized she needed a lawyer. Incredibly, except for the brief and abortive use of an attorney when she went before the university judicial committee, Rajender had managed the almost two years of appeals without one.

Out of the hundreds of attorneys in the Twin Cities, whom should she pick? She knew none personally. Earlier she had attended a meeting of the Women's Equity Action League, an organization she had now joined, and heard lawyer Ellen Dresselhuis, its chair, speak on sex discrimination. A feminist lawyer seemed appropriate, but in that era the lawsuit Rajender proposed was novel. Dresselhuis was a sole practitioner and would not take the case on a contingency basis. Rajender, therefore, had to come up with a substantial sum (about 75 percent of her previous year's salary) as a retainer.

EEOC did send a right-to-sue letter, but the complaint had to be filed in ninety days. When it was filed, it charged Moos, Hexter, and the regents with discrimination against Rajender on the basis of sex and national origin, and demanded a jury trial. It asked the court to give her a

> permanent position as Assistant Professor, back pay, compensation for interruption of career, loss of professional standing and reputation, and her physical and mental pain and anguish in the amount of $500,000; punitive damages of $250,000; and attorney fees.

The complaint, based on Civil Rights Act sections 1983 and 1985, modern Executive Orders 11,141 and 11,246, and Title VII, was narrowly and somewhat vaguely drawn, and the university immediately moved to have it dismissed for failing to specify a proper cause of action. At that point, Rajender contacted an EEOC Washington attorney, who flew to Minneapolis to argue against dismissal. Judge Miles Lord disallowed the university's petition, but the complaint was redrafted.

Gradually, Rajender became dissatisfied with her attorney. She felt Dresselhuis was not aggressive enough in developing the facts of the case. The last straw was when the chair of the ad hoc committee died after a prolonged struggle against cancer, before Dresselhuis could take her deposition.

In 1975, fifteen months after the original complaint was filed, Rajender made a trip to the Chicago EEOC office to seek advice about a new lawyer. EEOC knew a young attorney, Paul Sprenger, who had been working with them in a class action against the Minnesota Mining and Manufacturing Company (3M). Sprenger agreed to examine the case materials and immediately saw their potential as a class action. Furthermore, he was willing to take the case on a contingency basis and to advance costs. Rajender believed Sprenger's commitment was pragmatic rather than ideological, and the documents made the case seem like a winner.

Sprenger's law firm, Johnson and Sands, was a substantial firm with about fifteen lawyers, and he was a rising star who had negotiated a $4.5 million settlement in the discrimination suit against 3M. Now, with another young lawyer in the firm, Terry Cosgrove, he set out to create pressure for another settlement by documenting his case and escalating his legal tactics. But first there was an unexpected problem with Dresselhuis. She claimed she had invested considerable time in drafting and responding to interrogatories and was unwilling to give Sprenger the papers unless he paid her $75,000. Sprenger threatened to take the matter to Judge Lord, but then the papers were transferred on the understanding that Dresselhuis could apply to the court for attorney fees if Rajender was successful.

To test the waters, Sprenger offered the university a settlement for

$50,000. But the university did not even respond, as it had previously ignored Dresselhuis's offer of $35,000. Sprenger then amended the complaint in September, 1975, to make it a class action on behalf of all academic, nonstudent employees of the University of Minnesota.

The heat was turned up, but it takes a long time to develop a class action suit. So again in June, 1977, Sprenger proposed a settlement, although on broader grounds. Again the university turned it down. Sprenger began to realize that the class would have to be certified before any serious settlement negotiation could take place.

As the university prepared to respond, it faced a choice of legal representation. Its in-house counsel had been used mostly for routine legal problems and had limited trial experience. Since UM has constitutionally autonomous status, the state attorney general does not represent it in litigation. So, right after it received Rajender's complaint, a large downtown law firm, Leonard, Street and Deinard, was chosen, and Charles Mays, an experienced trial attorney, was selected to handle the defense.

After forcing the original complaint to be amended, Mays focused on the jurisdictional issues. The University of Minnesota, he argued, was protected by the Eleventh Amendment from lawsuits against it in federal courts, and the Executive Orders did not permit private parties to bring actions. He also tried to limit plaintiff's access to university data on grounds of privacy. But in December, 1973, the judge overruled defendant's objections to releasing university data, although such material was to be stamped confidential and was not to be given to anyone other than the plaintiff's attorney.[29] The university set the price of copying material at twenty cents a page, a figure it later had cause to regret. Mays did win other procedural points. In January, 1976, there was a stipulation dismissing the regents as individual defendants, though the board collectively could and would be sued. Also, Sprenger was forbidden to continue soliciting for additional class members.

The first critical task for the defense was to blunt Sprenger's attempt to get a class certified. Initially, it appeared that they would succeed. There was a question about Rajender's status as an appropriate representative of the class. Rajender's principal claim of discrimination involved events that had occurred before March 24, 1972, when Title VII was amended to cover all university faculty. And as the case dragged on, she had not been employed by the university for several years. The case had been thoroughly reviewed by university officials and was in any event arguably unique. Most of all, the university emphasized that there was no evidence that any real class of plaintiffs existed because no other women had stepped forward to join the suit. Asking for dismissal, Mays noted that the last person who got away with begging a class of one was Richard Nixon, and Shyamala Rajender should not be given such a status.

Sprenger felt vulnerable here. He and Rajender tried hard to find other plaintiffs, but none was forthcoming. Later, when he addressed various women's groups, he begged.

You don't have to join suit. You don't have to put your name to it. You don't have to testify. We realize you are scared. You don't know what the outcome of the case will be. But at least put some warm bodies in the courtroom so that when the judge looks up, there are a few women out there who are interested in the case. So when he says, "Do you have the same problems?", you can at least nod.[30]

Many agreed they would attend, but in fact none did.

Litigation Preparation

But the judge did not need a court full of women to convince him. In February, 1978, he ruled that a class did exist. In April he provided a twelve-page opinion explaining his decision and scheduled a five-day pilot trial. It was clear that the judge wanted to play an unusually aggressive role in the development of the litigation.

The federal courthouse in Minneapolis is 1950s Eisenhower-gray architecture, but there is nothing gray about Judge Miles Lord. Indeed, the press's adjectives for him almost always have been "colorful," followed by "controversial." He has been good copy in the Twin Cities for over three decades. His current newspaper names are "his grace," "his eminence," and "the warrior judge," but Lord prefers the sobriquet his old friend Hubert Humphrey gave him, "the people's judge," and it does seem the most explanatory.[31]

Judge Lord, the son of a lumberman on Minnesota's Mesabi Iron Range, had to struggle for his education. One reporter wrote,

As a college student, he worked from 1 to 5 p.m. as a janitor, from 6 to 10 p.m. as a postal clerk, and from 11 p.m. to 7 a.m. as a night watchman. He regarded sleep as a Republican conspiracy to be viewed skeptically.[32]

At UM Law School, he began to make friends in the Democrat-Farmer Labor (DFL) party hierarchy, which would eventually propel him to three elected terms as Minnesota attorney general. In 1966 the party got him a coveted federal judgeship appointment from Lyndon Johnson, but he always had one eye on a United States Senate seat.

On the bench, he has been described as "an unforgiving, unregenerate, unabashed Prairie Prophet of the old school as well as a fervent new-school environmentalist."[33] This ideology has brought him into fierce confrontations, particularly with pharmaceutical and mining corporations and with state and federal officials who wanted to cut food stamps and welfare checks. But it also made him visible and popular. In 1976 a statewide poll about him (itself an unusual exercise regarding a federal judge) found five times as many Minnesotans approved his performance as disapproved.[34]

The controversy over Judge Lord is not just about his ideology but also over his style. As one reporter described it:

> The man in the black robes does not just sit on the bench, he prowls it, sometimes moving from one chair to another, like a restless animal waiting to leap. He trades verbal jabs with lawyers, comments on new arrivals in the courtroom, regales spectators with off-the-cuff remarks that range from the amusing to the outlandish, and at times he seems to be directing a theatrical production instead of running a federal courtroom.[35]

There is direction to the production. Lord argues that he tries to "help" some attorneys by asking questions. "It evens out the sides if I look out at the litigants and I ask are they rich and powerful, or are they poor and oppressed?"[36] Sometimes the judge has gone too far. In one of his most important cases, *Reserve Mining v. Environmental Protection Agency,* the corporation appealed to the Eighth Circuit to have him recused, although the trial had already begun. The court of appeals agreed in unusually harsh language:

> Judge Lord seems to have shed the robe of the judge and to have assumed the mantle of the advocate. The court thus becomes lawyer, witness and judge in the same proceeding, and abandons the greatest virtue of a fair and conscientious judge—impartiality. . . .
>
>   . . . Our system of government is premised upon subservience to the rule of law. If a judge in the exercise of judicial power loses sight of these principles, the result is autocratic rule by lawless judicial action.[37]

In 1980, the *American Lawyer* magazine named Judge Lord as one of the eleven worst judges in the country.[38] But the next year the Association of Trial Lawyers of America (the plaintiffs' bar) gave him their award as the best federal trial judge. The citation commended him

> for being a staunch protector of the rights of the consumer, the environment, the worker, the citizen, and minorities; and for being in the forefront of judicial innovation, to insure that rights are protected and not forfeited or lost in a procedural morass.[39]

For both sides in the *Rajender* case, the reputation and character of Judge Lord was a major consideration as the state's university confronted the Indian immigrant in the federal court.

There are four federal judges in Minneapolis, so it was just a matter of luck that the case landed on Lord's docket. But the luck of that draw was extremely important. In addition to Judge Lord's general reputation and style, the university had specific reasons to be wary in trying its case before him. In 1971, prior to the enactment of Title IX, the judge had made a landmark sex discrimination decision by ruling that Minnesota high school girls had to be permitted participation on boy's tennis and cross-country teams if these sports were not otherwise available to girls.[40] A few years later, he presided over a large sex discrimination settlement involving the United States Fidelity and Guarantee Corporation by appointing special masters to oversee the integration of job categories in the company. Indeed, his activist temperament and liberal ideology were so well known that some corporations used the tactic of hiring his son-in-law's law firm so that Lord could not hear the case. But UM decided not to try to avoid him.

The plaintiffs were more sensitive to having the right judge. Lord is the senior district court judge and so assigns cases. After he had presided over preliminary rulings, he routinely assigned the trial to another judge. But the plantiffs personally confronted him and asked him to resume his role in the case, and he did.

In his ruling certifying the class, Judge Lord defined it as consisting of "approximately 1300 current female academic employees and all females, past, present, and future applicants for academic, non-student positions." Though Rajender's claim was factually unique, the judge found that it satisfied the requirement of commonality because the "central University administration exercises considerable control over each employment decision," including hers and those of all other members of the class. Furthermore, she had identified nine other women who had allegedly suffered sex discrimination, even though they were not formal parties. Most important, the judge cited and seemed impressed by the university's own statistics that showed the standard pattern in American higher education, in which women clustered at the bottom of the rank pyramid and were paid less than men in each rank.[41]

	Male	Female	Percentage Difference between Men's and Women's Median Salaries
Professors	892	58	11
Associate Professors	784	88	10
Assistant Professors	857	243	9
Instructors	542	371	12

Such a statistical disparity in favor of men, the judge found, necessarily implies sex discrimination and is a common threat to all past and potential women applicants. Without quite saying so, Lord appeared to accept fully plaintiff's prima facie case, and the burden shifted heavily to the defense.

Pretrial Impacts

The litigation process had so far had a devastating impact on Shyamala Rajender. Contrary to her impression, the university had decided not to pay for the attorney she used at the senate judicial committee. That cost her three to four thousand dollars. Then she had to raise another seventy-five hundred dollars to pay Ellen Dresselhuis. That required a bank loan, but in addition, she did what Indian women always have done in a crisis—she sold the gold jewelry she had brought with her to the United States. Now there was another lawyer to worry about and more court costs.

Even worse, her career as a scientist seemed shattered. When she continued to press her claims within the university, she received calls from top administrators warning her about the problem she was creating for them and herself as this matter became more and more public. But with a Ph.D., some publications, three post-docs, and three years teaching in a prestigious department, she thought a chemistry position would be available somewhere.

But it was not. She recalls:

> When this was going on, I would apply to other institutions even outside of Minnesota. When they saw my credentials, they would be very interested until they started making phone calls and finding out who I was and what I was doing. All of a sudden I had the image of being a trouble-maker and a rabble rouser. This kind of situation I came up against time and time again.[42]

After friends in other departments confirmed that the lawsuit had placed a "don't touch" sign on her, Rajender knew she must find another profession. One of her first offers was the position of affirmative action officer for the Minnesota state college system. Whether they were truly taken by her credentials or just interested in sticking a symbolic needle into the prestigious University of Minnesota by hiring its legal adversary is not known, but the job didn't work out. After a year, she began to feel it was a token position with no real power and resigned. In the interim, Rajender entered Hamline University Law School. Three years later she obtained her J.D., graduating at the top of her class, but she found practice difficult. She feels that her notoriety made the big firms uninterested in her, and after she hung out her own shingle it appeared it would take a long time to build up a successful solo practice.

So she and her husband migrated to California, where he found a position at San Francisco State University and she joined a law firm. By the time of the trial she had passed both the Minnesota and California bar examinations and, later, the patent bar, all on the first attempt. The immigrant chemist had become a much more formidable legal opponent.

But she had also paid a high price. At her age it was hard to change careers. And there was a heavy social cost. She remembers:

Even in the Chemistry Department I had lots of friends, very close friends, people that we socialized with, people that came to our house practically every other week or we went to their house for gourmet club. After it started, gradually they started drifting away and not having anything to do with me because having any friendship with me would be construed as being in sympathy with my position. Some were even openly hostile.

. . . All of the people who knew facts which would help me all of a sudden found their memories fading. It happened even with women not just men.[43]

One of her friends in the department said,

I sympathize with you but I have an obligation to protect the department, because I am a part of the department and you are not. But I will not lie either for you or for them.

Finally, she recalls:

Subtle pressures were put on my husband. "Why is she pursuing this? It could affect your career." He felt a little intimidated, but he said you do what you think is right and we are all 100% behind you. Don't worry about what they are doing to us; we'll take care of ourselves. I got a lot of support from my family. If I hadn't had that support . . . [She then discusses the family pressures which she believed led another prominent plaintiff to drop her case]. Everybody else was ridiculing, thinking what I was doing was silly and stupid, that I was one of those activist, bra-burning feminists who would cry foul at everything and didn't have anything much to go on. It was just a figment of my imagination and I would be thrown out on my face by the court.[44]

In the meantime, two of her adversaries, Hexter and Moos, resigned under fire, but people come and go in major administrative positions in universities all the time, and one needs to be careful not to confuse chronological sequence with cause and effect. During the trial Hexter was asked about the chairmanship.

> Q. Now is it fair to say that you left the Chairmanship under pressure. . . . Is that a fair characterization of what happened?

> A. Well, I've thought a lot about my decision at that time, both before and after, and I think the decision was a mutual one in which both the department and myself decided that they would be better served with new leadership.

When Sprenger pressed by asking about the lengthy faculty meeting on Hexter's chairmanship, Judge Lord interrupted and went off the record.
When they returned on the record, Sprenger asked point blank:

> I'd like to ask Dr. Hexter whether or not his affirmative action program—or lack of it—or his treatment of Shyamala Rajender had anything to do with his resignation.

> A. Absolutely not.

> Q. In other words when the department looked at that, they approved it?

> A. I believe so.

> Q. And they did look at it?

> A. I don't know that.[45]

Other departmental members confirm that Rajender was not the issue that ended Hexter's chairmanship. He had been given the difficult task of welding into a single department four divisions that had had considerable autonomy, even to the point of granting four separate Ph.D. programs. It was a job that made enemies, and opinions differ about how well he did it. Since Hexter came in 1969, the department has had five different chairs, and former occupants of that position acknowledge that the department is hard on its leaders, as they try to overcome the old divisional structure. It is also conceded that the paperwork created by the *Rajender* case generally and the climate of suspicion in which chemistry specifically functioned made the chairmanship doubly difficult.

Did the department approve of Hexter's handling of the Rajender controversy? The appointment decisions were made routinely by departmental consensus. But after the lawsuit was filed, the department, despite the bombshells of publicity on the case, never met to consider it. Members were constantly surprised at the litigation developments. Some believe that was a consequence of Hexter's tight administrative style (and after all, he was the named plaintiff); others acknowledge that it takes a lot to get chemists out of their labs.

Moos's presidency came to a conclusion in 1974, but he had resigned under pressure a year earlier. His last years at the university had not been happy ones.[46] After leaving Minnesota, he spent a year trying to rescue the Center for the Study of Democratic Institutions in Santa Barbara, but it was difficult to keep that organization afloat. When he came back to the Twin Cities, he made a quixotic effort to obtain the Republican senatorial nomination. By the time of the trial in 1978, he was, in his own words, "unemployed."

He died in 1982 alone in a cabin in northern Minnesota, estranged from his family and from the university he once served. Since he could not be interviewed, we cannot know the impact the case had on him. Presidents confront a lot of crises, and in the late sixties, Moos faced all the difficult campus upheavals—Vietnam, Black Power, and others. But in one of the last things he wrote before his death, he said:

> Litigation has spread like fire through universities. The result is an expansion of legal staffs at nearly every college and university, with the added expenses that go along. . . . What is especially costly is that the courts frequently place the burden of proof on the defendant, or university. This can sometimes cause such large legal costs and administrative and faculty time lost that several universities have decided to settle handsomely outside of court to avoid the much larger expense of contesting the case, even though they believe their case to be solid.[47]

Trial Impacts

The same day Judge Lord released his memorandum supporting the decision to certify the class, he scheduled the beginning of a pilot trial. This minitrial focused fairly specifically on the Rajender issue rather than on the whole class and was used by Judge Lord, in his words, to create a "tailwind for settlement." It was clear to all the parties that the judge preferred the case be settled. As it had developed over the last five years, the judge had acted consistently to accelerate settlement over an increased number of issues. There are several theories about why he did so. First, that is his style, particularly in complicated cases. It is quicker, more flexible, and nonreviewable by the Eighth Circuit. One doesn't have to be so particular about precedents from other jurisdictions in a settlement. Second, some thought the judge did not want to make a formal ruling that might be damaging to his alma mater. Judge

Lord bridled at the idea that he might be soft on the university, a concept university officials also found, under the circumstances, ridiculous. But, in fact, the judge has a considerable affection for the university and can quote almost verbatim the words from its charter that are carved on the granite pediment of Northrup Auditorium in the main quadrangle:

> The University of Minnesota, founded in the truth that men are enabled by understanding, dedicated to the advancement of learning and the search for truth, devoted to the instruction of youth and the welfare of the state.

By leading the university to justice, the Judge believed, he would fulfill that credo.

The plaintiffs also wanted a settlement. But since the class had been certified, that had become more complicated. Shyamala Rajender was living in California, no longer a practicing chemist. Her interests were not, as a practical matter, the same as those of her thirteen hundred sisters still working at UM.

From the university's perspective settlement was even more difficult. As Mays recalls, when a corporation is sued and its president gets a good cost-benefit analysis of settlement versus litigation, he can decide what to do. But who can decide for the university? President Moos, Chairman Hexter, and the regents were all named defendants, and they had different stakes in the matter. Furthermore, there were faculty governance and traditional academic personnel practices to be considered. Certain faculty rights could not be negotiated away.

Ultimately, the regents would have to decide, but there were twelve of them and consensus was difficult. Furthermore, being sued for sex discrimination was difficult to swallow after years of unpaid service to the state's university. Some regents wanted vindication. Finally, although most who had studied the matter knew that the university had some problems with sex discrimination (it was a large, decentralized organization, and most universities discriminated against women in those days), there was a consensus that Rajender did not have a good case and that there was an important issue of merit in protecting the chemistry department.

Formal settlement hearings had occurred in 1975 and 1977, before the class was certified, but each time the university backed away. So now, after certification, the university decided to tough it out, although it was aware that Judge Lord was going to be very difficult. But if a proper record could be created, perhaps relief would come from the Eighth Circuit.

When the pilot trial began in April, 1978, Judge Lord had already been handling the *Rajender* case for five years. But generally he had dealt face-to-face only with the attorneys. Except for Rajender, with whom he had talked several times, the other dramatis personae had been present only through depositions or other court materials. Now he would get a chance to see and personally question, as is his style, the other characters. Sprenger put on Rajender as his major witness. She thinks that the judge was initially skeptical but that as her testimony went on he became more and more receptive. Perhaps he would have been so disposed anyway, but it was a considerable advantage that she was now a lawyer and knew how to present her case. Frequently during the trial, the judge addressed questions to her and treated her as a cocounsel.

Sprenger decided that tactically he would get more out of Hexter and Moos if they were dismissed as defendants, so they would no longer fear any personal liability. Sprenger began with Moos, but the judge soon took over. After Moos's disastrous press release conceding chemistry department discrimination was put in the record, the judge began with his questions.

THE COURT. What do you think of this—we'll just visit here. . . . I don't want to embarrass you or anything.

A. You won't.

THE COURT. I am getting a look at this thing, really a new look at it that I haven't had before. Some surprises are coming to me, or things that I took for granted are now being pointed out in the context of affirmative action.[48]

The judge then went on to ask about the chances of women being hired in a major chemistry department anywhere in the country. Moos conceded that the traditionally all-male club made that difficult.

Then the judge turned to the problem as he now defined it.

THE COURT. Well, some rather broad allegations are made here against our own institution (UM), you know.

A. Well, I would say, Your Honor—with all respect—this is true of the judiciary in a way, too.

THE COURT. But that case is not before me now.

A. Of course not, Your Honor.

THE COURT. But the real question I have to resolve here is, at this time, what do we do about a state institution? This is really a big problem to me. And I am not so worried about the future; that can be taken care of. Even if we think the University is too inbred and there is too much collegiality there to take care of this—if we have that—now with the Court in there, we might be able to help out on that.

But the problem is: what do we do about people in the past who now want to come in on this class action, and make a claim for money, damages or to be tucked in there someplace in the hierarchy?[49]

After Sprenger and Lord were finished with Moos, Hexter was called to the stand. Sprenger had him describe the UM recruiting procedures and the small number of women that emerged from chemistry searches under that process; then the judge took over again.

THE COURT. Now Dr. Hexter,—please believe me—we don't have anything personal here now do we?

A. No.

THE COURT. I felt that you should be dismissed and out of the lawsuit as a person.

But I am looking at it as an institution and as a way of life, in the way of how we have proceeded.

Does this tell us then that of all the women who have ever applied to IT [Institute of Technology, the larger unit to which Chemistry belonged] only a very, very tiny number have ever had a spark of excellence in the mind's eye of those who were examining them?

A. Within chemistry, I think that is true.

I should add, Your Honor, that only on one occasion—as this process has developed—has one women been invited for the second stage of the process where that spark was clearly visible.[50]

The pilot trial was then recessed while the judge ordered the parties to draft a new settlement discussion. The interest on the university's part now was considerable. Moos's and Hexter's testimony made it unlikely that the university would prevail on any issue relating to discrimination in chemistry. But the university now had to worry about much more than Rajender. The class contained thirteen hundred potential plaintiffs, and Paul Sprenger and Terry Cosgrove were designated the class's attorneys.

For the next six weeks, attorneys for both sides hammered out a draft consent decree in which the university, while not conceding any guilt (as is the convention), would agree to make changes to avoid any future discrimination and would compensate Rajender. The draft was forty-nine pages long and was completed by June 28, 1978. In the next few days Joel Tierney, the university in-house counsel, who had a very limited participation in the nego-tiation, distributed his analysis of the proposed decree compared with what might be expected from a Judge Lord ruling. From Tierney's perspective, there were significant risks in a potential court order. For one thing, a finding of discrimination might endanger existing university contracts and lead to court-imposed quotas. Moreover, instead of university committees monitor-ing affirmative action procedures (particularly setting or meeting goals), Tierney thought the court or a special master might take on that activity. But there were also some advantages in the draft decree. Once the master had decided that a claimant had established a prima facie case, the issue would go to a peer review committee (one member selected by the claimant, one by the department, and the third chosen by the first two). The special master would preside but not vote, and if any party wanted to appeal, the matter would go directly to the Eighth Circuit, bypassing Judge Lord. Most important, a suc-cessful claimant would be awarded costs and attorney fees only up to $750. That provision would have a significant prophylactic effect on the number of claims and the willingness of the attorneys to get involved. Finally, both sides would have a veto power over the selection of the special master, while Tierney feared that once a decision on the merits had been made, Lord would appoint whomever he wished.

As for Rajender herself, the parties were not yet agreed. Her asking price at that time was a tenured position (under the circumstances any-thing less would give her no security at all) and $50,000. By this time, the university was willing and even eager to give her the money, but it would only let her compete for a position. Tierney, however, believed that if the judge were to decide the question, he might award Rajender tenure and a sub-stantial sum.

The draft and Tierney's analysis were then circulated to the vice-presi-dents, several faculty leaders, and Hexter. The chemist was the first to re-spond, and, not surprisingly, he was very critical. He wrote:

> It is difficult to imagine how the worst judgment the Court might itself order could be more onerous than this draft decree. . . . I have read the Consent Decree in the case of Lamphere *vs*. Brown University, and have discussed its effects with several of its faculty. In their opinion it has brought an end to the careers of many of its distinguished scholars. In comparison to that at Brown, the present draft Decree is *crushing* to the university as a whole. It is a document which proposes procedures that will be most costly and burdensome to the University, odious to its traditions of governance and destructive of its high standards based upon excellence and equal opportunity.[51]

In particular, he was critical of the new system of setting "rigid goals," which he thought inconsistent with the Bakke case just decided, and of the new hearing committees that would bypass the existing senate judiciary committees. He also thought that setting up all the special procedures for women would create the possibility of lawsuits by males. Finally, he prophesied that

> the draft Consent Decree proposes an onerous and punitive super-bureaucracy, the selection of which may well be biased, which will be costly and time-consuming, which is possibly illegal in several respects, and which supercedes [*sic*] well-established lines of authority and responsibility within the University. In both substance and spirit it suffers from its construction by individuals who do not know how universities, their faculties and administrations work and govern themselves. At best, the proposed procedures are costly and burdensome; at worst, they will involve the University in litigation which will make that to date appear microscopic in retrospect.[52]

The chairman of the senate judicial committee was also opposed. He wrote:

> The University should decline to accept any part of the decree. It simply violates too many of our established principles and structures of governance to be acceptable.[53]

He objected to the role of the special master and the bypassing of the traditional authority of the vice-president of academic affairs and the executive senate committee.

> Sex discrimination may only be part of a claim, yet forfeiture of other means of redress is total. Because of the burden of proof provisions, as well as some others, a female faculty member would be sorely tempted to plead only discrimination and use the proposed structures to hear the complaint. This can only be detrimental to the University. Any system which creates one judicial structure for a certain group and another for others is a system which goes counter to all our principles and one which is headed for grave difficulties.[54]

A month after the draft was completed, the vice-presidents were ready to report their verdicts to Charles Mays. In the way of vice-presidents, they did not flatly reject the proposal, but they said they could not affirmatively recommend it to the regents without a lot of changes. In particular, the vice-presidents objected to the power of the new hearing panel. They wrote:

The Panel, which is not constituted to provide subject-matter expertise, is called upon to determine which candidate is the ''best qualified.'' It is an inappropriate tribunal to do so. This strikes at the core of academic freedom.[55]

Finally, they thought that extending this provision until 1986, as the draft required, was far too long.

The vice-presidents had spoken, and new president Peter Magrath was preoccupied with other matters. Given the weight of their critique and the president's passive role, the regents could not accept the draft. Another attempt at settlement had collapsed.

The parties then went back to preparing to reopen the pilot trial. But Sprenger had to solve one problem. Suppose Rajender, in California, finally grew weary of waiting out the protracted process and wanted a settlement of her claims. Or suppose something happened to her; there were no other designated members of the class. But, since success seemed more probable, intervenors were not so hard to find now. In December, 1979, six years after Rajender had filed, five other women were added as named plaintiffs. Settling with Rajender would not be enough now.

Once again the pilot trial began. This time, Sprenger's principal point of attack was Lillian Williams, the university's affirmative action officer. Williams, who had come from Greensboro, North Carolina, began her career with the university hospital in 1948, gradually worked her way up the administrative ladder, and had become one of the most highly respected affirmative action officers in the country. But she did not have faculty rank or much authority over faculty decisions. This placed her in the difficult position of being responsible for monitoring equal employment opportunity activity without having any real power. On the witness stand, Sprenger began to pinpoint the dilemma, when once again Judge Lord took over the questioning.

First, he tried to assure Mrs. Williams that she could answer questions candidly.

THE COURT. I want you to relax.

A. All right.

THE COURT. I would doubt very much that the regents would fire you or that the president would fire you because of anything you say here. . . .

From what I've seen in your testimony here, you have done everything that a woman in your position can do. And I'm very sincere about that.

A. Thank you.

Sprenger and Judge Lord then proceeded to prod Williams to consider all of the weaknesses in the UM affirmative action system.

Q. Mrs. Williams, you said earlier in your testimony this morning that Dr. Hexter gave you the impression that there were no women or females qualified for appointment to regular positions in the chemistry department. Right?

A. That's true.

Q. And I'm wondering if you believe that, knowing what you know now?

A. Knowing what I know now, I know that there are women, I know that there are minorities who have obtained degrees in chemistry over the past five years—because I have statistics that have been compiled, so that I know it now.

The court then asked her whether she could think of an explanation for the fact that women were not being hired proportionally.

A. Yes. That men were just not into the habit of hiring women and hiring minorities, and so they didn't hire them.

THE COURT. Is the president powerless to change it, too, as the thing exists, as a practical matter?

A. My opinion, Judge Lord, is yes.

THE COURT. Then the only people that make the hiring decisions and effect compliance or non-compliance with the law are the tenured faculty people in the various departments?

A. Yes.

THE COURT. And apparently that can't ever change until somebody makes a rule or a decision that the regents are responsible for the University and are willing to change those decisions and go right into the hiring process, or send somebody into it that makes these evaluations to see that they are not biased sexually or racially?

A. That's true.

THE COURT. That may be what this lawsuit is about, as to whether or not a delegation of authority to a department head is appropriate and legal, or whether or not the regents have an affirmative duty not to so delegate when the results are as they seem to be in the chemistry department.[56]

Williams's concession, painfully given, was devastating to the university. But more threatening, Sprenger and Judge Lord had decided to subpoena the regents as a group to attend the trial, at which point it was likely that the judge would lecture them from the bench. That would have made headlines, ugly headlines. It was too much. The university threw in the towel. This time a settlement had to be reached.

A hard process was still ahead, but what became the *Rajender* consent decree was finally submitted to the court in June, 1980. This time some of the regents who were lawyers directly participated in the negotiation, and the faculty critics had little role. Once the regents acted decisively, dissent within the university was silenced, but gaining a consensus with the plaintiff class was not so easy. When the decree was published, the judge held a hearing at which a number of women faculty complained about the university's unwillingness to share information and open up procedures.[57] The judge was supportive. Consequently, a number of revisions were made to accommodate their criticisms. The final decree was not signed until August, 1980.

Decision Impacts

For Shyamala Rajender, the seven-year litigation process was over. She had won, but as she had told reporters, "I have to pinch myself to make myself believe it."[58] Some of her colleagues were more jubilant. Lois Erickson, an associate professor of educational psychology, declared, "It is the first step on a long road of justice. . . . Many women at the university feel the Chemistry building should be renamed Rajender Hall."[59]

On the day the decree was finally signed, Rajender flew from California to Minneapolis to attend a luncheon in her honor at the Campus Club. The fete was given by other women faculty who now stood to gain substantially from the case they had once regarded so skeptically.

When the applause died down, what had Rajender achieved for herself? The monetary proposals were split in half, and she received a modest $100,000. Even though she now had a successful legal career in California, until the end of the negotiating process she held out for at least a symbolic reinstatement in the chemistry department. Under Title VII law, she was clearly entitled to such a position, but chemistry was adamantly against it.

Judge Lord was skeptical about placing her back in "the snake pit." Finally she gave in so that the consent decree could move ahead.

Although its pattern is not uncommon in discrimination lawsuits against corporations or municipal governments, the scope of the *Rajender* consent decree is unprecedented in higher education. The thirty-four-page decree can only be summarized here. Among its principal requirements are:

1. That the existing university affirmative action plan be modified by requiring good-faith efforts to employ qualified women at levels to the point proportional to the number of women holding appropriate degrees or other qualifications. This "requires that preference be given to an approximately equally well qualified female candidate over another candidate who is not also a member of a protected class defined in this Decree."

2. That written sex neutral criteria for evaluating the qualification of all nonstudent employees be established.

3. That a university committee on equal employment opportunity for women be created with the full power of a university senate committee. That the plaintiffs be able to choose two of the seven members of the committee. The purpose of the committee is to see that the consent decree is fulfilled by proposing new policies, reviewing existing policies that may have disparate impact, and monitoring implementation procedures.

4. That each academic unit set two-year goals and timetables for hiring females. (The Decree then detailed the affirmative action rules governing hiring.) The University would provide information on statistical availability. The department must record application data (even the forms were specified) and the number of women seriously considered. If the special master determines that the university is not keeping the proper records, (s)he can order such tasks completed. The data must be kept so that any applicant for a faculty position may inspect it.

5. That in resolution of past claims, (*a*) any member of the class (all female nonstudent university employees) may file a claim for any act of sex discrimination that occurred after March 24, 1972; (*b*) such claims should go to the three special masters appointed by the judge; (*c*) the special masters shall defer action on such claims for up to 180 days, during which the university may act to resolve them; and (*d*) the special masters shall develop a list of qualified university faculty who can act as advisors to specific claimants.

6. That the special masters shall have subpoena power, that records be kept for all hearings, that the burden of proof be those used in federal courts, and that the proceeding may result in full equitable relief (back pay, promotions, attorney fees up to $6,000).

7. That any claimant may petition the special masters for a determination of whether any employment practice policy or procedure of the university violates Title VII or the decree.

8. That the decree shall last until January 1, 1989.

When university officials described the decree to their constituencies, they naturally put the best face on it. To some extent, they argued, it was no more than an agreement to live up to the terms of modern civil rights law.[60] Further, they suggested, it was better than the *Lamphere* settlement Brown University had signed.[61] Off the record, they explained, they feared that Judge Lord was losing all patience with the university and might write an overkill decision accusing it of all manner of offenses. Although they might expect the Eighth Circuit to overturn Lord, as it had in the past on other matters, that would take several years and hundreds of thousands of dollars in attorney fees. In the interim, the Lord opinion would be a public relations nightmare for the state's university. Resisting Shyamala Rajender was one thing, but in Minnesota a sustained fight with "women" was politically impossible.

Some of the university's initial assessment of the consequences of the decree may have been a sort of public whistling in the dark, but it is clear that even in private UM officials badly miscalculated. They estimated that only about twenty-five to forty claims would be filed and that most of those would be settled by internal university procedures and never go to the special masters. They were wrong on both counts. Indeed, they were so convinced of the limited potential of claims under the consent decree that the university vigorously opposed setting a monetary cap on its liability. They thought such a figure would become a target and would also add to the public relations problems when the headlines blared, "UM Settles Discrimination Claims for X Million Dollars." But the one cap the university wanted it did not get. At Judge Lord's insistence, the cap on attorney fees was increased from $750 in the 1978 draft to $6,000 in the final decree. The latter sum is not a lot of money in modern litigation terms, but it is enough to try a small claim and enough to develop a more complex one until other funds can be raised.

But the greatest miscalculation university officials made was in estimating the depth of the feeling of mistreatment UM women had.[62] The process started slowly. From August, 1980, to May 1, 1981, only about 25 claims were filed. Even then the university was not certain how to handle them. They were farmed out to a young attorney, but he had no way to obtain the settlements he thought best, because there was confusion in the university about who was authorized to reach agreements. Then in May and June before the end of the academic year, 150 new claims came in, overwhelming the attorney. He tried sending a case to the standing judicial committee of the faculty university senate, but that body could not even agree on its procedures before the 180 days ran out.

By June, 1984, about 300 claims had been filed: 120 were settled or decided by the special masters; 85 were dismissed by the court or abandoned by the claimants; and 17 individual claims are still pending.[63] The other 95 claims are class issues. About half of them relate to the School of Nursing, and the rest are petitions seeking to challenge university policy on civil rights grounds. Only one of the petitions has been decided, and the petitions are the most explosive part of the Rajender consent decree. Should the special master rule that various UM personnel procedures and criteria have adverse impacts on women, it will not only open up new claims against UM but will no doubt cause lawsuits on similar issues to be instigated elsewhere.

The single decided petition created a novel administrative-political arrangement. A new faculty assistance officer has been established whose task it will be to help individuals present their grievances effectively. This position reports to the faculty affairs committee of the university senate.

If the university has had some unpleasant surprises during the implementation process, many women have been vocal critics in frequent contact with the media. They feel that the university had been uncooperative in releasing materials, intolerably slow in its internal procedures, and still not committed to affirmative action in hiring and promotion. On the latter point, the matter is one of perspective. In the probationary rank where women traditionally have been most represented in universities, UM has hired women at about the 30 percent rate. But in the tenured ranks, change has been slower. Nor is it clear that salary equity has been achieved. UM is now in the midst of a major salary study, but comparable worth issues have made the outcome very complex. Women faculty in nursing and home economics have raised comparable worth issues through the petition route. Minnesota has state legislation requiring comparable worth studies. Although this law specifically exempts university faculty, courts may not be inclined to do so.

Furthermore, although the University was initially reluctant to challenge decisions of the special masters and thereby confront Judge Lord directly, it has begun to resist on some points. When claimants successfully argued before Lord that the $6,000 cap on attorney fees was making it difficult to find lawyers to raise some issues and that that was unfair since the university could spend as much of taxpayers' money as necessary to defend itself, the university appealed. The Eighth Circuit agreed that the $6,000 cap was a part of the give and take of the consent decree process and upheld it.[64]

Of course, the majority of claims that have been seriously pursued have been settled. As the university attorney has said, "It is very much in the University's interest to resolve cases (out of court) rather than with the bitterness that comes with a trial."[65] The university has established a screening process: a three-person committee of legal counsel, an affirmative action officer, and a female administrator in the office of the vice-president of academic affairs. When they recommend settlement, sometimes it is because investigation has proved the university wrong; sometimes it is because in the mix of facts there are elements that would be difficult to defend or embarrassing to expose; and sometimes it is because it is cheaper to settle. The university is also reshaping its internal governance procedures so that appropriate issues can be heard within the 180-day limit. Whether this pattern of acceptance/resistance at the midpoint in the span of the decree will continue is impossible to predict. Indeed, one cannot even be certain the decree will be lifted in 1989.

Posttrial Impacts

Just as the litigation process had various impacts on the parties involved, so it also affected their attorneys differently. For Paul Sprenger, who had been working on the *Rajender* case for five years on a contingency basis, the consent decree was an enormous victory. The decree received national publicity, and, as the winner, he found it very good for his business. Almost every discrimination claimant in the university and dozens in other parts of the country have contacted his office. But academic cases are too time consuming and are no longer high on his list. Sprenger currently is managing Title VII class actions against the Cargill and Burlington Northern companies.

There was still the matter of being paid for his work on *Rajender*. Sprenger had left Johnson and Sands in 1977 to form his own smaller firm, while his previous partner, Terry Cosgrove, remained with the parent firm. Together they estimated that they had spent 12,635 hours on the case, for a total of $701,675 in fees for pre- and postsettlement work. In addition, their expenses were $123,549. But the matter was not as straightforward as that. Because civil rights cases are often taken on a contingency basis with all the uncertainty that entails and because in theory plaintiffs' attorneys are acting in the public interest in enforcing civil rights laws, judges have the discretion to multiply the normal fee to reward the attorney and punish the offender. Sprenger and Cosgrove decided to appeal to that discretion by describing the risks they had run. First, they noted that over the years they had spent 21 percent and 30 percent of their time, respectively, on the case. More important, as their brief pointed out, citing a whole string of cases where academic plaintiffs had failed, the issues were novel and success unlikely.

The university opposed any bonus for them by arguing that the hours they had billed were excessive and that the decree generally just reaffirmed what the university did anyhow. But to challenge the significance of the decree was to attack not only the performance of plaintiff's attorney but of the judge who had been so active in its creation. Not surprisingly, the judge was quite taken with the importance of the *Rajender* outcome. He argued that such cases were difficult to win "because of the aura of liberalism that surrounds academic institutions."[66] He cited at length the provisions of the decree and suggested that $40 million might be the ultimate worth of the total package the claimants had won. If "the settlement on Rajender is the largest one ever negotiated in an academic setting" and if that "significant and unexpected result evidences the creation of outstanding advocacy," then the judge thought straightforward compensation for the attorneys was not enough. Consequently, he decided to triple the base fees of Sprenger and Cosgrove to make the total amount nearly $2 million plus interest.

In the university, there was considerable sentiment for appealing the attorney fees award. It was certainly unprecedented in academic discrimination litigation. Furthermore, the Eighth Circuit has expressed displeasure over civil rights "bounty hunters," so Mays drew up a brief for appeal. But the university decided the risks were too great. Judge Lord had ordered that "[i]n the event the payments are not made on February 1, 1983, or before, the Court shall find the University in violation of its order and impose such sanctions as it determines in its sole discretion." Of course, that would be appealable too. But would the chance of further affronting the judge who now had continuing jurisdiction over the university's personnel process until 1989 be worth it? And how much would the appeal cost in legal fees? Furthermore, the university had insurance. So the calculus of costs and benefits prevailed over the passion of principle, and a settlement was reached in which the plaintiff's attorneys got their money, but dropped the 11 percent interest that had accumulated.

The university then turned to its insurance company, a small Chicago firm, North River, and its co-insurers, Continental Casualty and Lloyd's of London. Like most insurance, the university's policy looked better before a claim had to be made. The companies argued that the university had not kept them apprised of the liability it was running, and so its policies were inappropriate. The matter was complex because of the difficulty of determining the effective date of the policies and because no one could estimate what future expenses might be. By January, 1983, the university had made forty-four settlements, which had cost $785,921, and there were still six years to go on the decree. So the university had to sue the companies. Here, for the first time, having a case heard by Judge Lord was an advantage, and, after a lengthy exchange of legal documents, the university and the companies reached settlement, which, over the years, has covered nearly $4 million of the litigation costs.

For Judge Lord, *Rajender* was not just another case. He estimated that for two years after the decree, 25 to 30 percent of his time was spent in sorting out *Rajender* questions. But although these issues continued to focus public attention on the judge, *Rajender* gradually was superseded by the controversy over lawsuits regarding an intrauterine birth control device, the Dalkon Shield. The day that case was settled for $4.5 million, Judge Lord ordered the three top executives of A. H. Robins, shield manufacturers, to the courtroom and said, "The Dalkon Shield was an instrument of death, mutilation, and disease . . . a deadly depth charge in the womb ready to explode at any time."[67]

The company, which had many other cases it wanted to settle, thought the judge's remarks prejudiced their position and responded with a very unusual lawsuit against him. Retaining Griffin Bell, President Carter's attorney general, the company sought to have Lord's remarks stricken from the record and the judge himself reprimanded and asked to retire. Lord, as usual, did not seem dismayed at the controversy. He hired Ramsey Clark, President Johnson's attorney general, to represent him. But the judge did confess that he found being a defendant and having to live at the whim of court calendars very uncomfortable.[68]

For the other attorneys in the case the outcome was more mixed. Dresselhuis never petitioned for a part of the fee settlement, and she announced in 1979 that she would no longer take any more academic discrimination cases, because they were too hard on the plaintiffs. Mays continued to do work for his firm on postsettlement claims, but gradually the university found that arrangement unsatisfactory and expensive. Consequently, UM shifted its legal work to in-house counsel and expanded its staff from three to eight. Its new chief counsel is Steve Dunham, who, after receiving his J.D. at Yale, became a member of the UM Law School faculty. Dunham's appointment and the staff expansion has not only signaled the university's attempt to get a better control of its legal affairs but represented a change in philosophy as well. The university's legal stance has been firmly prosettlement in most cases. The legal expenses and morale costs are simply too high to act otherwise. Also, Dunham accepts the fact (the state has tough laws about this) that a public university's records are public information. The data demands for evaluating all of the postdecree claims have been enormous and unprecedented, but UM now tries to be cooperative.

Although Hexter has played a role in critiquing the 1978 settlement draft, because he was at that time a defendant, no one in chemistry was consulted when the final consent decree was formulated. Some were not pleased. One senior member of the faculty wrote in a letter to the *Minneapolis Tribune:*

In the more than 20 years that I have been here, the chemistry department has definitely not discriminated against Rajender or anyone else because of sex or race. A high official of the university administration has admitted to me that "no one serious" in the administration actually thinks the department discriminated against Rajender.

It is clear that people with any sense of ethics at all would never have agreed to a settlement like this; but the president and the regents definitely did so. No doubt they thought they could protect themselves from future hassles by making a scapegoat of the chemistry department.[69]

But the more immediate problem was the decree's requirement that among the next five appointments in chemistry two women had to be included. The decree was not finally signed until August, 1980, and the department had already made a commitment to four males. The university was in a bind, so the decision was made to hire two of the males in tenure track positions and to make the other two temporary assistant professors until the two females were hired. That required some difficult negotiation to avoid a breach of contract and eventually some blood money to ease the pain of the two temporaries. The department hired its two women members and now has three female faculty out of forty altogether.

The fallout from the *Rajender* controversy has made hiring in chemistry more difficult overall. Some women chemists have been concerned that they would not be treated fairly, but the department also lost one strong female candidate who made it clear that she did not want to be perceived by others as being recruited as a female. She did not want "the Rajender Chair" and worried that she would always be under a cloud at Minnesota.

Some males have been concerned as well about whether they would be treated equally if the department has to be oversolicitous of its females. The department has been able to recruit some faculty, but nobody knows how long the double bind will exist.

How has the *Rajender* litigation process affected others at UM? The university is such a big place that many people have not been affected at all. Still, every administrator and every unit has been affected by increased paperwork and, the administration hopes, by increased sensitivity. Steve Dunham believes both are true. He is optimistic that by the end of the decree, the university will approach in each rank the percentage of women actually available. In many units, there are now more specific criteria for promotion and tenure, and since there is increased awareness of how the combination of subjectivity and decentralization can hide discrimination, he believes overall personnel decisions since the decree are more rational and, ultimately, more based on merit.

But he will also concede that there is a downside. Some chairs have become gun shy about exercising personnel discretion, and there has been some tendency to make across-the-board salary increases and to make close call tenure decisions in an atmosphere that suggests that everything may end up in court. Consequently, some faculty have said they don't want to be involved in personnel committees where decisions are going to be controversial. Overall, the amount of committee time and paperwork required to implement *Rajender* has been extraordinary even by the standards of a large university, but whether the improved procedures that have resulted are worth it is a matter of individual perception.

Dunham does recognize another problem in the recruiting and retaining of faculty stars. Since even in the current academic marketplace most stars are males, it is difficult, though not impossible, for Minnesota to make special arrangements for the person the university really wants without violating *Rajender* recruiting rules.

There are a lot of rumors floating around the campus about the impact of *Rajender* on different administrators. Some did look bad when the full price of the decree became known. For others *Rajender* speeded up administrative burn-out.

In November, 1984, Peter Magrath left Minnesota to become president of the University of Missouri system. Such events cause a lot of press speculation, especially since Magrath had been the subject of an external evaluation the previous spring, the results of which were not released to the public. The criticism most often voiced, however, was lack of decisiveness in leading the massive UM structure. In parting, Magrath gave an interview to two Minneapolis reporters in which he said, "I'm not big on self-flagellation," and he "reflected on what he would do differently if he could repeat his decade at Minnesota." He said that he wished he could have done more for faculty salaries and the humanities but that he was satisfied with his handling of budget cuts and football coaches (items for which he received criticism). But his hindsight now suggested that the main thing he should have done differently was to pay more attention to the *Rajender* case. Magrath noted that the lawsuit had cost $5 million in fees and settlement at the midpoint of the decree period. In retrospect, he conceded that he should have tried early involvement and attempted creative solutions "to reduce the number of trips the university took to court during his tenure."[70]

But *Rajender* became a problem unlike that faced by any previous university president. It is unprecedented to have three special masters reviewing every policy and every personnel decision affecting faculty women on the campus for ten years. *Rajender* is like a fire burning in a coal mine. It cannot be put out, although things appear to be normal on the surface. Just as you think you have learned to live with it and go on to other matters, it erupts in explosion and demands attention.

The consent decree continues to emerge in university decision making, sometimes in unpredictable ways. When Magrath resigned, Ken Keller, the incumbent vice-president for academic affairs, was appointed interim president. A condition was attached that he not be a candidate for the permanent presidential position lest his insider position scare attractive outside candidates from applying. Consequently, Keller did not apply for the job, but not surprisingly, since he had been a visible and strong leader on the campus for many years, several other people nominated him for the position.

Under the consent degree, every position at the university must have a hiring plan that specifies the terms and conditions of the search. After months of going through the search process, in April, 1985, Keller was appointed president of the University of Minnesota. Not everyone was pleased. Indeed, several persons, some of whom had claims under the decree (which then Vice-president Keller had opposed), believed that the process that selected him was flawed because it meant the university was abandoning its adherence to the decree and its procedures. Consequently, in May, with Paul Sprenger as their attorney, they filed suit with Judge Lord, arguing that the selection process amounted to a contempt of court and that Keller should be barred from the presidency now or ever. Lord, who is taking a reduced caseload as a senior judge, decided to give the case to his full-time successor. Judge Paul A. Magnuson found that President-elect Keller's selection was not, all things considered, a violation of the decree. He also expressed annoyance that such an issue would come into court and required the parties to come up with new procedures for high-level searches.

This use of the consent decree to challenge a new president has had an enormously polarizing impact on the university. Some are outraged that such an unprecedented action should be used to embarrass the institution and its leadership. Their opponents believe that if the line is not drawn on such a prominent position, the decree will become unenforceable. Others are concerned that the lawsuit itself will undermine support for the decree.

The irony is that all this should have happened at the University of Minnesota. It is not just that UM could so easily have afforded the $35,000 and the tenure track appointment Rajender wanted for settlement but that the university has had a special liberal tradition in a state that has been a national leader in civil rights legislation. Indeed, in 1976, the University of Minnesota was the first university in the country to have its affirmative action plan accepted by HEW. Perhaps that the suit did happen at UM is a sign of how deep and how complicated is the problem of sex discrimination in American universities.

Rajender has had an enormous impact not only on the University of Minnesota, but also on academic discrimination law. The case is frequently cited and has shaped other settlements. Judge Lord is not shy about publishing his decisions. One of the case's progeny is *Craik v. Minnesota State Univer-*

sity Board, in which women faculty won a class action on salary and promotion issues covering the system of regional public universities.[71] When the $7.5 million *Melani* settlement was signed between the female class and the City University of New York in 1984, the *Rajender* experience influenced both parties.[72]

Finally, what was the impact of the decree on Shyamala Rajender? She used the $100,000 settlement to buy a California house, but the case dogged her even on the coast. She joined a San Francisco law firm only to find another situation in which she thought women were unequally treated. When the decree was signed and the name Rajender became well known in legal circles as a feminist symbol, she felt a chill descend over her relationships in the firm. Later she left to become a patent attorney for Lawrence Livermore Laboratory, where she could use both her scientific and legal training. In this federally funded organization, she has finally found an employer who she feels treats her fairly.

Her notoriety often brings inquiries from other women who are contemplating litigation, and this has caused her to reflect on the decade-long experience. She says prospective plaintiffs need to think about the professional consequences of taking a case to court, the burden of proof, what will happen to their lives and their families.

> You need to think about all those things before you plunge into this. I didn't have that kind of advice. I was one of the first few people. Fools rush in where angels fear to tread and I was one of those fools who rushed in.
>
> I did this because there was nobody to advise me differently. I also relied on people telling me you go ahead and do these things and we will be solid behind you. But when you turn around who is behind me? There isn't anybody behind you. You are all by yourself out in the cold. How it is going to turn out you don't know. Fortunately for me, I developed a new occupation that occupied me emotionally and mentally so this thing didn't consume me and burn me up totally and completely.
>
> Knowing what I know now, what might I have done when all these problems came? I might say OK, to hell with it; I'm going to law school. I am sure the case is having an enormous impact in higher education, but from my personal point of view it was a terrible price to pay. I will carry the scars of battle for the rest of my life.[73]

Notes

1. 20 Employment Practices Decisions ¶ 30,214, 24 Fair Employment Practices Cases 1045 (D. Minn. 1978), 20 Employment Practices Decisions ¶ 30,225, 24

Fair Employment Practices Cases 1051 (D. Minn. 1979), 546 F. Supp. 158 (D. Minn. 1982), 563 F. Supp. 401 (D. Minn 1983).

2. The university's other song (its alma mater), "Hail! Minnesota," became the state's official anthem in 1949.
3. Jim Klobuchar, column in *Minneapolis Star and Tribune*, June 23, 1984, p. 1B.
4. Marilyn J. Taylor, "Stellar Contracts Lure Stars from University," *Minneapolis Star*, April 27, 1981, p. 1.
5. "Facts," University Relations Office, 1983.
6. Theodore C. Blegen, *The Land Lies Open* (Minneapolis: University of Minnesota Press, 1949), p. 156. See also James Gray, *The University of Minnesota* (Minneapolis: University of Minnesota Press, 1951).
7. Blegen, *The Land Lies Open*, p. 186.
8. The university is not reticent in telling Minnesotans about its contribution to their good life. See University Relations Office, *Return on Your Investment* (Minneapolis: University of Minnesota Publications, 1984).
9. As quoted in David S. Boyer, "Minnesota, Where Water Is the Magic Word," *National Geographic*, February, 1976, p. 204.
10. For a discussion of this unusual political climate, see G. Theodore Mitau, *Politics of Minnesota* (Minneapolis: University of Minnesota Press, 1970).
11. "The Living Legacy of One Good Chemist," *Update*, Spring, 1984, p. 13.
12. Robert Hexter, letter to Thomas Spencer, January 9, 1970.
13. Theodore Caplow and Reese McGee, *The Academic Marketplace* (New York: Doubleday and Co., 1965), p. 95.
14. *Chemical and Engineering News*, May 10, 1971, pp. 21–22.
15. In discounting Lumry's "smoking gun letter," it was suggested that it was the kind of overstatement solicitous mentors write for their post-docs and that in any event it represented only his personal opinions. The letter is dated November 24, 1969, and is in the Rajender Hearing File, University Archives.
16. It is now clear that civil rights statutes protect legal aliens, but it was not as certain then. Moreover, there is a psychological barrier for noncitizens to overcome in asserting rights.
17. Rajender Trial, Exhibit M.
18. Ibid.
19. Rajender Trial, Exhibit O.
20. Robert Hexter, letter to Warren E. Cheston, February 12, 1971.
21. These events were discussed under cross-examination in the Hexter testimony.
22. Robert Hexter, letter to Fred E. Lukerman, December 27, 1971. Hexter Deposition, Exhibit P, January 28, 1978, p. 5.
23. Ibid.
24. Ibid., p. 6.
25. Ibid., p. 8.
26. Ibid.
27. Moos testimony, May 10, 1978, p. 35.
28. The judicial committee decision is in the University Archives.
29. Rajender, 24 Fair Employment Practices Cases 1045.
30. Shyamala Rajender, tape-recorded interview with author, February 15, 1984.
31. As quoted by the *Minneapolis Star*, February 27, 1977, p. 4B. The occasion was

Judge Lord's restoration of $280 million in food stamps cut by the Nixon administration.

32. Jim Klobuchar, "Miles Lord: Judicial Godfather to Troubled Environment," *Minneapolis Star,* December 9, 1974, p. 1B.
33. August C. Wehrwein, article in *Minneapolis Star,* December 10, 1981, p. 12A.
34. *Minneapolis Tribune,* June 26, 1980, p. 1B.
35. Larry Millet, "Champion of the Underdog or Misguided Judicial Zealot?" *St. Paul Pioneer Press,* September 14, 1980, Focus section, p. 1.
36. Steve Berg and Doug Stone, "The Lord of Federal Court and His Life of Intrigue," *Minneapolis Tribune,* December 9, 1976, p. 12A.
37. Reserve Mining Co. v. Lord, 529 F.2d 181, 185, 186, 188 (8th Cir. 1976).
38. *American Lawyer,* July, 1980, p. 27.
39. *Minneapolis Tribune,* July 18, 1981, p. 5A.
40. Judge Lord regards himself as a converted male chauvinist. He likes to tell the story that he did not take the girls' sports suits very seriously until he had calls from his sister and daughter, who were then attorneys and who reminded him how badly they felt when they had been excluded from interscholastic athletics.
41. Rajender, 24 Fair Employment Practices Cases 1051.
42. Rajender, tape-recorded interview with author.
43. Ibid.
44. Ibid.
45. Hexter testimony, May 11, 1978, pp. 6–7.
46. Richard Gibson, "A Conversation with Malcolm Moos, 'The Golden Years of Higher Education Ended in 1968,' " *Minneapolis Star,* August 21, 1973, sec. A.
47. Malcolm Moos, *The Post Land Grant University* (Adelphi, Md.: University of Maryland Press, 1981), pp. 40–41.
48. Moos testimony, May 10, 1978, p. 36.
49. Ibid., p. 39.
50. Hexter testimony, May 10, 1978, p. 18.
51. Robert Hexter, letter to Robert A. Stein, July 6, 1978, p. 1.
52. Ibid., p. 2.
53. Peter Robinson, letter to Henry Koffler, July 17, 1978, p. 1.
54. Ibid., p. 2.
55. Robert A. Stein, letter to Charles Mays, July 27, 1978.
56. Williams's testimony is 102 pages long. These highlights are taken from pages 26, 44–49, 85, and 96.
57. *Minnesota Daily,* August 4, 1980.
58. *Minnesota Daily,* April 28, 1981.
59. Ibid. Erickson later sued the University for sex discrimination herself.
60. C. Peter Magrath, memo to other administrators, April 25, 1980. National commentators were not so sanguine. Sheldon Steinbach, an attorney for the American Council on Education, declared:

It's a disaster for higher education. It is part of the pattern of the erosion of the peer review process and the posture of the institution as the ultimate determiner of who is the most appropriate person to hold a position. (Quoted in William J. Broad, "Ending Sex Discrimination in Academia," *Science,* June 6, 1980, p. 1,120.)

61. Lamphere v. Brown University, 685 F.2d 743 (1st Cir. 1982).

62. Part of the university's underestimation came also from the fact that it did not foresee the consequences of the institutionalization of the grievance mechanism the decree required. By setting up a faculty advisory committee on women with a university-provided office, secretary, and $20,500 budget, the court created an effective system for publicizing and supporting sex discrimination claims. *Minnesota Daily*, June 16, 1981.

63. For a description of some of the plaintiffs and some of the outcomes, see Ellen Foley, "Six Women: Faculty Members Who Decided to Fight the System," *Minneapolis Tribune*, June 5, 1982, sec. B, and Suzanne Perry, "Sex Bias in Academe: A Sweeping Decree Helps Minnesota Women Press Claims, *Chronicle of Higher Education*, August 31, 1983, p. 15. The most controversial individual claim was that of a female librarian who was awarded faculty tenure by a special master; the university objected and got the recommendation reversed by a federal magistrate. The librarian lost her appeal in the Eighth Circuit.

64. *Minneapolis Star*, March 27, 1984, sec. A.

65. *Minneapolis Star*, June 5, 1982, p. 5C.

66. Rajender, 546 F. Supp. at 170.

67. Trial Transcript, February 28, 1984. See also Sheldon Engelmayer and Robert Waxman, *Lord's Justice: One Judge's War Against the Infamous Dalkon Shield* (New York: Doubleday and Co., 1985).

68. Judge Miles Lord, interview with author, June 11, 1984.

69. *Minneapolis Tribune*, June 19, 1980, sec. A.

70. *Minneapolis Star and Tribune*, June 21, 1984, p. 1A.

71. 731 F.2d 465 (8th Cir. 1984).

72. Melani v. Board of Higher Education, 561 F. Supp. 769 (S.D.N.Y. 1983).

73. Rajender, tape-recorded interview with author.

Chapter 8
Conclusions and Recommendations

In a recent monograph titled *Dispute Resolution in America,* the authors concluded that the fundamental problem in curing shortcomings in obtaining civil justice is that the system "at both the federal and state levels is, on the whole, unmeasured, undescribed, and unanalyzed."[1] Our research has focused on describing the various impacts of the civil litigation process on the participants. That focus was based on the assumption that the consequences of this process are important in ways often not reflected in judicial opinions. We believe the previous case studies bear out that assertion. For example, although the *Rajender* case produced four printed decisions, reading them would reveal very little about what finally happened to the plaintiff and the university. Nothing in those opinions would indicate that Rajender, though victorious, was forced to give up her profession as a chemist or that she felt the litigation process had a very negative impact on her life. Nor would the opinions explain the effect the process has had on the university's personnel policies and bureaucratic structure and the continuing interrelationship between the university and Judge Lord. Indeed, even though there is an unusual published opinion on the subject of the attorney fees in the case, the reader would not know that despite the $2 million award, the winning lawyer became reluctant to take further academic discrimination cases.

Additional examples of the gap between the printed opinion and social reality could be drawn from other case studies, but it is more important to ask the question: What systematically can be learned from the approach of focusing on the impact of the litigation process? To answer that question, one must avoid over-generalizing from five cases, particularly since they were not randomly selected, so we have gathered data from two larger surveys.

As in all case study research, some sacrifice of quantitative validity had to be made in order to depict the uniqueness and richness of particular cases. But by blending information drawn from the case studies with data from the larger samples of plaintiffs and university attorneys gathered in the mail-telephone

220

surveys described in chapter 2, we are now able to discuss the impact of the litigation process in more comprehensive terms.

Impact on Plaintiffs

How has the litigation process worked and what have been its consequences from the perspective of plaintiffs? As the analytical framework we used for our research suggests, the first problem the prospective plaintiff has is understanding enough about the negative personnel action that has occurred to decide whether discrimination is involved. Felsteiner, Abel, and Sarat have described this process as naming, blaming, and claiming.[2] Our data do not suggest a pattern for how this occurs, probably because the plaintiffs ranged from persons who did not get hired at all to persons who could not get promoted to full professor and because the issues covered everything from denial of tenure (which is usually a bit mysterious) to the differences in pension payments for males and females (which is quite public). Sometimes the plaintiff wandered around talking to whoever would listen without ever getting competent advice or clarification on the issues. Sometimes, as at Montana State University, informal conversations among female faculty about salary and promotion decisions led to the formation of a formal consciousness-raising group, which resulted in some women filing a legal complaint.

Selecting an Attorney

Once the prospective plaintiff has decided that he or she has been discriminated against, a choice has to be made whether to contact a governmental agency for help, whether to consult a national or regional civil rights organization, and whether to go through a campus grievance procedure or try to litigate as soon as possible. The plaintiffs we have studied have chosen among each of these options, some simultaneously, but sooner or later, an attorney must be selected if a lawsuit is to be initiated. The plaintiffs' survey reports the not surprising fact that various methods of selection were used. Most common were recommendations from family, friends, or local civil rights organizations. In 20 percent of the cases, a litigating organization or government agency provided the attorney and paid most or all of the costs.

Most surprising is the reported amount of tension and even conflict between plaintiffs and attorneys. Almost half of the plaintiffs were dissatisfied with some or all of their attorneys to the point that four of the plaintiffs in our five case studies changed their initially chosen lawyers, as did half of the plaintiffs in our larger survey. (We are not aware of other research on this subject that would allow comparison of our sample to some larger norm.) It may be that faculty clients are unusually hard to work with or, more likely, as attorneys report, that academic cases are particularly difficult to litigate, but the fact of the conflict exists. Usually the issue was the plaintiff's perception that the attorney was not proceeding expeditiously. Frequently the problem was that the plaintiff did not feel sufficiently informed about the development of the case. Often the issue was money. Sometimes the fee arrangement was negotiated clearly from the beginning, but frequently it was not (a sure recipe for conflict). Even when the hourly amount is precisely stated, what does that figure mean if the process drags out over several years, if the defense engages in tactics that make discovery unpredictably expensive, or if there are appeals? That cost can be uncomfortably high when the appeal is on the merits, but when there are also motions, cross-motions, and appeals on procedural and jurisdictional issues, the delays and the costs can be excruciating. Naturally all this often creates tension between lawyer and client. As one plaintiff who thought he had formed a close team with his lawyer said, "Up until the final fee setting, I regarded the attorney to be a friend of the 'brother category.'" The plaintiff is now engaged in a retaliation case and has a new lawyer.

Another factor that influences the impact of the process is whether support groups exist and what function they play. The support groups may be formal or informal and provide financial and/or emotional support, advice, or contacts.

Almost inevitably, family and close friends will be involved in the litigation process. Over 90 percent of those surveyed said they had support from these sources. In turn the family will often be affected by the financial expense and, generally, the emotional trauma as well. One plaintiff reported,

> Yes, my family was willing to forego vacations, new car, remodeling, and any extensive wardrobe changes. They also recognized that I was carrying a heavy emotional load. They listened when I wanted to talk things out and respected my withdrawal when I needed isolation.[3]

But in any stressful situation, not all families hold together, and litigation can exacerbate strains that already exist. One plaintiff who lost his case and a tenured position and is now living alone in a foreign country wrote: "The family broke apart. Wife filed for divorce. I still owe $35,000 to my attorney."

In our case studies, some national or regional organizations were active. The Connecticut Women's Educational and Legal Fund helped Lieberman with her appeal. The EEOC took up Scott's cause, but the NAACP offered only token assistance. Some plaintiffs, such as those at Montana State, formed local ad hoc organizations important to them. Others, such as Acosta (see chap. 2), Kunda, and Rajender, operated virtually alone.

Plaintiff support networks, where they exist, can play an enormously important role. The Cornell Seven's (*Zahorik v. Cornell*)[4] local network met almost every week to discuss legal issues, how to get information, and how to finance the case. One problem they had to resolve was whether to accept a $5,000 donation from the Playboy Foundation, a somewhat tainted source for those committed feminists. Eventually they said yes. In professor and social activist Nancy Shaw's suit against the University of California, Santa Cruz, she asked for financial and publicity commitments from her campus and community supporters before deciding to proceed. They, in fact, responded with a three-day sit-in of the chancellor's office, the "redoing" (i.e., repainting) of several commercial billboards to support her cause, and major financial support. In another case, a support group bought shares of a home mortgage for a professor who had lost a tenure decision, so she could stay in the area to litigate.

One of the most difficult decisions a plaintiff faces is whether to publicize the case and seek widespread support or to work quietly inside. For both emotional and financial reasons, a broad support network can be desirable, but this strategy can also create problems. Becoming a symbol or cause for another group risks distorting the plaintiff's priorities. Or plaintiffs may find they spend more energy nurturing their group than they receive back from it. Most of all, ongoing publicity is required to keep the support group going. Caricaturing the defendant is a common tactic, but that can reduce the possibility of settlement or of functioning effectively in the work setting if a verdict is won.

The other strategy is to try to be only as confrontational and noisy as necessary to get the attention of authorities, so that the case can be settled. One former plaintiff wrote Diana Paul, who sued Stanford, alleging sex discrimination, "I avoided all PR on my case as my lawyer advised against becoming a cause celebre. This did aid me—especially upon my return as I had to work with the very people who had tried to oust me." In fact, the strategy worked. The case was settled, and the plaintiff has become reconciled to her former colleagues. Kunda also decided to avoid publicity, and she believes that this decision contributed significantly to the ease with which she fit back into her faculty position.

Former professor Paul has chosen the more public strategy. Indeed, her husband, Doug Paul, an attorney, has founded a network for plaintiffs and their attorneys that sends out periodic newsletters.

As the trial approaches, many plaintiffs report being consumed by the practical necessities of preparation and the emotional implications of the event. One plaintiff, whose field was foreign languages, suddenly found herself reading Emanuel law outlines and talking to as many people who had sued or were poised to sue as possible. In retrospect she has no regrets about her labors.

It is a full-time job. Once your decision [to litigate] is firm, approach the matter as though you were doing it for someone else. One form at a time, one statement at a time, one day at a time. With the full conviction that what you are doing needs to be done. Get everything in writing, in ink, pencil, or cranberry juice.

Almost all plaintiffs reported some personal activity in trial preparation, and half were intensively involved in acquiring documents, making studies, and contacting supporters. They did this because they were well placed to obtain information and possessed or developed the skills to analyze it. Further, they needed to be involved to save costs. Frequently, plaintiffs and their friends spent many hours of their labor during the litigation process.

The Cost to Plaintiffs

Plaintiffs frequently do not know the whole financial cost of lawsuits for their side and have even less information about defendants' costs. In our survey and case studies, plaintiffs' costs ranged from "a few thousand" to, in the *Rajender* case, actual legal fees of $825,224 and, as assessed by the judge against the university, $2,000,000. Plaintiffs reported a median cost of $52,000 per case, but that is surely an underestimation, since it does not cover cases paid for by government or litigating agencies or through contingent fee agreements, where fees are unrelated to costs.

Estimating the social and career costs of a lawsuit is even more difficult.[5] One winner said, "Many of my colleagues seem to shun me or would express the thought of not wanting to be seen with me. Some feared retaliation by higher administrators." Another winner remarked, "For five years I was a leper—I discovered that if there is a war the College Professor is the last person on earth I'll share a foxhole with." But the dynamics of the relationship between the plaintiff and academic colleagues during the litigation process is not just a simple matter of cowardice or lack of consideration. For plaintiffs, the litigation process often becomes the central thrust of their lives. Even if colleagues are initially supportive, in time their ardor must cool, and they must make their peace with administrators who are defendants and the institution itself. Then the plaintiff often feels betrayed. One winner reported the alienation that occurred during the litigation process: "Nothing has changed but I avoid them (colleagues and administration) at all costs."

Nor were plaintiffs satisfied with the legal process. Two-thirds of them were critical of its fairness, speed, efficiency, and cost. The losers characteristically believed that some of their best evidence never got in the record or was considered and that the judges were partial to the institution. One losing plaintiff wrote:

I found the attitudes of both judges condescending and arrogant. The first, always late, kept saying in a surreal way, "Let's move this along, now. Remember, you only rent the hall for a little while," although he seemed infinitely patient with the university people who explained procedures (all documented) at great length and cracked jokes on the witness stand. The second judge had at least some semblance of judicial demeanor, although he seemed totally puzzled about why a nice, well-educated white lady should be suing her former employers when she had another perfectly nice job. . . .

Frankly, I came away from the trials angrier at the judicial system than I had been at the University system. By that time I had learned that a fair hearing was a kind of accident in a personnel action in academe; somehow I had expected at least a judicious consideration of my whole case in court. . . . I could turn around at the end of the second trial and shake hands with the division chair and the chancellor of my university; I had nothing but contempt for the people who conducted the proceedings.

The winners were more inclined to think judges were fair but were still critical of the process. One winner said, "If it's justice you seek [in court], you'll not get it, but if you want to see the law enforced, then the legal process works."

Over 90 percent of the plaintiffs testified during the trial. The effect of that experience was mixed though predominantly negative. The impact does not seem to be dependent on ultimately winning or losing. For some the process of being deposed or testifying was particularly stressful. One unsuccessful plaintiff referred to her pretrial deposition as a "horrendous experience" and another who lost remembered her trial examination with "rage and frustration." Still another losing plaintiff recalled, "I felt like I was a criminal in a murder trial ready to be executed. It was an awful feeling." Even one winner said that the "pre-trial processes were quite difficult because the attorneys of the institution tried to wear me out in depositions for hours and hours." But for other plaintiffs, finally getting their day in court was rewarding. One winner said, "Physically, mentally, emotionally draining, but in my case a great relief. It had taken five years [to get to court]." One plaintiff who eventually lost still recalled that her testimony "gave me a good feeling. It was my chance to publicize the kind of things that went on at the institution." Another plaintiff said, "I didn't know I had the 'spunk.' I was amazingly pleased with my testimony. I think that as a result of that experience, I am a stronger person, and my self-image has improved."

More than half of the plaintiffs made employment changes after the litigation, which is not so surprising because most of them lost when they challenged negative personnel decisions in court. But a third of the plaintiffs found that the litigation process itself, not necessarily the decisions, caused them to change careers or institutions. Even winners found themselves moving on, often out of academic life. Perhaps some of them were not well suited for that life in the first place. That is hard to judge, but it can be said that winning a lawsuit in an academic institution does not necessarily make it possible to work for the defendant again. Indeed, one of the most disturbing findings in our research is that so many of the winners have had to or felt inclined to file retaliation charges after the initial litigation. Is this because they are paranoid or litigation prone? Or is it because a very visible plaintiff cannot really win litigation against an academic institution? Was Judge Lord right in saying that Shyamala Rajender, even though entitled to rejoin the University of Minnesota chemistry department, could not as a practical matter function there? Is the nature of the academic workplace such that faculty are so dependent on the voluntary cooperation of colleagues and administrators to do their job that no judge can restore a person to that workplace if hostility remains? That was the conclusion of one court when a professor of business administration sued the University of Massachusetts. The district judge found in his favor, but conceded that

> the fashioning of an appropriate remedy for the defendant's unlawful discrimination against plaintiff presents an apparently unique problem. At trial, plaintiff through counsel informed the Court that he no longer sought reinstatement as a tenured professor at the University of Massachusetts. This decision of the plaintiff is understandable to the Court, and indeed appears reasonable in light of the animosities and hostilities generated during review of this tenure case and perhaps the subsequent litigation as well. It cannot be gainsaid that collegiality is the goal of every faculty and administration. Kumar no doubt has every reason to suspect that his collegial participation in the academic and administrative functions of the University of Massachusetts is at this juncture a lost opportunity.[6]

For plaintiffs, then, the litigation generally has a negative effect on their finances; their relationships with family, friends, and colleagues; their attitudes towards lawyers and the legal process in general; and most of all on their careers. Even for those few who win a judicial decision, the interruptions in their careers are substantial and costly. In our survey, two out of three plaintiffs reported that the process had had an overall negative impact on their lives, but we believe even this result underestimates the reality. In the universe of federal court decisions on academic discrimination, only about 20 percent of the plaintiffs won on the merits. Yet 40 percent of the respondents in our survey won. Those who prevailed in the litigation process were naturally more willing to discuss it than those who did not. Furthermore, a substantial proportion of those who lost in court have also lost touch with their lawyers, professional associates, colleagues, and former employers and proved impossible for us to locate. It is reasonable to expect that the litigation experience was even more negative for them than for our respondents. Plaintiffs who lost were more inclined not to return the questionnaires, and a few wrote to tell us specifically that they did not wish to think about such an unpleasant experience again. One plaintiff in that category declared,

> I was extremely upset when I received the papers of your survey. The questions are far too personal. I would not even answer some of these questions if they were asked by my best friend.
>
> I looked over them once, held back the tears and permitted myself to get angry instead. What dreadful timing, too, I thought—minutes after the verdict has been cast.

The case had actually been concluded six months earlier.

Despite the negative impacts of the process, most plaintiffs said that even with the benefit of hindsight they would still litigate again (albeit with more caution than they had originally entered this process). A few would not. One who lost wrote, "No. NEVER. If I could start all over again, I would never litigate. . . . Keep your job. Accept the circumstances as they are peacefully." This plaintiff, who was fired from a tenured full professorship after he filed suit, has not, in the subsequent four years, found a full-time position. A few winners, on the other hand, even found the experience exhilarating. But a more common response was, as one winner wrote, "I would dread the hurt, isolation, pain and suffering, but I cannot reasonably expect others to defend our rights. I was right in persisting and would feel cowardly not to do it again, if necessary."

As difficult as litigation was, most plaintiffs said they would do it again to vindicate their own sense of integrity or to improve the situation of others in the institutions or in higher education generally. One plaintiff, a winner, though now teaching part time and delivering pizza during the off hours, wrote at the bottom of her questionnaire, "Thank you for caring and excuse my dyspeptic handwriting about it [the litigation process]. . . . [The questionnaire] brought it all back, it is sad. . . . [W]e must not lose faith."

Impact on Defendants

In our case studies and our surveys of defense counsel, we acquired some broader information on the impact of litigation on the institutions' organization and procedures. In contrast to the willingness of many plaintiffs to talk openly and at length about the often negative consequences of litigation, many respondent administrators and defense counsel were unable or unwilling to recall specific details. For them the process was less personal and the results more diffuse, particularly since they were usually on the winning side. Nevertheless, it is possible to make some generalizations about the impact on defendants.

Making the Decision to Defend

Litigation frequently catches the institution by surprise, even if the plaintiff has used internal grievance mechanisms and/or generated external publicity. Once a faculty member has filed a lawsuit against a college or university, who decides whether to defend the litigation or to attempt settlement? It is a critical management decision, and our survey indicates that it is rarely made by one individual, but instead usually by a group including the president or campus chancellor, the university counsel (if the institution has one), the dean of the academic unit in which the plaintiff was employed, and often the trustees as well. The decision involves judgments about the chances of prevailing, the expense of defending a lengthy and complicated lawsuit, and the effect of the litigation on the college or university's public image and relationships with donors (including state government funding sources) and its impact on the morale of faculty still employed at the institution (as well as whether a settlement might encourage other faculty to litigate in the future). Several counsel reported that when they thought the institution had wronged the plaintiff, they advised the administrators to settle rather than to defend. Counsel also indicated that they themselves tended to view such litigation more objectively than did academic administrators and faculty, who tended to talk about "principles" and "defending the academic evaluation system."

If the college believes its administrators and faculty have behaved appropriately, as was the case in *Scott* and *Lieberman,* the college may decide to defend in order to receive judicial endorsement of its practices in an effort both to establish a principle and to avoid future litigation by faculty. At Muhlenberg College, the trustees had settled an earlier case of alleged discrimination, and the memory of that settlement was an important factor in the college's decision to defend the *Kunda* litigation. In all of these cases, a modest settlement would have cost the college far less than the expenses incurred, even in a successful defense (for example, *Lieberman* cost the University of Connecticut well over half a million dollars); but litigation decisions are not always made on the basis of financial considerations, especially in academe. Sometimes, however, as in *Rajender* and *Mecklenberg,* the possibilities of settlement are never clearly decided by anyone, and the institution drifts into litigation it could have avoided. Inaction by the defendant will almost always result in a trial.

The Selection of Counsel

When sued for employment discrimination, most of the colleges surveyed tended to select outside counsel, at least for the trial portion of the litigation. In some cases, institutions were covered by insurance and used the insurance carrier's attorney for both the discovery process and the trial itself. Furthermore, many public colleges and universities must use the office of the state attorney general and are not permitted to make the attorney selection decision. In some cases they are not even permitted to create a position of university counsel but instead place an attorney in a position called special assistant to the president. When asked why and how they would decide to use outside counsel, many inside counsel responded that discrimination cases required special expertise, which they often did not possess, and consumed tremendous numbers of hours in preparation and in trial. In fact, one counsel, an assistant attorney general who defended the college himself, noted that ''[the case] exhausted the budget [and] it consumed all staff time for months. . . . [I]t was partly responsible for the creation of the position of general counsel.''

Litigation about discrimination and other issues has resulted in a major increase in the number of lawyers working for higher education institutions and in their prominence within the institutional decision-making structure. Academic attorneys have their own support network, the National Association of College and University Attorneys (NACUA). This organization is well organized and well financed, sponsoring its own law review, the *Journal of College and University Law,* and holding an annual convention. The NACUA communication network gives the defense a significant advantage over plaintiffs in this field.

The Costs to Defendants

Being sued for discrimination against faculty generally has a negative impact on defendants at several levels. First, the publicity is harmful. Here the plaintiffs have an advantage, because they are free to say whatever they want to. They can allege all manner of things, even if they have no intention of proving them in court. A discrimination charge against an institution of higher learning is good copy, and the plaintiff's story will usually receive media attention. The defendant, on the advice of counsel, will generally not be able to reply. Since the validity of the charges may not be settled by the courts for several years, the perceived fairness of the institution may be under a cloud for that period. Not only may there be bad local publicity, as the University of Minnesota suffered in the *Rajender* case, but there may be national reports as well. When the American Association of University Women (AAUW) decided to support the Cornell plaintiffs, the university was criticized in the pages of *Graduate Woman,* the organization's national publication.

Second, discrimination litigation that drags on for several years is bad for institutional morale. If the charge is a class action and has credibility, it may destabilize an administration or a department. As in the *Rajender* aftermath, litigation may give groups leverage within the institution to gain objectives not necessarily related to the original charge. On close calls, some decision makers may feel timid about enforcing standards for fear of dragging the institution through the courts again. Even if the institution wins, the struggle may harm recruiting of students and faculty and even fund-raising activities. Trustees who are motivated by a sense of public service or by the status of the position, and who are generally unpaid, find it most unpleasant to be a named defendant in a discrimination suit.

Third, litigation can be very hard on the plaintiff's peers. If the negative decision was made at the department level and the department was split, replaying the conflicts in open court under oath will not heal any wounds. The plaintiff's attorneys will try to show that the department's procedures were inadequate or erratically followed, its judgment capricious, and some of its members biased and vindictive. If the negative decision was made by the administration, the department may be torn between supporting a colleague and aligning itself with those who control the resources the department requires. One particularly painful aspect of the academic discrimination process is that, to win many types of Title VII or equal pay cases, the plaintiff's attorney must pair the plaintiff with one or more of her colleagues to show that the institution's treatment of the plaintiff was discriminatory. This means that counsel must attempt to show in court that the person or persons paired are not as competent as the plaintiff. The consequence is that an innocent bystander who had no direct relationship to the personnel decisions that went against the plaintiff may be asked to take the witness stand to defend his career. Why were some of your teaching evaluations negative? Why was there a lapse in your publication record? Why are so many of your articles coauthored? Is that a vanity press? Or even, is your degree legitimate?[7] The witness is unlikely to win this exchange, since if his academic record had been impeccable plaintiff's counsel would not have picked him for a pair. No, the pair will have been chosen because he has some weakness that will make the plaintiff look good by comparison. The only defense is for the defendant's attorney to tear into the plaintiff's record when she gets on the stand. After days of this kind of examination and cross-examination, several careers may be in tatters that no judge can mend.

Finally, the costs in time and money are substantial. Driven by the need to uncover the institution's personnel closet skeletons and to impose a burden on the defendant during the discovery process in order to induce a settlement, the plaintiff's attorney will ask for as much information and as many records as possible. An inexperienced counsel may not even know what to ask for and so will err on the side of comprehensiveness. The defense, on the other hand, will seek to limit discovery and sometimes will find it even has a difficult time finding a copy of its faculty handbook. The judge will be called upon to establish the ground rules, but that requires motions and pretrial hearings, which are expensive. Some universities have spent hundreds of thousands of dollars simply to restrict discovery in the class action suits. If and when the trial takes place, in addition to the normal legal fees, university officials may have to be on hold for days in case their appearance is necessary. Should the case be lost, there will be settlement costs, back pay, the plaintiffs' attorney fees, and other expenditures. Even if the case is won, the institutional costs mentioned before still have to be paid.

Although hard data could not be obtained, it is our impression that defendants' financial costs were higher than plaintiffs'. Consequently, most major institutions carry insurance to cover litigation expenses—but, of course, that costs money. As the University of Minnesota discovered, when you are actually sued, coverage is sometimes uncertain. Further, in 1985, two major insurers informed academic institutions that they would no longer underwrite policies covering costs of discrimination suits or provide liability insurance for trustees and officers generally.[8] For the affluent persons in leadership positions most likely to be asked to become trustees or regents, this new exposure to lawsuits and personal liability is a most unpleasant disincentive. Consequently, the Association of Governing Boards and others are seriously exploring the creation of new organizations to self-insure academic institutions from litigation costs.

Yet one should not overstate the significance of litigation in the life of an institution. Most universities have not been involved in a major discrimination lawsuit. One can take the perspective that many problems can arise in operating a higher education institution, and being sued is just one of them. As one president of a medium-size university replied when asked if he was being sued at the moment, "I suppose so, I usually am."[9] At some point a lawsuit becomes a potential nuisance like an auditor's report, an accreditation visit, or any other external threat. The institution creates a bureaucracy and a procedure to handle the threat, and life goes on.

Impacts on Defendants' Procedures and Organizations

The complexity of decision making in institutions of higher education makes tracing all the consequences of defending an employment discrimination lawsuit difficult. In only a few cases, such as *Rajender* and *Mecklenberg*, where the court has ordered specific changes, can exact cause and effect be seen.

Even at other institutions where litigation played a role in changing promotion and tenure decisions and/or in requiring greater accountability of participants in the process, cause and effect are not simple to establish, because litigation against other institutions, the demands of federal equal employment regulations, unionization, or the advent of new and (presumably) more enlightened administrators who wished to avoid future litigation also influenced changes. Since decision making in the academic setting involves many layers of participants, there may be multiple causes of any particular change.

Furthermore, most colleges and universities are successful in their defense of these lawsuits, and thus the impetus to change what has been found to be lawful practice is understandably weak. Despite this disincentive, several institutions that have prevailed have altered their procedures or their accountability requirements, at least in part as a result of living with the consequences of earlier decisions.

Decisions made at the University of Connecticut (*Lieberman*) and the University of Delaware (*Scott*) to strengthen the accountability of the entire faculty personnel decision-making process can be attributed primarily to the arrival of new academic vice-presidents after the litigation commenced. At Delaware, the provost took office after Scott filed his lawsuit, but before trial, so he was intimately involved in collecting evidence and assisting the university's attorney in building the university's defense. The provost attributed his concern for accountability and procedural compliance at least as much to the presence of a faculty union (and a contractual grievance system) as to the outcome of the litigation against the university. Although the university prevailed in the Scott case, it had lost several earlier cases brought by faculty, and the importance of documentation and procedural compliance in faculty personnel decisions was obvious to the university administration.

Similar circumstances convinced the new academic vice-president at the University of Connecticut to require greater accountability of the individuals participating in faculty personnel decisions. At both institutions, the following has happened:

1. Probationary faculty are evaluated annually by either the department chair or a group of senior faculty, using the promotion standards appropriate to their department or discipline.
2. The results of the annual evaluation are forwarded to the dean and to the academic vice-president.
3. Both the dean and the academic vice-president review the evidence supporting the evaluation. Should the evaluation be positive but accompanied by little evidence of successful performance, the academic vice-president (or the dean) calls the faculty member, the department chair, and the dean together and conducts a joint review of the faculty member's performance.

4. The performance of department chairs and deans in the annual evaluation of probationary faculty (i.e., their documentation and the quality
of their review) becomes one criterion upon which these individuals
are reviewed for continuation or termination of their administrative
appointments.

University counsel, at least, report few instances in which, as a result of
a particular case or as a response to federal regulatory agency requirements,
they recommended changes in hiring, promotion, tenure, or salary policies of
an institution that has undergone discrimination litigation. The typical response by counsel to questions about the impact of the litigation was, "We
won the case, and therefore it wasn't necessary to change our procedures or
policies." As one counsel noted, however, it is a part of the ethos of defense
counsel not to concede that they were forced to make changes. Further,
counsel often face resistance from academics when they recommend changes
in criteria or procedures for hiring, promotion, or tenure. One counsel suggested some reforms "before the cases arose, during litigation and after
settlement . . . [but they] mostly fall on deaf ears because educators do not
want advice from their attorney." Another respondent counsel appeared especially frustrated with apparently unsuccessful efforts to improve the faculty
personnel decision-making process, saying:

Educators resent lawyers and only call on them when problems come up
that are generally political or have gone too far to stay out of court—then
they want help and advice. The workload has continued to increase
without a significant salary increase or the hiring of assistants. Educators
want too much from their lawyers and refuse to give credit for good
work.

However, other counsel reported some success in persuading administrators
to document their decisions more carefully, to seek the advice of counsel
when a particularly sensitive personnel decision was pending, or to be more
candid with faculty, "letting people know where they stand." The counsel's
responses suggested a high level of concern for procedural consistency and
institutional accountability in faculty personnel decisions. Others reported
activities targeted at educating department chairs and deans to the requirements of equal employment opportunity laws and also reported efforts to train
chairs to use the promotion and tenure process correctly and to conduct the
evaluation properly and with attention to documentation.

In many institutions these tasks are given to the affirmative action officer.
Litigation has generally strengthened their role on campus—for example, by
specific judicial mandate as in the *Rajender* and *Mecklenberg* cases. Else-

where, the need to avoid litigation still gives clout to affirmative action officials as federal administrative enforcement efforts have weakened.

Impact on Judges, Litigation Agencies, and Lawyers

For almost all academic plaintiffs and most individual defendants, being involved in a major lawsuit is a once-in-a-lifetime experience, and one would expect that the impact might be dramatic. For judges, litigating agencies, and lawyers, on the other hand, lawsuits are a continuous activity. Still, they are affected in discernible ways by particular cases or classes of cases. In our research we inquired about the impact of academic discrimination lawsuits on these legal officials.

Although it is not possible to document in hard comparative terms, the evidence from their opinions suggests that most judges are uncomfortable with academic discrimination cases. This has been articulated in several ways. Sometimes judges have expressed their frustration through sarcasm. In 1974, in one of the earliest cases, *Faro v. New York University* Judge Leonard P. Moore said, writing for the Second Circuit,

> Dr. Faro, in effect, envisions herself as a modern Jeanne d'Arc fighting for the right of embattled womanhood on the academic battlefield, facing a solid phalanx of men and male faculty prejudice. . . .
>
> Of all fields which the federal courts should hesitate to invade and to take over, education and faculty appointments at a University level are probably the least suited for federal court supervision. Dr. Faro would remove any subjective judgments by her faculty colleagues in the decision-making process by having the courts examine "the University's recruitment, compensation, promotion and termination and by analyzing the way these procedures are applied to the claimant personally."[10]

A few years later, in 1977, a federal district judge in *Johnson v. University of Pittsburgh* expressed the problem in more functional terms:

> During the trial, the court has been required to make excursions through the very frontiers of human knowledge in an ever advancing field of biochemistry. The case is also an example of the devastating effects of sex discrimination cases of this kind against universities upon the work and calendars of the United States' courts, and the commitments and time of trial counsel. Attempts to curtail the case proved fruitless in view of plaintiff's claim, for which there appeared to be a reasonable basis that because of sex discrimination, males had been hired and promoted in her department who were less qualified than she was to receive promotion

and tenure. This necessitated the examination of the professional credentials of numerous professors, a task for which the court, like probably
most federal judges, was ill suited.[11]

Even when a statistical approach is taken to provide more objective
evidence about academic personnel decisions, judges have been frustrated. As
one judge said after listening to several days of testimony by statisticians in a
case brought by the EEOC:

The best that can be said about all of the statistical testimony concerning
promotions is that, in this case, it is a very difficult area to harness
statistically and the various results do not provide a reliable
measurement. . . .[12]

As a consequence of these attitudes, it appeared for a while that even
though Congress had specifically amended the Equal Pay Act and the Civil
Rights Act of 1964 to cover faculties, the courts were not going to take
responsibility for enforcement. Statistical patterns that effectively shifted the
burden of proof in other areas of employment were not found convincing in
academic cases. Most important, the elaborate process of review that characterizes most faculty personnel decisions, the complexity and subjectivity of
factors considered, and the status of the deans, chairmen, and senior faculty
who testified seemed to spellbind federal judges. It was almost as though the
honorable men in the judicial robes could not bring themselves to believe that
the distinguished men in the academic gowns could discriminate. By 1977,
plaintiffs had lost thirty of the thirty-six cases the federal courts had tried.

Then in 1978, the Second Circuit reevaluated the trend of judicial deference to academic practices. It said,

This anti-interventionist policy has rendered colleges and universities virtually immune to charges of employment bias, at least when that
bias is not expressed overtly. We fear, however, that the common-sense
position we took in *Faro,* namely that courts must be ever-mindful of
relative institutional competences, has been pressed beyond all reasonable limits, and may be employed to undercut the explicit legislative
intent of the Civil Rights Act of 1964. In affirming here, we do not rely
on any such policy of self-abnegation where colleges are concerned.[13]

Despite this language, the Second Circuit has recently turned much cooler
toward academic discrimination cases. In *Lieberman,* Judge Friendly, writing
for that circuit, warned that the courts should not engage in "tired-eye review" of tenure decisions.[14] In 1984, Judge Ralph Winter, a former Yale

Law School professor, wrote an opinion for the Second Circuit strongly affirming traditional academic personnel procedures in a case against Cornell University.[15]

Although plaintiffs have improved slightly their won-lost record (56 victories out of 166) in cases decided by federal courts after 1977, their general chances of success are obviously not promising. That reality and the complexity of their cases has affected the decisions of litigating agencies and lawyers about whether to commit resources to these lawsuits. The role of litigating agencies in the development of civil rights law has been well documented.[16] But these agencies, whether public or private, have limited resources and cannot meet all the requests for their support. In that circumstance, they will try to pick cases that are likely to establish a new and favorable rule of law, that affect a larger number of parties, or that may gain publicity or political support for the agency.

No matter how rational the resource allocation decisions may appear to the agency boards or to nonlitigants, the denial of financial or legal assistance is often viewed by plaintiffs as indifference at best or betrayal at worst. Especially in cases where plaintiffs have been vocal and hard-working supporters of civil rights causes, their inability to garner support from civil rights organizations has been a bitter pill.

As a generalization, the public agencies have not played a great role in academic discrimination cases. The EEOC is the largest such agency. Although at one time it had a backlog of thousands of academic discrimination cases, its role has been modest. It was involved in some cases early on, but not only did the plaintiffs lose most of them, the agency failed even to get courts to apply existing civil rights legal rules or to establish new ones. Furthermore, academic plaintiffs were often very critical about the performance of EEOC lawyers. Consequently, the agency has become very selective about the cases it will take.[17] Most plaintiffs simply receive a right-to-sue letter, although a few have benefited from EEOC investigation or conciliation attempts.

The private litigating agencies have not fared much better. Given its constituency of professional women, NOW was naturally interested in academic discrimination cases. It invested heavily in two early cases decided in 1977, *Johnson v. University of Pittsburgh*[18] and *Cussler v. University of Maryland*[19] and provided a noted feminist attorney, Sylvia Roberts, for the plaintiffs. When those cases resulted in disastrous defeats, NOW cut its losses in this field and has rarely been involved in subsequent cases. Similarly, the National Women's Law Center has decided not to pursue Title VII claims but is focusing instead on equity for girls and women under Title IX of the education amendments of 1972.[20]

Their place has been partially filled by the legal defense fund of the

AAUW, which assisted in the Cornell Seven case and hopes to adopt about three cases a year. Some disciplinary organizations have proved helpful to plaintiffs, but the one to organize formally in this area has been the National Women's Studies Association. To establish a pool of resources, it has created a fund from settlements received by women plaintiffs. One such beneficiary was a former plaintiff who wrote a current plaintiff:

> It is with a mixture of pleasure and regret that I send along the enclosed check. Pleasure because this contribution from the National Women's Studies Association Task Force on Discrimination may, in some way, help you win both a personal victory and a victory for women all across academia. Regret because I know too well the pain, anxiety, and soul-consuming demands a Title VII case inevitably entails.

The AAUP has historically played a major role in protecting faculty rights, but it is finding its resources severely tested in this litigious era.[21] In discrimination suits, the organization has been most active on pension equity issues, actually intervening in *Spirt* (a case challenging sex-based pension computations) as a plaintiff. In its winning effort to force the Teachers Insurance Annuity Association to use sex-neutral tables, the AAUP invested fifteen hundred attorney hours. The national organization has also made modest grants to support a few other cases, and some local chapters have been involved with discrimination issues on their campuses as well. Nevertheless, the AAUP has participated in only a handful of the discrimination lawsuits so far.

Winning or losing a case generally affects a lawyer's career and income as well. The attorney in private practice must make a constant calculus about where to invest time and reputation. Since these cases are unusually time consuming and complex and most plaintiff lawyers have lost, there is naturally some disincentive to continue working in this area. Neither George Sprenger nor Gregory Morgan, who were financially and legally successful in the *Rajender* and *Mecklenberg* lawsuits, respectively, will any longer take new academic discrimination cases, because they are so chancy and laborious. In two other instances we studied, winning lawyers had a falling out with their firms even though they were awarded attorney fees, because the cases were so time consuming. Finally, a loss in another one of these cases led to financial difficulty and the eventual dissolution of a law firm. Consequently, some plaintiffs report difficulty in finding lawyers.

Apart from the financial consequences, many lawyers who become involved with academic plaintiffs have an ideological stake in the case. However, they must weigh the time and other costs required to participate in academic suits against larger ideological goals. For that reason, the San Francisco law firm Equal Rights Associates, which has handled several academic cases, has grown very cautious about accepting new ones. Another plaintiff's attorney wrote us,

> I have represented a number of academics in discrimination cases with a lack of success totally disproportionate to all other areas of my practice. It is my opinion that the unwillingness of the courts to "call a spade a spade" is extremely detrimental to the plaintiffs, to the integrity of the institutions sued and to our society at large.
>
> It is never pleasant to lose a lawsuit but that is quite different from the sense of outrage I have felt, and I know my clients have experienced in this area. It appears that the judiciary has made a pact with institutions of higher education to pay lip service to the law. It is my hunch that your research will uncover some fairly embittered plaintiffs.

The impact of discrimination litigation on attorneys who work in academic institutions has been different. This type of litigation, among others, has changed the number and the role of university attorneys. Larry Thompson, special assistant to the president of Ohio State University,[22] notes that from 1946 to 1956 there were about fifteen decisions involving a variety of claims against colleges and universities every year; by 1969 that number had jumped to ninety-nine a year, and it has increased dramatically since then. More lawsuits against academic institutions mean more lawyers. In 1984 NACUA found that nearly half of the institutions surveyed had a full-time resident legal counsel, double the number of such lawyers in 1972. Thompson concluded that "by the mid-1970s most institutions were accustomed to consulting lawyers on major decisions, so that lawyers often become participants in policy making and governance." There are many causes for this development, but there is nothing like a class action discrimination suit to focus an institution's mind on getting legal advice.

How Could the System Be Improved?

The civil litigation process in place in the United States has developed over centuries. Modifications of it will not be easy or quick. Clearly, there are many benefits to the adversary system with its careful articulation of rules of evidence, checks and balances. Yet as this study shows, the litigation process imposes heavy costs on both winners and losers. If the reader is tempted to believe that the participants in the study were unusually sensitive to the costs of the process, it might be well to remember that someone as experienced and prudent as Judge Learned Hand once remarked, "I must say as a litigant, I should dread a lawsuit beyond almost anything short of sickness and of death."[23]

What could be done to minimize the costs of litigation without diminishing its potential to achieve justice? One problem is that there are too many lawsuits. It is easy to see that some of these cases should never have been brought. They were not close calls, academically or legally. Yet one must be wary of the illusion of the perfect vision hindsight provides. The plaintiff, even if clear-minded and objective (an unusual condition when one feels threatened by discrimination) in assessing the evidence, will rarely be in possession of all the relevant facts when the lawsuit is initiated. It may take hours of discovery and sometimes considerable cross-examination during the trial before the strength or weakness of a case is fully apparent to the participants. By that time, much of the cost has been borne, and it is difficult to back away from a wrong-headed position and save face. Trials create a momentum like a political campaign or even a war. It is difficult to question the cause once the battle starts.

One way to reduce the number of lawsuits is to increase the candor and comprehensiveness of communications between lawyer and clients when the litigation decision is made. If, as this research documents, the litigation process often has multiple negative effects on the participants whether they win or lose, full knowledge of those effects might well encourage the parties to use other devices to settle conflicts. It should be the lawyer's task to explain those realities and alternatives for the clients. George C. Paine II, now chief judge of the United States Bankruptcy Court in the middle district of Tennessee, wrote us about an academic discrimination case he handled when he was a lawyer:

> [T]his litigation had a tremendous impact on X, both emotionally and professionally. From the former standpoint, we lawyers forget and take for granted the stresses of any lawsuit, which a "real person" is unable to do. X held up remarkably well during this lengthy process, but I know it was, in fact, very trying for him, no pun intended. Further, from a professional standpoint, nothing can be more disruptive than to be in an adversarial position with your school with both sides seeking help from the other faculty members.

Some of the lawyers in our case studies were knowledgeable and conscientious in informing their clients about the hazards of the litigation process; others saw their role as simply to maximize the chances of winning, using all the tactics litigation allows.

In their relationship with their clients, lawyers face the problems of incentives and information. Litigation produces stress for lawyers and, if the case is taken on a contingency basis, financial risk as well, but a complex lawsuit can also be a source of considerable income and status. Therefore, to detail the potential negative effects of the litigation process and to outline quicker and cheaper alternatives for the client may not be in the lawyer's own best interest. In an overcrowded profession scrambling for customers, it may be unrealistic to expect attorneys to volunteer very much negative information about the multiple costs of litigation. Nevertheless, we believe clients should have the same right to be informed about the side effects of litigation as patients have to be informed about the side effects of medical procedures. The lawyers' code of ethics should establish that right.

But if a lawyer conscientiously tried to explain the potential impacts of the litigation process to clients, where would the lawyer learn that information? As a generalization, not in law school, according to the literature on the legal curriculum and our interviews on the subject. Administrators from five law schools in Baltimore and Detroit were interviewed regarding their schools' attitudes toward teaching about the impacts of the litigation process.[24] Law schools vary in the way they place the goals for their curriculum on the continuum from legal scholar to practitioner. But in both kinds of schools, administrators recognized that the impact of the litigation process is an important factor in dealing with clients. A few believed some of this information is transmitted in clinical courses; others said it is taught in all courses episodically but in none specifically. When pressed, all conceded that what, if anything, is taught about this subject is unsystematic and not purposeful. In response to the question why, if the impact of the litigation process is an important topic, more attention is not paid to it in the curriculum, we received three replies: (1) the curriculum is already crowded; (2) nothing systematic can be taught about this subject; and (3) young lawyers learn about this in law firms from senior partners. All professional schools think their curricula are full of critical professional knowledge, and an outsider can only ask faculty to examine their priorities. The impacts on clients of a key process lawyers use to serve client interests would seem to be a central concern. The contention that nothing systematic can be gathered and transmitted about these impacts would be a naive rejection of social science, except that, in fact, social scientists have produced little information about this subject. When such information is developed, then law schools will be challenged to make good use of it. Nor is it satisfactory to say that that is the law firm's task. Not all young lawyers are employed in environments where senior lawyers are available to impart such knowledge. But even where they are, experience is no substitute for science in understanding the complex impacts of litigation. We agree with Harvard president and lawyer Derek Bok, who declared, in assessing problems in contemporary law school curriculum,

> [W]e ignore the social sciences at our peril, for their techniques grow steadily more refined. Doctors work with statisticians to measure the

costs and benefits of protracted hospitalization, or coronary bypass surgery, or mastectomy, or CAT scanning; one cannot help but wonder
whether similar techniques might not help to assess the usefulness of
legal procedures as well.

As yet, this work is largely overlooked by our great schools of law.
One can argue that such studies are not the proper province of the legal
scholar and that it is better to wait for social scientists in other parts of the
university to do the necessary research. But experience shows how empty
this observation is. Law professors cannot stand idly by and expect others
to investigate their problems.

. . . Throughout the curriculum, professors spend vast amounts of
time examining the decisions of appellate courts, but make little effort to
explore new voluntary mechanisms that might enable parties to resolve
various types of disputes without going to court in the first place.[25]

But even if a client is fully informed about the impacts of litigation,
sometimes he or she will still choose to proceed. If so, hard choices must be
made. The first task of the plaintiff is to develop a statement of the facts
around the triggering incident as carefully and comprehensively as possible
and then secure competent advice about how to interpret those facts. Getting
good advice is not very easy. The obvious source is a lawyer, but there are
problems. Legal advice is expensive, though not so costly as embarking on a
fruitless lawsuit. Finding the right lawyer is tricky. Because of the cost and
uncertainty of this kind of litigation, many lawyers are reluctant to be involved in academic discrimination cases. Although inexperienced lawyers
and lawyers who are ideologically committed to the cause may be willing to
take the case, they have obvious liabilities. Even a veteran lawyer skilled in
employment discrimination law may know little about the nuances of academic personnel practices and so may not be a good evaluator of whether a
university's refusal to release reference letters or to credit opinions from
former students is a facade for discrimination.

Nor is it easy to obtain help from government agencies, although the
strength of state and local agencies varies dramatically from region to region.
The federal agency, EEOC, is rarely doing more than issuing right-to-sue
letters these days. Very few plaintiffs get government attorneys anymore. If
the plaintiff can get a government agency involved, then it is possible a
serious investigation may result. If so, that will substantially reduce the costs
of discovery should the case go to trial. The investigation may produce a
finding of probable cause, which generally requires some conciliation activity. If the investigation yields no probable cause outcome, then that should
be a powerful caution that the plaintiff should ponder before investing in a
lawyer to seek more discovery.

Another place for evaluation of the claim is on the campus, in the affirmative action office or grievance committee. In theory, affirmative action officers know the campus and civil rights law well enough to be effective evaluators. Perhaps they have played that role and have effectively negotiated settlements or discouraged suits on some campuses, but since our data are drawn from cases actually tried, it does not show them playing major roles in solving these conflicts. Realistically, however, there are limitations on the effectiveness of affirmative action officers even if they are well trained (an uncertain condition). They are almost always members of the administrative staff, often assistants to the president. That certainly produces a cross-pressure on an officer should an objective evaluation produce a recommendation to sue the institution. On the other hand, they are often viewed as partisan members of protected classes, or at least some classes (women or blacks but not necessarily both), and that perception may affect the ability of an officer to obtain information about the alleged discrimination or to be viewed as objective once the evaluation is made.

Still another option is the use of the campus grievance procedure to hear the claim. Again, since we are considering only cases that have gone to trial, the role of such procedures in screening or settling cases is not fully apparent. In the one instance, *Rajender*, where a plaintiff tried to use the existing procedure, the administration was not responsive to its conclusions. Even if the administration does not honor the results of the grievance procedures, there are often major benefits for a plaintiff who pursues a claim through that forum if it is organized properly. First, the financial cost is usually free or low, and the procedure may result in significant discovery of documents that otherwise would be expensive to have produced. Through the grievance procedure, Rajender obtained critical evidence that helped her enlist the aid of an attorney. Second, a good procedure should result in a reasonably objective evaluation of the claim in a fairly expeditious manner. If the plaintiff prevails and the administration will not settle the case, that usually will increase the possibility of creating a support network. Further, a grievance committee victory may effectively undermine the administration's contention that the plaintiff is challenging the principle of peer review, a principle to which the courts have generally been quite deferential. Should the plaintiff lose in the grievance committee, then very serious consideration should be given to dropping the claim. The record of plaintiffs in federal courts makes it very unlikely that he or she would prevail.

Taking all of these concerns into consideration, we would suggest that plaintiffs consider carefully the following questions before deciding to file a lawsuit:

- Do I know or can I find a competent, experienced, affordable attorney?
- Can I involve strong local or national support networks in my case?

- Can I form a class of similarly affected individuals?
- Does the institution have a pattern of settling employment disputes such as this one?
- Am I raising a new point of law, or is my case purely a matter of whether the negative decision was correct and fairly reached?
- Are the results of peer review or a grievance process in my favor?
- Do my faculty colleagues support me against the administration?
- Am I willing to endure a lengthy, expensive, time-consuming process with the knowledge that plaintiffs rarely have won in these cases?
- Can I begin a career in a new (or different) organization or field as a cushion in the event of either a loss or a judge's refusal to reinstate me?
- Do my family and friends support a decision to litigate after reading these questions?

These questions reflect the advice of plaintiffs in our case studies and national survey. They suggest that factual, legal, and emotional issues are all important components of the decisions that have to be made in the litigation process.

It takes two to make a lawsuit. Sometimes the defense forces a trial when a settlement would be in everyone's best interest. Our data show that many persons at different institutional levels play roles in the decision to defend or settle. Since academe's tradition is collegial, that may be appropriate, even rational. But it also may lead to loss of accountability or decisiveness. Considering the multiple costs of litigation to the defendants even when they win, the decision to defend or settle is a major one. It should be made by the president.

At the initial stage the president, however, faces the same problem as the plaintiff: how to obtain accurate information about the facts surrounding the triggering incident and to interpret their legal significance. There also may be ethical questions. Not everything that is legally defensible may be consistent with the institution's moral or social commitments, and those factors may influence the litigation decision. Making the decision early is obviously better than later. The president of Montana State University did not realize the seriousness or the validity of the charges against his institution until he attended three days of the trial, and it was only after the court imposed a decade-long consent decree that Minnesota's president realized the stakes involved in that litigation.

Contemporary university presidents are enormously busy, but litigation poses a threat to the institution that requires their attention. The institutions should have rules in place similar to those business and government use to manage potential crises. Reports on any lost-time injury anywhere in the worldwide DuPont Corporation must be submitted to the executive committee in Wilmington within twenty-four hours. One consequence of this high visibility policy is that DuPont's accident rate is one-seventeenth of the chemical industry average.[26] Martha McSteen, the current commissioner of the Social Security Administration, which has about eighty thousand employees, has a policy that any time a congressman writes the agency about a case, the answer is to be on her desk within forty-eight hours.[27] Similarly, the president of a university should require comprehensive reports on litigable issues to be in his or her office within a short time.

The president must realize, however, that each of the report writers will have his or her own vested interests, and none of them will have a complete view of the controverted events. For that reason, the president may want to convene a meeting of the institution's legal counsel and the plaintiff's counsel for an informal discussion of the facts of the case. That meeting may provide the president with a sense of the stakes and costs of proceeding with a full-scale defense. Irving R. Shapiro, in recommending the use of alternatives to litigation for corporations, recalls that

> TRW, Inc. and Telecredit resolved a patent-infringement difference in a two-day hearing conducted in private before a neutral adviser. After each side had made its case the president of Telecredit and a vice president of TRW worked out a compromise settlement in half an hour. The savings in legal fees are estimated at more than $1 million.[28]

Not every attack is worth repelling. Given the significance of tenure and the basic validity of its procedures, the University of Connecticut's expensive and vigorous defense may have been justified, but one may question whether it was rational to defend an ad hoc procedure and failure to promote at the University of the District of Columbia in the *Acosta* case.[29]

Our findings from the case studies and the counsel surveys suggest that those who make the decision to defend or settle (usually a group of administrators with the help of counsel) should answer the following questions after their own internal investigation:

- Are the institution's procedures for faculty employment decisions consistent with recognized external standards (such as AAUP guidelines)?
- Have other external bodies, such as governmental agencies, accrediting bodies, or professional associations, found the institution in violation of accepted personnel standards?
- Has the institution settled other, similar cases in a manner that could be suggestive of fault in this case?
- If the case is filed as a class action, what proportion of the faculty are potential class members? What is the likelihood of class certification? How representative are the plaintiffs of the purported class?

- Are there statistical studies that suggest that the institution faculty is unusually nonrepresentative in racial or gender categories?
- In an individual claim did the plaintiff's departmental colleagues recommend for or against the hiring/promotion/tenure/salary increase?
- How well documented is the decision, and to what degree did each level of the decision process agree with other levels?
- In cases where a peer committee decision is being challenged, to what degree has the plaintiff's department or college applied criteria consistently to similarly qualified faculty?
- Does the alleged violation appear to be an isolated incident, or are there examples of similar problems in other departments?
- Can the litigation be settled for a moderate monetary amount without requiring reinstatement or major adjustments in rank and salary?

Other issues may be important as well, such as the degree to which the institution will be affected by negative publicity, or the possibility that academic freedom violations have been also alleged. Campus leaders may decide that the lawsuit must be defended in order to affirm an important principle, to discourage other litigation, or for some other reason. But in making such a decision, college administrators and their counsel may wish to consider the words of Thomas H. Wright, Jr., counsel for Princeton University and a respected scholar of higher education law:

> Institutions that have been through a full-scale legal battle really know it. Class action and tenure disputes can just rip the department and even an institution apart in ways that take years and years to rebuild. Faculty members threatened by lawsuits often develop a new wariness . . . shying away from hard decisions. These are not healthy instincts in a university.[30]

It is unlikely that plaintiffs will consider the long-term interests of the institution when making a decision to litigate. It is imperative that college administrators and their counsel do.

What about using some other alternatives to litigation in settling conflicts over alleged discrimination? Perhaps because they have been subjected to much litigation only recently, universities have been more conservative than other organizations in exploring mediation or arbitration alternatives. In 1978, the Ford Foundation and the Sloane Commission on Government and Education funded the Center for Mediation in Higher Education, housed within the American Arbitration Association. The experiment was not successful, largely because higher education institutions refused to use its services.[31]

Nearly all the counsel surveyed noted the expense and length of these cases, but when asked whether a nonlitigative dispute resolution process would be preferable, many were doubtful. Several noted that they and the university preferred litigation to mediation or arbitration because few plaintiffs' cases were strong ones, and the university preferred a judicial ruling affirming the appropriateness of the university's decision rather than the compromise mediation or arbitration might provide. Most were very much against binding arbitration—either because it weakened institutional autonomy or because it permitted an outsider to make a decision binding on the institution. It is not clear why outsider federal judges are preferable to outsider arbitrators, except that the judiciary has been very respectful of academic institutions. Others noted that the Supreme Court, in *Alexander v. Gardner-Denver*,[32] had removed the traditional judicial deference to arbitrators' findings in employment discrimination cases, thus undermining any incentive to use that tool.

Despite the doubts of some of his counterparts, one counsel proclaimed eloquently that he would prefer a nonlitigative dispute resolution process, but he did not believe that either the institution or the faculty would favor such an alternative. He noted that

> educational institutions are different from profit-making ones—they don't use money as part of making decisions, and see principles that must be upheld where individuals in other kinds of organizations would not.

Another experienced counsel who has litigated several discrimination cases favored mediation and arbitration as well. She said that

> these suits are very destructive, especially when filed by tenured faculty who will remain at the university. Especially in discrimination cases, people are emotionally convinced that they've been mistreated. At my institution, we've had trouble finding people to serve on [tenure and promotion] committees in departments which have been involved in litigation. Mediation and arbitration might help defuse the emotion and resolve the dispute more quickly.

Perhaps when academic administrators learn more about litigation, they will realize they may lose more control of institutional autonomy in the courtroom than in any other arena. Federal judges have taken charge of public school systems, mental hospitals, and prisons. Judge Lord has proven they can control a university faculty personnel system as well.

Further, there are a lot of other alternatives. As the historian Jerold Auerbach said, "The American pattern of dispute settlement is and always has been, more varied and complex than our currently constructed legal perspectives would suggest."[33] Currently, the field of inventing and implementing alternatives to litigation is booming. In addition to the older American Arbitration Association, there are the newer National Academy of Conciliators and the Society of Professionals in Dispute Resolution. The field has spawned its own law review, the *Ohio State University Journal of Dispute Resolution*. Several national foundations have funded the National Institute of Dispute Resolution so that it can operate a clearinghouse for information on litigation alternatives. There is also a Center for Public Resources,

> which offers judicial panels, including some of the best-known names in the law, to sit as neutral advisers or judges in "minitrials." One law professor, Frank Sander of Harvard, has suggested that the courthouse of the future will have many doors, bearing such labels as Arbitrator, Mediator, Ombudsman, and Malpractice Panel, as well as Courtroom.[34]

The TRW Corporation has used a Washington consulting company, Endispute, to analyze pending cases against it to see if they could be resolved without going to trial. Two professors at the University of Maryland, Elizabeth Koopman and Joan Hunt, have developed a mediation system for child custody cases that

> replaces the traditional adversary system of lawyer-negotiated custody and visitation plans with cooperative parental decision-making regarding post-divorce care of minor children. Through mediation, couples are led away from win-lose confrontations and moved toward mutual and binding agreements.[35]

Even law schools are beginning to train their students in alternatives to litigation. The National Institute for Dispute Resolution has raised $250,000 from large corporations to stimulate law schools to develop course materials on alternatives.[36]

Universities should not be so hesitant in using alternatives to litigation. In any well-run institution, an alternative is already in place—campus grievance procedures.[37] A grievance system benefits the college or university as well as potential plaintiffs. Its procedures can provide a forum for a disappointed or angry faculty member to be listened to, and the opportunity to blow off steam has been found beneficial irrespective of the outcome of the grievance.[38] Moreover, research that does exist on both business[39] and academic[40] organizations has shown that implementing a grievance system leads to more responsible and fairer organizational personnel policies and more consistent treatment of employees. It would be valuable if we had more comprehensive research on how such procedures are working.[41] We need a national study to publicize successful grievance models and illuminate pitfalls at various types of institutions. This much seems clear: to perform their function effectively in the civil rights era, the campus grievance process must be able to go beyond procedural reviews to examine the substance of a decision in order to determine whether discrimination exists. A well-ordered grievance process and carefully articulated set of personnel procedures will not eliminate all lawsuits, but some will be settled and the rest will be easier and cheaper to win.

Almost every academic administrator would affirm that an institution's faculty is its most valuable asset, but higher education consistently has underinvested in developing its academic personnel systems.[42] Although litigation, threatened or real, has probably improved these personnel systems, there is much more that can be done.

Research Conclusions

It is important to explore practical alternatives that can minimize the costs of litigation for both parties, but the necessary and primary first step is description. Only then can informed change take place. Social scientists use models for both descriptive and predictive purposes. The ten-stage analytical framework developed in chapter 1 was intended to be a descriptive tool, and one purpose of this project was to test its effectiveness.

Researchers who wish to examine the impacts of the litigation process face a difficult task, which may be why such studies have been done so rarely. The events of a major lawsuit usually take place over several years, involve a dozen or more participants, and produce thousands of pages of documents. Often the interpretation of these events is clouded by charged emotions and faulty memories. Simple chronology may confuse cause and effect and, in any event, does not reveal the relationship between the parties' decisions and the impacts of the process. Some mechanism for compiling and sorting through the enormous amount of data in order to illuminate important questions is necessary. The ten-stage litigation process framework was useful for developing the inquiry, gathering the data, and then reporting it. In field research intuition and chance sometimes produce valuable insights, but the structure and discipline provided by the framework were consistently valuable. Not infrequently, the framework caused the researchers to ask about decisions the participants had not, at the time, consciously realized they had made or had long since moved to the rear of their memories.

The framework was also helpful in organizing the case studies in a manner that permitted comparisons. In general, what the comparisons show is that although there were major variations in the issues, characteristics of the parties, and legal outcomes of the suits, the decision-making process and the types of costs involved in the litigation process were much the same in all cases. Although there were substantial differences in degree, most of the impacts of the litigation process were negative for most parties. Experienced attorneys are generally familiar with the sequence of litigation and its potential outcomes; most parties are not. The ten stages in the framework may prove to be a useful device for helping parties to understand the process, their place in it, and where they should be making decisions and anticipating impacts. In particular, the parties need to be clear about the consequences of pursuing the case and of settling it, about the effects of discovery and trial conduct on post-decision relationships, and about the nature of public statements and support networks in the conflict. The next step is to develop a research program to test specific hypotheses about impacts of various decisions and procedures in the litigation process. At that point, we may be able to predict some of these consequences more precisely for the participants.

We believe social scientists must continue inquiring into the impact of the litigation process. The quantity and scope of civil litigation in contemporary American society is so great that better tools are needed to measure the consequences of the process. Research on criminal justice has looked at the impact of that process, and changes have occurred in the way both accused and accusers are treated. In rape and child abuse cases, for example, awareness of the harmful effects that the traditional trial process has had on witnesses has led to reforms in many jurisdictions.

In most civil litigation, the impact of the process is probably not nearly as traumatic as in criminal cases, but, as this research has demonstrated, the consequences may still be damaging. Since our research covers only a particular species of civil litigation, we cannot generalize with certainty beyond academic discrimination cases. Many civil lawsuits are arm's-length affairs in which the parties have no great emotional or financial stakes, and therefore the consequences of the process may be marginal. But there are other types of civil litigation whose impacts may resemble those reported here. The key, we think, is whether there was a long-term personal relationship between the parties before the lawsuit began. In that circumstance, the stakes are often not just money or power but also an affirmation of self-worth and integrity. Rarely will the courts be able to satisfy the latter demand, and sorting through these issues in an adversary process can be very harmful. Cases in this category might be divorce, child custody, disputes between neighbors or property-holding associations (condominiums), disputes between organizations and their members (especially over ideological issues), client-professional disagreement (medical malpractice), and, of course, employment controversies of many kinds. It is also in these areas that there has been the most experimentation with the use of alternative mechanisms for dispute resolution. The time has come to forge a stronger link between empirical research on the consequences of the litigation process and attempts to reform that process or to seek alternatives.

NOTES

1. Jonathan B. Marks, Earl Johnson, Jr., and Peter L. Szanton, *Dispute Resolution in America: Processes in Evolution* (Washington, D.C.: National Institute for Dispute Resolution, 1984).
2. William L. F. Felsteiner, Richard L. Abel, and Austin Sarat, "The Emergence and Transformation of Disputes: Naming, Blaming, Claiming . . . ," *Law and Society Review* 15 (1980–81): 632–54. See also Sandra E. Gleason, "The Decision to File a Sex Discrimination Complaint in the Federal Government: The Benefits and Costs of 'Voice,' " in *36th Annual Proceedings* (Industrial Relations Research Association, Madison, Wis., 1983), pp. 189–97.
3. This quotation, and the ones that follow, unless otherwise identified, come from the surveys of plaintiffs or university attorneys. The completed questionnaires are in the project's research files.
4. Zahorik v. Cornell University, 579 F. Supp. 349 (N.D.N.Y. 1983), *aff'd,* 729 F.2d 85 (2d Cir. 1984).
5. Good research on the financial and time costs of a lawsuit has been done by the Civil Litigation Research Project at the University of Wisconsin. See David M. Trubeck et al., "The Costs of Ordinary Litigation" (Civil Litigation Research Project, University of Wisconsin, 1983).
6. Kumar v. Board of Trustees, 566 F. Supp. 1299, 1320 (D. Mass. 1983), *rev'd,* 774 F.2d 1 (1st Cir. 1985). Although the trial court awarded Kumar seven years of back pay, minus the amount he earned during the period, and attorney fees, the award was reversed on appeal and the university's decision to deny him tenure upheld.
7. In Acosta v. University of the District of Columbia, 528 F. Supp. 1215 (D.D.C. 1981), the plaintiff was turned down for promotion ostensibly because he lacked a doctorate. During the pretrial discovery process, however, it was revealed that one of the members of Acosta's promotion committee had probably falsely claimed possession of a Ph.D. degree. The person later left the university under pressure. Trial Transcript, p. 290.
8. See Association of Governing Boards, *Reports,* July/August, September/October, 1985.
9. Clark Kerr has noted that President Richard Lyman of Stanford claims that in his last year at the university there were more lawsuits against him and Stanford than during the whole twenty years Wallace Sterling had been president of Stanford before him. "Impressions 1984: Higher Education Once Again in Transition," address given for the Earl V. Pullias Lectures in Higher Education, University of Southern California, March 10, 1984.
10. 502 F.2d 1229, 1231–32 (2d Cir. 1974).
11. 435 F. Supp. 1328, 1332 (W.D. Pa. 1977).
12. Presseisen v. Swarthmore College, 442 F. Supp. 593, 613 (E.D. Pa. 1977).
13. Powell v. Syracuse University, 580 F.2d 1150, 1153 (2d Cir. 1978), *cert. denied,* 439 U.S. 984 (1978).
14. 630 F.2d 60, 68 (2d Cir. 1980).
15. Zahorik v. Cornell University, 579 F. Supp. 349 (N.D.N.Y. 1983), *aff'd,* 729 F.2d 85 (2d Cir. 1984).

16. Clement Vose, *Caucasians Only: The Supreme Court, the NAACP and the Restrictive Covenant Cases* (Berkeley: University of California Press, 1959), and Timothy J. O'Neill, *Bakke and the Politics of Equality* (Middletown, Conn.: Wesleyan University Press, 1985).

17. Gaynelle Evans and Cheryl M. Fields, "Equal Employment Agency to Focus Its Probes on Individuals," *Chronicle of Higher Education,* February 20, 1985, p. 25.

18. 359 F. Supp. 1002 (W.D. Pa. 1973), 435 F. Supp. 1328 (W.D. Pa. 1977).

19. 430 F. Supp. 602 (D. Md. 1977).

20. Karen Childers et al., "A Network of One's Own," in *Rocking the Boat,* ed. Gloria DeSole and Leonore Hoffman (New York: Modern Language Association, 1981).

21. In the 1985–86 academic year, Committee A, which handles issues related to academic freedom and tenure, received 1,222 complaints, of which, by the year's end, 265 had been settled, dismissed or withdrawn, 37 had been mediated, and 987 were unresolved. This number of complaints was the highest since 1976; Jordan E. Kurland, AAUP associate general secretary believes that is because faculty are increasingly interested in using nonlitigative means of resolving disputes. *Chronicle of Higher Education,* June 25, 1986, p. 20.

22. Thompson's speech was given at the 1984 NACUA Convention and was reported by Cheryl Fields, "Academics' Increased Reliance on Legal Advice Documented by College Attorney's Association," *Chronicle of Higher Education,* July 17, 1985, p. 15.

23. Quoted in Jerome Frank, *Courts on Trial* (Princeton, N.J.: Princeton University Press, 1949), p. 40.

24. Most of these interviews were conducted by Isaac Sperka, a student at the University of Maryland.

25. Derek Bok, "What Are American Law Schools Doing Wrong? A Lot," *Student Lawyer,* September, 1985, p. 50. Bok is a former dean of Harvard Law School.

26. Irving S. Shapiro, *America's Third Revolution: Public Interest and the Private Role* (New York: Harper and Row, 1984), p. 264.

27. Renato DiPentima, deputy associate commissioner, Social Security Administration, interview with author, November 5, 1984.

28. Shapiro, *America's Third Revolution,* p. 190.

29. The court described the procedures being defended: "Subjectivity and conflict of interest pervaded the entire promotion process." She found the process "discriminatory" and "invalid" and awarded Acosta a full professorship.

30. Quoted in Fields, "Academics' Increased Reliance on Legal Advice."

31. The project did produce a useful publication: Jane McCarthy, Irving Ladimer, and Josef P. Sirefman, *Managing Faculty Disputes* (San Francisco: Jossey-Bass, 1984).

32. 415 U.S. 36 (1974).

33. Jerold S. Auerbach, *Justice Without Law? Resolving Disputes Without Lawyers* (New York: Oxford University Press, 1983), p. 1.

34. Shapiro, *America's Third Revolution,* p. 190. See also Larry Ray with Anne L. Clark, "The Multi-Door Courthouse Idea: Building the Courthouse of the Future Today," *Ohio State Journal of Dispute Resolution* 1, no. 1 (1985): 3–29.

35. "Reducing Custody Conflicts," *Precis* 14, no. 31 (May 7, 1984): 2–3 (publication of the University of Maryland at College Park). Compare with Brigette M. Bodenheimer, "The Rights of Children and the Crisis of Custody Litigation: Modifications of Custody In and Out of State," *Colorado Law Review* 46 (1976): 495–505.

36. Daniel B. Moskowitz, "Alternatives to Litigation Gain Support," *Washington Post,* February 6, 1984, p. A-23.

37. A variety of forms exist. Eighty campuses have created ombudsmen. The University and College Ombudsmen Association is at Southern Illinois University, Carbondale, Illinois.

38. A. W. J. Thompson and V. V. Murray, *Grievance Procedures* (Westmead, U.K.: Saxon House, D.C. Heath, 1976).

39. Sumner H. Slichter, James J. Healy, and E. Robert Livernash, *The Impact of Collective Bargaining on Management* (Washington, D.C.: Brookings Institution, 1960).

40. James P. Begin, "Grievance Procedures and Faculty Collegiality: The Rutgers Case," *Industrial and Labor Relations Review* 31, no. 1 (1978): 295–309.

41. A very useful beginning can be found in the work of Martin Estey as reported in "Faculty Grievance Procedures Outside Collective Bargaining: The Experience at AAU Campuses," *Academe,* May/June, 1986, pp. 6–15. The data are drawn from 17 major public and private research universities, and the conclusions are fairly optimistic about the utility of such procedures. Whether these data and conclusions reflect the reality elsewhere in the universe of 3,100 institutions of higher education in the United States is not certain.

42. For a comprehensive analysis of the underinvestment problem in salary, working conditions, and opportunity for professional growth, see Howard R. Bowen and Jack H. Schuster, *American Professors: A National Resource Imperiled* (New York: Oxford University Press, 1986).

Appendix
Academic Discrimination Cases, 1969–84

This list was compiled from the authors' research, a LEXIS search of the federal courts file from 1970 through 1984, and a search of *Education Law Reporter* from its inception in 1982 through the end of 1984.

Abrams v. Baylor College of Medicine, 32 Fair Employment Practices Cases 935 (S.D. Tex. 1983), 581 F. Supp. 1570 (S.D. Tex. 1984)

Abramson v. University of Hawaii, 548 P.2d 253 (Hawaii 1976), 594 F.2d 202 (9th Cir. 1979)

Acosta v. University of the District of Columbia, 528 F. Supp. 1215 (D.D.C. 1981)

Adler v. John Carroll University, 549 F. Supp. 652 (N.D. Ohio, 1982)

Al-Hamdami v. SUNY, 438 F. Supp. 299 (W.D.N.Y. 1977)

Al-Khazraji v. Saint Francis College, 523 F. Supp. 386 (W.D. Pa. 1981)

Araujo v. Trustees of Boston College, 34 Employment Practices Decisions ¶ 34,409 (D. Mass. 1983)

Banerjee v. Smith College, 495 F. Supp. 1148 (D. Mass. 1980), *aff'd,* 648 F.2d 61 (1st Cir. 1981), *cert. denied,* 454 U.S. 1098 (1981)

Barding v. Board of Curators, 497 F. Supp. 1013 (W.D. Mo. 1980)

Baruah v. Young, 536 F. Supp. 356 (D. Md. 1982)

Behlar v. Smith, 544 F. Supp. 1085 (E.D. Ark. 1982), *aff'd,* 719 F.2d 950 (8th Cir. 1983), *cert. denied,* 104 S. Ct. 2169 (1984)

Bennun v. Rutgers, 413 F. Supp. 1274 (D. N.J. 1976)

Bernhard v. Dutchess Community College, 28 Employment Practices Decisions ¶ 32,540 (S.D.N.Y. 1982)

Berry v. Board of Supervisors, Louisiana State University, 715 F.2d 971 (5th Cir. 1983), 783 F.2d 1270 (5th Cir. 1986)

Beverly v. Douglas, 591 F. Supp. 1321 (S.D.N.Y. 1984)

Bickley v. University of Maryland, 527 F. Supp. 174 (D. Md. 1981)

Billings v. Wichita State University, 557 F. Supp. 1348 (D. Kan. 1983)

Bireline v. Seagondollar, 567 F.2d 260 (4th Cir. 1977), *cert. denied,* 444 U.S. 842 (1980)

Black Faculty Association v. San Diego Community College District, 664 F.2d 1153 (9th Cir. 1981)

253

Board of Governors v. Perry, 17 Employment Practices Decisions ¶ 8530 (E.D. Mich. 1976)

Board of Regents v. Dawes, 370 F. Supp. 1190 (D. Neb. 1975), *rev'd*, 522 F.2d 380 (8th Cir. 1976), *cert. denied*, 424 U.S. 914 (1976)

Braden v. University of Pittsburgh, 343 F. Supp. 836 (W.D. Pa. 1972), 477 F.2d 1 (3d Cir. 1973); 392 F. Supp. 118 (W.D. Pa. 1975), *aff'd*, 552 F.2d 948 (3d Cir. 1977)

Byron v. University of Florida, 403 F. Supp. 49 (N.D. Fla. 1975)

Campbell v. Ramsey, 484 F. Supp. 190 (E.D. Ark. 1980), *aff'd*, 631 F.2d 597 (8th Cir. 1980)

Cap v. Lehigh University, 433 F. Supp. 1275 (E.D. Pa. 1977), 450 F. Supp. 460 (E.D. Pa. 1978)

Carpenter v. Board of Regents, 529 F. Supp. 525 (W.D. Wis. 1982), *aff'd*, 728 F.2d 911 (7th Cir. 1984)

Carton v. Trustees of Tufts College, 25 Fair Employment Practices Cases 1114 (D. Mass. 1981)

Chai v. Michigan Technological University, 493 F. Supp. 1137 (W.D. Mich. 1980)

Chambliss v. Foote, 421 F. Supp. 12 (E.D. La. 1976), *aff'd*, 562 F.2d 1015 (5th Cir. 1977), *cert. denied*, 439 U.S. 839 (1978)

Chang v. University of Rhode Island, 554 F. Supp. 1203 (D.R.I. 1983), 606 F. Supp. 1161 (D.R.I. 1985)

Chung v. Morehouse College, 11 Employment Practices Decisions ¶ 10,657 (N.D. Ga. 1975)

Citron v. Jackson State University, 456 F. Supp. 3 (S.D. Miss. 1977), *aff'd*, 577 F.2d 1132 (5th Cir. 1978)

Clark v. Atlanta University, 65 F.R.D. 414 (N.D. Ga. 1974), *aff'd*, 15 Employment Practices Decisions ¶ 9951 (5th Cir. 1977)

Cohen v. Community College of Philadelphia, 484 F. Supp. 411 (E.D. Pa. 1980)

Cohen v. Illinois Institute of Technology, 384 F. Supp. 202 (N.D. Ill. 1974), *aff'd*, 524 F.2d 818 (7th Cir. 1975), *cert. denied*, 425 U.S. 943 (1976)

Cohen v. Temple University, 578 F. Supp. 1371 (E.D. Pa. 1984)

Cole v. University of Hartford, 391 F. Supp. 88 (D. Conn. 1975)

Cooper v. University of Texas, Dallas, 482 F. Supp. 187 (N.D. Tex. 1979), *aff'd*, 648 F.2d 1039 (5th Cir. 1981)

Coser v. Moore, 587 F. Supp. 572 (E.D.N.Y. 1983), *aff'd*, 739 F.2d 746 (2d Cir. 1984)

Craig v. Alabama State University, 451 F. Supp. 1207 (M.D. Ala. 1978), *aff'd*, 614 F.2d 1295 (5th Cir. 1980), *cert. denied*, 449 U.S. 862 (1980)

Craik v. Minnesota State University Board, 731 F.2d 465 (8th Cir. 1984)

Cramer v. Virginia Commonwealth University, 415 F. Supp. 673 (E.D. Va. 1976), *vacated*, 586 F.2d 297 (4th Cir. 1978), 486 F. Supp. 187 (D. Va. 1980)

Croushorn v. Board of Trustees of University of Tennessee, 518 F. Supp. 9 (M.D. Tenn. 1980)

Cussler v. University of Maryland, 430 F. Supp. 602 (D. Md. 1977)

Davis v. State Board for Community Colleges, 27 Fair Employment Practices Cases 215 (E.D. Va. 1981)

Davis v. Weidner, 421 F. Supp. 594 (E.D. Wis. 1976), *aff'd*, 596 F.2d 726 (7th Cir. 1979)

Denny v. Westfield State College, 25 Fair Employment Practices Cases 957 (D. Mass. 1981)

Dewey v. University of New Hampshire, 694 F.2d 1 (1st Cir. 1982), *cert. denied*, 461 U.S. 944 (1983)

Duke v. University of Texas, El Paso, 663 F.2d 522 (5th Cir. 1981), 729 F.2d 994 (5th Cir. 1984), *cert. denied*, 105 S. Ct. 386 (1984)

Duncan v. Maryland, 21 Employment Practices Decisions ¶ 30,554 (D. Md. 1978)

Dyson v. Lavery, 417 F. Supp. 103 (E.D. Va. 1976)

EEOC v. Colby College, 439 F. Supp. 631 (D. Me. 1977), *rev'd*, 589 F.2d 1139 (1st Cir. 1978)

EEOC v. Cleveland State University, 29 Employment Practices Decisions ¶ 32,783 (N.D. Ohio 1982)

EEOC v. McCarthy, 578 F. Supp. 45 (D. Mass. 1983)

EEOC v. Mississippi College, 451 F. Supp. 564 (D. Miss. 1978), *vacated and remanded*, 626 F.2d 477 (5th Cir. 1980), *cert. denied*, 453 U.S. 912 (1981)

EEOC v. University of New Mexico, 504 F.2d 1296 (10th Cir. 1974)

EEOC v. University of Notre Dame, 551 F. Supp. 737 (N.D. Ind. 1982), *rev'd*, 715 F.2d 331 (7th Cir. 1983)

EEOC v. University of Pittsburgh, 487 F. Supp. 1071 (W.D. Pa. 1980), *aff'd*, 643 F.2d 983 (3d Cir. 1981), *cert. denied*, 454 U.S. 880 (1981)

EEOC v. Southwest Baptist Seminary, 485 F. Supp. 255 (N.D. Tex. 1980), *modified*, 651 F.2d 277 (5th Cir. 1981), *cert. denied*, 456 U.S. 905 (1982)

EEOC v. Troy State University, 693 F.2d 1353 (11th Cir. 1982), *cert. denied*, 463 U.S. 1207 (1983)

EEOC v. Tufts University, 421 F. Supp. 152 (D. Mass. 1975)

Egelston v. SUNY Geneseo, 535 F.2d 752 (2d Cir. 1976)

Eichmann v. Indiana State University, 597 F.2d 1104 (7th Cir. 1979)

Elias v. El Paso County Community College District, 556 F. Supp. 248 (W.D. Tex. 1982)

Ende v. Board of Regents, 565 F. Supp. 501 (N.D. Ill. 1983), *aff'd*, 757 F.2d 176 (7th Cir. 1985)

Faro v. New York University, 6 Employment Practices Decisions ¶ 8940 (S.D.N.Y. 1973), *aff'd*, 502 F.2d 1229 (2d Cir. 1974)

Felton v. Trustees of California State University, 708 F.2d 1507 (9th Cir. 1983)

Fisher v. Dillard University, 499 F. Supp. 525 (E.D. La. 1980)

Fisher v. Flynn, 598 F.2d 663 (1st Cir. 1979)

Ford v. Nicks, 741 F.2d 858 (6th Cir. 1984)

Francis-Sobel v. University of Maine, 597 F.2d 15 (1st Cir. 1979), *cert. denied*, 444 U.S. 949 (1980)

Franklin v. Herbert Lehman College, 508 F. Supp. 945 (S.D.N.Y. 1981)

Garcia v. University of Kansas, 31 Fair Employment Practices Cases 277 (10th Cir. 1983)

Gellman v. State of Maryland, 538 F.2d 603 (4th Cir. 1976)

Ghosh v. New York University Medical Center, 576 F. Supp. 86 (S.D.N.Y. 1983)

Gilinsky v. Columbia University, 440 F. Supp. 1120 (S.D.N.Y. 1977), 488 F. Supp. 1309 (S.D.N.Y. 1980), *aff'd,* 652 F.2d 53 (2d Cir. 1981)

Gladney v. Thomas, 573 F. Supp. 1232 (N.D. Ala. 1983)

Gray v. Board of Higher Education, 92 F.R.D. 87 (S.D.N.Y. 1981), *rev'd,* 692 F.2d 901 (2d Cir. 1982)

Green v. Board of Regents, 335 F. Supp. 249 (N.D. Tex. 1971), *aff'd,* 474 F.2d 594 (5th Cir. 1973)

Greer v. University of Arkansas Board of Trustees, 544 F. Supp. 1685 (E.D. Ark. 1982), *modified,* 719 F.2d 950 (8th Cir. 1983), *cert. denied,* 466 U.S. 958 (1984)

Gresham v. Chambers, 501 F.2d 687 (2d Cir. 1974)

Guerra v. Board of Trustees, 567 F.2d 352 (9th Cir. 1977)

Guertin v. Hackerman, 496 F. Supp. 593 (S.D. Tex. 1980), 25 Fair Employment Practices Cases 207 (S.D. Tex. 1981)

Gupta v. East Texas State University, 654 F.2d 411 (5th Cir. 1981)

Hanshaw v. Delaware Tech, 405 F. Supp. 292 (D. Del. 1975)

Harmond v. Board of Regents, 31 Fair Employment Practices Cases 940 (S.D. Ga. 1983)

Haugh v. Iona College, 22 Employment Practices Decisions ¶ 30,790 (S.D.N.Y. 1980)

Hein v. Oregon College of Education, 718 F.2d 910 (9th Cir. 1982)

Henry v. Texas Tech, 466 F. Supp. 141 (N.D. Tex. 1979)

Hernandez-Cruz v. Fordham University, 521 F. Supp. 1059 (S.D.N.Y. 1981)

Herrmann v. Moore, 576 F.2d 453 (2d Cir. 1978), *cert. denied,* 439 U.S. 1003 (1978)

Hill v. Nettleton, 455 F. Supp. 514 (D. Colo. 1978)

Hooker v. Tufts University, 581 F. Supp. 98 (D. Mass. 1983), 581 F. Supp. 104 (D. Mass. 1983)

Hoth v. Grinnell College, 23 Fair Employment Practices Cases 528 (S.D. Iowa 1980)

Hou v. Slippery Rock State College, 573 F. Supp. 1539 (W.D. Pa. 1983)

Huang v. College of Holy Cross, 436 F. Supp. 639 (D. Mass. 1977)

Hudak v. Curators of University of Missouri, 586 F.2d 105 (8th Cir. 1978), *cert. denied,* 440 U.S. 985 (1979)

Hunter v. Ward, 476 F. Supp. 913 (E.D. Ark. 1979)

Hyatt v. Agricultural and Technical College, 21 Employment Practices Decisions ¶ 30,509 (E.D.N.Y. 1979).

Ishigami v. University of Hawaii, 469 F. Supp. 443 (D. Hawaii 1979)

Jackson v. University of Pittsburgh, 405 F. Supp. 607 (W.D. Pa. 1975)

Jacobs v. Board of Regents, 473 F. Supp. 663 (S.D. Fla. 1979)

Jacobs v. College of William and Mary, 495 F. Supp. 183 (E.D. Va. 1980), *aff'd,* 661 F.2d 922 (4th Cir. 1981)

Jamerson v. Board of Trustees, 662 F.2d 320 (5th Cir. 1981)

Jaroch v. University of Wisconsin, 372 F. Supp. 106 (E.D. Wis. 1974)

Jawa v. Fayetteville State University, 426 F. Supp. 218 (E.D.N.C. 1976)

Jepsen v. Florida Board of Regents, 21 Fair Employment Practices Cases 1695 (N.D. Fla. 1977), *rev'd,* 610 F.2d 1379 (5th Cir. 1980), 754 F.2d 924 (5th Cir. 1985)

Johnson v. Michigan State University, 547 F. Supp. 429 (W.D. Mich. 1982), *aff'd,* 723 F.2d 909 (6th Cir. 1983)

Johnson v. University of Pittsburgh, 359 F. Supp. 1002 (W.D. Pa. 1973), 435 F. Supp. 1328 (W.D. Pa. 1977)

Joshi v. Florida State University, 486 F. Supp. 86 (N.D. Fla. 1980), *rev'd*, 646 F.2d 981 (5th Cir. 1981), *cert. denied*, 456 U.S. 972 (1982), 763 F.2d 1227 (11th Cir. 1985)

Kaplowitz v. University of Chicago, 387 F. Supp. 42 (N.D. Ill. 1974)

Karlen v. New York University, 464 F. Supp. 704 (S.D.N.Y. 1979)

Keyes v. Lenoir Rhyne College, 15 Fair Employment Practices Cases 914 (W.D.N.C. 1976), *aff'd*, 552 F.2d 579 (4th Cir. 1977), *cert. denied*, 434 U.S. 904 (1977)

Kim v. Coppin State College, 662 F.2d 1055 (4th Cir. 1981)

Klain v. Pennsylvania State University, 15 Employment Practices Decisions ¶ 7979 (M.D. Pa. 1977)

Kumar v. Board of Trustees, 566 F. Supp. 1299 (D. Mass. 1983), *rev'd*, 774 F.2d 1 (1st Cir. 1985)

Kunda v. Muhlenberg College, 463 F. Supp. 294 (E.D. Pa. 1978), *aff'd*, 621 F.2d 532 (3d Cir. 1980)

Kureshy v. City University of New York, 561 F. Supp. 1098 (E.D.N.Y. 1983)

Kutska v. California State College, 410 F. Supp. 48 (W.D. Pa. 1976), *aff'd*, 549 F.2d 795 (3d Cir. 1977)

Labat v. Board of Higher Education, 401 F. Supp. 753 (S.D.N.Y. 1975)

Laborde v. Regents, University of California, 495 F. Supp. 1067 (C.D. Cal. 1980), *aff'd*, 686 F.2d 715 (9th Cir. 1982), *cert. denied*, 459 U.S. 1173 (1983)

Lamb v. Rantoul, 421 F. Supp. 492 (D.R.I. 1976), *aff'd*, 561 F.2d 409 (1st Cir. 1977), 538 F. Supp. 34 (D.R.I. 1981)

Lamb v. Scripps College, 627 F.2d 1015 (9th Cir. 1980)

Lamphere v. Brown University, 71 F.R.D. 641 (D.R.I. 1976), 553 F.2d 714 (1st Cir. 1977), 610 F.2d 46 (1st Cir. 1979), 491 F. Supp. 232 (D.R.I. 1980), *aff'd*, 685 F.2d 743 (1st Cir. 1982), 613 F. Supp. 971 (D.R.I. 1985)

Langland v. Vanderbilt University, 589 F. Supp. 995 (M.D. Tenn. 1984), *aff'd*, 772 F.2d 907 (6th Cir. 1985)

Larsen v. Kirkham, 499 F. Supp. 960 (D. Utah 1980), *cert. denied*, 464 U.S. 849 (1983)

Lazic v. University of Pennsylvania, 513 F. Supp. 761 (E.D. Pa. 1981)

League of Academic Women v. Regents, University of California, 343 F. Supp. 636 (N.D. Cal. 1972)

Leake v. University of Cincinnati, 93 F.R.D. 460 (S.D. Ohio 1976), 605 F.2d 255 (6th Cir. 1979)

Leftwich v. Harris-Stowe State College, 540 F. Supp. 37 (E.D. Mo. 1982), *modified*, 702 F.2d 686 (8th Cir. 1983)

Levine v. Fairleigh Dickinson University, 646 F.2d 825 (3d Cir. 1981)

Lewis v. Central Piedmont Community College, 689 F.2d 1207 (4th Cir. 1982), *cert. denied*, 460 U.S. 1040 (1983)

Lewis v. Chicago State, 299 F. Supp. 1357 (N.D. Ill. 1969)

Lewis v. St. Louis University, 573 F. Supp. 300 (E.D. Mo. 1983), *aff'd*, 744 F.2d 1368 (8th Cir. 1984)

Lieberman v. Gant, 474 F. Supp. 848 (D. Conn. 1979), *aff'd*, 630 F.2d 60 (2d Cir. 1980)

Lincoln v. Board of Regents, 697 F.2d 928 (11th Cir. 1983), *cert. denied,* 464 U.S. 826 (1983)

Lucky v. Board of Regents, 34 Fair Employment Practices Cases 986 (S.D. Fla. 1981)

Lynn v. Board of Regents, 21 Employment Practices Decisions ¶ 30,558 (C.D. Cal. 1979), *rev'd,* 656 F.2d 1337 (9th Cir. 1981), *cert. denied,* 459 U.S. 823 (1982)

Lyon v. Temple University, 507 F. Supp. 471 (E.D. Pa. 1981), 543 F. Supp. 1372 (E.D. Pa. 1982)

McAdoo v. Toll, 591 F. Supp. 1399 (D. Md. 1984)

McAloon v. Bryant College of Business Administration, 520 F. Supp. 103 (D.N.H. 1981)

McKillop v. Regents, University of California, 386 F. Supp. 1270 (N.D. Cal. 1975)

McMillan v. Rust College, 710 F.2d 1112 (5th Cir. 1983)

Manning v. Tufts University, 613 F.2d 1200 (1st Cir. 1980)

Marshall v. Georgia Southwestern College, 489 F. Supp. 1322 (M.D. Ga. 1980), 580 F. Supp. 859 (D. Ga. 1984), *modified,* 765 F.2d 1026 (11th Cir. 1985)

Marshall v. Kent State, 13 Employment Practices Decisions ¶ 11,374 (D. Ohio 1976), *aff'd,* 589 F.2d 255 (6th Cir. 1978)

Marshall v. University of Texas, El Paso, 25 Fair Employment Practices Cases 1048 (W.D. Tex. 1978)

Mecklenberg v. Montana State University, 13 Employment Practices Decisions ¶ 11,438 (D. Mont. 1976)

Meehan v. New England School of Law, 522 F. Supp. 484 (D. Mass. 1981), *aff'd,* 705 F.2d 439 (1st Cir. 1983)

Melani v. Board of Higher Education, 561 F. Supp. 769 (S.D.N.Y. 1983)

Melanson v. Rantoul, 421 F. Supp. 492 (D.R.I. 1976), *aff'd,* 561 F.2d 409 (1st Cir. 1977), 536 F. Supp. 271 (D.R.I. 1982)

Michigan State University Faculty Association v. Michigan State University, 93 F.R.D. 54 (W.D. Mich. 1981)

Middleton-Keirn v. Stone, 655 F.2d 609 (5th Cir. 1981)

Mitchell v. Visser, 529 F. Supp. 1034 (D. Kan. 1981)

Mittelstaedt v. University of Arkansas, 487 F. Supp. 960 (E.D. Ark. 1980)

Molthan v. Temple University, 442 F. Supp 448 (E.D. Pa. 1977), 83 F.R.D. 368 (E.D. Pa. 1979), *aff'd,* 778 F.2d 955 (3d Cir. 1985)

Mosby v. Webster College, 423 F. Supp. 615 (E.D. Mo. 1976), *aff'd,* 563 F.2d 901 (8th Cir. 1977)

Muhich v. Allen, 603 F.2d 1247 (7th Cir. 1979)

O'Connell v. Teachers College of Columbia, 63 F.R.D. 638 (S.D.N.Y. 1974)

Ottaviani v. SUNY (New Paltz), 19 Employment Practices Decisions ¶ 9199 (S.D.N.Y. 1979), 26 Employment Practices Decisions ¶ 31,954 (S.D.N.Y. 1981)

Palmer v. District Board of Trustees, 748 F.2d 595 (11th Cir. 1984)

Pande v. Johns Hopkins University, 598 F. Supp. 1084 (D. Md. 1984)

Pendrell v. Chatham College, 370 F. Supp. 494 (W.D. Pa. 1974)

Penk v. Oregon State Board of Education, 93 F.R.D. 45 (D. Or. 1981), 99 F.R.D. 495, 497, 500, 501, 504, 506, 508, 511 (D. Or. 1982)

Perham v. Ladd, 436 F. Supp. 1101 (N.D. Ill. 1977)

Peters v. Middlebury College, 12 Fair Employment Practices Cases 295 (D. Vt. 1974), 409 F. Supp. 857 (D. Vt. 1976)

Peters v. Wayne State University, 476 F. Supp. 1343 (E.D. Mich. 1979), *rev'd*, 691 F.2d 235 (6th Cir. 1982), *vacated and remanded*, 463 U.S. 1223 (1983)

Pime v. Loyola University of Chicago, 585 F. Supp. 435 (D. Ill. 1984)

Planells v. Howard University, 32 Fair Employment Practices Cases 336 (D.D.C. 1983)

Powell v. Syracuse University, 580 F.2d 1150 (2d Cir. 1978), *cert. denied*, 439 U.S. 984 (1978)

Presseisen v. Swarthmore College, 386 F. Supp. 1337 (E.D. Pa. 1974), 442 F. Supp. 593 (E.D. Pa. 1977), *aff'd*, 582 F.2d 1275 (3d Cir. 1978)

Rackin v. University of Pennsylvania, 386 F. Supp. 992 (E.D. Pa. 1974)

Rajender v. University of Minnesota, 20 Employment Practices Decisions ¶ 30,214, 24 Fair Employment Practices Cases 1045 (D. Minn. 1978), 20 Employment Practices Decisions ¶ 30,225, 24 Fair Employment Practices Cases 1051 (D. Minn. 1979), 546 F. Supp. 158 (D. Minn. 1982), 563 F. Supp. 401 (D. Minn. 1983)

Ricks v. Delaware State College, 605 F.2d 710 (3d Cir. 1979), *rev'd*, 444 U.S. 250 (1980)

Riley v. University of Lowell, 651 F.2d 822 (1st Cir. 1981), *cert. denied*, 454 U.S. 1125 (1981)

Ritter v. Mt. St. Mary's College, 495 F. Supp. 724 (D. Md. 1980)

Rivas v. State Board for Community Colleges, 517 F. Supp. 467 (D. Colo. 1981)

Rubenstein v. University of Wisconsin Board of Regents, 422 F. Supp. 61 (E.D. Wis. 1976)

Rubin v. University of Minnesota, 653 F.2d 351 (8th Cir. 1981)

Russell v. Belmont College, 554 F. Supp. 667 (M.D. Tenn. 1982)

St. Louis v. Alverno College, 744 F.2d 1314 (7th Cir. 1984)

Sanday v. Carnegie-Mellon, 11 Employment Practices Decisions ¶ 10,659 (W.D. Pa. 1975), 15 Employment Practices Decisions ¶ 8088 (W.D. Pa. 1976)

Sanders v. Duke University, 538 F. Supp. 1143 (M.D.N.C. 1982)

Savage v. Kibbee, 405 F. Supp. 307 (S.D.N.Y. 1975), 426 F. Supp. 760 (S.D.N.Y. 1976)

Scagnelli v. Whiting, 554 F. Supp. 77 (M.D.N.C. 1982)

Schwartz v. Florida, 494 F. Supp. 574 (N.D. Fla. 1980)

Scott v. University of Delaware, 385 F. Supp. 937 (D. Del. 1974), 68 F.R.D. 606 (D. Del. 1975), 16 Fair Employment Practices Cases 737 (D. Del. 1976), 455 F. Supp. 1102 (D. Del. 1978), *modified*, 601 F.2d 76 (3d Cir. 1979), *cert. denied*, 444 U.S. 931 (1979)

Sessum v. Houston Community College, 94 F.R.D. 316 (S.D. Tex. 1982)

Shawer v. Indiana University, 602 F.2d 1161 (3d Cir. 1979)

Shipley v. Fisk University, 8 Employment Practices Decisions ¶ 9538 (M.D. Tenn. 1973)

Silverman v. Lehigh University, 19 Fair Employment Practices Cases 983 (E.D. Pa. 1976)

Sime v. Trustees, California State University and Colleges, 526 F.2d 1112 (9th Cir. 1975)

Smith v. University of North Carolina, 18 Fair Employment Practices Cases 913 (M.D.N.C. 1978), 19 Employment Practices Decisions ¶ 9040 (M.D.N.C. 1979), *aff'd,* 632 F.2d 316 (4th Cir. 1980)

Sobel v. Yeshiva University, 438 F. Supp. 625 (S.D.N.Y. 1976), 21 Employment Practices Decisions ¶ 30,360 (S.D.N.Y. 1979), 22 Employment Practices Decisions ¶ 30,653 (S.D.N.Y. 1980), 566 F. Supp. 1166 (S.D.N.Y. 1983)

Soble v. University of Maryland, 572 F. Supp. 1509 (D. Md. 1983), *aff'd,* 778 F.2d 164 (4th Cir. 1985)

Solin v. State University of New York, 416 F. Supp. 536 (S.D.N.Y. 1976)

Spaulding v. University of Washington, 676 F.2d 1232 (9th Cir. 1982), 740 F.2d 686 (9th Cir. 1984), *cert. denied,* 105 S. Ct. 511 (1984)

Spieldoch v. Maryville College, 13 Fair Employment Practices Cases 660 (E.D. Mo. 1975)

Spirt v. Teachers Insurance and Annuity Association, 475 F. Supp. 1298 (S.D.N.Y. 1979), *aff'd in part and rev'd in part,* 691 F.2d 1054 (2d Cir. 1982), *vacated and remanded,* 103 S. Ct. 3565 (1983), 735 F.2d 23 (2d Cir. 1984), *cert. denied,* 105 S. Ct. 274 (1984)

Strunk v. Western Kentucky University, 11 Fair Employment Practices Cases 355 (E.D. Ky. 1975)

Sweeney v. Board of Trustees, 569 F.2d 169 (1st Cir. 1978), *vacated,* 439 U.S. 24 (1979), 604 F.2d 106 (1st Cir. 1979), *cert. denied,* 444 U.S. 1045 (1980)

Taliaferro v. Dykstra, 7 Employment Practices Decisions ¶ 9343 (E.D. Va. 1974), 388 F. Supp. 937 (E.D. Va. 1975)

Taylor v. Southern University of New Orleans, 554 F. Supp. 334 (E.D. La. 1982), *aff'd,* 721 F.2d 816 (5th Cir. 1983)

Theodore v. Elmhurst College, 421 F. Supp. 355 (N.D. Ill. 1976)

Timper v. Board of Regents, 512 F. Supp. 384 (W.D. Wis. 1981)

Tolliver v. Yeargan, 567 F. Supp. 116 (W.D. Ark. 1983), *aff'd,* 728 F.2d 1076 (8th Cir. 1984)

Townsel v. University of Alabama, 80 F.R.D. 741 (N.D. Ala. 1978)

Turgeon v. Howard University, 571 F. Supp. 679 (D.D.C. 1983)

United States v. University of Maryland, 438 F. Supp. 742 (D. Md. 1977)

Usery v. Memphis State University, 13 Employment Practices Decisions ¶ 11,451 (W.D. Tenn. 1976)

Valentine v. Smith, 654 F.2d 503 (8th Cir. 1981), *cert. denied,* 454 U.S. 1124 (1981)

Van de Vate v. Boling, 379 F. Supp. 925 (E.D. Tenn. 1974)

Vaughn v. Regents, University of California, 504 F. Supp. 1349 (E.D. Cal. 1981)

Veeder v. Trustees of Boston College, 85 F.R.D. 13 (D. Mass 1979)

Wagner v. Long Island University, 419 F. Supp. 618 (E.D.N.Y. 1976)

Walton v. St. Louis Community College, 583 F. Supp. 458 (E.D. Mo. 1984)

Weise v. Syracuse University, 522 F.2d 397 (2d Cir. 1975), 553 F. Supp. 675 (N.D.N.Y. 1982)

Whitaker v. Board of Higher Education, 461 F. Supp. 99 (E.D.N.Y. 1978)

White v. University of Massachusetts, 28 Employment Practices Decisions ¶ 32,415 (D. Mass. 1981)

Whiting v. Jackson State University, 616 F.2d 116 (5th Cir. 1980)

Wilkens v. University of Houston, 471 F. Supp. 1054 (S.D. Tex. 1979), *aff'd in part and rev'd in part,* 654 F.2d 388 (5th Cir. 1981), *vacated,* 459 U.S. 809 (1982), 695 F.2d 134 (5th Cir. 1983)

Winkes v. Brown University, 491 F. Supp. 232 (D.R.I. 1980), 747 F.2d 792 (1st Cir. 1984)

Winsey v. Pace College, 394 F. Supp. 1324 (S.D.N.Y. 1975)

Zahorik v. Cornell University, 34 Fair Employment Practices Cases 147 (N.D.N.Y. 1981), 579 F. Supp. 349 (N.D.N.Y. 1983), *aff'd,* 729 F.2d 85 (2d Cir. 1984)

Zaustinsky v. University of California, 96 F.R.D. 622 (N.D. Cal. 1983), *aff'd,* 782 F.2d 1055 (9th Cir. 1985)

Bibliography

ARTICLES

Aiken, Ray J. "Legal Liabilities in Higher Education: Their Scope and Management." *Journal of College and University Law* 3 (November, 1977): 225.
Allentown Call Chronicle, December 23, 1979.
Allentown Morning Call, October 4, 1979, December 7, 1979.
American Lawyer, July, 1980, p. 27.
Association of Governing Boards. *Reports.* July/August, September/October, 1985.
Auerbach, Jerold S. "Welcome to Litigation." *New Republic,* January 17, 1983, p. 21.
Bartholet, Elizabeth. "Application of Title VII to Jobs in High Places." *Harvard Law Review* 95 (1982): 945–1,027.
Begin, James P. "Grievance Procedures and Faculty Collegiality: The Rutgers Case." *Industrial and Labor Relations Review* 31, no. 1 (1978): 295–309.
Berg, Steve, and Doug Stone. "The Lord of Federal Court and His Life of Intrigue." *Minneapolis Tribune,* December 9, 1976.
Bodenheimer, Brigette. "The Rights of Children and the Crisis of Custody Litigation: Modifications of Custody In and Out of State." *Colorado Law Review* 46 (1976): 495–505.
Bok, Derek. "What Are American Law Schools Doing Wrong? A Lot." *Student Lawyer,* September, 1983, pp. 46–51.
Boyer, David S. "Minnesota, Where Water Is the Magic Word." *National Geographic,* February, 1976, pp. 200–229.
Bozeman Chronicle, June 6, 1976, July 7, 1977, February 9, 1984.
Brazil, Wayne D. "The Attorney as Victim: Toward More Candor about the Psychological Price Tag of Litigation Practice." *Journal of the Legal Profession* 3 (1978): 107–17.
Broad, William J. "Ending Sex Discrimination in Academia." *Science,* June 6, 1980, pp. 1,120–22.
Brodeur, Paul. "The Asbestos Industry on Trial." *New Yorker,* June 10, 17, 24, July 1, 1985, pp. 49, 45, 37, 36.

Burger, Warren. Address to the American Bar Association, August 10, 1970. Reprinted in Howard James, *Crisis in the Courts*. New York: David McKay Co., 1971.

Carr, David. "Consolidated Dalkon Shield Cases: Playing for Keeps." *Twin Cities Reader*, February 15, 1984.

Caughey, Peter. "MSU Jobs Record Criticized." *Bozeman Chronicle*, November 15, 1981.

Chemical and Engineering News, May 10, 1971.

Chronicle of Higher Education, May 11, 1983, July 17, 1985, June 25, 1986.

Clark, Donald L. "Discrimination Suits: A Unique Settlement." *Educational Record* 58 (Summer, 1977), 233–49.

Estey, Martin. "Faculty Grievance Procedures Outside Collective Bargaining: The Experience at AAU Campuses." *Academe*, May/June, 1986, pp. 6–15.

Evans, Gaynelle, and Cheryl M. Fields. "Equal Employment Agency to Focus Its Probes on Individuals." *Chronicle of Higher Education*, February 20, 1985.

Farrell, Charles S. "University of Delaware Tries to Live Down 'Racist' Image." *Chronicle of Higher Education*, November 9, 1983.

Felsteiner, William L. F., Richard L. Abel, and Austin Sarat. "The Emergence and Transformation of Disputes: Naming, Blaming, Claiming. . . ." *Law and Society Review* 15 (1980–81): 632–54.

Fields, Cheryl. "Academics' Increased Reliance on Legal Advice Documented by College Attorney's Association." *Chronicle of Higher Education*, July 17, 1985.

Foley, Ellen. "Six Women: Faculty Members Who Decided to Fight the System." *Minneapolis Tribune*, June 5, 1982.

Galanter, Marc. "Reading the Landscape of Disputes: What We Know and Don't Know about Our Allegedly Contentious and Litigious Society." *U.C.L.A. Law Review* 31 (October, 1983): 4–71.

Gibson, Richard. "A Conversation with Malcolm Moos, 'The Golden Years of Higher Education Ended in 1968.'" *Minneapolis Star*, August 21, 1973.

Glazer, Nathan. "Toward an Imperial Judiciary." *Public Interest* 41 (1975): 104–23.

Gleason, Sandra E. "The Decision to File a Sex Discrimination Complaint in the Federal Government: The Benefits and Costs of 'Voice.'" In *36th Annual Proceedings*. Industrial Relations Research Association, Madison, Wis., 1983, pp. 189–97.

Gouldner, Helen. "The Social Impact of Campus Litigation." *Journal of Higher Education* 51, no. 3 (1980): 328–36.

Hatfield, Robert S. "The Impact of Antitrust on the Large Corporation." *Vital Speeches* 45, no. 22 (September, 1979): 699–702.

Johnson, Charles S., and Arthur Hutchinson. "MSU Squabble Gives Rare Glimpse in System." *Sunday Missoulan*, March 28, 1976.

"Judging the Judges: An Outsized Job Getting Bigger." *Time*, August 20, 1979, p. 49.

Kerr, Clark. "Impressions 1984: Higher Education Once Again in Transition." Address given for the Earl V. Pullias Lectures in Higher Education, University of Southern California, 1984.

Klobuchar, Jim. Column in *Minneapolis Star and Tribune*, June 23, 1984.

————. "Miles Lord: Judicial Godfather to Troubled Environment." *Minneapolis Star,* December 9, 1974.

Kramer, George R. "Title VII on Campus." *Columbia Law Review* 82 (1982): 1,206–35.

LaNoue, George R. "The Federal Judiciary, Discrimination, and Academic Personnel Policy." *Policy Studies Journal* 10 (September, 1981): 105–23.

————. "Tenure and Title VII." *Journal of College and University Law* 1 (Spring, 1974): 206–21.

Lasorte, Michael A. "Academic Women's Salaries: Equal Pay for Equal Work?" *Journal of Higher Education* 42 (1971): 265–78.

Lee, Barbara A. "Balancing Confidentiality and Disclosure in Faculty Peer Review: Impact of Title VII Litigation." *Journal of College and University Law* 9 (1982–83): 279–314.

————. "Raising the Hurdles: Judicial Response to Heightened Standards for Promotion and Tenure." *Education Law Reporter* 20 (1984): 357–64.

————. "Threshold Qualifications in Academic Discrimination Litigation: How Onerous Is the Burden?" *Education Law Reporter* vol. 30 (1986): 1–9.

"The Living Legacy of One Good Chemist." *Update,* Spring, 1984, p. 1.

McFadden, Robert D. "U.S. Court Rules Against City U. in Sex-Bias Suit." *New York Times,* March 19, 1983.

McMillen, Liz. "Legal Experts Eye 2 Sex-Bias Lawsuits Brought by Women's-Studies Scholars." *Chronicle of Higher Education,* April 9, 1986.

Mather, Lynn, and Barbara Yngvesson. "Language, Audience, and the Transformation of Disputes." *Law and Society Review* 15 (1980–81): 775–824.

Miller, Richard E., and Austin Sarat. "Grievances, Charges and Disputes: Assessing the Adversary Culture." *Law and Society Review* 15 (1980–81): 562–65.

Millet, Larry. "Champion of the Underdog or Misguided Judicial Zealot?" *St. Paul Pioneer Press,* September 14, 1980.

Minneapolis Star, February 27, 1977, June 5, 1982, March 27, 1984.

Minneapolis Star and Tribune, June 21, 1984.

Minneapolis Tribune, June 19, 1980, June 26, 1980, July 18, 1981.

Minnesota Daily, August 4, 1980, April 28, 1981, June 16, 1981.

Mnookin, Robert H., and Lewis A. Kornhauser. "Bargaining in the Shadow of the Law: The Case of Divorce." *Yale Law Journal* 88 (1979): 950–97.

Moskowitz, Daniel B. "Alternatives to Litigation Gain Support." *Washington Post,* February 6, 1984.

Naftulin, Donald M. "Psychological Effects of Litigation on the Industrially Impaired Patient." *Industrial Medicine and Surgery* 39, no. 4 (April, 1970): 26–29.

Note. "Academic Freedom, Secrecy, and Subjectivity as Obstacles to Proving a Title VII Sex Discrimination Case in Academia." *University of North Carolina Law Journal* 60 (1982): 438–50.

Note. "Preventing Unnecessary Intrusions on University Autonomy: A Proposed Academic Freedom Privilege." *California Law Review* 69 (1981): 1,538–68.

Parker, Frederick. "Outline of the History of Sociology at the University of Delaware—1913–1966." University of Delaware, Newark, Del., 1973.

Peale, Roger. "Litigation as a Means of Improving Treatment: Is It the Best Approach?" *Hospital and Community Psychiatry* 26, no. 3 (March, 1975): 170–71.

Perry, Suzanne. "Sex Bias in Academe: A Sweeping Decree Helps Minnesota Women Press Claims." *Chronicle of Higher Education,* August 31, 1983.

Ray, Larry, with Anne L. Clark. "The Multi-Door Courthouse Idea: Building the Courthouse of the Future Today." *Ohio State Journal of Dispute Resolution* 1, no. 1 (1985): 3–29.

Reagan, Ronald. Address to the American Tort Reform Association. Reprinted in the *Washington Post,* May 31, 1986.

"Reducing Custody Conflicts." *Precis* 14, no. 31 (May 7, 1984): 2–3.

Roper, Robert T. "A Preliminary Examination of Available Civil and Criminal Trend Data in State Trial Courts for 1978, 1981 and 1984." National Center for State Courts, Williamsburg, Va., April, 1986.

Scarpitti, Frank. "The Black Student and the University of Delaware." University of Delaware, Newark, Del., 1969.

Shavell, Steven. "Suite, Settlement, and Trial: A Theoretical Analysis under Alternative Methods for the Allocation of Legal Costs." *Journal of Legal Studies* 11 (January, 1982): 435–58.

Taylor, Marilyn J. "Stellar Contracts Lure Stars from University." *Minneapolis Star,* April 27, 1981.

"Too Much Law." *Newsweek,* January 10, 1977, p. 42.

Trout, Florence. "MSU Women Seek Better Breaks in Job." *Bozeman Daily Chronicle,* July 30, 1974.

Trubeck, David, et al. "Civil Litigation Research Project: Final Report." University of Wisconsin, 1983.

"Uniform Guidelines on Employee Selection Procedures." 29 C.F.R. §1607.1 et seq.

Waintroob, Andrea R. "The Developing Law of Equal Employment Opportunity at the White Collar and Professional Level." *William and Mary Law Review* 21 (1979–80): 45–119.

Ware, Ciji. "The Silkwood Connection." *New West,* June 18, 1979, pp. 23, 25–26, 28, 30, 33–35.

Watkins, Beverly. "What the High Court's 'Yeshiva' Decision Has Meant to Yeshiva University Itself." *Chronicle of Higher Education,* February 20, 1985, pp. 27–28.

Wehrwein, August C. Article in the *Minneapolis Star,* December 10, 1981.

Weick, Karl E. "Educational Organizations as Loosely-Coupled Systems." *Administrative Science Quarterly* 21 (1976): 1–19.

Wiltse, Eric. "MSU Female Faculty Lags." *Bozeman Chronicle,* January 29, 1981.

Wood, Robert. "Professionals at Bay: Managing Boston's Public Schools." *Journal of Policy Analysis and Management* 1, no. 4 (Summer, 1982): 454–68.

BOOKS

Abramson, Joan. *Old Boys, New Women.* New York: Praeger Publishers, 1979.

Allison, Graham T. *Essence of Decision: Exploring the Cuban Missile Crisis.* Boston: Little, Brown and Co., 1971.

Auerbach, Jerold S. *Justice Without Law? Resolving Disputes Without Lawyers*. New York: Oxford University Press, 1983.

Belth, Marc. "The Study of Education as the Study of Models." In *The Social Studies: Structure, Models, and Categories*, edited by Martin Feldman and Eli Seifman. Englewood Cliffs, N.J.: Prentice-Hall, 1969.

Bennack, F., Jr. *The American Public, the Media, and the Judicial System*. Hearst Corporation Report New York: Hearst Corporation, 1983.

Berger, Raoul. *Government by Judiciary*. Cambridge, Mass.: Harvard University Press, 1977.

Blau, Peter M. *The Organization of Academic Work*. New York: John Wiley and Sons, 1973.

Blegen, Theodore C. *The Land Lies Open*. Minneapolis: University of Minnesota Press, 1949.

Bowen, Howard R., and Jack H. Schuster. *American Professors: A National Resource Imperiled*. New York: Oxford University Press, 1986.

Boyum, Keith O., and Lynn Mather, eds. *Empirical Theories about Courts*. New York: Longman, 1983.

Brewer, Garry D., and Peter de Leon. *The Foundations of Policy Analysis*. Homewood, Ill.: Dorsey Press, 1983.

Burlingame, Merril G. *A History of Montana State University*. Bozeman, Mont.: Office of Information Publications, 1968.

Caplow, Theodore, and Reese McGee. *The Academic Marketplace*. New York: Doubleday and Co., 1965.

Carcopino, Jerome. *The Daily Life of Rome*. New Haven: Yale University Press, 1940.

Childers, Karen, et al. "A Network of One's Own." In *Rocking the Boat*, edited by Gloria DeSole and Leonore Hoffman. New York: Modern Language Association, 1981.

Cohen, Michael, and James March. *Leadership and Ambiguity*. New York: McGraw-Hill, 1976.

Easton, David. *A Systems Analysis of Political Life*. New York: John Wiley and Sons, 1965.

Edwards, Harry T. *Higher Education and the Unholy Crusade Against Governmental Regulation*. Cambridge, Mass.: Institute for Educational Management, 1980.

Engelmayer, Sheldon, and Robert Waxman. *Lord's Justice: One Judge's War Against the Infamous Dalkon Shield*. New York: Doubleday and Co., 1985.

Flango, Victor E., et al. *The Business of State Trial Courts*. Williamsburg, Va.: National Center for State Courts, 1983.

Frank, Jerome. *Courts on Trial*. Princeton, N.J.: Princeton University Press, 1949.

Frohock, Fred M. *The Nature of Political Inquiry*. Homewood, Ill.: Dorsey Press, 1967.

Glasscock, Carl B. *The War of the Copper Kings: Builders of Butte and Wolves of Wall Street*. New York: Grosset and Dunlap, 1966.

Goldman, Sheldon, and Thomas P. Jahinge. *The Federal Courts as a Political System*. New York: Harper and Row, 1971.

————. *The Federal Judicial System*. New York: Holt, Rinehart and Winston, 1968.

Gray, James. *The University of Minnesota*. Minneapolis: University of Minnesota Press, 1951.

Halpern, Stephen C., and Charles M. Lamb. *Supreme Court: Activism and Restraint*. Lexington, Mass.: Lexington Books, 1982.

Hobbs, Walter C. "The Courts." In *Higher Education and American Society*, edited by P. G. Altbach and R. O. Berdahl. Buffalo: Prometheus Books, 1981.

Horowitz, Donald. *The Courts and Social Policy*. Washington, D.C.: Brookings Institution, 1977.

Jacob, Herb. *Debtors in Court: The Consumption of Government Services*. Chicago: Rand McNally, 1969.

James, Howard. *Crisis in the Courts*. New York: David McKay Co., 1971.

Jones, Charles O. *An Introduction to the Policy Process*. North Scituate, Mass.: Duxbury Press, 1977.

Kaplin, William A. *The Law of Higher Education*. 2d ed. San Francisco: Jossey-Bass, 1985.

Kluger, Richard. *Simple Justice*. New York: Alfred A. Knopf, 1975.

Kolasa, Blair J., and Bernadine Meyer. *Legal Systems*. Englewood Cliffs, N.J.: Prentice-Hall, 1978.

Lieberman, Jethro K. *The Litigious Society*. New York: Basic Books, 1981.

Lieberman, Marcia. "The Most Important Thing for You to Know." In *Rocking the Boat*, edited by Gloria DeSole and Leonore Hoffman. New York: Modern Language Association, 1981.

Lewis, Anthony. *Gideon's Trumpet*. New York: Vintage Books, 1964.

McCarthy, Jane, Irving Ladimer, and Josef P. Sirefman. *Managing Faculty Disputes*. San Francisco: Jossey-Bass, 1984.

Marks, Jonathan B., Earl Johnson, Jr., and Peter L. Szanton. *Dispute Resolution in America: Processes in Evolution*. Washington, D.C.: National Institute for Dispute Resolution, 1984.

Marks, Marlene Adler. *The Suing of America*. New York: Seaview Books, 1981.

May, Judith V., and Aaron B. Wildavsky. *The Policy Cycle*. Beverly Hills: Sage, 1978.

Metzger, Walter P. "Academic Tenure in America: A Historical Essay." In *Faculty Tenure*, edited by the Commission on Academic Tenure. San Francisco: Jossey-Bass, 1973, pp. 93–159.

Mitau, G. Theodore. *Politics of Minnesota*. Minneapolis: University of Minnesota Press, 1970.

Moos, Malcolm. *The Post Land Grant University*. Adelphi, Md.: University of Maryland Press, 1981.

Moroney, Robert M. "Policy Analysis within a Value Theoretical Framework." In *Models for Analysis of Social Policy*, edited by Ron Haskin and James J. Gallagher. Norwood, N.J.: Ablex Publishing, 1981.

Nader, Laura, and Harry F. Todd, Jr., eds. *The Disputing Process—Law in Ten Societies*. New York: Columbia University Press, 1978.

Neier, Aryeh. *Only Judgement*. Middletown, Conn.: Wesleyan University Press, 1982.

O'Neill, Timothy J. *Bakke and the Politics of Equality*. Middletown, Conn.: Wesleyan University Press, 1985.

Pezzullo, Thomas R., and Barbara E. Brittingham. *Salary Equity: Detecting Sex Bias in Salary AmongCollege and University Professors.* Lexington, Mass.: D.C. Heath–Lexington, 1979.

President's Commission on Law Enforcement and Administration of Justice. *Challenge of Crime in Free Society.* Washington, D.C., 1967.

Rackin, Phyllis. "Not by Lawyers Alone: Ten Practical Lessons for Academic Litigants." In *Rocking the Boat,* edited by Gloria DeSole and Leonore Hoffman. New York: Modern Language Association, 1981.

Rebell, Michael A., and Arthur R. Block. *Educational Policy-Making and the Courts.* Chicago: University of Chicago Press, 1982.

Shapiro, Irving S. *America's Third Revolution: Public Interest and the Private Role.* New York: Harper and Row, 1984.

Shaw, B. N. *Academic Tenure in American Higher Education.* Chicago: Adams Press, 1971.

Sigler, Jay A. *An Introduction to the Legal System.* Homewood, Ill.: Dorsey Press, 1968.

Sindler, Allan. *Bakke, De Funis, and Minority Admissions.* New York: Longman, 1978.

Slavin, Sarah, and Jacqueline Macaulay. "Joan Roberts and the University." In *Rocking the Boat,* edited by Gloria DeSole and Leonore Hoffman. New York: Modern Language Association, 1981.

Slichter, Sumner H., James J. Healy, and E. Robert Livernash. *The Impact of Collective Bargaining on Management.* Washington, D.C.: Brookings Institution, 1960.

Stern, Gerald. *The Buffalo Creek Disaster.* New York: Random House, 1977.

Stewart, James B. *The Partners.* New York: Simon and Schuster, 1983.

Taylor, Jean G., et al. *Data Analysis and Simulation of the District of Columbia Trial Court Systems for the Processing of Felony Defendants.* Arlington, Va.: Institute for Defense Analysis, 1968.

Thompson, A. W. J., and V. V. Murray. *Grievance Procedures.* Westmead, U.K.: Saxon House, D. C. Heath, 1976.

Tocqueville, Alexis de. *Democracy in America.* Edited by J. P. Mayer and M. Lerner. New York: Harper and Row, 1966.

Toole, K. Ross. *Twentieth Century Montana: A State of Extremes.* Norman, Okla.: University of Oklahoma Press, 1972.

University Relations Office. *Return on Your Investment.* Minneapolis: University of Minnesota Publications, 1984.

Vose, Clement. *Caucasians Only: The Supreme Court, the NAACP and the Restrictive Covenant Cases.* Berkeley: University of California Press, 1959.

Wessel, Milton R. *The Rule of Reason: A New Approach to Corporate Litigation.* Boston: Addison-Wesley Publishing Co., 1976.

Westin, Alan. *Youngstown v. Sawyer.* New York: Macmillan Co., 1958.

CASES

Acosta v. University of the District of Columbia, 528 F. Supp. 1215 (D.D.C. 1981)

Alexander v. Gardner-Denver, 415 U.S. 36 (1974)

Anapol v. University of Delaware, 412 F. Supp. 675 (D. Del. 1976)
Aumiller v. University of Delaware, 434 F. Supp. 1273 (D. Del. 1977)
Baxter v. Savannah Sugar Refining Corp. 495 F.2d 437 (5th Cir. 1974)
Board of Regents v. Roth, 408 U S 464 (1972)
Castaneda v. Partida, 430 U.S. 482 (1977)
Commonwealth v. Tate, 432 A.2d 1382 (Pa. 1981)
Craik v. Minnesota State University Board, 731 F.2d 465 (8th Cir. 1984)
Cussler v. University of Maryland, 430 F. Supp. 602 (D. Md. 1977)
EEOC v. University of Notre Dame, 551 F. Supp. 737 (N.D. Ind. 1982), *rev'd*, 715
    F.2d 331 (7th Cir. 1983)
Faro v. New York University, 6 Employment Practices Decisions ¶ 8940 (S.D.N.Y.
    1973), *aff'd*, 502 F.2d 1229 (2d Cir. 1974)
Firefighters Local Union No. 1784 v. Stotts, 467 U.S. 561 (1984)
Griggs v. Duke Power Co., 401 U.S. 424 (1971)
Hester v. Southern Ry., 497 F.2d 1374 (5th Cir. 1974)
Johnson v. University of Pittsburgh, 359 F. Supp. 1002. (W.D. Pa. 1973), 435 F.
    Supp. 1328 (W.D. Pa. 1977)
Joseph v. Norman's Health Club, Inc., 582 F.2d 86 (8th Cir. 1976)
Keddie v. Pennsylvania State University, 412 F. Supp. 1264 (M.D. Pa. 1976)
Keegan v. University of Delaware, 349 A.2d 14 (Del. Super. Ct. 1975)
Kumar v. Board of Trustees, 566 F. Supp. 1299 (D. Mass. 1983), *rev'd*, 774 F.2d 1
    (1st Cir. 1985)
Kunda v. Muhlenberg College, 463 F. Supp. 294 (E.D. Pa. 1978), *aff'd*, 621 F.2d
    532 (3d Cir. 1980)
Lamphere v. Brown University, 71 F.R.D. 641 (D.R.I. 1976), 553 F.2d 714 (1st Cir.
    1977), 610 F.2d 464 (1st Cir. 1979), 491 F. Supp. 232 (D.R.I. 1980), *aff'd*, 685
    F.2d 743 (1st Cir. 1982), 613 F. Supp. 971 (D.R.I. 1985)
Lieberman v. Gant, 474 F. Supp. 848 (D. Conn. 1979), *aff'd*, 630 F.2d 60 (2d Cir.
    1980)
Lynn v. Board of Regents, 21 Employment Practices Decisions ¶ 30,558 (C.D. Cal.
    1979), *rev'd*, 656 F.2d 1337 (9th Cir. 1981), *cert. denied*, 459 U.S. 823 (1982)
McDonnell-Douglas Co. v. Green, 411 U.S. 792 (1973)
Mecklenberg v. Montana State University, 13 Employment Practices Decisions
    ¶ 11,438 (D. Mont. 1976)
Melani v. Board of Higher Education, 561 F. Supp. 769 (S.D.N.Y. 1983)
Parker v. University of Delaware, 75 A.2d 225 (Del. Ch. 1950)
Powell v. Syracuse University, 580 F.2d 1150 (2d Cir. 1978), *cert. denied*, 439 U.S.
    984 (1978)
Presseisen v. Swarthmore College, 336 F. Supp. 1337 (E.D. Pa. 1974), 442 F. Supp.
    593 (E.D. Pa. 1977), *aff'd*, 582 F.2d 1275 (3d Cir. 1978)
Rajender v. University of Minnesota, 20 Employment Practices Decisions ¶ 30,214,
    24 Fair Employment Practices Cases 1045 (D. Minn. 1978), 20 Employment
    Practices Decisions ¶ 30,225, 24 Fair Employment Practices Cases 1051 (D.
    Minn. 1979), 546 F. Supp. 158 (D. Minn. 1982), 563 F. Supp. 401 (D. Minn.
    1983)
Reserve Mining Co. v. Lord, 529 F.2d 181 (8th Cir. 1976)

Rowe v. General Motors, 457 F.2d 348 (5th Cir. 1972)

Scott v. University of Delaware, 385 F. Supp. 937 (D. Del. 1974), 68 F.R.D. 606 (D. Del. 1975), 16 Fair Employment Practices Cases 737 (D. Del. 1976), 455 F. Supp. 1102 (D. Del. 1978), *modified*, 601 F.2d 76 (3d Cir. 1979), *cert. denied*, 444 U.S. 931 (1979)

Shea v. Gant, 22 Fair Employment Practices Cases 371 (D. Conn. 1979)

Smith v. University of North Carolina, 18 Fair Employment Practices Cases 913 (M.D.N.C. 1978), 19 Employment Practices Decisions ¶ 9040 (M.D.N.C. 1979), *aff'd*, 632 F.2d 316 (4th Cir. 1980)

Sobel v. Yeshiva University, 438 F. Supp. 625 (S.D.N.Y. 1976), 21 Employment Practices Decisions ¶ 30,360 (S.D.N.Y. 1979), 22 Employment Practices Decisions ¶ 30,653 (S.D.N.Y. 1980), 566 F. Supp. 1166 (S.D.N.Y. 1983)

Tanton v. McKinney, 197 N.W. 510 (Mich. 1929)

Texas Department of Community Affairs v. Burdine, 450 U.S. 248 (1981)

Townsend v. Nassau County Medical Center, 558 F.2d 117 (2d Cir. 1977), *cert. denied*, 434 U.S. 1015 (1977)

United States v. Ironworkers Local 86, 3 Employment Practices Decisions ¶ 8213 (9th Cir. 1971)

Washington v. Davis, 426 U.S. 229 (1976)

Wilkens v. University of Houston, 471 F. Supp. 1054 (S.D. Tex. 1979), *aff'd in part and rev'd in part*, 654 F.2d 388 (5th Cir. 1981), *vacated*, 459 U.S. 809 (1982), 695 F.2d 134 (5th Cir. 1983)

Wood v. Strickland, 420 U.S. 308 (1975)

Zahorik v. Cornell University, 34 Fair Employment Practices Cases 147 (N.D.N.Y. 1981), 579 F. Supp. 349 (N.D.N.Y. 1983), *aff'd*, 729 F.2d 85 (2d Cir. 1984)

Index

DATE DUE

MAY 31 '90			
CHECKED	*OUT BY*		
HAND — S. Wilks			
MAY 31 '01			
MAY 31 '93			
MAY 31 '94			
MAY 31 '95			
APR 26 '96			
	261-2500		Printed in USA